American Missions
in Bicentennial Perspective

Contributors

Professor Catherine L. Albanese, *Wright State University*

Professor R. Pierce Beaver, *emeritus, University of Chicago Divinity School*

Professor Henry Warner Bowden, *Douglass College, Rutgers University*

Professor J. Walter Cason, *Garrett-Evangelical Theological School*

Dr. Charles L. Chaney, *Director, Division of Church Extension, Illinois Baptist State Convention (Southern)*

Professor Edward M. Cook, *Department of History, The University of Chicago*

Professor Charles W. Forman, *Yale University Divinity School*

Dr. Charles H. Germany, *World Division, Board of Global Ministries, United Methodist Church*

Professor W. Richie Hogg, *Perkins School of Theology, Southern Methodist University*

Mr. Stephen C. Knapp, *Partnership in Mission*

President Louis J. Luzbetak, S. V. D., *Divine Word College, and President of the American Society of Missiology*

Dr. Emmanuel L. McCall, *Home Mission Board, Southern Baptist Convention*

Rev. Tim Ryan, *Scarboro Fathers, Toronto*

Professor James A. Scherer, *The Lutheran School of Theology at Chicago*

Rev. Simon E. Smith, S. J., *Executive Secretary, Jesuit Missions*

American Missions
in Bicentennial Perspective

Papers presented at the fourth
annual meeting of the American
Society of Missiology at Trinity
Evangelical Divinity School, Deerfield, Illinois, June 18 - 20, 1976.

R. Pierce Beaver
Editor

William Carey Library

533 HERMOSA STREET • SOUTH PASADENA, CALIF. 91030

**Published by the William Carey Library
533 Hermosa Street
South Pasadena, Calif. 91030
Telephone 213-682-2047**

In accord with some of the most recent thinking in the academic press, the William Carey Library is pleased to present
this scholarly book which has been prepared from an author-
edited and author-prepared camera-ready manuscript.

Library of Congress Cataloging in Publication Data

American Society of Missiology.
    American missions in Bicentennial perspective.

    Includes bibliographies.
    1. Missions, American--History--Congresses.
I. Beaver, Robert Pierce, 1906-   II. Title.
BV2410.A43 1977   266'.023   77-7569
ISBN 0-87808-153-4

PRINTED IN THE UNITED STATES OF AMERICA

Contents

Foreword

The selection of a theme and the preparation of a program for the annual meeting of the American Society of Missiology in 1976 was committed to a committee which included Professor James A. Scherer of the Lutheran School of Theology at Chicago, Dr. Charles L. Chaney, director of the Division of Church Extension of the Illinois Baptist State Association, Rev. Fr. Lawrence Nemer of the Catholic Theological Union, and the undersigned as convener. The Bicentennial Anniversary celebration of the nation suggested the theme, American Missions in Bicentennial Perspective.

American world mission or cross-cultural mission has had a history longer than that of the nation in its independent state since it has been in operation for three hundred fifty years. However, a new period began with the end of the War for Independence and soon the overseas mission was launched. Nearly all the missionary societies founded between 1787 and 1820 declared that they had three objectives, namely to evangelize the American Indians, the people of the frontier settlements, and the heathen at the ends of the earth. The worldwide mission of the American, British, and, to a considerable degree, the European churches developed out of the Indian mission. The evangelization of African slaves was a small effort, and the American Blacks converted themselves through the work of the Holy Spirit and shaped their own distinctive form of Christianity. The Blacks and Indians have continued to be the largest ethnic communities in the United States, and they are included in this program. It is the foreign or overseas mission beginning in 1810 that is primarily under review. That is an enterprise in which Americans held first place among Protestants by 1914. Roman Catholics began sending missionaries from the United

States quite late. The overseas mission has been the greatest
vehicle for extending American altruism abroad. The Protestant
portion of it taught the churchmen stewardship and called forth
the resources in personnel and money to develop all the other denominational agencies and to occupy the continent. It also formed
in the minds of Americans the images of distant lands and peoples.

Mission (singular) here refers to the total task of the Church
in witness. Missions (plural) connotes the agencies and operations
by which mission is implemented.

The program of the assembly as the Table of Contents shows began with a review of the state of mission during the period of the
Revolution and moved to attention to certain factors which affected the course and shape of mission. An overview of two centuries
of mission theory was paired with a panel on contemporary understanding of mission. Black Christianity and the mission to the
Indians brought attention to the two largest ethnic minorities.
The Presidential Address is always a high point in the annual assembly of the Society and the paper by Father Louis J. Luzbetak
will be found here. The final session was given to the Role of
the American Churches in World Mission, both Protestant and Roman
Catholic. Each paper was distributed in advance of the meeting at
Trinity Evangelical Divinity School at Deerfield, Illinois, on June
18-20. Each author introduced his paper briefly, and general discussion was introduced by a response by a critic.

The Executive Committee committed the gathering of the papers
into a volume to the undersigned. Note well that this is not a
book developed through successive chapters. It is a collection of
independent program papers related to a general theme. Each writer submitted a text supposed to be ready for the camera and typed
to certain directions. But secretaries interpret directions differently and typewriters are not uniform. Therefore, there is
marked variety in size and style of type, in the systems of references and citations, and other matters. Uniformity -- admittedly
very desirable -- could have been achieved only by retyping, and
that expense would have made publication of the papers impossible.
The responses of Sister Margaret Hawk, C. A. of Pine Ridge, S. D.,
and Dr. Nirmal Minz of Ranchi, Bihar, India, were unfortunately
lost in the mails. Brother Joseph Davis was unable to provide his
text.

Warm thanks are extended to Mrs. Patricia McCrossan at the
William Carey Library for her skill, and patience in handling a
late and very uneven typescript.

R. Pierce Beaver
Editor

1

The Missionary Situation in the Revolutionary Era

Charles L. Chaney

This chapter describes the various commitments of men and money
to missionary activity, in what is now the United States of
America, during the generation of the American Revolution. An
effort will be made to accent both action and attitude. If there
was any considerable involvement in missionary pursuits, what
motivated that action? Was there a *missionary* spirit among the
American churches in the quarter century between 1763 and 1787?
Were there groups of Christians in Europe challenged to make disciples of Jesus Christ and gather churches among the different
peoples of the American continent? What was the extent of that
commitment and what kind of success did they experience in the
Revolutionary Era?

A truism of popular American church historiography affirms
that missionary activity toward pagan peoples by Protestants before the nineteenth century was almost non-existent. It is true
that this activity was nothing like the flood of evangelical
effort that developed after 1800. Nevertheless, such activity
was considerable.

A corollary to this historiographical "axiom" says that church
extension efforts among European peoples in the colonial period
were not in reality "missions". This assertion too needs more
careful evaluation. There was a widespread commitment to win
dispersed European immigrants to vital faith in Christ and to
active church membership before the Revolutionary War. Much
of this activity was construed as finding and getting back in the
fold those who were already a part of the flock of God. But to
insist that the proliferation of churches in the eighteenth century among Europeans was only church extension among those already
Christian is to overlook the Evangelical Revival and some of its
major tenets. Philosophically these missionary evangelists and

church planters made no distinction between the Europeans destitute of lively faith in Christ and the totally ungospelized
Indians or Negroes. Most of those who gathered churches in communities "destitute of the means of grace" also considered themselves on a mission.

The tendency among historians to evaluate American Christianity in the colonial period almost totally by the statements and
activities of those identified with the various ecclesiastical
establishments has contributed to this historical distortion. The
growth of the sectarians in the years immediately before the
Revolution, even through the years of war and on through the years
of the Confederation, has been largely overlooked. No comprehensive survey of the missionary situation at the end of the American
Colonial Period can fail to consider them.

The missionary activity of Roman Catholics beyond the frontiers
of English Colonial America is well known in general outlines, and
it has documentation in tomes. This paper attempts to bring all
the various strands together and take a look at what was being
done with a missionary purpose during the struggle for independence and nationhood--Protestant and Catholic, establishment
and sectarian, and among the various non-English speaking churches.

I.   THE ROMAN CATHOLIC RIM

The fantastic story of Roman Catholic missionary achievements
on the southern, western and northern perimeters of the United
States in the two centuries before the Revoluationary War has been
told with literary flair and exacting scholarship. This paper
will scan only the years before the Revolution to sketch the conditions of the missions and briefly note any considerable change
by the end of the Confederation period.

For the Roman Catholic Church the North American continent was
an important land for missionary endeavor during the eighteenth
century. The diversity of colonial settlements divided it into
several fields of missionary activity. Missionaries from Spain,
France and England were the primary agents responsible for laying
the foundation for what has become a great church in the twentieth
century.

General Considerations

Several factors in western civilization had tremendous effect
on the missionary situation of Roman Catholics in North America
during the Revolutionary era. These factors were determinative
no matter where the missions were located or their national origin.

Relations between church and state, the roots of which reach
back to the break-up of the old Roman Empire, *can hardly be over-
emphasized as a formative influence in both missionary advance
and retreat in the eighteenth century.*[1] The right of lay patronage grew from an expression of lay concern for accessibility to
the church and sacraments to a practice that spread throughout
the Catholic world and embraced some of the richest churches and
religious foundations of Europe. By the sixteenth century the
Church had acquired vast land holdings throughout Europe that
were administered by bishops, abbots and other high clergy. The
rise of national monarchies and the period of the secular control
of the church led to royal demands that sovereigns had the right
to name those men who should, with papal approval, occupy the
various ecclesiastical benefices within their dominion. This was
an expansion and nationalization of the right of patronage.

These rights were secured from the papacy in several struggles
throughout the fifteenth and early sixteenth centuries. By the
time Francois Laval was appointed Vicar Apostolic of New France
in 1658, French kings had enjoyed the right to present candidates
for papal approval almost 150 years. At no time were the missionary activities in New France totally free from the hindrances and
restrictions of lay authorities.

The lay control of the Church in Spain came even earlier and
had a more pronounced bearing on Spanish missions in North
America. In 1493, among the various actions that Alexander VI
took to protect and encourage the Spanish explorations, Ferdinand
and Isabella were granted the right to name all missionaries who
should go to the New World. In 1508, the right of the ruler to
nominate all ecclesiastical benefices without exceptions and in
perpetuity, was given by Julius II.[2] The Spanish sovereign had,
in effect, as much authority over the Spanish Church as over the
Spanish army. The implications of these grants, so minuscule at
the beginning of the sixteenth century, had tremendous influence
on the mission over the next three centuries.

*Competition for empire among European nations during the
eighteenth century marks the ebb and flow of Roman Catholic
missionary activity.* From the War of Spanish Succession, 1702,
until the American Revolution England, France and Spain were
almost constantly embroiled in war--often involving all three
nations. The struggle was not primarily for military conquest
and invariably led to a negotiated peace. Some wars, therefore,
had direct and often devastating effects on the North American
colonies of these nations.

The Peace of Paris, 1763, eliminated France as a colonial
power in North America during the eighteenth century. Spain's
expansive colonial empire was in decline through the entire

century. Though it continued to manage vast areas of land and
even explore, claim and occupy some new areas in the Revolutionary era, the sun was setting on the Spanish empire. The effect
on the efficiency and success of the mission was obvious.

England, too, lost considerable of its colonial empire in North
America in the century. The Revolutionary War itself took care
of that.

The suppression of the Society of Jesus by various European
sovereigns during the third quarter of the century, and the
eventual dissolution of the order by Clement XIV in 1773, *was a
salient factor that shaped Roman Catholic missions in 1776.*[3]
What had begun at mid-century in Portugal as part of a determined
effort to destroy all barriers to royal rule and restore that
country to a nation of rank, became an international crusade.
Rationalism, humanitarian liberalism, nationalistic patriotism
and enlightened despotism combined with inter-order competition
and conflict of dogma within the Church to bring the Jesuits down.
In 1759, they were expelled from Portugal. In 1762, the Society
was found subversive to the French State. In 1767, Charles III
decreed that the Jesuits be expelled from all Spanish dominions.
This was executed in New Spain in 1768. The withdrawal of the
Jesuits meant the further decline of most missions in the Spanish
Southwest.

Spanish Missions

The cultural, military and religious dynamic of Spain for two
centuries after the final expulsion of the Moors from Granada is
absolutely incredible. In less than seventy years the broad
boundaries of a vast colonial empire were marked off. Spanish
culture and religion had begun to make an indelible mark on much
of the New World. More missionaries, by far, went from Spain than
from any other European country. More successful conquests were
made for king and cross by Spanish army and Church than by any
other western power. The penetration of North America was only an
insignificant and small part of a vast enterprise.

*The missionary epoch in Florida had already passed before the
middle of the eighteenth century.* The first successful Spanish
colony at St. Augustine was a political and military necessity.
The French colony at the mouth of St. John's River posed a serious
threat to the route of the Spanish treasue ships. A Jesuit
missionary contingent arrived in 1566, but was withdrawn five
years later. The Franciscans, who sent their first missionary to
Florida in 1573, provided the spiritual dynamic for Spanish
Florida.

Within the next century the Francisans had considerable success
among the Indians. When Bishop Caldiron of Santiago visited

Florida in 1674, the mission was just beyond its zenith.   There
were about 30 villages of Christian Indians, and the bishop reported that he confirmed over 13,000 Christians.[4]

In 1670 the English had begun their colonization of the
Carolinas.   The Spanish settlements and missions were henceforth
under almost constant pressure.   The French arrival in Louisana
at the end of the century posed a threat from the west.   The War
of Spanish Succession made Florida open game for the English.   By
the end of those hostilities the Indian missions were all but
obliterated.   There was little peace until 1763, when, in the
Peace of Paris Spain surrendered Florida to the English.   The
Franciscan missionaries left Florida for Mexico.

During the American Revolution there was no Indian mission in
Florida.   Spain regained Florida in 1783.   But the Indian mission
was not reopened except in a very limited way around St. Augustine
and Pensacola.

New Mexico was the next arena of missionary action for the
Spanish Church.   The vanguard was led by the Franciscans.   *By the
time of the American Revolution this mission had already passed
its apogee in the colonial period.*   It left a religious and
cultural mark on the Southwest that has continued.   The mission
laid foundations for a strong Catholic Church among most of the
peoples in this area of the United States.

Several factors distinguish the mission to New Mexico from that
in Florida.   It was launched from Mexico instead of Spain.   The
personnel came from those colleges of friars in New Spain which
were founded for educational and evangelistic ministries in the
New World.   The Indians in New Mexico had a much more advanced
social structure than those in Florida.   The missionaries found,
already in existence, the building blocks from which to create a
civilization.   The New Mexico mission was, therefore, closer to
its base of support and had brighter prospects for success than
any other mission within the present United States.

Permanent missionary settlement came in 1598, when nine Franciscans accompanied Don Juan de Onate in the conquest of New
Mexico.   The mission had extraordinary success during the first
half of the seventeenth century and rapid decline in the second
half, which climaxed in the Indian revolt of 1680.   Serious tension between the civil authorities and the missionary establishment characterized the first five decades of the eighteenth century.   After 1725, the Bishop of Durango attempted to extend his
control over New Mexico.   The Franciscan superiors had held, from
the beginning, the faculties for conferring the Sacrament of Confirmation.   This produced a half-century of disruptive conflict
within the New Mexico mission.

The reports of the various visiting bishops between 1725 and 1760 do not flatter the missionaries. In 1775, the Franciscan superior in Mexico sent Francisco Dominguez on an inspection tour of the province. He spent 1775 in his tour. His report gives a unique picture of the situation at the beginning of the American Revolution. He found 2,014 Spaniards in Santa Fe and its environs. In the scattered missions he found almost 18,000 Indians in the care of 20 Franciscan brothers. The disinclination of the mission-aries to learn the native languages that had been criticized by earlier visitors was still a problem. He found the missionaries generally in a low spiritual condition.[5]

His visit did not produce renewal but reaction. Many of his brothers rejected his suggestions of reform, and some attempted to discredit him. Decline of the mission stations continued. By the 1790's, New Mexico's European population increased, and the Indian mission was no longer the central concern of the Spanish Church in New Mexico.

Texas became the third field of missionary effort for Spanish Christianity in what has become the United States.[6] The first efforts at Christianizing Texas Indians began after 1675. Fran-ciscans from two significant colleges of missionary friars in Mexico were the manpower for the Texas apostolate. The College of Our Lady of Guadalupe in Zacatecas and the College of the Holy Cross in Queretano provided personnel for the Franciscan missions throughout Mexico and the American Southwest. These two commun-ities recruited and trained the missionaries for New Mexico, as well as Texas. The College of San Fernando in Mexico City also produced missionary preachers on a smaller scale for Texas.

The missions in Texas were, in comparison with other areas of Spanish America, largely unsuccessful. They were plagued with tension between military leaders and the missionaries, crippled by repeated changes in royal policy, hindered by uncooperative tribal culture and often violent warfare, and were continually anemic and undermanned because of the distances between mission stations and the lack of interest of civil authorities in New Mexico and Spain.

By 1775, the end of the first century, the missionary situa-tion was one of general retreat. Four developments were of pri-mary importance.

Repeated failure in planting permanent missions among the small tribes of Central and Western Texas and almost total hostility from the dominant and fearsome Apache and Comanche tribes kept the Texas mission from expansion. The Apaches in Texas were on the southern plains because of pressure from the Comanches. Mission outposts and Christian villages were subject to sudden

and devastating attack. At one time, the Apaches sought detente
with the Spanish. A mission was established among them at mid-
century on the San Saba River. In less than a decade, after repeated attacks by the Comanches, it was totally wiped out by the
Apaches themselves. Growth was impossible.

The attitude of the Spanish government toward Texas in general
and East Texas in particular, after 1763, led to the dissolution
of the East Texas missions in 1772. The government had assisted
in the establishment of a line of missions and presidios in the
"piney woods" area of Texas after 1690, because of the fear of
French penetration from Louisiana. In the Peace of Paris, Spain
secured Louisiana as a part of the settlement. East Texas was no
longer a frontier to guard against foreign aggression, but an interior province. In 1772, the governor's residence was withdrawn
to San Antonio, and the missions closed.

The expulsion of the Jesuits from the domain of Charles III,
in 1767, meant the withdrawal of missionary personnel from Texas.
The Spanish crown insisted that both Louisiana and Upper California be occupied by Spanish missionaries. Upper California became
a priority of the government after 1769, and many of the posts of
the Jesuits in Arizona were filled by Franciscans. Some were withdrawn from Texas. No new recruits were sent in.

Finally, the Queretano friars began, in 1769, to request to be
relieved of temporal administration of their six missions. They
did not wish to continue to manage farms, ranches and conduct
other commercial enterprises. In 1772 their work was turned over
to the Zacatecas missionaries. However, the Indian population
from San Antonio south was in decline, especially around the
missions. Those Indians remaining were able to manage their own
affairs. The pressure of Whites for the mission lands was constant. By the end of the American Revolution the Zacatecas friars
were wishing to be relieved of all temporal responsibility. This
was the first step toward total secularization of the Texas
missions after 1790.

Arizona was a fourth area of Spanish missionary activity.
Primeria Alta, as the Spanish called the area of Northern Sonora
and Arizona of the Gadsden Purchase, was penetrated by Francicans,
indeed, before missions in Texas were undertaken. But their work
was confined almost exclusively to what is now Northern Sonora.
The Jesuits, led by Eusebio Kino, rapidly advanced into what is
now Arizona after 1700. Kino established three missions between
the present Nogales and Tucson.

By 1710, he was confident that "the blessed time is now coming
when not only the conquest and conversion of the Californias is
being accomplished, but also . . . that of these other extensive
lands and nations of this North America."[7]

Kino died a year later and the mission experienced serious decline. This frontier was all but abandoned. When the missions
were turned over to the Franciscans in 1768, Kino's three missions
were all that were left to transfer, and they were in a very
feeble state.

The Franciscans made little progress in Arizona. Tucson was
established as a presidio in 1776. The missionaries attempted to
establish a route that would tie Primeria Alta to California during the years that followed. They made plans for establishing
missions along that road. But four of the Franciscans were killed by the Yumas in 1781, and the missionary efforts came virtually to a standstill.

While 1763 brought an end to Spanish Catholic missions in
Florida, *it brought a much greater land under the sway of the
Spanish Church in Western Louisiana*. Spain took a different
approach toward the Indian tribes in Louisiana than in the Southwest. The Indians of the North, as they had learned in Texas,
did not settle into missions as most did in New Spain and New
Mexico. In the short period that Spain controlled Louisiana, the
classical missions establishment was not the frontier policy.[8]
The Spanish mission to the Indians of the Mississippi Valley was
insignificant during the Revolutionary era.

Constant military and political tensions, plus the decline of
Spanish national and religious vitality kept significant growth
from occurring in the various European settlements. First, it
was almost seven years before the Spanish political control was
secured in the new colonial acquisitions. A small band of French
Capuchins held ecclesiastical affairs together during this period.
Not until 1772, did the Bishop of Santiago begin to provide some
of the priests needed to maintain the churches established by the
French. When the first contingent of Spanish Capuchins arrived,
a period of inter-Capuchin feuding, on the basis of national
origin, continued until 1776, when the French superior died. Representation of the Spanish Church actually only gained control
of the Louisiana churches about the same time that the Declaration of Independence was being signed.

Spain entered the war against England in 1779. Spanish forces
were involved in the capture of the Floridas from England. But
that new area only added to the problem of the Spanish Church in
Louisiana. There was a severe shortage of priests and a growing
population. The French-speaking Acadian community continued to
increase all through the period. They held themselves aloof from
the old French of Louisiana. There were also growing German-
speaking and English-speaking colonies that came under the care
of the Church.

In 1785, Capuchin superior, Cirillo de Barcelona was conse-
crated auxiliary bishop of Santiago with residence in New Orleans.
On his return from consecration in Cuba, he took steps to raise
the level of Christian obedience in the churches. But he soon
returned to Cuba for a three-year stint. When he did return, he
found ecclesiastical affairs largely in control of his assistant,
Antonio de Sebella. A struggle began that lasted until Sebella
was deported in 1790.

Almost constant military, political and ecclesiastical intrigue
dominated the Church in Louisiana during the Revolutionary era.
There were new churches opened among the European colonies, but
little of it resulted from deliberate missionary effort.

*The most exciting story of Roman Catholic missions in the
Revolutionary period is that of the Franciscan penetration of
California.* The Jesuits left thirteen missions in the hands of
the Franciscans when they were expelled from Baja California in
1768. Junipero Serra was the Franciscan superior for the California missions. He was 56 years old, a veteran of 21 years in
the missions of New Spain and the College of San Fernando in
Mexico City. He is by far the most outstanding Catholic missionary in America during the Revolutionary era.

Russian encroachments from the north--beginning about 1740--
and closer ties between Russia and England motivated the Spanish
government to occupy Upper California with a series of presidios
and missions. San Diego was established in July, 1769,

In April, 1772, the Dominicans assumed all the missions in
Baja California. This left the Franciscans free to give full
attention to Upper California. By the time the Continental Congress began circulating the Articles of Confederation in November,
1977, eight missions had been established as far north as San
Francisco. A period of conflict between Serra and the newly
appointed governor of California that lasted until Serra's death
in 1784 slowed down the advance. Nevertheless, Serra formulated
a bold plan for missionary expansion up the coast of California.
He wanted to see one mission at about every 25 leagues. "This
would," he said, "provide a great increase of Christianity."[9]
By the time of his death in 1784, nine missions had been established. Something very like his plan was carried out. By 1787,
thirteen missions were established between San Diego and San
Francisco.[10]

Serra formulated no missionary theory in his numerous letters.
But they do reveal something of the missionary motivation that
characterized the man and many of those who labored with him. For
him the mission was always a holy and apostolic enterprise. "Nothing else but the love of God," he insisted prompted him to devote his life to the missionary vocation.[11] His purpose in

California was evangelical. He went there to take the gospel of
Christ. He was on a spiritual conquest, though often cast in
imperial dress. He attempted to fan "the flames on all sides,"
so that "new and immense territories" might be "gathered into the
bosom of Holy Mother the Church and subjected to the Crown of
Spain."[12] At the time of the first mass in Monterey, a cross was
erected. Serra reported that "after raising aloft the standard
of the King of Heaven, we unfurled the flag of our Catholic
Monarch likewise."[13] The stories of what took place in California,
he said, should "stir up the world to undertake the spiritual
conquest of this New World, and give to God, before very long,
thousands of souls."[14]

Serra was moved to missionary labor without dreading the possibility of martyrdom. Suffering and labor, he insisted, had to
be faced with a joyful attitude. New missionaries, he wrote a
brother in Mexico City, must not be men who "put on a glum face
whenever there is work to be done, and are scarcely here before
they become . . .anxious to return. Hardships they will have to
face--these men who come to sacrifice themselves in so holy an
enterprise."[15] His biographers have stressed the phrase from his
farewell letter to his family, "go ahead and never turn back," as
a kind of prophecy of the character of his life. They are probably correct. He and many of the missionaries of his age were
committed to sharing Christ with pagans, even at the expense of
their lives.

The most stimulating statement of missionary motivation of
this era that I have read is from the pen of a Jesuit, Johann
Jakob Baegert who published his *Observations on Lower California*
in 1771. He attacked Protestantism for its obvious lack of commitment to the Gentile mission. The crux of his barrage was a
series of questions investigating the lack of Protestant martyrs
in the apostolate. One paragraph will express the idealized
spirit of Roman Catholic missionary motivation in the Revolutionary era.

> Hence among the Roman Catholic clergy Christ has his
> helpers and the Apostles have their faithful successors,
> in the person of the missionaries, dedicated to the con-
> version of heathen. To teach and baptize unbelievers,
> the missionaries travel throughout the world, penetrating
> into regions where no profit-hungary merchant nor daring
> pioneer has ever been before. They work and sweat with
> Christ for the salvation of souls; they wait to see their
> Faith spread into all corners of the world and make
> Christians of all men, no matter who they might be. Some
> they instruct and baptize, others they prepare for Heaven.
> They preach the gospel to those who are nothing to them,
> from whom they get nothing, and from whom they expect
> nothing but death and martyrdom.[16]

The French Residue

The exclusion of the French from North America did not suddenly happen in 1763. The struggle had been going on for almost a century. The French always eventually lost ground. The explusion of French Roman Catholics from what is now the United States took place in some areas before the Peace of Paris.

The French Jesuits had three missions among the Abenaki tribes in Maine during the first quarter of the eighteenth century. The Treaty of Utrecht of 1713 gave Acadia to Great Britain. But due to vagueness about its boundaries, trouble developed. As New England settlers moved up toward the Kennebec River, the Abenakis retaliated. The Indians burned Georgetown and Brunswick. This led to a declaration of war by Massachusetts. By 1725, the War had effectively destroyed the Jesuit missions.

These events are important for this story, not only because they contributed to the exclusion of French missions from what was to become the United States, but because they are also the occasion for the renewal of the languishing New England mission to the Indians.

The Abenaki held staunchly to their Catholic faith, and when New France was handed over to Great Britain in 1763, they requested priests from the new English governor in Quebec. He referred them to Francis Barnard, Governor of Massachusetts, in whose province their lands were located. Barnard met with them in 1764, but was unwilling to attempt to get a Catholic priest for them and unable to persuade them to accept a Protestant minister.

An effort was made in the early 1770's to win them away from their Catholic faith. The Massachusetts General Court appointed trustees of an Eastern Mission, who assisted Daniel Little of Wells in a preaching tour among the Abenakis in 1772 and again in 1774. After the Revolution the Abenakis were still without a priest. Louis Rouselett, of Boston, visited them several times during the '80's. They did not get a priest until John Carroll assigned a French refugee to them after 1792.

French Roman Catholic mission work was effectively excluded from New York before Britain took over Canada. The last mission, at La Presentation, on the St. Lawrence, was abandoned in 1775, during the French and Indian War.

The French missions were never as elaborate, extensive or successful as the Spanish missions. The religious revival that was so pervasive in France during the mid-seventeenth century began to subside after 1680. By the end of the century religious

fervor was in decline. The severe conflict between the Society
of Jesus and other groups of religious as well as with French
political factions produced further deterioration of mission interest. In general, by the time the French domains in the Western Great Lakes and the Mississippi Valley were handed over to
the English and Spanish, the work among the Indian tribes in
those areas was insignificant, and the major work of the missionaries was in the scattered settlements of Europeans along the
Mississippi and around the Lakes. The suppression of the Jesuits
in French domains was followed immediately by the transfer of
North American possessions to England and Spain. These two events
were like twin blows in a missionary situation already languishing in the North and West. [17]

The village of Detroit was served by a Franciscan through the
Revolutionary War. Simplicius Bocquet and his parish remained
solidly pro-British. Pierre Potier, a former Jesuit serving as
a secular priest, settled a remnant of the Hurons across the
river from Detroit in Canada.

In the Illinois Country there were five small villages. Three
priests were present through most of the Revolutionary era.
Sebastian Meurin, a Jesuit, returned in 1764 to serve in Illinois
as a secular priest. He was appointed vicar-general by Bishop
Joseph Briand in Quebec in 1768. With the various priests in
that country he attempted to coordinate the work in Kaskaskia,
Prairie du Rocher, Cahokia, Fort deChartes and St. Genevieve, now
in Spanish territory. St. Louis was founded in 1764, and they
also provided some religious direction there. When the Spanish
finally assumed control of western Louisiana, they excluded the
ministrations of any priest under the jurisdiction of a bishop
in British controlled territory. In 1768, Pierre Gibault arrived
from Canada and re-established a Christian ministry in Vincennes.
He continued to serve the church there and those in Illinois
throughout the Revolution. The only significant inroad into an
Indian tribe was with the Kaskaskia branch of the Illinois tribe.
But by the time of the Revolution their numbers had declined, and
the primary ministry of the missionaries was to the increasing
number of white settlers.

Lower Louisiana is a similar story. As in Illinois, the first
missionary thrust was an effort to plant the Christian faith
among the various Indian tribes. This large field was primarily
divided between the Jesuits and the Capuchins after 1725. A community of Ursulines pursued a mission of mercy and education in
New Orleans.

The Capuchins maintained a mission near Natchitoches on the
Red River on the Spanish frontier. It was abandoned when Spain
took over western Louisiana. The Capuchins had no other missions
among the Indians after 1750.

The Jesuits began missions among several tribes in the second
quarter of the century.   Outposts were located on the Yazoo and
Arkansas Rivers, among the Indians of that name.   In what is now
Alabama there were largely unsuccessful missions among the Ali-
bamons and Choctaws.   By mid-century no siginificant advance had
been made in any tribe.   When the Jesuits were suppressed only
four remained in lower Louisiana.

At the dawn of the American Revolution the missionary efforts
that French Roman Catholics had pursued in what is now the United
States for 150 years had almost faded from existence.   It was
insignificant by 1776 because it had been in serious decline for
almost the entire century.

The English Foothold

At the beginning of the generation of the Revolution Roman
Catholics had only a foothold in the English colonies.   The English mission was a Jesuit mission and had been since the founding of Maryland.   Their strength was confined almost totally to
that state and Pennsylvania.   Rhode Island had few Catholics.
Every other colony, except Pennsylvania, had legal restrictions
on the free exercise of the Roman Catholic faith and full citizenship for its adherents.

The end of the French and Indian War brought a general peace
to Roman Catholics in the colonies until the Quebec Act of 1773.
But the American reaction to these events was short-lived due to
the rising war spirit, the desire to enlist Roman Catholic Canada on the side of the colonies, and the rising commitment to
radical freedom up and down the eastern seaboard.   At its peak,
during the decade before the Declaration of Independence, there
were eighteen Jesuits serving in the mission--four in Pennsylvania and fourteen in Maryland.

During this period, through normal attrition, the number of
personnel declined.   The Jesuits, already expelled from France,
Spain and Portugal, were under mounting pressure.   Few new recruits came.   But the suppression of the Society of Jesus by the
Pope did not bring a serious change in the colonies. The Jesuits
went on serving as ex-Jesuits with the same superior.

Several factors combined to make 1770-1790 a very significant
period in the history of the Roman Catholic Church in America.
Roman Catholics went into the era legally excluded from full
citizenship in most states, and came out with full legal citizenship and the free exercise of religion nationally.   State legal
restrictions had been abolished in most states.   The zealous
participation of most Roman Catholics in the Revolutionary cause
along with the contribution of Roman Catholic France to the War
had a good effect on the general attitude toward Roman Catholics

in the new nation. Not until the 19th Century and the great influx of Roman Catholics from Ireland and southern and eastern
Europe did rabid anti-Catholicism again raise its head.

The response of Rome to the change in circumstances brought on
by the Revolution made it possible for the Church to emerge from
the Revolution with credentials sufficient to begin the organization of an American church. John Carroll's acceptance of his
appointment as Superior of the American missions in 1784 was the
first step toward an American bishopric.

Struggles to bring order out of disorder in thirteen states
and to regulate and control the influx of new, sometimes rene-
gade, priests from Europe convinced American Roman Catholic
leadership of the need for a bishop. American priests had resisted the idea of an American bishop because of the widespread
prejudice against bishops in the colonies and their own distrust
of the Congregation for the Propagation of the Faith. Nevertheless,
the clergy requested the erection of a see from Rome in 1786, to
be filled by someone they would nominate. The request was
granted, and John Carroll was appointed the first bishop in 1789.

Due to the coming explosion in France, the Roman Catholic
Church in America was on the eve of a period of significant advance.

In general, the missionary situation of the Roman Catholics
during the era of the Revolution was not good. Only the Franciscan mission to the Indians of California was in a flourishing
state. There was new hope and vigor for the fledgling Church in
the new nation. But the personnel or resources to begin to expand into all of the new states were not in sight in 1789.

II.   THE COLONIAL ESTABLISHMENTS AND
THE BRITISH MISSIONARY SOCIETIES

The story of religion in America can be described, Franklin
Littel has said, as a movement from state church to pluralism.
During the colonial period the religious pattern was one of establishment. In the English colonies, magisterial Protestant-
ism--legally, at least--reigned supreme.

During the era of the Revolution, Standing Order Congregationalism dominated all of New England except Rhode Island, and the
Anglican Church was established in the remainder of the colonies
except New Jersey and Pennsylvania. Through the action of Governors, General Courts and Assemblies and with the assistance of
missionary societies in England and Scotland, these groups
gathered churches throughout the colonies among Europeans and
attempted in particular places to win pagan Indians and Blacks to
faith in Christ.

New England Missions

The earliest effort to evangelize the American Indians by Protestants was launched in New England in 1642, on Martha's Vineyard, and greatly enlarged on the mainland by John Eliot in 1646. The New England Company (NEC) was founded in England to underwrite this mission. Organized in 1649, it is the oldest Protestant Society exclusively for missionary purposes.

The NEC functioned in America through a Board of Commissioners who recruited missionaries, determined fields and gave general direction to the missions. There was invariably a very close relationship between the action of the Commissioners and the General Courts, especially of Massachusetts.

The Indian mission suffered significant discouragements during the French and Indian War. In the decade before the Revolution the NEC, through its Commissioners, gave primary support to four missions.

On Martha's Vineyard, Zechariah Mayhew was about halfway through his long ministry as the last Mayhew missionary on the Vineyard.[18] Mayhew itinerated among the five small congregations. He was assisted by two or three Indian preachers. The mission experienced great privations during the Revolution. Mayhew was seldom paid. An American missionary society assumed his support after 1787, though most of the Indians, concentrated at Gay Head, had become Baptists.

In 1764, the Commissioners sent Ebenezer Moseley and James Deane to Onohoquaga (Broom County, New York) to found a mission. Moseley remained until 1773. Aaron Crosley, recently graduated from Dartmouth College, took up the mission in 1774 and remained until 1777. The mission was closed that year.[19]

In 1770, Samuel Kirkland, the most effective missionary trained by Eleazor Wheelock, broke with his mentor. He had been supported by the Society in Scotland for Promoting Christian Knowledge (SSPCK). While the SSPCK continued to give some support to Kirkland, from 1770 until the Revolution began, the NEC provided his major support.

The most important mission in New England directed by the NEC Board of Commissioners was the Stockbridge Mission on the Housatonic in Western Massachusetts. Founded in 1735 by John Sergeant, it had been the show case Indian mission in New England. Jonathan Edwards became the missionary in 1751, after Sergeant's death. Stockbridge had by that time become a major outpost on the edge of the wilderness.

Stephen West became the missionary after Edward's resignation. Settled in 1758, he served until 1775. By the time the Revolution began, the number of whites in Stockbridge had increased so that the Indians were a minority. John Sergeant, Jr. became the Indian teacher in 1773 and, in 1775, took over the entire mission.

In 1770, Samson Occom, the best known and best trained Indian preacher in the eighteenth century, and his son-in-law, Joseph Johnson united the Indians in five small Indian communities in coastal New England and purchased land from the Onedias in northwestern New York. In 1774, they founded Brothertown. When the Revolution came these Indians withdrew to Stockbridge and remained there through the war. At the close of hostilities the Stockbridge community had moving fever. The Revolution effectively marked the end of significant Indian missions in New England. The stage had moved farther West.

The second missionary thrust in New England from Standing Order Churches came originally from Connecticut. It was not, however, as closely related to civil government. Eleazar Wheelock began a private school in 1743, at Lebanon. By 1754, after teaching Samson Occom for four years, he conceived a plan to train English and Indian young people together and to send them out as teams to evangelize the Pagan Tribes. Moor's Charity School was not intended to be an establishment institution, but was an enterprise of faith modeled after Francke's various charity institutions at Halle in Germany and George Whitfield's Orphanage in Georgia. Originally, Wheelock's mission was more an expression of the volunteerism and spontaneity of the Great Awakening than a project designed to be supported and promoted by the acts of magistrates.

The decade of the sixties were the most fruitful years of the Wheelock mission. Numerous young men were sent out, but they mostly itinerated, and few considered themselves missionaries for life. Samuel Kirkland was one outstanding exception.

The SSPCK had established a Board of Correspondents in Boston in 1734, in an effort to become involved in an Indian mission. A large bequest depended on this kind of activity. That mission failed after a few years, and the Boston Correspondents had ceased to function. In 1764, in the flush of victory over the French, Wheelock was able to get himself and several of his associates appointed on a Board of Correspondents in Connectict. Thus the SSPCK became the major supporter of his mission work. Samuel Kirkland was the most successful of all of Wheelock's missionaries, but the two came to a parting of their ways in 1770. The Wheelock enterprise had only itinerant missionaries at the beginning of the Revolution. After the establishment of Dartmouth in 1770, Wheelock's major interest was with English settlers in Western New England. Moor's Charity School did continue as a part of Dartmouth into the second quarter of the nineteenth century.[20]

Wheelock's break with Kirkland was followed by conflict with the SSPCK. With his removal to New Hampshire the Correspondents of which he was a part dissolved, and the SSPCK appointed a second Boston Board. This Board began to give limited support to Kirkland after 1773.

When the Revolution was over, the NEC refused to continue support in the new nation. Kirland petitioned the SSPCK, and its Board of Correspondents in Boston was formed for a third time. The SSPCK provided support for Christian teachers in several small Indian communities in New England, but primary support was given to John Sergeant, Jr. Kirkland did get a limited stipend.

Occom, Kirkland and Sergeant all located in the Oneida Country and attempted to relate themselves to the two churches in New Stockbridge and Brothertown. An unfortunate struggle ensued, and John Sergeant, Jr. emerged the victor.

The return of the SSPCK to missionary support stimulated Standing Order leaders in Boston to form a distinctively American missionary society. The effort had been made before. A society was formed in Boston in 1762 that failed to get the approbation of the King. Samuel Hopkins and Ezra Stiles had joined together in 1773 in proposing a society to send American Blacks as missionaries to Africa. Bristol Yamma and John Quamire were actually sent to Princeton to be trained for the mission. However, with Shay's Rebellion in the background and the disturbing news that Strict Congregationalist and Separtists and Baptists were growing alarmingly in the frontier communities, the Society for Propagating the Gospel among the Indians and Others in North America (SPGNA) was formed. It was a Standing Order Society that got its funds for frontier missions from the General Court of Massachusetts during the first decade of its existence. Because of an unexpected bequest, this society was able to begin at once to support Indian missions.

During the generation of the Revolution, Standing Order Churches began to organize for a determined missionary approach to the white settlers in frontier communities. Before this time the formation of new churches had primarily been a part of the legal proceeding in setting up new towns. Land was set aside for the church and the pastor, and legal arrangements were made for his support. One church for each community was the prevailing pattern.

Several things happened to change that pattern. Nascent pluralism was introduced. A few Baptist and Anglican churches had been in existence in New England since the seventeenth century. However, through the Society for Propagating the Gospel (SPG), the Church of England began to make determined efforts to form churches in New England before mid-century. The Great Awakening

produced two new situations. First, it gave renewed emphasis to
the new birth, which essentially meant a new definition of
"Christian." The revivalists rejected the Half-way Covenant and
insisted on a "lively" personal faith as the means of vital, saving union with Jesus Christ. Secondly, new churches began to be
organized, voluntarily supported, of those who could not find a
home for their new religious enthusiasm and convictions within
the Standing Order Churches. In the quarter century before the
Revolution strict Congregational, Baptist and Anglican churches
were proliferating all over New England.

The first reaction was legal retaliation against these new
congregations. The quarter century after 1750 was punctuated by
legal action against the various dissenters from the New England
way. Forced support, through taxes, of the pastors of the established churches made it a quarter century of conflict and actually stimulated the growth of these dissenting groups.

In the 1770's the Standing Order Church in Connecticut began
to react in another fashion. In 1774, the General Association in
that state took action to send to missionaries to the frontier
communities. None actually went because of the political unrest.
But a new direction was set.

When the General Association met in 1786, it offered to use
mission money collected before the Revolution for men willing to
preach in the "New-formed or forming Settlements." For the next
ten years the various local associations sent itinerant missionaries to the new communities annually. Thus the Standing Order
Churches in New England, by the end of the Confederation period,
were involved in a limited fashion in an Indian mission, and had
begun to take seriously church planting on the frontier.

Anglican Missions

The Church of England had no bishop in America during the
colonial period. In spite of the fact that it was favored by
civil government in a majority of the colonies, the Church had
little vigor in many areas, failed to penetrate beyond the larger
coastal communities in most colonies, and continually required
nourishment in money and personnel from England.

All the ills that the Church experienced were usually blamed
on the lack of a colonial episcopate. In 1766, Hugh Neill
lamented,

> whilst the Dissenters can send out an innumerable tribe
> of teachers of all sorts without any expenses, we must
> send three thousand miles cross the Atlantic Ocean, at
> the expense of all we are worth . . .before we can have

ordination--this is a difficulty that has, and always
will, prevent the growth of the Church in America.[21]

The lack of a resident bishop certainly contributed to some of
the problems of the Church. Nevertheless, the Church did experience growth right up to the beginning of the Revolution.

The Society for Propagating the Gospel (SPG), organized in
1701, was the principle missionary agent of the Church of England
in the colonies. Designed first of all "to settle the State of
Religion as well as may be among (its) *own People*," its secondary purpose was to "proceed in the best Methods . . .toward the
Conversion of the *Natives*."[22]

There was plenty to do among the colonials. In 1701, only
eight Anglican priests served the colonies outside Virginia (25)
and Maryland (17). During the next 75 years, 309 missionaries
served in America. There were 77 under appointment at the time
the War began, and 400 churches.

The Revolution, however, all but devasted the Church as it was
then constituted. Most SPG missionaries and many of the other
settled clergy were loyalists. Expansion came to a standstill.
Further, the most successful Protestant mission to American Indians in the colonial period, supported by the SPG, was lost to
Canada.

The SPG was reasonably successful in maintaining a mission to
the Mohawks, near Albany, from 1709 onward.[23] But few inroads
were made in bringing them into the Christian faith until Sir
William Johnson began to give his attention to it after 1760.
Johnson was made a member of the SPG, and he took a personal interest in the progress in evangelization. He did, in fact, recruit most of the missionaries and teachers for the Mohawk mission
until his death just before the Revolution.

By the time the Revolution began most of this tribe had become
Anglican Christians. Several factors contributed to this success.
The influence of Johnson himself over the tribe was considerable
and of long duration. Johnson had a genuine appreciation of Indian culture, and no effort was made to force the Mohawks to cease
being Indians and become Englishmen. Finally, in Joseph Brant the
Indians had a chief who was himself an articulate spokesman for
the Christian faith and stood with Johnson in persuading the
Mohawks--almost as a tribe--to become Christians.

When the Revolution came the Indians moved across the border
into Canada and were in the service of the King throughout the
War. They never moved back to the valley of the Mohawk in great
numbers.

The SPG also had an extensive ministry to Blacks, especially in New York. Joseph Hildreth was the teacher of the school in New York City where many were taught to read, write and the rudiments of the Christian faith. As in other missions, the leadership either left during the Revolution or refused to stay after the end of the War.[24]

Where there had been a strong Indian mission, a significant effort to Christianize pagan Blacks, and an aggressive program—in some colonies—of church planting was all but wiped out at the end of the Revolution.

However, steps were taken rapidly to form an American Church. Samuel Seabury was ordained in 1784. The Protestant Episcopal Church of America was formed in 1785. By 1790, the American church had four bishops and was on the way to recovery.

III. THE REVIVALISTIC CHURCHES

"The Great Awakening," said Robert E. Thompson almost a century ago, "terminated the Puritan and inaugurated the Pietist or Methodist age of American church history."[25] More recently Alan Heimert has insisted that the Great Awakening launched a new era in the evolution of the American mind.[26] That explosion of religious faith left a mark on all American religious groups existing at the time.

It had a formative effect on the Baptists and Presbyterians in America. American Baptists and Presbyterians in 1775 were of a different order from those in 1725. The Great Awakening *established* Calvinism among the Baptists, but it united it with the fire and fervor of Whitfield.[27]

The New Side Presbyterians, Leonard Trinterud has said, being "intensely missionary-minded, . . .by their unparalleled zeal and efforts, far outstripped the Old World Presbyterians that had been transplanted into the colonies and gave birth to a new order of Presbyterianism, an American Church."[28]

At the beginning of the Revolutionary era a new group, born out of the Evangelical Awakening in England, came upon the American scene. They were forced very quickly to become an American church. The Methodists, the Baptists and the Presybterians were all revivalistic churches. What was their missionary attitude, what were they doing, and what did they do as the American Revolution progressed, to express the missionary spirit that they shared?

The Presbyterians

During the decade before the Revolution, the Synod of New York and Philadelphia was involved in support of an Indian mission and in church planting on the frontier. John Brainerd had continued the missions of his brother for several years. But in the 1760's, the New Jersey government purchased land for the scattered Indian groups, and Brainerd became their superintendent and missionary. The Synod regularly gave support to Brainerd and to the school that he established among the Indians. Samson Occom also received some support for several itinerant missionary journeys after the defeat of France and the Pontiac Confederacy.

This Synod continued each year to send itinerant missionaries through the southern colonies, and during the 1760's began to send men regularly north into New York and across the mountains into western Pennsylvania. In 1767 Charles Beatty and George Duffield returned from a mission that carried them into Ohio. Their report called for the Synod to undertake extensive efforts to evangelize the Indian and white settlers and form them into churches. The Revolution opened before anything extensive was done.

The Synod as an effective national organization was adversely affected by the Revolution. In 1778 only fourteen members were present. No missionaries were sent out after 1777. But the Synod charged the various presbyteries to pursue the frontier mission with as much vigor as possible and to establish schools to train men on the frontier for the ministry. Those were extremely effective instructions. This diffused missionary philosophy continued for ten years.

The Presbyterian Church began to grow dramatically even while the War continued. In five years, 1781-86, five new presbyteries were erected on the frontier. In 1781, revival began in Red Stone Presbytery and seemed to move from church to church across the frontier until 1785. Then in 1787, the revival which Baptists and Methodists had been experiencing in Virginia broke loose among Presybterians.

The Presbyterians came to their first delegated national body in 1789, confident, refreshed and growing.

The Methodists

The Methodist story can be told quickly. The movement was launched in the colonies after numerous requests from people who were already Methodists. At least three lay preachers had already established a preaching ministry in Albany and New York City, and in Maryland before the first agents from the British Conference arrived. A few classes were already organized.

The decision to send two preachers in 1769 was conceived as an evangelistic mission designed not only to win Englishmen to faith in Christ, but to help them live a disciplined Christian life. The sending of missionaries was discontinued after 1774. The coming of the Methodists was not an effort to plant new churches. That tendency was resisted by Wesley and the appointed leadership in America until the War was over.

The Methodist approach—preach everywhere and gather those who respond into cells of mutual discipline and care—is a method calculated for growth and one that will inevitably produce churches. By the time the Revolution began, numerous lay preachers had been raised up, and there was already a strong feeling that the societies should have the sacraments. This opinion was so strong, especially in the South, that preachers in a Southern Conference ordained themselves in 1779, and began to administer the sacraments. Asbury was able to heal the schism and this practice was discontinued.

One reason for the problem in the Southern colonies was the fantastic growth that took place there. By 1775, over two-thirds of the 3,148 society members were in the South. The work was carried on not by Wesley's missionaries but by men considered irregular and by native American preachers. By 1780, 7,800 of the 8,500 Methodists were in the South. Revival started in the Anglican parish of Devereaux Jarratt in 1772. By 1774, it had begun in the Methodist circuits in the area and continued into the early years of the War. Dramatic growth continued in the midst of war.

The War had a detrimental effect. Methodist leaders were suspected of being Tories, and many were. All of Wesley's missionaries except Asbury had returned to England by 1778. Because of the war there was a sharp decline in membership in the middle colonies, especially New York. Nevertheless, by the Christmas Conference, 1784, there were 82 preachers at the disposal of the conference and 15,000 members. These were men who itinerated, evangelists, and very soon to become church planters. They functioned exactly as the itinerant missionaries sent out by other larger ecclesiastical bodies in the new nation at that time, except they functioned for twelve months instead of two or three. By 1788, there were enough Methodists across the mountains to have an annual conference in Tennessee. By 1790, there were 227 itinerants and 57,600 members.[29]

Methodists in America had not organized for a mission to pagan peoples. Thomas Coke was attempting to get the British Conference to take overseas missions seriously. They did preach effectively to Blacks. But no distinction was made between their work among the Black and white Americans until the end of the century.

The Baptists

Sometime about 1790, Baptists became the largest religious
group in the new nation. Significant growth began after 1750.
Several factors contributed to the growth. The progressive trek
in New England from Strict Congregationalism to the Baptist position helped. But Baptists aggressively gathered new churches at
the same time. In the South the introduction of the spirit of
the Great Awakening into the back country by the Separatist Baptists caused proliferation of churches from 1756 to the end of the
century. The aggressive work of itinerant missionaries, first
from the Philadelphia Association and gradually from other
associations that were formed, made the growth--both in coastal
areas and on the frontier--a reality.

Itinerant, unsalaried preachers and little, scattered missionary-minded associations were the agents of expansion. Before 1776,
there were eight associations in the colonies. By 1787, there
were fourteen more. Growth continued through the Revolution. In
fact, the Baptists were probably able to use the mobility made
necessary by the War as a means of spreading their faith. The
Warren Association, for example, at the beginning of the Revolution had 27 churches and 1,393 members. When the War was over it
had 44 churches and 3,570 members. Only Baptists in the Middle
colonies were seriously hindered from growth by the War. The
attack on the Regulation Movement in North Carolina before the
Revolution effectively dispersed Baptists from North Carolina, but
that only meant greater growth in other places.

Was their expansion planned, organized and deliberate or spontaneous, accidental and chaotic? Both.

There were deliberate, planned efforts to evangelize and gather
churches both by individuals and associations. However, revivals
that contributed to the growth of Methodists and, later, Presbyterians in the South had a tremendous effect on Baptist growth in
those areas. During the later years of the Revolution there was
a revival among the Baptists in New England. Warren Association
reported in 1780 that in the past year 765 new members had been
added to their churches. Over 1,000 had been baptized who did
not unite with their churches.[30]

The pattern of deliberate expansion was remarkably identical
in all of the associations. The churches of the Philadelphia
Association experienced a decline of 1,200 members from 1775 to
1783, but the number of churches increased by three. Even during
the War and occupation the association raised a fund for the express purpose of "preaching the gospel in destitute places, (and)
among the back settlements."[31] The addition of new churches to
the association at each annual meeting stopped during the war,

but as soon as Cornwallis had surrendered, newly constituted
churches were added every year. By 1787, there were 55 churches
and 3,198 members.

The Warren Association was even more aggressive. In 1778,
three missionaries were sent, and their expenses paid, to the
"northern part of our county." In 1779, and for the two years
following, missionary preachers were sent to New Hampshire. In
1782, Isaac Chase was sent to the District of Maine. He found
two other Baptist preachers there before him. They all remained.
In 1787, the Bowdoinham Association was formed, and a program of
itineracy was adopted at the first meeing.[32]

Baptists in America undertook no mission to pagan people in the
Revolutionary era. They did, along with Methodists and Presbyterians, develop a method of sending missionaries to frontier
settlements that set the stage for greater missionary involvement
in the nineteenth century.

IV THE NON-ENGLISH CHURCHES

Reformed and Lutheran churches composed the bulk of the non-
English speaking congregations in America at the time of the
Revolution. The growth of these *Lutheran and Reformed* Churches
in colonial America reflects the missionary interest of several
different groups in Europe.

By the time of the Revolution, Lutheran, German Reformed and
Dutch Reformed synods had already been organized or were being
organized in America. The parent bodies in Europe maintained
close control over all ecclesiastical affairs in the colonies.
This tended to retard development toward maturity in the colonial
bodies. Generally, the last half of the eighteenth century was a
time of tension between European ecclesiastical parents and
American daughters. This affected the missionary situation of
these churches during the Revolutionary era.

These American churches, struggling to bring order out of
cultural and geographical diversity and to gain their own independence from European superiors, did not develop a distinctly
missionary approach to the American Indian during the eighteenth
century. If they did engage in evangelism among Indians and
Blacks, it was spontaneous and without organization or persistence.

Dutch Reformed

Dutch Reformed churches in America were placed under the oversight of the Classis of Amsterdam in the seventeenth century. The
eighteenth century was a struggle, first toward an organized,
extra-congregational expression of the Church, and then toward

full independence from the Classis of Amsterdam and the Synod of
North Holland. Permission to form a Coetus, requested in 1738,
was finally granted in 1747. Actual independence from the Church
of Holland was secured in 1792.

The Classis of Amsterdam was the most active missionary body
of the Reformed Church of the Netherlands. At the same time it
had oversight of the young churches in America, it directed work
in South Africa and in various places in the Orient. This classis
had a standing committee of commissioners to care for the overseas
churches.

The Amsterdam body not only attempted to provide personnel, it
steadfastly insisted on approving all who were ordained ministers.
It provided not only some monetary assistance but also ecclesiastical discipline.

The General Body of the Reformed Church in New York and New
Jersey experienced little expansion during the revolutionary era.
A serious division occurred in 1754 that was not healed until
1771. Twelve years later the Synod was still trying to get some
consistories to sign the articles of union.

In 1784, a committee presented a long report on the condition
of the Church. It called attention to the new settlements and
challenged the Synod to double the number of its congregations
by missionary activity.

There was a great deal of discussion and oral planning, but
no missionary went out until 1792.33

German Reformed

The German Reformed Church is a somewhat different story. In
1728, these churches came under the oversight of the Reformed
Church in Holland. More support and more freedom was given to
the German churches, mainly in Pennsylvania, than to the Dutch
churches in New York and New Jersey.

The Church in Holland, as with the Dutch-speaking churches,
became the missionary body responsible for the effort to evangelize and plant churches among the German immigrants in America.
With the German church, not just the Classis of Amsterdam, but
both the Synod of North and of South Holland were directly involved. A group of deputies from each synod met together to give
direction to the mission.

Numerous churches had already been established in 1746, when
Michael Schlatter was sent to Pennsylvania with explicit orders
to form the scattered churches into a Coetus. This was accomplished in 1747.

Beginning in 1753 and continuing until 1791, the parent body in Holland sent money for pastoral support every year without exception--a total of over $25,000. Personnel was sent every year, even through the Revolution. Nevertheless, the American churches made a break with Holland in 1791. A Synod was organized in 1792, and the German Reformed body became an independent church.

This church was shaped much more by evangelical pietism than the Dutch Reformed church. Pastors were more active in evangelistic travels. This was especially true of those numerous pastors who came from the University of Herborn, a pietistic institution that had an influence among German Reformed people in America like the University of Halle had on early Lutherans in America.

In the Revolutionary era, the pietistic party within the Reformed Church and the Methodists, in the person of Francis Asbury, joined in evangelistic efforts in Maryland. Led by Phillip William Otterbein, a class system was employed in most of the Maryland churches modeled after the Methodist pattern. There were stirring results and there was significant growth from 1770 to 1775. The Reformed churches came to the beginning of the Revolution filled with optimism and in a position of strength.

The Revolution was more devastating among the churches of the Middle Colonies than in either the South or New England. The Coetus was unable to meet every year during the War. It emerged from the War facing several internal problems: gaining its independence from Holland, which meant renouncing the annual stipend; dealing with the threat posed by independents and pietists; and handling the matter of union churches with Lutherans. Faced with these problems no plan was developed that could be described as distinctly missionary by the time the Synod was organized in 1792.

The Lutherans

The development of larger ecclesiastical fellowship among Lutherans centered in Pennsylvania, though there were significant numbers of Lutherans in other colonies. The progress and shape of early American Lutheranism was influenced by people with missionary intent in England and Germany.

The Lutheran movement in America was primarily a missionary project of the Halle institutions in Germany, mediated through the large Lutheran community attached to the House of Hanover in London. It is difficult to understand this relationship without realizing that the Hanoverian kings--while directly related to the Church of England--were, in sympathy at least, also Lutherans. If the kings themselves were not devoted Lutherans, there were many in their courts who were. The Royal German St. James Chapel had two pastors whose ministry spanned the first three quarters

of the seventeenth century. Both were close friends of the two
Frankes. Both had the missionary passion so characteristic of
early Halle pietism. Anton W. Bohme, the first pastor and court
Chaplain at St. James, took a personal interest in German immi-
grants from the Palatinate who came through England on the way to
Pennsylvania. Then Frederick Michael Ziegenhagen, his successor
became a sort of German bishop over the scattered Lutherans in
Pennsylvania. They wrote him for ministers and other assistance.
He was the person contacted when a call was extended to Henry M.
Muhlenburg to come to Philadelphia.

Ziegenhagen invariably turned to the younger Franke for personnel. The community in Halle gave direction to the missionary
pastors and received from Pennsylvania annually reports of their
activity. In all, Halle sent twenty-four missionaries and leaders
to minister in Pennsylvania.[34]

The Society for Promoting Christian Knowledge (SPCK) became
directly involved in the support of the Lutherans in Georgia from
the beginning, and later provided support for some of the churches
in Pennsylvania. Until 1783, the Church of Sweden provided support
and provost for the Swedish Lutheran Church on the Delaware.

In Muhlenburg, G. A. Franke found not only an effective evangelist, but a devoted church planter. His often repeated motto,
"the church must be planted," is a mark of his missionary commitment. At the beginning of the Revolution he was supervising
seventy congregations in the Middle Colonies. About 30 other
congregations were located in the South.

The Revolutionary period for Lutherans, as with Dutch and
Reformed Churches, was the time for breaking ties with parent
bodies in Europe. There was no organized plan with missionary
intent by the Ministerium of Pennsylvania during the Revolutionary
generation.

V.   THE PEACE CHURCHES

The final group of Protestant churches to be surveyed are those
that can be called the Peace Churches. This discussion will be
confined to the Quakers and the Moravians.

Society of Friends

The account of the founding of Quakerism in colonial America is
an exciting story of men and women who knew themselves sent on a
divine mission to bear witness to the Christ within. They were
sent to America not just to spy out the land but to take possession
of it. They did it very successfully. By the time of the Revolution there were almost 50,000 Quakers in the colonies.

During the period of the *"First Publishers,"* people were gathered
into the fellowship of Friends through direct evangelism. During
the eighteenth century the Society of Friends adopted a policy of
birthright membership that effectively transformed them from a
church of believers to an association of people, some of whom
might be unconverted. Growth during the last 75 years of the
century was predominately natural increase from families.

In the decade before the American Revolution Quakers experienced
a great deal of internal difficulty maintaining their peace witness.
They also struggled to have one voice against slavery and to manifest the anti-slavery witness with practice.

Only sporadically between the Fox-Penn era and the Revolution
did the possibility of helping the American Indian by teaching him
Christianity occur to Friends. The visit of John Woolman to the
Indians on the Susquehanna in 1763 was only a single occurrence,
and his visit was among Indians already won to Christian faith by
the Moravians. Zebulon Heston visited the Delawares in 1773 with
a message from the Meeting for Sufferings at Philadelphia. The
Indians urged upon him a need for religious teachers. The Meeting
replied that they would send teachers, but only if they could go
with a sense of duty. No Friends had the inner prompting to
evangelize the Indians in 1774.[35]

The important step made by the Quakers toward a renewed missionary spirit in the Revolutionary era was in the creation of the
Meetings for Sufferings. The first to be established in America
was in Philadelphia in 1756. The original purpose of these meetings was to meet emergency conditions related to war, relief and/or
legal aid. They were composed of leaders appointed at the Quarterly
and Yearly Meetings.

The evolution of these Meetings for Suffering to take up the
cause of the Indians and the Blacks in the years after the War
involved Quakers in deliberate and concerted missionary activity
again, after almost a century of disinterest in those matters.

The Unitas Fratrum, The Unity of the Brethren

The missionary character of the Moravian Church in America is
well known. What was the situation in reference to missions in
1776?

First, at the General Synod meeting in Europe in 1775, action
was taken that hindered the growth of the Church in America for
over forty years. The consequences of that action were not imposed
on the American branch of the Church until 1779.

Bishop Johann F. Reichel arrived in April, and in August he convened a conference of ministers, in which steps were taken to bring the affairs of the Church into conformity with Synodical decisions. An era of centralization was introduced that effectively hindered American Moravians from planting churches among Europeans.

There had been steady growth and the addition of new congregations from Rhode Island to North Carolina almost every year in the decade before the Revolution.

The Wachovia project in North Carolina had begun in earnest in 1758. During the same time that Separatist Baptists were exploding in the back country of North Carolina, the Moravians were also gathering congregations.

However, the decision of the Synod determined that these outlying small societies would not be considered congregations. They were training schools. Those in them who proved themselves regenerate might then be admitted to full membership in the churches within Moravian settlements. At the same time that Methodists, Episcopalians, Reformed, and Lutheran groups were being set free from European control, the United Brethren were brought under a stricter discipline.

In terms of the mission to pagan peoples, no group in America was as committed in theory, resources and actual performance to cross cultural evangelism as were the Moravians. No group in America was more successful. No missionary effort was more tragically destroyed by the war than that of the Moravians.

The Wachovia tract was purchased to become a base for evangelizing the Cherokee, Catawba, Creek and Chickasaw tribes as Bethlehem was intended for the northern tribes. No significant inroads were made into the southern tribes before or immediately after the Revolution.

In 1775, immediately before the War an attempt was made to begin a mission to slaves in Georgia. War effectively put an end to the effort.

In David Zeisberger, already a veteran missionary among the northern tribes, the Moravians had a missionary of the caliber of Serra in California. He is the only Protestant missionary in the generation of the Revolution who stands out as a man able to communicate the Gospel of Christ across cultural lines. As with Serra, Zeisberger had excellent men with whom he worked.

His work among the Delawares was beset with hardships from the time that the Pontiac Rebellion was brought to a conclusion.[36] Progressively the band of Christian Indians moved from the north

branch of the Susquehanna to Beaver River, across the Ohio to the
Tuscarawas River. Another village of Christian Indians from the
Allegheny Valley followed them. There, in three different communities, in 1773-1778, may Delaware Indians became Christians and
great peace, prosperity and growth ensued.

However, the villages were located between Detroit and Pittsburgh.
The missionaries and the Indians were first taken captive and marched
to Sandusky by the British. The villages were destroyed. Weeks
later, the Indians were permitted to return to harvest what was left
of their crops. There, working in the fields, they were discovered
by a troop of American militiamen, herded into barns and massacred.
The tragedy took place March 8, 1781, a few weeks before the surren-
der of Cornwallis.

Zeisberger, of course, continued. In four years he planted a
successful mission from the remnants of his people, just north of
Detroit. In 1786, New Salem was begun near Cleveland.

                    * * * * * * * * * *

It is impossible in a brief paragraph to characterize the missionary spirit of these differing Protestant groups. I believe that one
of the greatest missionary sermons preached in America in the last
quarter of the eighteenth century was delivered by Samuel Hopkins
before the Providence Society for Abolishing the Slave Trade, May 17,
1793. It was based on Matthew 28:19-20, and should be ranked alongside the great sermon by William Carey a few months earlier. A
few lines will illustrate the convictions that motivated a large
number of the men who manned the Protestant missionary effort during
the Revolution.

> This command of Christ respects not only the apostles and
> disciples who then heard him . . . and the ministers . . .
> who have since been, . . . but is extended to all Christians,
> in every age of the church, requireing them in all proper
> ways, according to their ability, stations, and opportunities,
> to promote this benevolent design, and exert themselves for
> the furtherance of the gospel, that, if possible all may hear
> and share in the happy effects of it.
> . . . .
> He ordered that this good news should be published through
> the whole world, and the offer of his salvation be made to
> all mankind, whatever nation or complexion, whether Jews or
> Gentiles, the more civilized or barbarians, rich or poor,
> white or black, this being the only remedy for lost man,
> suited to recover him from that state of darkness, sin and
> misery in which the world of mankind lay.[37]

VI.   SUMMING UP

How shall we sum up all this diverse, and often unrelated, detail? Two or three observations will suffice.

1. At the time of the American Revolution the great mission of
European Christians toward pagan peoples in North America, that
characterized the sixteenth and seventeenth centuries, was almost
in demise. The bulk of this heroic mission period stemmed from
Roman Catholic countries. Only the Franciscan mission in California
and the Moravian mission among the Delawares flourished. Their vigor was expressed only in great hardship. Perhaps the Anglican
mission among the Mohawks should also be included. It did effectively Christianize a tribe. It was, however, not so much the work
of missionaries sent to communicate the faith across barriers of
language, race and culture as it was the sharing of faith by
leaders inside that culture. This is always the most effective
way of communicating the faith. Reading the source material on
this mission, one gets the feeling that the Mohawks became Christians
almost in spite of their missionaries.

2. In the English colonies the most pervasive influence on missionary activity at the time of the Revolution was the Evangelical Awakening that surged through the Atlantic Community during the eighteenth
century. Whether effected by German Pietism, England's Evangelical
Revival, or the Great Awakening in the colonies the spiritual motivation of Protestants stemmed primarily from this source. It also
informed their understanding of the missionary task, defined the
missionary message and provided goals for missionary effort.

3. This survey exposes the missionary commitment of European
groups and suggests the contribution that they made to shaping
American Christianity. Often overlooked in accounts of developing
denominationalism, the contribution of these European missionary
societies and church bodies was very often an expression of real evangelical concern, as much as an effort to reproduce like kind on
American soil. During the period of the Revolution, however, the
participation of these groups was often oppressive and possessive.
In the Revolutionary era they often had a negative effect on the
missionary situation. Christians almost always prefer debating
about the faith to sharing it with others.

4. Among Protestants, the missionary situation at the time of the
Revolution was most favorable among the revivalistic, free churches.
There was a marriage, as Sidney Mead has suggested, of rationalism and
pietism during the Revolutionary epoch.[38] The home they built for
themselves was national religious freedom. Magisterial Protestantism
was at its lowest ebb from 1775 to 1795. Methodists, Baptists and
Presbyterians (to a lesser degree) continued to expand in that age of
infidelity, even before the Second Great Awakening began. These
groups found themselves in an ethos of responsiveness.

NOTES

[1] I am greatly indebted to John Tracy Ellis, Catholics in Colonial America (Benedictine Studies; Baltimore: Helicar Press, 1965), pp. 11-18, for the discussion that follows.

[2] John Tracy Ellis, ed., Documents of American Catholic History (Milwaukee: The Bruce Publishing Company, 1956), pp. 5-7.

[3] Leo Gershog, From Despotism to Revolution (Harper Torchbooks; New York: Harper and Row, Publishers, 1963) pp. 142-161, 264-295, has been very helpful to me.

[4] Report of Bishop Caldiron of Santiago to Queen Mother Marie Anne on The Florida Missions, August 14, 1674, in Tracy, Documents, pp. 18-23.

[5] Eleanor B. Adams and Angelico Chaves, The Mission of New Mexico, 1776 (Albuquerque:1956), pp. 12-43.

[6] Carlos E. Castaneda, Our Catholic Heritage in Texas (6 vols.; Austin:1936) contains a massive account of the colonial history of Roman Catholicism in Texas.

[7] Report of Eusebio Francisco Kino on the Missions at Primeria Alta, Ellis, Documents pp. 25-26.

[8] John Francis Brannon, "The Spaniards and the Illinois Country, 1762-1800," Journal of The Illinois State Historical Society, LXIX (May, 1976) pp. 115-116.

[9]Letter to Rafael Verger, June 20, 1771, in Antonine Tibesas, ed., Writings of Junopero Serra (3 vols.; Washington: Academy of American Franciscan History, 1955), I, 217.

[10]Ibid., note 78, III, 449.

[11]Letter to Francesch Serra, August 20, 1979, ibid., III, 3.

[12]Letter to Francisco Carlos de Croix, June 8, 1771, ibid., I, 209.

[13]Letter to Juan Andres, June 12, 1779, ibid., I, 169.

[14]Ibid., p. 153.

[15]Ibid., p. 173.

[16]Quoted in Ralph D. Winter, "Jesuits Yes, Presbyterians No!," Church Growth Bulletin, VI (May, 1970), 69.

[17]Mary Doris Mulvey, French Catholic Missionaries in the Present United States (Washington, D.C.: The Catholic University of America, 1936), p. 105.

[18]See Margery Ruth Johnson, The Mayhew Mission to the Indians, 1643-1806, doctoral dissertation, Clark University, Worcester, Massachusetts, 1966, pp. 283-308.

[19]William Kellaway, The New England Company 1649-1776 (New York: Barnes and Noble, Inc., 1961), p. 267.

[20]See Charles Chaney, The Birth of Missions in America (Pasadena: William Carey Library, 1976) pp. 111-113 for a much more detailed account of these developments.

[21]C. F. Pascoe, Two Hundred Years of the S.P.G. (London: Published at the Societies Office, 1901), p. 35.

[22]Ibid., p. 7.

[23]See John W. Lydekker, The Faithful Mohawks (New York: The Macmillan Company, 1938) for a very readable account of this mission.

[24]See Frank J. Klingberg, Anglican Humanitarianism in Colonial New York (Philadelphia: The Church Historical Society, 1940), pp. 120-190.

[25]Robert E. Thompson, A History of the Presbyterian Churches in the United States (New York: Charles Scribners Sons, 1895), p. 34.

[26]Alan Heimert and Perry Miller, eds., The Great Awakening (New York: The Bobbs-Merril Company, Inc., 1967), p. xiv.

[27]See T. B. Matson, Isaac Backus: Pioneer of Religious Liberty (Rochester, N.Y.: American Baptist Historical Society, 1962), p.34.

[28]Leonard Trinterud, The Forming of An American Tradition (Philadelphia: The Westminster Press, 1954), p. 122.

[29]Wade Crawford Barclay, History of Methodist Missions (6 vols., New York: Board of Missions and Church Extension of the Methodist Church, 1949), pp. 4-120, and W. W. Sweet, Methodism in American History (New York: The Methodist Book Concern, 1933), pp. 47-99, have guided me in this discussion.

[30]A. D. Gillette, ed., Minutes of the Philadelphia Baptist Association (Philadelphia: American Baptist Publication Society, 1851), p. 169.

[31]Ibid., p. 159.

[32]Henry S. Bunnage, A History of Baptists in New England (Philadelphia: American Baptist Publication Society, 1894), pp. 800-803.

[33]Chaney, op. cit, pp. 148-149. See E. T. Corwin, A History of the Reformed Church, Dutch (New York: The Christian Literature Co., 1894), pp. 131-183.

[34]Theodore E. Schmank, A History of the Lutheran Church in Pennsylvania (Philadelphia: General Council Publication House, 1903), pp. 176-207.

[35]Sidney V. James, A People Among Peoples (Cambridge, Mass.: Harvard University Press, 1963), pp. 298-299.

[36]See Elma E. Gray, Wilderness Christians (Ithaca, New York: Cornell University Press, 1956).

[37]Samuel Hopkins, A Discourse on the Slave Trade and the Slavery of the Africans, Works of Samuel Hopkins, D. D., Edward Parks, ed. (3 vols.; Boston: Doctrinal Tract and Book Society, 1854), II, 598-599.

[38]Sidney Mead, The Lively Experiment (New York: Harper and Row, Publishers, 1963), p. 38.

2

Response to Dr. Chaney

Edward M. Cook

In the paper just presented, Mr. Chaney gives a broad survey of missionary activities in North America on the eve of the American Revolution. Within his purview falls not only the missionary work of the Catholic Spanish and French among the Indians west of the Mississippi and on the fringes of the English settlements, but also the rivalry of various English Protestant groups for the conversion of some of the same Indians and the efforts of various sects and national churches to enlarge their followings among the inhabitants of English America. The paper effectively demonstrates that the volume of missionary work carried on in the eighteenth century was indeed large and is quite successful in describing how that work varied in intensity from place to place and from time to time over the century. Because Mr. Chaney has surveyed the situation well, I propose in the next few minutes to amplify his discussion in two ways rather than to review the specifics of his account.

My first line of commentary involves looking at the missionary situation from an eighteenth century point of view. In his presentation Mr. Chaney has adopted the stance of a twentieth century ecumenical historian, and has defined missionary activity in terms of the converting activities of <u>all</u> Christian groups. Such a notion, of course, would have seemed alien, if not downright perverse, to eighteenth century Christians, who remained bitterly divided along sectarian lines. Sectarian divisions influenced missionary perceptions in at least three significant ways. Most broadly historical and theological differences encouraged Catholics and Protestants to continue to view one another as heretics and tools of Satan. In the North American context and elsewhere, these identifications meant that

no selfrespecting Protestant would identify the activities of
the French and Spanish as legitimate missionary work, and the
same attitude was reciprocated by the Catholics. Conversion by
the religious enemy was in many respects worse than leaving
non-Christians in their heathen state.

Even within the two great camps, national differences implied large problems for the missions. On the eve of the
American Revolution, Europeans viewed religion as a major instrument of political order and authority, and thus the legitimate concern of governments that sustained religious institutions and required the religious authorities to support state
power. The Protestant nations of England, Scotland, Holland,
Sweden, and Germany all had established churches that were
active in America and the Catholic nations of France and Spain
had nationally distinct religious hierarchies. The political
authorities of each country manipulated missions for territorial aggrandizement as well as for pious ends. The nationali-
ties of missionary clergy were as important within the Catholic
or Protestant groupings as they were between the two: all
national groups viewed the missions of foreigners as alien and
threatening enterprises.

Even apart from nationalistic tensions, relatively narrow
differences in faith or practice provided grounds for sharp divisions. In English America evangelical groups competed as
intensely among themselves as they did with formalist or sac-
rimentalist bodies. Similarly the history of Catholic missions
is marked by the rivalries of Jesuits, Franciscans, Dominicans,
and other missionary groups.

The key point about the eighteenth century view of missions
is to stress the intensely competitive nature of the situation.
Converters were not under the impression that their rivals
were involved in a common, constructive enterprise. They would
not have asked about the broad existence of a missionary spirit,
about the general scale of the commitment, or about the aggregate success of Christians in gaining converts among the
pagan peoples of America, although all of these questions seem
relevant and sensible to us today. Rather, they would have
viewed missions in a far more competitive fashion, keeping
score not for the general enterprise, but for their particular
sect. This historical viewpoint must be clear in the reader's
minds when they deal with accounts of missionary activity such
as that presented here.

My second line of commentary uses this competitive perspective to make a connection implied in the definition of Mr.
Chaney's topic but entirely outside the scope of his paper. I

am speaking of the relationship between missionary activity and the beginning of the American Revolution itself. Some mention of this aspect of the missionary situation is not only appropriate in itself, but also illustrates clearly the tensions involved in eighteen century missions.

The most direct source of missionary involvement in the origin of the Revolution was the Anglican church and particularly its missionary arm, the Society for the Propagation of the Gospel in Foreign Parts (S.P.G.). As Mr. Chaney has related, the S.P.G. was founded in 1702 with two primary purposes: first, to convert the pagan Indians and African slaves to Anglican Christianity, and second, to minister to "unchurched" European settlers which in practice came to mean anyone not served by an Anglican church. Missions to the slaves and Indians continued throughout the colonial period, but as the eighteenth century wore on the goal of converting Europeans gradually became paramount. S.P.G. missionaries assisted in the development of the established church in newer colonies such as the Carolinas, and then increasingly turned their attention to converting the Protestant dissenters in the non-Anglican colonies north of the Mason-Dixon line.

The growing concentration of Anglican missions among northern Christians stemmed from two factors. First, groups of Anglicans in the colonies were persistent in their petitions to the S.P.G., while the heathen were obviously less importunate. The Society could not ignore the pleas of believers in the colonies, especially when groups of them offered partial support for a mission and often a potential candidate for the post. Typically, the S.P.G. would contribute to such a mission as long as the local congregation remained unable to support a church and clergyman by themselves. By mid-century the S.P.G. was devoting major resources to serving minorities of immigrant Anglicans and colonial converts in the non-Anglican colonies. The second factor in the allocation of resources was the belief of the English policy makers in the efficacy of church-state relations. As the colonies grew in size and self-reliance, officials became apprehensive about their inability to secure consistent cooperation with imperial policies. Because the role of an established church in indoctrinating subjects in the religiously sanctioned standards of order and subordination was axiomatic to the eighteenth century, policy experts advocated extension of the Anglican establishment in America, and government officials encouraged the church to aim its missionary work at dissenters. If dissenters could be converted to orderly Anglicans, the theory held, government authority and social control in the colonies would increase greatly.

As Anglican missionary pressure grew, American dissenters experienced increasing friction. In New York, Anglican missionaries continued to block the incorporation of a Presbyterian
organization designed to facilitate the church's property
management, and supported an amazingly ill-advised scheme to
require that non-Anglicans be married by Anglican clergymen.
In both New York and Pennsylvania dissenters resented Anglican
control of the only colleges in the colony. In New England,
hostility was most intense. There, the S.P.G. engineered Privy
Council disallowance of the Charter of a Congregational mission
to the Indians setting in stark relief the contrast between
S.P.G. rhetoric about Indian missions and S.P.G. actions in
proselytizing Christians. Anglican missions were especially
obtrusive in that region, because its religious complexion
was relatively homogeneous and because its native trained clergy
were numerous enough to meet basic religious needs. Abrasive
Anglican missionaries made public pronouncements that conflicted
sharply with New England's views about the quality of Congregational institutions and especially about the seventeenth
century history of Puritan and Anglican relations. Persistent
friction engendered distrust, and brought out the latent sus-
picions about Anglican motives that English dissenters retained
from the seventeenth century history of persecution. By the
1760's dissenters throughout the colonies were prepared to see
sinister indications of impending persecution in the pleas
of Anglican clergymen for appointment of an American bishop and
in the obvious government support for Anglican missionary enterprises.

By 1765, suspicion of Anglican missions fed the Revolutionary
movement, and provided explanations for allegedly oppressive
acts of the authorities. Dissenters found Anglican missionaries' calls for obedience to the Stamp Act entirely consistent
with the S.P.G. presumed goals of forcing an American establishment: one historical function of the Anglican establishment had
been to lend religious sanction to government actions during
periods of royal tyranny. Seventeenth century associations between tyrannical rule and Catholic influence and fear that government supported missions would overthrow religious liberty
contributed to American discovery of a grievance in the Quebec
Act, which legalized the Roman Catholic Church in Canada. To
suspicious colonists the slightest government concession to
"popery" reinforced the conclusion that the authorities sought
to establish, in English America as well as in Canada, the kind
authoritarian religious system that the Catholic church represented for dissenting Protestants.

That there was a missionary contribution to 1776 as well as a missionary situation in 1776 underscores the need for constant attention to the culture and definitions of past society when we look into history. Seeking answers about missions in the current understanding of the term is a useful exercise, but it is only partially revelatory about past situations.

3

An Overview of Cultural Factors in the American Protestant Missionary Enterprise

Henry Warner Bowden

Before we consider several major forces which have affected the scope and character of American missionary activities, a few preliminary distinctions are in order. The missionary impulse in its entirety is a complex one, stemming from varied motivational factors and involving a wide variety of individuals. If someone wished to conduct a thorough survey of missions, he would have to cover at least four important headings: the "great commission," the persons who volunteer for individual service, those who stay behind but support missionaries through boards or coordinating agencies and finally those in host cultures who often perceive Christianity quite differently from the ones bringing it to them.

Each of these comprehensive categories deserves lengthy attention. To begin with, one should be thoroughly acquainted with the basic missionary thrust that has been an essential part of Christian life through the centuries. On a theological level --it often seems on a confessional level too--a commitment to share with others the message of God's Son as savior of all mankind has been close to the heart of vibrant, witnessing faith. The gospel lives primarily by personal affirmation, by being embodied in the private lives and congregational response of believers. But in most cases the New Testament message has also been one which thrives on reaching new listeners. Despite the fact that some Christian groups have tried to restrict gospel precepts as their own elitist badge of ethnic or social privilege, church history is full of examples which show missionaries breaking out of those patterns to share salvation's story with those yet unacquainted with it. On the whole then, Christianity means missions. It cannot compromise with finitude or accept

the idea that some people on this globe remain properly outside
its ken. If it were to admit such limitations, something in its
fundamental construction as a universal faith would be lost.
There is a quality within its kerygmatic affirmation that cannot
long deny the impulse to proclaim saving truth with others. Anyone wishing to understand missions must appreciate this theological imperative as endemic to its ideological base.

The second broad category useful for interpreting missionary
movements has to do with the agents themselves. In addition to
embodying the fundamental energy of continuous outreach found in
their confession, they always bring to their various tasks a
host of other motivations: spiritual, psychological and theological. The careful student of missions would want as adequate an
understanding as possible of the persons actually involved in
day-to-day exercises. Why did they volunteer? How did they
conceive of the missionary enterprise in general and of their
relation to it in particular? What did they hope to accomplish?
How did they go about it? Why did they choose certain fields of
endeavor rather than other likely mission stations? What im-
pelled them to leave home, and what compelled them to accept
tasks in specific new homes? What forms of Christianity did
they embody through years of self-sacrificing toil? Did they
persevere or despair, remain inflexible or adapt to new conditions? These questions represent only a few of the things we
need to know about the agents themselves before we can penetrate
to the living core of missions activity.

A third category of interest, and one on which the bulk of
this essay will concentrate, has to do with those who materially
supported missions over the years. Whether we look at vast numbers of laymen who contributed funds for pursuing missions at
home and abroad, or whether we investigate the coordinating
boards, this level of inquiry allows us to see massive cultural
forces at work. Some of these mission boards were interdenominational in conception and operation; most of them shaped policy
within independent denominational units. But managerial decisions made in both of these alignments reflected dominant cultural patterns of their day. The men who constituted those
boards represented commonly held assumptions about what missions
were supposed to accomplish and how those goals could best be
achieved. Whom did they accept as missionaries and where did
they send them? With what objectives did they charge those under
their jurisdiction, and how did they evaluate success or failure
in light of those concerns? How did priorities change? What
goals succeeded earlier ones, and how did those shifting perspectives on civilization coincide with the underlying constant,
"pure Christianity"? Knowledge about this aspect of missions
can lead us to a greater appreciation of the way in which American cultural factors gave particular nuances to corporate evangelism in earlier times.

Finally, a thorough student of missions should be mindful of of those who receive the Christian message as presented by individual volunteers who are influenced by far-off managerial boards. This is so primarily because such hosts already stand within a cultural framework. They have formed basic notions about personal identity, group orientation, definitions of right and wrong, the consequences of fulfilling or violating cultural sanctions, and with that distinctive mind-set they confront new data brought by the missionary. From their perspective Christianity might represent a radical thrust at all their learned values; it may reaffirm certain principles while calling for reform in a limited number of areas; for some it could appear less sophisticated than the combination of religious teachings and civilized deportment already in operation. Since the Christian missionary hardly ever conveys a message of salvation to his listeners without practical lessons as to how religion applies in everyday life, it is inevitable that the preacher as well as his audience embodies a set of priorities tied to specific cultural orientations. Tension between cultural systems result, sometimes deliberately as with expectations regarding morals, worship patterns and family life, sometimes unwittingly as with concepts of territorial identity, assumptions about productive work and what one can expect in the afterlife.

The interaction of host and missionary cultures is an essential element in comprehending the total picture of missions because new religious forms arise in the interstices. As host cultures prove receptive to imported doctrine and behavioral standards, they assimilate precepts within their old cultural framework and create new modes of Christian living. Of course neither the old culture nor Christianity as represented by the missionary remains entirely as it was prior to interaction. There is a mix of old and new, native and imported, which constitutes the growing edge of expanded Christian witness. The important thing to notice in this process is that it is mutually affective. The gospel does not remake the entire fabric of native cultures; host systems do not restructure Christian teaching into antithetical or unrecognizable versions. Multiple expressions and varying emphases abound, but underlying all of them there is a shared faith which allows us to speak of the missionary enterprise as a single though complex topic. So a study of missions will include not only those who bring the message to a new people; it will also look at the results of missionary activity in the host culture, knowing all the while that as Christianity is assimilated in a new setting, it will form the basis for another cycle of mission outreach. Those who once heard a strange gospel will be transformed into a base from which the great commission once again summons volunteer evangelists and inaugurates the process over again.

These four categories, then, pertain to a thoroughgoing survey

of missions within more circumscribed limits, the rest of this
essay shall devote itself to factors at work in the third area
mentioned above.

Except for a few anomalies in states such as Connecticut and
Massachusetts, the revolutionary epoch produced a new circumstance on the American continent: ecclesiastical and civil powers
were separated, and churches were thrown on their own resources
to succeed or fail by themselves. Mission activity as well as
other ecclesiastical programs followed plans of their own making
without the benefit of state aid, and they can legitimately be
viewed as grass-roots movements. Voluntary support for missions
programs came from people who constituted the backbone of both
evangelical Protestantism and American culture. The ideas, plans,
hopes and prejudices which they embodied had an impact on mission
work. Many of those factors are considered in the following
pages.

EARLY NATIONAL PERIOD, 1790-1865

The years of revolutionary struggle and those immediately following did not bode well for American churches. Times of actual
warfare and attendant economic depression caused a great deal of
tumult in organized religion, disrupting in some areas the pattern of regular church life beyond the hope of speedy recovery.
Property damage, demographic shifts and patriot-versus-loyalist
antagonism had crippled many parishes. Ardor for secular aims
of the rebellion also absorbed the interests of most American
citizens; whatever influence church leaders had in colonial life,
and that was admittedly considerable, such dominance gave place
to spokesmen in the political arena as socio-economic issues
pressed themselves onto the public mind with increased urgency.
Though churchmen exerted more influence than their numbers might
indicate, still no more than 10% of the total population belonged
officially to a formal congregation. Such a small proportion of
the general citizenry appeared inadequate to cope with the challenge of new circumstances which followed in the aftermath of
war.

Another factor confronting evangelical work in this period
was the widely acknowledged respect for Enlightenment philosophy.
Whether this attitude affected cultural values in the form of
Newtonian science, Lockean psychology or assumptions regarding
human nature and a benevolent deity, a major intellectual tradition in 1790 placed a premium on rationality as a criterion of
truth. In the eyes of most religious leaders such rationalism
was indicative of a deistic perspective which had little place
for faith, or worse of "infidelity" which rejected the essential
tenets of a Christian belief system. National leaders such as
Thomas Jefferson gave prominence to rationalistic ideas that undermined the confessional aspects of biblical religion; polemi-

cists such as Ethan Allen, Elihu Palmer and Joseph Priestley argued the cogency of their position to the apparent detriment of orthodox perspectives. To make matters worse, "infidelity" was linked in the popular mind with France, the country which granted material aid in wartime and cultural leadership thereafter. But after 1789 France exhibited by her own inner turmoil the disastrous consequences of "infidel philosophy": upheaval, terror and ruin. Deism as an alternative ideology was bad enough, but churchmen perceived it to be a social threat as well. The fabric of both religion and society hung in the balance, and many church leaders were diffident about their chances of counteracting this outwardly urbane but inwardly corrupt philosophical orientation.

The final condition challenging churches in this early period was one fraught with consequences. Just at the time when religious leaders recognized more than ever (prompted by the French Revolution) that Christian morals were a necessary base for sound social structure, governmental aid for enhancing such a moral buttress was withdrawn. The separation of church and state seemed at first blush to threaten what contribution two churches (Anglican and Congregationalist) had already made to building a humane civilization on the best ethical precepts. Of course the dissenting bodies viewed disestablishment with less alarm, but each of them faced an unknown future because "free religion" was virtually untried in the annals of Christian history. So the challenge to all ecclesiastical units was to attempt a transformation of the non-churchgoing body politic by persuasive means rather than by statutory regulation. For many this meant utilizing unfamiliar methods and working within an unanticipated psychological framework. The unique circumstance of competing religious groups with voluntary membership taking the place of one official body with preferential cultural emoluments doubtless heightened an atmosphere of apprehension in post-revolutionary times.

At the same time this situation of competing churches proved to be a stimulus to greater activity in later decades. Once acclimated to the shock of disestablishment, Christian spokesmen found that loss of support also meant freedom from control. Baptists, Quakers and Moravians had always known this; Congregationalists, Anglicans and Catholics came to recognize genuine benefits in the new way of doing things. All were determined to recover from damages incurred during the war, and they solicited voluntary contributions to rebuild membership as well as edifices. They grimly resolved to combat myriad forms of "infidelity" as manifested in rationalistic religion or loose republican talk about social policies bereft of Protestant morality. Christian leaders of all confessions accepted the task of persuading audiences to accept biblical faith rather than Enlightenment tenets or the dangerous social tendencies attributable to deism. And, like it or not, they also faced up to disestablishment--fact as

well as theory--declaring in time that free churches in a free
state provided the best situation for expansion and growth.
Whatever obstacles the future held, whatever disadvantages in
the lively experiment of voluntaryism, they produced a ground-
swell of positive response to meet those challenges. Sometimes
clerical activity took the form of careful argumentation, but
more often it found expression in fervent revival sermons or
heated tirades against Jefferson as an enemy to all that was
dear in American culture. The important fact to notice is that
churches at first seemed intimidated by their circumstances, op-
ponents and lack of official encouragement. But they responded
to the situation with courage born of faith in the gospel and
developed a practical program centering on missionary outreach
which eventually turned the tide in their favor.

Western land constituted another factor in this early phase
of American missions. In fact for one hundred years the reced-
ing frontier was continually present as an elemental ingredient
in national life. At first population moved into territory already claimed by seaboard states, notably New York, Pennsylvania
and Virginia; then Tennessee and Kentucky were quickly filled by
settlers who poured through the Cumberland Gap. Rich prairie
country north of the Ohio River lured thousands of others to
populate expanses from Zanesville, Ohio, to Rock Island, Illinois.
Sober commentators on the Peace of Paris (1783) observed that the
Mississippi River would long stand as this country's western
boundary and comfortably hold all the nation's people for another
century. But a scant two decades later the Louisiana Purchase
opened wide new vistas for westward expansion. After a second
war with England, more robust optimism developed regarding the
vibrant federal political system. Whetted by Jackson's policy
of Indian removal, whites clamored for more and more land. In
1844 they elected James K. Polk to the presidency chiefly because he promised to extend American hegemony to the Rio Grande
and on to the Pacific.

That year marks something of a watershed in American expansionist sentiment. Polk's election over the more famous Clay
indicated how pioneer enthusiasm had grown to continental proportions. Key indicators were that the majority of citizens
demanded the annexation of Texas, the occupation of Oregon and
the acquisition of California by any means, fair or foul. An
advantageous war with Mexico, discovery of gold in the Sierra
Nevadas plus determined efforts to bind east and west with a
network of railroads solidified the idea that America ought to
be a continental power. These were the times when "manifest
destiny" was first used as a slogan. Ironically enough, 1844
was also the year when two of the largest denominations (Methodists and Baptists) split apart because sectional interests predominated over national ones. But the dream of manifest destiny
continued, and it reminds us that a prominent theme in pre-Civil

War history was that of subduing the continent and establishing throughout its breadth the white man's conception of civilized life.

Within that context American missions took its cue and perfected its technique. Briefly stated, the primary task was to move west with pioneers, evangelizing the frontier as clergymen tried to keep pace with an expanding nation. Just as with circumstances in 1790, "the West" presented churches with both a challenge and an opportunity. At times the positive aspect was emphasized, and interdenominational boards such as the American Home Missionary Society (1826) sponsored preachers eager to canvass fields of unchurched westerners. At other times the negative theme predominated, and spokesmen such as Lyman Beecher (1830) or Horace Bushnell (1847) would issue a strong "plea for the West" or warning about "barbarism the first danger." But regardless of which emotional pole was stressed, clergymen placed common emphasis on national growth, western land and the need for Christian congregations all across the American continent. It was plain to see that mission agencies were determined to move west with the people and mold distant communities as much as possible according to traditional Protestant standards of thought and action.

The technique utilized to accomplish much of this task was the revival. In a real sense every local exhorter and traveling evangelist were participants in missionary activity because they sought to Christianize western populations through revival sermons. Interdenominational camp meetings were a unique western feature for a while, but even when revivals were incorporated into denominational patterns and made a regular part of town or city life, the central appeal remained on conversion. White audiences, listening to Peter Cartwright in Kentucky or Charles G. Finney at New York's Broadway Tabernacle, received a message born of the Second Great Awakening. They were urged to recognize their need of personal salvation and to do something about it that very day in free reformatory response. Traditional Calvinist emphases in theology were seriously eroded by this missionary impulse; either that or their sponsoring groups had little to do with westward expansion in the early national period. The stress on individual conversions, personal decisions of markedly Arminian tendency, and the need to build new churches on voluntary principles coincided very well with westward movement, democratic liberty and material advancement won through the efforts of common men.

After being persuaded to accept the bare outlines of a Christian perspective, converts were further urged to align themselves with specific churches. Revivalistic missionary activity was both an attempt to garner as many souls as possible for Christianity and also a practical program for extending the number of

denominational units. In fact most missionary effort during
this period had a denominational base--with somewhat narrow motivations and self-centered objectives. There were some cooperative ventures, but competition between churches was often a more
recognized motivating factor than the shared challenge of unconverted thousands who cared for no religious orientation at all.
The important thing to notice is that western missionaries were
expected to raise churches in the hinterlands which corresponded
to more settled patterns back East. Evangelical preaching,
whether initial device or continuing supplement, was a technique
used to gather new members into church systems already comfortable with distinctive forms of liturgy, polity and confessional
articulation. The revivals helped spread Christianity through a
mobile and rapidly growing population, but it did not materially
affect the content of religious action. It was a means used by
churches to extend their influence and control greater numbers
of people by applying disciplinary standards bound within ecclesiastical structures.

Normal church growth in the early national period took on the
air of missionary endeavor in the sense that all denominational
spokesmen were responsible for recruiting new members and establishing new congregations, especially but not exclusively in the
West. Freed from Calvinist theology they offered easy plans of
personal salvation but compensated for excessive forgiveness by
emphasizing vigorous moral restraints on individual behavior.
Thus missions to the white man from 1800 to 1865 constituted a
broad "united evangelical front" calculated to preserve Protestant
standards of morality in private and public sectors. Work of the
American Bible Society (1816) and the American Tract Society
(1825) becomes more intelligible in this context. Its agents
spread literature among groups and individual families with this
overarching end in view. Ante-bellum eleemosynary societies and
state or municipal reform bodies of countless localities also
fit this dominant cultural pattern. Missionaries sought to transform the barbaric frontier, convert great numbers who had no religious affiliation; but more importantly they tried to mold successive generations of Americans along conservative lines of moral
conduct that were already in vogue on the eastern seaboard.

Three exceptions to the major trend must be noted: work on
southern plantations, among Indians and in foreign missions. The
South was different because of slavery. Missionaries there usually changed their message to fit separate audiences. After the
usual evangelical exhortation, slaveowners were urged to be humane regarding the needs of those entrusted to their care.
Blacks too were offered the spiritual reward of salvation from a
God who loved them as much as He did white men. But upon conversion, bondmen were enjoined to exhibit patience and meekness in
their menial status. Missionary efforts on the plantations themselves tried to avoid arousing bitter feelings over the slavery

question, apparently on the ground that it was more important to save souls than to reform local customs. With the exception of making room for chattel slavery, southern missionary programs resembled those in other parts of the country as far as doctrine, organization structure and worship practices were concerned, even among the blacks whether freedmen or bond.

By the 1830s, however, another cultural factor exerted pressure in this area. Antislavery sentiment began to accelerate, and that agitation strongly influenced southern missions. Agents supported by southern churches usually continued the old format, but northern spokesmen began to call for an end to the "peculiar institution." In retrospect it seems clear that many representatives of the Home Mission, Bible, and Tract Societies embodied abolitionist proclivities as they tried to conduct their primary function in the South. Those individuals were received with increasing suspicion in many states as sectional tensions mounted. Some of the more uncompromising became identified with societies specifically concerned for slave welfare and thereafter the freedman, notably the American Missionary Association (1846). But whether this missionary impulse found expression in radical abolition groups or in milder forms, it was characterized by the same general feature of attempts to make social behavior conform to ruling patterns set by northern and eastern churches.

Missionary work among Indians made similar demands, but they cut much deeper because of differences between red and white cultures. Conversion of Indians to Christianity meant not only their accepting a new worldview replete with referential symbols and an otherworldly orientation; it also involved adopting a new ethos with unfamiliar economic routines, work ethic, family structure, the English language and untested conceptions of personal fulfillment. The accepted phrasing was that red men had to be "civilized" before they could be "Christianized." Religious and cultural factors were so uncritically intertwined by white missionaries, they insisted that both aspects were parts of a single framework, advantageous to all who adopted the total package. The fact that such a view often caused serious trouble within tribes or villages and produced cultural disorientation in individuals did not alter the missionary's attitude about his task   This was the case among, for example, the Cherokee in Georgia, the Wyandot in Ohio, the Dakota in Minnesota and a host of nations after their removal to Oklahoma. For white audiences Christian missions invited them to assume a lifestyle with which they were already familiar, if not entirely supportive of it. For red audiences missionary teachings demanded a change of belief and action so thoroughgoing, it constituted an almost entirely new basis for individual or ethnic identity. So one still finds the common theme of conservative Protestant dominance in moral suasion at work in Indian missions, but it is preceded by a more basic thrust, viz., to transform the host culture before molding it according to standards of the white man's making.

American participation in foreign missions does not conform exactly to cultural norms of the early national period either. No expansionist enthusiasm supported Judson, Rice and three others as first appointees of the American Board of Commissioners for Foreign Missions in 1812. No territorial ambitions were discernible as one denomination after another inaugurated programs and sent individuals to Africa, South America or the Far East. Of course agents in Liberia, Chile or Hawaii often clashed with local customs related to dress, sexual habits, personal hygiene and traditional belief systems. But on the whole they were less assertive of a single cultural standard, less insistent on Americanizing variant forms of human existence than their stay-at-home counterparts. Judged in terms of the national setting in which they emerged and developed strength by means of voluntary support, foreign missions constituted the purest form of missionary altruism--an anomaly in their day.

TIME OF EXTERNAL GROWTH AND INTERNAL PROBLEMS, 1865-1920

Decades between the end of the Civil War and that of World War I carry a number of partially enlightening secular labels; whether characterized as "the gilded age" or "the Victorian era," it was a time marked by industrialism, cities and ever increasing immigration. As far as Protestant activity was concerned, these fifty-five years were a period of outward confidence and continued expansion. But at the same time strong winds of change in both theology and social attitudes began to affect the course of missions. At the beginning of this era it seemed as if things would go on largely as they had in the past. Establishing new churches in western territory, reiterating the gospel of free salvation by means of revival sermons and influencing American life through the persuasive tactics of voluntary societies--all these endeavors promised to continue unabated.

Indeed, the war itself had not hampered missions but rather opened new opportunities for service. The Sanitary Commissions (U.S. and Western) as well as the Christian Commission coordinated material resources to distribute everything from Bibles to toilet articles, bandages to ministerial consolation at Union army camps. Revivals in hospitals, prisons and training depots were not uncommon. Victory for the North appeared to most citizens as a vindication of their conception of a Christian civilization (now making ambiguous room for the black man if not yet the red or yellow), a laissez-faire economy able to produce great quantities of both guns and butter, and open competition among churches which shared similar views about the conservative function of religion in cultural progress. Such ideas had formed part of the widespread "united evangelical front" before the war, and national trauma over secession and slavery only made these elements stand out in higher relief. The God of battles had proved the righteousness of northern ideals, and churches in the Reconstruction era looked forward to pressing their advantage as far as manpower and physical resources would allow.

So the dominant theme in 1865 was one of continuance: a satisfaction with methods and goals plus a determination to use proven techniques as the burgeoning quality of American life offered occasion. There was still territory between the oceans to populate, and churches still needed building. A westering orientation still guided denominational mission agencies, and they concentrated much of their effort along that line. Church extension and Protestant morality continued to have priority; separate denominations persisted in following independent courses of action. One new variation was the greater initiative displayed by women. During the 1870s and 80s independent women's missionary societies appeared in major denominations including the Baptists, Methodists, Presbyterians, Episcopalians, Congregationalists and Disciples of Christ. Sometimes they concentrated on specialized tasks such as evangelizing minority groups or more thorough educational programs in existing churches. In other situations they provided supplementary outlets for supporting established activities in home or foreign missions. Either way, women's work gave additional impetus to Protestant action in pursuit of common objectives articulated in the all-embracing ideal, "a Christian America."

As time passed, foreign missions were affected by this energy and optimism. By 1890 essentially the same expansionist sentiments which had earlier defended a continental vision of manifest destiny now pushed that view to broader scope. Imperialistic policies were a natural outgrowth of post-war developments; North America contained the best achievement of divinely approved democratic institutions, and many thought it was time to export those exemplary patterns as befitting a nation grown into a world power by its naval prowess. After a glorious little war against Spain the United States found that it controlled the Philippines, Puerto Rico, Hawaii and other Pacific islands. With protectorates over Cuba, Nicaragua and Panama plus concessions in China, this country indicated a willingness to shoulder "the white man's burden" and benefit lesser civilizations around the globe. The Caribbean became an American lake; the Far East became our neighbor across a foreshortened Pacific Ocean. Missionary work within this context assumed unparalleled optimism and reflected corresponding imperialistic tendencies until the carnage of World War I ended expansionist motivations with terrible finality.

There were times when missionary outreach expressed itself in terms which, hindsight allows us to say, bordered on racism. Josiah Strong is perhaps the best example of those who equated help to foreign countries with a thoroughgoing transferal of Anglo-Saxon lifestyle and institutions. As the epitome of all WASP mentality, he had no difficulty in identifying Christianity with American (occasionally British) customs and then championing that amalgam as the one viable culture for anyone wishing to live effectively in the modern world. Strong even seemed at times to maintain a genetic connection between spiritual attainment and capacities brought to fruition in the white man. But even in his more expansive moments he represented a frame of mind which insisted that other peoples copy the socio-religious achievements of Americans, if not improve their bloodlines through intermarriage. He articulated a climate of opinion that fed on triumphalist predictions of how American life as a vehicle for Christian ideals would conquer the superstitions and base passions of other countries. This would come largely through other peoples' recognizing the obvious superiority of American accomplishments, but voluntary though such conversions might be, in his eyes they were still victories for a righteous cause won by a master race.

Of course most elements of public opinion did not go to the extremes of Strong's uncritical equation of America as world power and world savior. But church agencies for foreign missions did draw a measure of confidence from the increased prestige which their country had acquired among other nations of the world. The best examples of sanguine hope for spiritual conquest around the globe were the Student Volunteer Movement (1886) and the World's Student Christian Federation (1895). Highly gifted young men such as John R. Mott, Luther D. Wishard and Robert P. Wilder represented a new wave of student volunteers (2,106 in the first year alone) who were intensely dedicated to world evangelization. They were in no sense self-conscious agents of an imperialist government, but their time of efflorescence did correspond to the general chronological framework in which their country enjoyed a tremendous increase of influence around the globe. It would be difficult to imagine any other time before or after this happy juxtaposition of missionary upsurge and American international prestige for Mott to popularize in 1901 the revealing motto: "the evangelization of the world in this generation." Whether missioners volunteered for work in denominational field stations, student cooperative societies or diversified programs like the YMCA, the favorable conditions of international peace and American ascendance seemed to make that motto a practicable objective. Theological motivations lay behind the hope of stamping all nations with a Christian character; for a time physical conditions made that hope seem a tangible reality.

Within the territorial United States, however, changes were occurring which altered the face of mission work there for all time. Most importantly population increased fourteen times in the half century after Appomattox, and most of those people

massed together in large urban areas. The growth of industrialism in America (antecedent factor for the rise of cities),
coupled with a strong wave of immigration from southern and eastern Europe, produced an inner revolution in this country. By the
1880s many were beginning to see that the really challenging frontier confronting the churches was the city, not forest or prairie
any longer. For scores of analysts the goal was still to Christianize America, but America was rapidly changing character before their eyes. Urban problems caused a shift of focus for the
missionary impulse at home, and they elicited new emphases which
added unanticipated dimensions to responsible denominational
work in the cities.

The major problem with dense urban population is that it
tends to perpetuate unequal distribution of goods. Of course
cities held all the opportunities for vice which healthy individuals could find in rural settings too; barrooms and brothels,
gambling and shady business transactions flourished among large
numbers of people as lustily (but probably not more so) as they
did in thinly populated towns or villages. Standard temptations
could be found in cities but in no greater proportion than outside them—beyond that derived from demographic concentration.
The radically new thing about cities was that economic, social
and often political stratification produced miserable conditions
for those at lower levels of society, and those strata seemed
impervious to reform. In short, city conditions exploited the
poor and made them despair of improvement in any foreseeable
future. Perpetual slums, grinding poverty, intransigent hostility between capitalism and organized labor: add these to the
culture shock and language difficulties experienced by millions
of immigrants pouring into cities at the turn of this century,
and one begins to see the problem faced by the missionary in
the city.

New conditions presented new needs; they in turn spawned new
strategies which added to the evangelistic-moralistic character
of missions in earlier days. Profound social changes had produced squalor, poverty and human exploitation in an aggregate
too large to ignore. Many spokesmen such as Washington Gladden,
Josiah Strong (who saw conditions more as a threat to WASP dominance but nevertheless a concrete problem that needed solving)
and Walter Rauschenbusch called attention to human needs not being met in the impersonal city. They helped instill the idea
that Christian missions should aid people with basic social services in addition to preaching a time-honored gospel. City missions espoused the idea of caring for elemental problems such as
food, clothing and shelter as if they were of equal (at time pre-
eminent) importance to a ministry among the down-and-out. Those
concerned about human life amid urban blight developed a new
category of ethical thought, one resisted by old guard conservatives but one that accepted some measure of corporate responsi-

bility for the casualties of city existence. Most theorists
just spoke of ameliorating the situation; others moved from
charity as a personalistic response and approached the concept
of justice as an adequately shared standpoint for group action.
But whether social ethics emphasized the need for more "institutional churches" and their many services to tenement neighbor-
hoods or the need for legislated reform in areas such as minimum
wages and labor conditions, the point is that such concerns were
concomitant with the area chosen by home missionaries as their
latest field of endeavor.

Another aspect of changing perspectives at work by the turn
of this century was an increased emphasis on interdenominational
cooperation. The growth of cities did not initiate this line of
thinking, but urban problems may have accelerated the process
and provided some of the earliest occasions for experimentation.
A more likely source for ecumenical urgings was practical missionary experience, whether in Montana hamlets, suburbs around
Baltimore or the Five Points district in New York. Agents in
such fields had long noticed the waste of competition, the folly
of overchurched towns and the theological scandal of churches
working against each other in pursuit of a supposedly common
cause. An early paradigm emerged in 1893 when the Interdenominational Conference on Foreign Missions Societies of the U.S.A.
and Canada (later the Foreign Missions Conference of North America) was formed. By 1908 pragmatic considerations were a dominant factor behind forming both the Home Missions Council and
the Federal Council of Churches, each a product of creative
leadership but taken together as a monument to cooperation for
the sake of efficiency.

A short time later the World Missionary Conference (1910)
gave additional weight and wider notice to a cooperative concept
come of age. Such ecumenical bodies may have exerted subsequent
influence on the more theoretical aspects of Christian union,
but in America at the turn of this century their worth lay in
practical strength to get a job done. It is tempting to fall
back on easy assumptions and say that the FCC, indeed ecumenical
ventures in general, patterned themselves after Standard Oil,
Swift Packing Co. or other efficient business cartels. But the
idea of church cooperation was not new at that time, nor did
secular patterns in banking or management provide any noticeable
stimulus. This was a time rather when men still shared a moral
idealism about solving human problems; they were optimistic regarding victory in good causes, and they were zealous in seeking
better means of reaching their goals. In days when cities presented dilemmas larger than any single church could handle, when
differences between churches were considered not worth the jeal-
ousy and strife wasted on them in the past, this was a time for
unprecedented cooperation to solve problems of unprecedented size.
Major denominations such as Baptists, Methodists, Lutherans, Con-

gregationalists, Presbyterians and Reformed continued to operate
separate mission boards, but they agreed that ecumenical action
was another valuable means of evangelical work. And while each
group often seemed to pursue denominational objectives much as
before, thoughts about the church universal and themselves as
discrete units within it could never be the same again. There
is more than a grain of truth in the observation that 1908 was
annus mirabilis.

Theological currents, particularly those called "liberal" in
the early 1900s also contributed to the new shape of missions in
this country. Beginning in the days of Horace Bushnell (1802-
1876) and gathering momentum through decades when natural science
developed immense bodies of new knowledge, some religious thinkers initiated a deliberate process of restating Christian tenets
in ways acceptable to contemporary intellectual standards. One
of the broad philosophical emphases that made sense in modern
times--due to everything from random strands of transcendental
romanticism to minute classificatory studies in biology--was a
recognition of continuity in life. Many found it no longer fash-
ionable to draw sharp distinctions between nature and the supernatural, for example, or churches and society at large, or humanity and the rest of mammalian life. Many strains of thought entered into this intellectual development (some more determinative
than others for certain thinkers), but by and large liberal theologians emphasized the organic wholeness of major categories such
as nature, man and God while conservatives insisted on fundamental ontological distinctions between them.

Other doctrinal perspectives built on the basic theme of continuity to flesh out a distinctively liberal attitude toward
missions. One was an acceptance of man's goodness instead of
any stress on innate depravity. Evolutionary patterns of change
blended with widespread satisfaction in human achievements (moral
as well as artistic and industrial) to produce glowing affirmation of "progress." Good people were getting better and better
in ways that encouraged further effort toward improving the quality of civilized life. Another part of this liberal scenario
was to consider religion primarily a set of moral teachings.
The religion of Jesus was based on his exemplary life and the
moral guidance he offered during an all-too-brief earthly ministry. His attempt to illustrate how men could be perfect even as
their Father in heaven was perfect left an inspiring system of
moral precepts, applicable to all ages and conditions of men.
Liberals thus selected elements of Christianity which they found
compatible with an age manifestly triumphant over old ignorance
and old failures. They defined their optimistic faith in the
light of man's goodness which could be guided by tested ethical
rubrics to eventual perfection in individuals and beyond.

Emphases on basic tenets such as continuity, human ability

and Christianity as essentially a moral code led many liberals to new conceptions of missionary endeavor. They were not inclined to stress the need of <u>churches</u> in missionary work because a number of other agencies might do the job just as well, maybe better since they need not have denominational interests lurking in the background. The liberal thrust at the turn of this century (stemming from an admittedly long evangelical heritage) was to blur distinctions between ecclesiastical and cultural life, all to the good because advancement in one meant improvement in both. Liberals viewed the general Protestant attempt to move men along a continuum from nature to grace, from moral capacity to more concrete expressions of brotherhood, and they held that churches had no real significance in the process other than way-stations. Some of them went so far as to eliminate differences between gathered Christian bodies and society at large, focusing rather on all of society as the place where religious guidance could be most effectively administered. Their optimism in man, in progress and in the superiority of Christian ethics culminated in visions of a perfect society, a Kingdom of God realized in America through the patient ministrations of liberal missionaries in contemporary life Sometimes this line of thought produced a general affirmation of work in cities; occasionally it resulted in elaborate theologies of the Social Gospel. But whether meliorative or transformationist, it was firmly based on a liberal view of man and society which looked forward confidently to the eventual permeation of all human life with the social teachings of Jesus.

Curiously enough, at the time one group of liberals backed the Social Gospel and envisioned saving all of society, a smaller contingent followed more reductionistic tendencies in that perspective and threatened to obliterate the most elemental assumption of missionary activity. They drew on similar tenets such as continuity and human goodness, but their general conclusion was to lessen the importance of Christianity as distinctive or superior to other viewpoints. Historians had been stockpiling information for some time that showed similarities between Hebrew religion and other faiths in Mesopotamia and Egypt; Christian chronicles disclosed repeated examples of cultural factors' twisting the gospel into now this message, now that. Furthermore, historical understanding of other classical systems such as Hinduism and Buddhism revealed them to be viable attempts to regulate human lives by high-minded ideals. On the basis of such information many thought of the Judeo-Christian tradition as just one among several human belief systems, denying its claim to an authoritative revelation in much the same pattern of reasoning that posited man as part of nature and churches as part of larger social contexts.

Liberals of this frame of mind viewed all religions as more or less equal systems, conditioned by varying cultures but shar-

ing basically similar injunctions and appeals to transcendental
(or humanistic) sanctions. There was for them no finality in
Christ nor any obvious superiority in gospels associated with
his name. In short, one aspect of knowledge about world religions was a relativism that denied qualitative differences between them. One of the best expressions of this attitude appeared late (1932), but it was the end product of a liberal ferment begun perhaps fifty years earlier. After surveying modern
missionary techniques, a laymen's board of inquiry led by Harvard
professor, William E. Hocking, recommended that Christian groups
not emphasize distinct claims over against native religions.
They urged in a document entitled *Re-thinking Missions* that
educational and philanthropic work be separated from self-conscious evangelizing and that missions concentrate on material
aid <u>without</u> <u>any</u> <u>preaching</u>. In keeping with the relativity of
religions, Hocking's report suggested that Christian groups cur-
tail their self-centered recruiting and just try to "cooperate
with non-Christian agencies for social improvement." This attitude was not shared by a large number of Protestant thinkers,
liberal or conservative. A more representative spokesman was
Robert E. Speer who retained an emphasis on unique qualities
found in the Christian message and its global impulse. But in
the last analysis this liberal cul de sac should be mentioned
here to round off the imperialistic age because it illustrates
some of the confusion and cross-purposes with which Protestants
faced modern trends after World War I.

END OF THE PROTESTANT ERA, SINCE 1920

War against the Kaiser ended victoriously; the world had been
made safe for democracy. For a brief time after 1918 it seemed
that American culture might extend its influence untroubled in a
world preserved by force of arms for the continued advance of
righteous causes. In that year the Interchurch World Movement
announced a campaign of united missionary efforts unequalled in
scope, financial backing and hopes for global success, expanding
within two years to an operating budget of 336 million dollars.
In 1920 the Eighteenth Amendment went into effect, signaling the
end of saloons and climaxing the largest modern Protestant crusade to legislate moral standards into the fabric of American
civilization. Optimism about possible achievements along custom-
ary lines of WASP dominance never quite reached the same high
mark again.

In retrospect it seems that such optimism was hollow and bound
to end in disappointment, but in the early days of 1920 such a
disillusioning trend was not apparent. A rapid succession of
events, however, set the tone for "a return to normalcy." For
one thing the Interchurch cooperative program failed to collect
even a respectable fraction of its supporting budget and col-
lapsed ingloriously. In 1921 Congress enacted immigrant re-

striction legislation which virtually ended earlier patterns of
an open-ended American society. Three years later another set
of stringent quotas were established, showing that the American
people were then determined to exclude (not just regulate) as
many foreigners as possible from their country. Another indication of changing perceptions was that the idealism expressed so
altruistically in Prohibition settled into grim enforcement of
the Volstead Act. What began as a noble experiment in moral reform wound up as a display not of persuasion but of power, often
ineffective, used to make the public accept uniform behavioral
standards. The crusading passion of progressive evangelism seems
to have lost its bouyancy--and its following. Even pre-war urban
revivalists of the old individualistic stripe, such as William A.
"Billy" Sunday, lost their magic appeal. The arrangement of religious priorities in American churches was changing internally
while the character of American society simultaneously developed
new contours of its own.

   This set of events points more to an altered psychological
mood than to a physical state of affairs. It embodied a general
decline of idealism, a loss of confidence that political or religious leadership could secure reforms and sometimes even disillusionment with the idea that reform was a viable goal. The
Social Gospel terminology of saving society had lost much of its
potency; enthusiasm for mission programs, whether of practical
aid or evangelical outreach, was seriously undermined. During
the 1920s American Protestantism turned in on itself and in so
doing turned its back on most of the Christian programs so carefully nurtured through previous decades.

   Concurrent with this withering of idealism and action on the
home front, foreign missions also faced the future rather un-
certainly. New nations, formerly under colonial management of
western powers, began asserting their independence. These politically assertive entities emerged to fill a power vacuum created
after World War I, and they often drew strength from resurgent
native religions. Thus American missionaries had to face a revitalized self-consciousness in host countries, not unmixed with
pride in non-white traditions and hostile memories of cultural
domination endured as part of the white man's burden. Foreign
missionaries themselves did not lose heart, nor did many of them
redefine their ultimate conversionist objectives. But amid the
rising nationalism of non-industrial countries they confronted
energetic forms of cultural awareness that demanded less agres-
sive tactics and more modest expectation of results. The inter-
mission between wars did not witness much outright failure on
various mission fields, but it served as background for a certain curtailment of action, this congruent with the more radical
collapse of religious influence in America itself.

   Things turned from bad to worse after 1925 and entered a

period of spiritual recession long before economic decline could
be used as an excuse for its occurrence. By mid-decade financial
support for missions began to plummet; decreased numbers of volunteers for mission work served as a gauge of evangelical indifference. The Scopes courtroom drama in 1925 showed that liberals
and conservatives were still willing to fly at each other for the
sake of doctrine, but unlike earlier discussions the "monkey
trial" provided a low point of acrid debate without any productive resolution of issues. Three years later Protestants in-
dulged their nativist sentiments by voting against Alfred E.
Smith, the first Catholic presidential nominee of a major political party. Despite the fact that Hoover won in 1928, Protestant
leaders did not regain a measure of their cultural influence; it
eroded all the more due to faltering confidence in their programs.
Protestant churches reached their nadir in early years of the
Great Depression primarily because their identification with
American civilization no longer corresponded to the hard facts
of modern life. The population was no longer ethnically homoge-
nous; laissez-faire capitalism proved ruinous; confessional diversity defied all attempts to promote a common body of public
values, and all efforts to Christianize society had to be acknowledged as failures. These circumstances indicated that the
Protestant era had ended, a reality which brought about renewal
in churches instead of collapse, revitalized missions instead of
despair.

Though spokesmen for old perceptions and goals continued into
the fourth decade (some persist today in isolated pockets),
others began calling for ecclesiastical disengsgement from cultural alliances. Much of this new conception of the churches
in-but-not-of the world came from theologians, generally those
associated with the broad stream of thought known as "neo-orthodoxy." It is equally important to notice, however, that a wide
spectrum of cultural events helped shape the climate of opinion
in which renewed emphasis on liturgy, ecclesiology and doctrinal
integrity made greater headway. Theological renewal came from
the wreck of cultural Protestantism. Dreams of a coterminous
religion and civilization had never been successfully realized;
to compound the error, such dreams had encouraged compromises
with secular affairs until Protestantism almost forfeited its
birthright as a distinctively religious force. Of all the theologians who articulated this critique of Protestant compromise,
none were more effective than the brothers Neibuhr, Reinhold and
Richard. The Niebuhrian stress on divine sovereignty, human
finitude and the primacy of faith in confessional orientations
helped give a new sense of direction to churches in the late 30s
and 40s. It is worth noting that these two thinkers were also
masters at establishing a reciprocal relationship between concrete situations of modern existence as both supplement to biblical sources ideas and as a proving ground if resultant thoughts
offered guidance in any practical way. Politics, social condi-

tions and secular forces were important elements in theological
renewal, but culture no longer dictated norms or defined ultimate priorities.

Paradoxically, when churches began avoiding fatal entangle-
ments with secular objectives, they found a new theological base
for social service. Once Protestants acquired a certain detach-
ment regarding society, they learned to serve it without losing
their integrity or transcendental vision. Churches (and mission
programs following suit) did their best for society when they developed a proper, theologically reinforced disdain for worldly
values. This did not mean that religious groups had no concern
for worldly problems. Indeed, once they were free from cultural
objectives, practical programs of social aid were possible in an
atmosphere of heightened ecumenical consciousness. Since Protestants agreed that it was both necessary and good to abandon competitive designs of cultural domination, they found they could
cooperate on joint projects, all this accomplished with the additional dividend of sophisticated theological justification for
such a trend. In 1948 the World Council of Churches exemplified
this new attitude on an international scale. In 1950 the National Council of Churches embodied a more localized counterpart;
it is indicative of ecumenical awareness that the Home Missionary
Council and the Foreign Missions Conference disbanded to become
major divisions in this larger organization. Missions at mid-
century came to be viewed not as a loose collection of denominational enterprises and services but primarily as a significant
aspect of cooperative witness. They were put forth by the Christian church as a whole, a united work expressing a notable part
of its perennial message.

As we approach contemporary times, it becomes more difficult
to discern trends and speak about them with assurance. On the
International scene there seems to be more critical self-aware-
ness than in earlier periods. Up through World War I Protestant
forces identified their interests virtually without reservation
with the aims of this country. They idealized the war and its
purposes to an extreme degree, but national policy by the time
of World War II, Korea and thereafter was not idealized as much.
Military action was accepted more out of necessity as the nasty
business it is rather than as a righteous crusade to eradicate
evil. This is probably only a quantitative change from the old
imperialism, but it bears the healthy sign of creative tension
between religion and cultural goals instead of an uncritical
blending of the two categories. Another imponderable in foreign
missions is related to the Cold War. For the past two decades
there may have been instances in which Christian missions were
viewed (by workers in the field as well as those at home supporting their efforts) as outposts against the spread of Communist
influence. In a curious way this is imperialism in reverse: we
no longer want to establish an American hegemony in Indonesia,

e.g., but we must assert our presence there to make sure the
Russians or Chinese don't control the area. Disengagement from
the world has given foreign missions greater integrity; the new
perception of things has not, however, removed programs from the
complicated superpowers and emerging national pride in "the
Third World."

Another fairly clear trend posing a problem for contemporary
Protestants is the fact that cities have begun to erode seriously. The 1960 census showed that population declined in eight
out of ten major cities. Beginning in the early 50s stable
groups of wage earners and businesses started moving to the
suburbs, while foreign immigrants and migrating rural poor took
their places in the inner city. This created a downward spiral,
calling for more financial aid to continue social services while
the tax base for such support was reduced because of population
shifts. An ongoing vicious circle confronts cities today: needs
increase, and support for meeting needs is drying up. Social
services are worsening, and there seems to be no remedy in sight
other than federal funding. Home missionaries are certainly a-
ware of this trend. While there are no easy answers to this
situation, missionary efforts continue in the face of deteriorat-
ing conditions. It could be that settlement houses, store front
chapels and skid row soup kitchens are conducting a holding action, just giving tentative responses to a labyrinth of complex
problems.

The other major development of contemporary times has to do
with race relations. Since 1954 this country has been forced,
largely through court actions, to confront its unfinished agenda
regarding the civil rights of black Americans. Churches did not
generate this form of action, but they responded quickly enough
to win recognition as positive supporters more often than negative reactionaries. Of course black churches formed a predominant source of leadership, with Martin Luther King and the SCLC
heading the list. Beyond that core of moral inspiration, though,
white religious leaders also began to see a new practical way to
express the social implications of evangelical faith. Espousing
civil rights for black Americans has not meant the same thing
for all Protestants. Some ended their crusade after integrating
buses and lunch counters; others continue to seek equal opportunity in jobs, housing and voter registration. Not all denominations (or all churches within them) are integrated yet, but
the main point is that Protestantism as a whole has experienced
a massive shift of opinion on the race question during the 1960s.
It continues as an issue today, though any return to separate
denominations along color lines appears unlikely.

There have been many other events worth noting as we consider
the present status and future prospects of missions in American
life. The Billy Graham revivals, a post-war boom in church mem-

bership, the positive thinking fad of Norman Vincent Peale, new religions from the East ranging from Hare Krishna to the Rev. Moon, fresh impulses over women's ordination or old scraps over biblical literalism versus academic freedom--all these are parts of the kaleidoscope which forms our recent past. This background stands as a conditioning factor, not by any means a fully determinative principle, necessary for understanding the complex nature of missionary activity. It must be studied seriously as one of the four areas of missions analysis because the various contexts out of which missions emerge will always shed light on their objectives, methods, and criteria of ultimate success.

SUGGESTED READING LIST

Aaron I. Abell, The Urban Impact on American Protestantism, 1865-1900 (Cambridge MA, 1943).

Robert P. Beaver, The Missionary Between the Times (New York, 1968).

Robert F. Berkhofer, Salvation and the Savage: An Analysis of Protestant Missions and American Indian Response, 1787-1862 (Lexington KY, 1965).

Kenneth Cauthen, The Impact of American Religious Liberalism (New York, 1962).

Oliver W. Elsbree, The Rise of the Missionary Spirit in America (Williamsport PA, 1928).

Charles I. Foster, An Errand of Mercy: The United Evangelical Front, 1790-1837 (Chapel Hill, 1960).

Alan Geyer, Piety and Politics: American Protestantism in the World Arena (Richmond VA, 1963).

Colin B. Goodykoontz, Home Missions on the American Frontier (Caldwell ID, 1939; New York, 1971).

Clifford S. Griffin, Their Brothers' Keepers: Moral Stewardship in the United States, 1800-1865 (New Brunswick NJ, 1960).

Robert T. Handy, We Worship Together: A History of Cooperative Home Missions (New York, 1966).

_____, A Christian America; Protestant Hopes and Historical Realities (New York, 1971).

William E. Hocking (ed.), Re-Thinking Missions: A Laymen's Inquiry after One Hundred Years (New York, 1932).

Charles H. Hopkins, The Rise of the Social Gospel in American Protestantism, 1865-1915 (New Haven, 1940).

_____, History of the YMCA in North America (New York, 1951).

Hendrick Kraemer, The Christian Message in a Non-Christian World (London, 1938).

Martin E. Marty, Righteous Empire: The Protestant Experience in America (New York, 1970).

_____, Second Chance for American Protestants (New York, 1963).

Donald B. Meyer, The Protestant Search for Political Realism, 1919-1941 (Berkeley CA, 1960).

T. Scott Miyakawa, Protestants and Pioneers: Individualism and Conformity on the American Frontier (Chicago, 1964).

David M. Reimers, White Protestantism and the Negro (New York, 1965).

Milton C. Sernett, Black Religion and American Evangelism ..., 1787-1865 (Metuchen NJ, 1975).

4

Response to Dr. Bowden

Catherine L. Albanese

When I was invited to respond to Henry Bowden's paper, I was to say the least honored--as well as very much surprised. Studies in American Transcendentalism, the civil religion of the American Revolution, and contemporary popular religion hardly seem central to an understanding of the American Protestant missionary enterprise. So it is by no means as an expert in missiology that I approach the task of responding to Henry Bowden's very competent contribution. Yet there is a point at which my own interests and abilities may intersect with those of the presentation. My work in the areas I have mentioned has been less in the direction of discovering new facts than in illuminating old ones by suggesting new interpretations based on different categories --categories gleaned from disciplines such as the history of religions, the sociology of knowledge, and cultural and structural anthropology.

For the sake of raising what may be some significant issues for discussion, I should like to review Henry Bowden's paper from the perspective of these categories. The very excellence of Professor Bowden's "overview" is one element which urges me on in such a direction. While those who specialize in missions may want to add their insights--perhaps, for example, the influence of eschatological and millennial religion in the missionary thrust--on the whole, Bowden's presentation strikes me as inclusive rather than otherwise. Hence, let us see what results emerge from examining the categories which inform Professor Bowden's essay.

Bowden's pervasive theme seems to be that religion is an ingredient separable in theory and in fact from culture, so that

it stands over against culture as something which is quite definitely "other." Let me illustrate with some quotations from the
text of the discussion. On page 41, Bowden asks concerning the
history of mission boards, "What goals succeeded earlier ones,
and how did those shifting perspectives on civilization coincide
with the underlying constant, 'pure Christianity?'" Again, on
page 48, he tells us that, in working with American Indians,
"religious and cultural factors were so uncritically intertwined
by white missionaries, they insisted that both aspects were parts
of a single framework, advantageous to all who adopted the total
package." And on page 55, Bowden arrives at an evaluative judgment concerning nineteenth-century foreign mission efforts: they
"constituted the purest form of missionary altruism--an anomaly
in their day."

Bowden continues his survey with, on page 55, a comment on
liberalism: "The liberal thrust at the turn of this century
. . . was to blur distinctions between ecclesiastical and cultural life, all for the good because advancement in one meant
improvement in both." Then, on page 59, Bowden applauds the
demise of liberalism and the development of Neo-Orthodoxy:
"Indeed, once they were free from cultural objectives, practical
programs of social aid were possible in an atmosphere of heightened ecumenical consciousness." Finally, Bowden writes of the
new missionary posture vis à vis militarism in World War II and
thereafter (on page 59): "It bears healthy signs of creative
tension between religion and cultural goals instead of an uncritical blending of the two categories."

Now it is clear from Bowden's initial invocation of "pure
Christianity" to his conclusion about "uncritical blending" of
religion and culture that he sees these as two separate and different entities although capable of combination. What I should
like to do here is to direct attention to the possible sources
of Professor Bowden's understanding and then suggest alternative
constructions for category formation. Theologically, I would
locate the language of Professor Bowden's paper more or less
within the worldview of Neo-Orthodoxy. That is, it seems to
rise out of the perception of a revelation which transcends the
processes of history and yet appears over and over again within
them. Philosophically, it seems to me, Bowden's paper emerges
as representative of the Neo-Kantian heritage which pervades the
work of such eminent religion scholars as Ernst Troeltsch,
Max Weber, and even Joachim Wach, whom I shall forthwith be
quoting. Here, I refer to an enduring Platonism which discerns
the Idea as the pure and powerful motive force behind history,
the "really real" in the midst of objects and events which by
implication have relatively less reality. At the same time,
with the Neo-Kantians, the Idea reveals itself now in the onward

march of history. Hence, Bowden as historian receives license
to seek the Idea (religion and specifically Christianity) in the
midst of culture.

I have no wish to engage in either theological or philosophical controversy, but let me--having tried to identify Professor
Bowden's position--move to the level of more pragmatic discussion. Quite simply, despite the theological nicety and logical
attractiveness of these Neo-Orthodox and Platonic understandings,
I think that there are practical reasons to consider the use of
other categories. First of all, if we view religion as separate
from culture, we may face the impossibility of certain forms of
dialogue with other disciplines which offer valid and illuminating insights into some dimensions of the religious impulse. We
can go so far and no further before we cry "halt" before the
sacred preserve which is the domain of revelation or the Idea.
Secondly, if we view religion as separate from culture, we may
make it well nigh impossible to perceive the presence of common
meaning and value orientations in organized religion and the rest
of culture, orientations which--if discovered--may further raise
the question of their own priority to both the Christian churches
and the secular world.

In light of these considerations, I wish tentatively to intro-
duce some alternate understandings of the relationship between
religion and the rest of culture. One such possibility comes
from a reformulation of the very Neo-Kantian Platonism we have
been discussing. Joachim Wach, the great sociologist and historian of religions, tried to enunciate the role of religion within
the rest of culture by locating the "holy" in a position more
fundamental than the Platonic Ideas, the Good, the True, and the
Beautiful. Religion was not a fourth value to be added to the
Ideas. Rather, said Wach, "figuratively speaking, religion is
not a branch but the trunk of the tree. Therefore, the analysis
of any given culture entails not only the search for theologou-
mena, myths, or rites as a means of deciphering the religious
attitude but also a process of sensing and exploring the very
atmosphere and a careful study of the general attitudes revealed
in the integral expression of its life."[1]

From the other end of the spectrum, the anthropologist
Clifford Geertz has explored the meaning of religion as a cultural system in his now classical article by that title (1966).
For Geertz, sacred symbols function "to synthesize a people's
ethos--the tone, character, and quality of their life, its moral
and aesthetic style and mood--and their world view--the picture
they have of the way things in sheer actuality are, their most
comprehensive ideas of order." Therefore, concludes Geertz,
"religious symbols formulate a basic congruence between a

particular style of life and a specific (if, most often, implicit) metaphysic, and in so doing sustain each with the borrowed authority of the other."[2] Religion is thus in essence a part of culture since it functions to unify and integrate other aspects of that culture. Far from being itself a thing apart, it exists at the very core of cultural exchanges. In sum, while Wach sees religion as the trunk of the tree of culture, Geertz would reverse the proposition. Culture is the trunk of the tree of religion.

While it would be interesting to pursue the contrast between the two positions and investigate their respective ramifications, here it is sufficient to note what the two discussions have in common. Both view religion as inseparable in substance from the rest of culture, although--for purposes of empirical description-- both scholars have had few difficulties in identifying the religious aspect of culture and elucidating it brilliantly. But at this juncture, it may be useful to "try out" their mutual insight on the material of Professor Bowden's paper. What follows is suggestive more than conclusive--but it may aid us in coming to terms with some of the issues I have addressed.

If, for heuristic purposes, we assume that religion is part of culture or conversely, that culture is part of religion, the major religio-cultural categories which emerge from the Bowden discussion are from one point of view the categories of "history-makers." Let me explicate. Throughout Bowden's paper, we read of rational constructions such as Enlightenment philosophy, Calvinist theology, the idea of manifest destiny. We read also of institutions--the Protestant churches, the American Home Mission Society, the American Bible Society, the American Tract Society, the American Missionary Association. Again, we read of significant actions: the Revolutionary War, land expansion on the frontier, revival techniques, Indian mission techniques, to name but a few. I think it would be fair to say that the religious style which Bowden is articulating so well is one that is highly involved with social structure, putting its premium on a world of persons existing in communal patterns--the arena in which events unfold and history comes to be. Further, the style is one of task-orientation with faith in a projected future and sacrifice in the present to attain that future--the call of destiny or, in Bowden's terms, the "great commission." In this context, it is clear that discipline is required, and law and order--the guarantors of that discipline--are primary values. Bowden's survey reveals indeed a history of missions in which discipline becomes a fine art with institutions rising, seemingly spontaneously, and interacting superbly. Similarly, the mental projection of this law and order means that conscious explication of the religious tradition is important, and theological precision is prized. Bowden's discussion proceeds in an atmosphere sensitive to theological and philosophical currents. Finally, the style which Bowden exemplifies involves mastery over nature in order to build and stabilize human structures. And, of course, the technical prowess of missionaries, as Bowden has indicated, has been considerable.

I have borrowed the phrase, "history-makers," from Mircea Eliade in order to identify the religio-cultural style embodied in the Bowden discussion. Mircea Eliade has also linked this style of religion in which "history is on the march" with kings, heroes, and empires,[3] describing the character of its symbolism in terms analogous to those of missionary effort. In other words, the thrust toward extension, expansion, and encompassment belongs to the substantive meaning of nineteenth- and twentieth-century American Protestantism. Because Jesus suffered, died, and rose in history, history itself becomes valuable. So, too, does making history and the means to that end. But it would take only a cursory glance at the American story to see that these categories apply to the republican enterprise of the United States as well. Finally, the meanings and values are intrinsic to Professor Bowden's paper—a presentation cast overwhelmingly in the language of rational constructions, institutions, and actions, as we have seen.

It is significant that the nineteenth century also boasted another discovery, a "cultural factor" if you will, which is not mentioned in Professor Bowden's discussion. The nineteenth century was the great century of the discovery of the unconscious. We need not turn to Sigmund Freud in Vienna for confirmation, since America has been rich in exploration on its own. We can look to the unforgettable William James, but even earlier, in the writings of such American romantics as Nathaniel Hawthorne and Herman Melville, to name but two, the unconscious, if not called by name, was nonetheless visible and vigorous. It is of course clear that the concern for the unconscious which has touched many sensitive Americans has on the whole proved secondary in importance to history-making in American culture. My point in raising the issue here is that Professor Bowden's paper gives us very little sense of how introspection and the inner life figured in the missionary impulse of the last two centuries. My further and more important point is that the reason seems to be bound up with the religio-cultural categories which inform the presentation.

This expedition into alternative ways of viewing religio-cultural questions must hasten to a close. I have tried to illuminate that problematic from a somewhat different perspective. From this point of view, the religio-cultural matrix is inseparable. It becomes not so easy to distinguish teaching "culture" from teaching "religion." When Professor Bowden discusses latter-day missionaries who, after World War II, became disenchanted with imparting their "culture" along with their "religion," he is perhaps discussing only one level of the question. At deeper levels, the hidden springs of consciousness, the structures of meaning and value which lie embedded in language, can never be suppressed. They can only be conveyed more subtly. There is a good deal more continuity than at first glance appears between, not only missionaries past and missionaries present, but between missionaries and American scholars and these scholars and other Americans.

NOTES

[1] Joachim Wach, *Sociology of Religion* (1944) (Chicago: University of Chicago Press, Phoenix Books, 1967), p. 16.

[2] Clifford Geertz, "Religion as a Cultural System" (1966), in *The Interpretation of Cultures* (New York: Basic Books, 1973), pp. 89-90.

[3] Mircea Eliade, *Patterns in Comparative Religion,* translated by Rosemary Sheed (1958) (Cleveland: World Publishing Company, Meridian Books, 1967), p. 124.

5

A History of Foreign Mission Theory in America

Charles W. Forman

Christian missions, though they are a very practical activity, involve inevitably a great deal of theory and theology. The methods they use, the goals they work for, the way they treat people, all are based on theories and theologies whether these are fully articulated or not. And this is true of even so notoriously practical a people as the Americans and of their missions. America's mission theory has not attracted as much attention as America's mission work.[1] The historians' interest has always been turned to the operations and effects of missionary activity, whether in Asia, Africa, Latin America or Oceania. Yet the theory needs to be examined simultaneously if the activity is to be properly understood.

Let us follow then the history of that theory, starting with the beginning of America's foreign missions at the organization of the American Board of Commissioners for Foreign Missions in 1810 and continuing up to the middle years of the present century,

---

[1]

The only historical works on America's foreign mission theory are by R. Pierce Beaver 1952, 1966, 1967, 1968, and Charles L. Chaney 1976. Somewhat useful anthologies of mission thought are Stow 1846 and Ray 1907. Useful sections on mission theory are found in Elsbree 1928, Varg 1958 and Phillips 1969. The books by Berg 1956 and Jong 1970 provide useful comparative material though the one deals only with Britain and the other stops short of the beginning of foreign missions.

after which the story ceases to be history in the usual sense
and becomes a branch of contemporary thought. The history divides itself naturally into four quite distinct periods. The
first period can be regarded as extending from 1810 to about
1890. A fairly constant set of ideas accompanied the movement
during those eighty years. About 1890 the climate of opinion
changed markedly and from then to 1918, in what may be called
the heyday of American missions, there was a burst of new ideas
and an enormously increased quantity of literature expressing
those ideas. The third period was clearly the time between the
First and Second World Wars, a troubled era with some altogether
unique expressions of mission theory. And at the end we will
have to deal with the realm of thought emerging during and immediately after the Second World War. This was in some respects a
culmination because it brought some thorough and profound statements of mission theory and, in 1952, the only effort ever made
by American missions jointly and fully to express their theory
and theology. With that we may appropriately bring our survey
to a close.

Certain things will have to be excluded from attention. Books
on mission history obviously do not fall within the boundaries
envisaged here, which means that some of the greatest American
writers on missions will receive little or no attention. Writings dealing only with a particular country have also been omit-
ted except in cases where they had a much wider relevance. Our
concern is with those works which handle mission theory in more
general terms. It is also with those which do this in a more
serious way, not with the superficial works which are often very
popular. Let it be said, however, that there are numbers of very
popular works which are in fact quite serious and these we should
consider. They may not be scholarly in the ordinary sense, but
they are far from superficial and they can provide an excellent
gauge of the direction in which mission thought is moving. Some
of the books issued by the Missionary Education Movement and the
Friendship Press have been of this nature.

There is one field closely related to what is considered here
which we cannot examine. That is the whole field of missionary
thought in Europe. Our topic is American missionary thought
which obviously leaves out other countries. But we need to recognize that those who thought about missions in this country
were very much aware of what others were thinking abroad. This
is particularly true in regard to Britain. American writers refer frequently to what British writers have been saying and learn
from them or oppose them. In the twentieth century this became
increasingly true in relation to the European continent, especially Germany. Continental writers became the main inspiration or
the challenge for many people. However, Americans primarily had

their own ideas. There has been plenty of intellectual ferment
in this country regarding missions over the century and a half
we are covering and to that we must turn.

I

Admittedly, American missions to the world began with a minimum of theory and a maximum of practice. There were no long
treatises, major studies or extensive research programs at the
beginnings of the world missionary movement. There was, indeed,
a powerful new appropriation of the Christian message. But Evangelicalism, as that appropriation is called, emphasized the emotions more than the intellect and personal response more than
correct doctrine. Hence it did not lend itself to theorizing.
The start of a new program of action was not, in any case, a time
conducive to the development of theory. There were plans to be
made and enthusiasm to be stirred and support to be marshalled.
The literature which was appropriate to this activity consisted
of sermons and tracts, not scholarly theses.

Yet the Evangelicalism out of which the missions grew, for all
its stress on the emotions, had a strong intellectual heritage in
the work of Americans like Jonathan Edwards and Samuel Hopkins.
Behind those writers lay the intellectual foundation provided by
the Puritan scholars of early New England. The mission publi-
cists of the period following 1810 developed their thought in
this framework. (Chaney 1976: 9-56, 181.) Jonathan Edwards was
the primary source of their ideas, but Samuel Hopkins, Edward's
great disciple, lived nearer to their time and Hopkinsianism became the system of thought which directly moulded the foreign
missionary enthusiasts. It taught them that the Christian should
be actuated by "universal disinterested benevolence." This meant
an eagerness to do the will of God with no thought of reward on
earth or even in heaven, and with no limits on those who were to
be helped. It looked forward to the time when all men would be
united in one happy society each seeking and rejoicing in the
public good. This teaching served very effectively to break down
the acceptance of human suffering and the indifference to missions which had been present among some contemporary Calvinists.
(Hopkins 1852: I, 389, 399; III, 16. Chaney 1976: 57-84, 234-
237. Elsbree 1928: 139-148.)

Sermons and tracts packed with these ideas as well as with a
good dose of emotions, poured forth in large numbers during the
early years of the movement. They were eagerly received and

widely circulated. The sermon by Francis Wayland, the young
Baptist minister from Boston who later became the president of
Brown University, dealing with "The Moral Dignity of the Missionary Enterprise," was one of the most widely known. It was frequently reprinted not only in this country but in Britain and
appeared in collections later in the nineteenth century and even
in the twentieth (Wayland 1826, 1846, 1907). The Evangelical
Magazine in Britain said of it: "Well may America glory in the
man who could have reared such an imperishable monument to perpetuate his memory as a Christian teacher, and as a man of
taste." (Wayland: 1826: 2) Similarly influential was the
tract by the early medical missionary to India, Rev. John Scudder
of the Reformed Church. In The Redeemer's Last Command he
appealed to the church to devote its full energies to mission
work. Both these examples were strongly emotional statements,
though Wayland was chiefly interested in the emotions of exalta-
tion stirred by missionary heroism while Schudder wanted to stir
emotions of pity for the people to whom the missionary went.

The most obvious thing which strikes a reader of the missionary literature of that period, beyond its emotional quality, is
its tremendous altruistic emphasis and world embracing concern.
Those who thought about missions did indeed follow the Hopkinsian view in that they had little or nothing to say about advantages or benefits which might be derived from missionary activity
for the Christians of America either in this world or the next.
There was no talk about church aggrandizement which would appeal
to human pride or any offer of a reduction of punishment after
death, although there were occasional asides wondering about the
integrity of the salvation of those who showed no concern for
the salvation of others. The emphasis throughout was on the
needs of others, the fact that every soul in the most remote
corner of the world was as valuable as any close at hand,

2

One exception was provided by Warren 1870 which described
the political and economic as well as other gains accruing to
those who sent out foreign missionaries. Baird's brief mention
of missionary motivation in his general treatment of religion in
America (1844: 666) may also be seen as an exception, though his
reference to blessings resulting from missions is decidedly subordinate to his statement of other motives. Williams 1856,
which appears to be an exception, however, was actually an appeal for that higher blessedness which comes from giving rather
than receiving, and so fitted in with the usual altruistic
emphasis.

the reminder that all human beings belong to one family under
God and that we should therefore be as solicitous to help a
child subjected to the disabilities of some foreign customs and
religions as we would be to help our own child if he were caught
in similar toils. This altruism was simultaneously concerned
for the "temporal needs and eternal happiness" of those it
served. (Campbell 1827: 9-11. Tuckerman 1826: 31-32. Abeel
1838: 17-31. L. Woods in Beaver 1966: 257-259. Missionary
Offering 1843: 10-11, 64-76. Irwin 1866: 10-12. Beaver 1968:
144-45. Phillips 1969: 263-264.)

But altruism has its negative side in the sense of superiority and condescension and this was glaringly evident in the
nineteenth century understanding of missions. The picture which
was drawn of the non-Christian lands was one of unmitigated misery. "Beyond the boundaries of Christendom," said Francis Wayland, "on every side the dark places of the earth are filled
with the habitations of cruelty." (Wayland 1826: 7-8.) The
children thrown to the crocodiles in the sacred Ganges provided
one of the standard objects of sympathy (L. Woods 1812 in Beaver
1966: 259. Wayland 1826: 8. Scudder n.d.: 22-23.). They also
provided a clear example of the unfairness of the picture which
the mission writers drew. What was past or rare was reported
as present and typical. The missionary picture was decidedly
more negative than that drawn by other travelers. The pastor
of Broadway Tabernacle noted in 1851 that the public had for a
time been confused by the more appreciative accounts of these
other travelers who, he said, were interested in entertainment
or fame, but that now that reports were available from honest
missionaries, the degredation of the heathen was finally being
acknowledged. (Thompson 1851: 14-17.) By the 1890s a preacher,
even in a denomination which had no missionaries, could confidently say, "Now everyone knows what frightful misery prevails
among the heathen." (Leuking 1964: 154. cf. Anderson 1967: 77.
Phillips 1969: 270-279.)

Not surprisingly, the religions of the East were nearly always seen as evil as well as illusory. They were a "refuge for
lies." (Anderson 1967: 102.) They were "delusive...fictions."
(Hall and Newell 1818: 8.) A work on comparative religions
published by William Sprague in 1837 stated that the relations
between Christianity and paganism were the relations between
light and darkness and that with the spread of missions the
kingdom of darkness was being routed and its ruler was in panic.
(Sprague 1837: 70-71.) This book consisted entirely of a cata-
logue of unfavorable comparisons between Christianity and other
religions.

Few doubted that "the unbelieving heathen perished in everlasting torment." (Beaver 1968: 127.) But there was some

refinement of thought on this point by certain writers. Francis
Wayland and the Unitarian, Joseph Tuckerman, alike made the
point that those heathen who led a holy life according to their
faith might or, in the Unitarian view, would be saved. But both
agreed that among those people there was such a failure to live
up to their own teachings and human nature had become so
degraded and darkened that they needed to be redeemed and missions should therefore be sent to them. (Wayland 1826: 9.
Tuckerman 1826: 3, 18-22.) Even if we allow for some uncertainty on this point, another writer explained, if we are not completely sure about the salvation of non-Christians, "the only
safe and charitable plan is to assume that they all must perish
and then to exert ourselves to the utmost for their recovery."
(Abeel 1838: 67, 71-72.)

The missiology of those times, while it was highly critical
of Asia and Africa was not inclined to level criticisms against
life in America or Protestant Europe. Herein it differed sharply from the missiology of the following century. The Western
lands were painted in bright colors and the hope was sometimes
expressed that all the world would one day be as pleasant and
attractive as a New England village, a Scottish hamlet or the
German countryside. (Happer 1880: 2. Wayland 1826: 8-9. Phillips 1969: 242-246.) The new nation of America had strongly
nationalistic feelings and a sense of great destiny and these
things had their effect on American thought about missions.
They led mission writers to see a great destiny for America in
terms of service, however, and not of domination. There was
little desire expressed to relate missions to the operations of
the American government or other American interests.[3] In general there was far more emphasis on the dreadful state of the
"heathen" and the needs they represented than on the virtues
or greatness of the United States.

More important than any of these considerations regarding
the world and its peoples were the references in missionary
thinking to the love of Christ and his command to his church.
Sometimes these were expressed with a heavier emphasis on the

---

[3]
    Beaver 1968: 134-137. Phillips 1969: 289-290. Some impor-
tant missionaries in East Asia were exceptions to this. Varg
1958: 5. The statement is true, however, of the missionary
writing produced in America.

element of love and sometimes with a heavier emphasis on the command. Jesus' love for all humanity brought forth a responding love in the heart of the believer and a consequent desire to see Christ known and his honor proclaimed throughout the world. R. Pierce Beaver has remarked on the disappearance of the concern for the glory of God from missionary thinking at about the time that foreign missions were launched. (Beaver 1968: 139-140.) Yet the love for Christ and zeal for his honor can be seen as providing a closely parallel element in missionary thought.

Sometimes the emphasis was much more on Christ's command, especially his Great Commission, and this could give a very different cast to the theology of missions. Usually the element of command was kept in balance with other elements such as love and the Great Commission was seen as important only because it expressed something central in the whole of Christ's ministry, not because it stood alone as an arbitrary order. This was true both in the period we are studying and in the later periods. But on occasion, particularly in the later period between 1890 and 1918, the treatment of Christ's command was explicitly in terms of unquestioning duty or military obedience. The Victorian glorification of duty evidently had its effect on missionary motivation. (Pierson 1891: 154-155. Trible 1892: 7. Barton 1908: 194. Elsbree 1928: 152. For the more balanced statement on Christ's command, see Pierson 1886: 305. Speer 1910: 7. Brown 1908: 11. Zwemer 1943: 91. Barclay 1949-1973: 180-184.) Yet whenever, in any period, there was an extended or thoughtful elaboration of the grounds of missionary activity it is amazing how repeatedly and consistently it brought together the three bases of (1) obedience to Christ's command, (2) love for Christ and (3) compassion for the world. (Martin 1895:40-45. L. Woods 1812 in Beaver 1966: 258-260. R. Anderson in Beaver 1968: 141-142. Brown 1908: 6-10. D.J. Fleming in Goddard 1917: 24. Goddard 1917: 57-60.) It is well that it was so for the three were indeed interdependent. Obedience without love would be desiccated, love without obedience would be sentimental and either of them without a compassion for people would divert attention from the persons served to the act of serving.

As these fundamental grounds for mission remained fairly constant throughout the periods of this study, so a confidence in the final outcome of the missionary effort remained strong all through the years. To be sure it carried some important variations in outlook from time to time, just as the grounding of missions included some occasional variations which we shall discover. But basically there has always been a strong sense of assurance that because the One whose nature is love as revealed in Jesus Christ is indeed God, the creator and ruler of this

world, in the end his kingdom of righteousness and peace and
joy will be established and that the labors of the mission to
make God known and loved and obeyed will be gathered up in the
final consummation. Therefore American theology of missions
has never had any doubts as to the final outcome to which missions are related.

The variations which have appeared in missionary writing have
to do with the relative immediacy of this outcome and the dir-
ectness of the connection between the mission and the consummation. In the very early years there was much feeling that the
new age of God's kingdom was about to dawn and that the work of
missions for converting the nations would therefore be rapidly
successful. Missions were regarded as part of the pre-ordained
direction of God's great work of redemption. The church was
cooperating with God in bringing in the millennial era of peace
and brotherhood when all nations would serve Christ. Missions
and the world-wide turmoil of the early nineteenth century were
seen as signs of the end of the old age and the dawn of the new.
The thinkers of this period stressed that the new age was going
to come through the use of ordinary means and not through mira-
cles. But since it was God who was using these means the outcome was assured. The nations would be won for Christ. (Chaney 1976: 218, 243-244, 257-259, 262, 271. Elsbree 1928: 126-
127. Phillips 1969: 234. Abeel 1838: 24. Scudder n.d.: 6.
Anderson 1967: 59-63. Lueking 1964: 124.)

After the middle of the nineteenth century mission thinkers
wrestled with the problem of why this expectation had not been
realized and missions had not met a quick success. They generally came to the conclusion that for some reason in God's providence the age of mission work was to be a long one. The
length of time suggested by some of the earlier thinkers had
been two hundred years, so the reevaluations could easily resort
to that time-frame. The examples of the conversion of the Roman empire and of northern Europe were pointed to as models both
for the long time needed and the certainty of success. Contemporary examples of the conversion of whole nations, particularly Polynesia and Madagascar, were offered to show the direction
in which the world was going and the assurance of eventual triumph. (Thompson 1851: 12-13, 52-53. Happer 1880: 2-21. Martin 1895: 227-233. Thoburn 1895: 44-70. Barrows 1899: x.
Brown 1908: 140-142.) Dispensationalism which was popular in
some circles also came in with an explanation of the long time
involved in missions, for millenia were believed to lie between
the steps of the different dispensations. (Gordon 1893: 15-19.)

Around the end of the century there was a revival of talk
about those signs of the times which indicated a rapid opening

of the world to the Gospel. We will deal with that more fully
when examining that period, but for the present it is enough
to say that it had certain similarities to the early expectations of rapid success signaled in the events at the beginning
of the nineteenth century. In the years after 1918, however,
that kind of speculation decreased and even the assurance about
the success of the missionary enterprise was gradually trans-
muted--or attenuated--into assurance about the eventual triumph
of God's kingdom in which the mission of the church would find
fulfillment.[4]

The topics just considered have taken us beyond the nineteenth century into later periods. But before we leave that
earlier time entirely we should give some separate attention
to its greatest thinker and statesman in the field of missions,
Rufus Anderson, a secretary of the American Board from 1826 to
1866. Many of Anderson's views were of a piece with those of
his contemporaries and have, accordingly, been already noted.
He had, however, certain distinctive ideas which need recognition.

The point at which Anderson was far ahead of his age was in
his understanding of the way missions should work. Others had
a conviction that the faith should be presented to all mankind
but they did not define their goal more specifically. Some
believed that people had to be "civilized" before they could
receive the gospel, but most thought that mission work should
be essentially a matter of preaching. (Hall and Newell 1818:
7-8. Wayland 1826: 14-15. Thompson 1851: 43-46. Seeley 1875:
128-144. Happer 1880: 1-3. Varg 1958: 21.) Anderson agreed
with the overriding emphasis on preaching. The reconciliation
with God effected by Christ's atonement was the great theme of
missions and it needed to be presented in person by the preacher. (Anderson 1967: 25, 75, 79.) Social service or the so-
called civilizing work of missions was deprecated by him. The

---

4

Latourette 36: 214-215. Soper 1943: 286-290. Mott 1939:
95-96 can be seen as something of a holdover of the earlier
view anticipating the rapid triumph of the mission. This view
had also continued in some circles throughout the nineteenth
century before it returned to popularity at the end of that
time. (Beaver 1968: 131.)

social consequences of the gospel would gradually appear in
later generations out of the lives of indigenous Christians.
Anderson was well ahead of his time in seeing the confusion
involved in the identification of Christianity with Western
culture and seeing the long term incompatibility of the Christian faith with Western imperialism. (Ibid. 13, 14, 36, 78,
81-2. Phillips 1969: 253.)

Yet a concentration on preaching did not mean for Anderson,
as it did for some others, an absence of strategy and an end-
less, unlimited goal. He was the first American to recognize
the decisive importance of the founding of an indigenous church
and of the shaping of all policies toward that goal. He saw
that foreign missions could not continue to proliferate and
expand endlessly. They must have a limited objective, namely,
to establish a church which would itself take over responsibility for mission in its area, enabling the foreign mission to
close its own work there and move on to new fields. The missionary should not try to be a leader but should train the
future indigenous leaders. The church should support its own
leadership and advance its own mission. He did allow for a
period of missionary tutelage during which the new leadership
would be trained and self-support developed. It was Anderson,
along with Henry Venn of England, who formulated the goal of
missions which came to be generally accepted, i.e., the creation
of self-governing, self-supporting and self-propagating churches. (Anderson 1967: 15-16, 23, 27-28, 31, 34-35, 76, 89-99,
103-106.)

The greatest diversion from Anderson's emphasis on the national church came through the development of mission schools.
The school issue came to prominence in 1854 when Anderson went
to India to try to shift the direction of the missions there.
On his recommendation the missionaries agreed to close down
some of their schools and to concentrate more on preaching for
church development. He was not in fact opposed to all mission
schools. He believed that some were necessary for the training
of Christian leaders and the upbuilding of Christians in the
faith. But he did not as a rule support the effort to establish schools as a means for the introduction of Christianity.
He was convinced that this had proved itself an ineffective
method in countries like India. He also resisted the trend toward providing an English-language education since that could
only de-nationalize people reather than provide a strong national Christian leadership for the church. (Anderson 1967: 79-80,
101, 147-167. Jimeson 1855: 4-5.)

If we may glance ahead at this point it will be evident
that Anderson's philosophy on schools failed to be decisive in

the later thought on American missions. In the years after
1890 when missions were expanding and expending so much, the
schools were the most notable feature of their work. The
schools and colleges in Asia were devoted chiefly to educating
non-Christians rather than to producing an educated leadership
for the church as Anderson had recommended. The more conservative writers of that time justified this practice by asserting
that these schools could be effective agencies of evangelization if they were kept strongly Christian in spirit and in
practice, providing an excellent education and a close, personal contact between teacher and student.[5] The more liberal
writers did not try to defend the schools in these terms
but they still supported them simply as a Christian contribution to the development of the country, providing an education that would broaden the intellect and inculcate a spirit
of Christian service.[6] For one reason or the other schools
for the general public were vigorously advanced.

In 1922 the American mission boards sponsored two famous
educational commissions, one sent to China and the other to
Africa. (Christian Education in China 1922. Education in
Africa 1922.) Both took the liberal stance of regarding mission schools as contributions to the good of the whole people
rather than to the development of the Christian community or
to the winning of members for the church. The China commission
expressed the hope that schools would make China Christian in
principle and practice through inculcating the spirit of
Christian service. The Africa commission pressed for a type
of education which would be closely related to the physical
environment and social groupings of the people, which would

5
   Baldwin 1900: 69-70. Brown 1908: 124-126. Speer 1910:
93-98. Speer 1919: 179-183. In an earlier statement Speer
followed Anderson's view. Speer 1902: 54-56.
   6
   Barton 1913. Goucher 1912. Wherry 1912. Barton, a secretary of the American Board, saw one contribution of Christian
colleges in India as the provision of law-abiding leaders
whom the government was at last beginning to recognize and
employ instead of the irreligious and rebellious products
which the government's own colleges were producing, p. 158.
John Goucher, the Methodist clergy man and philanthropist who
served as president of and contributed so much to the college
which was later named for him, was an eager supporter of mission education, bearing the costs of 120 mission schools at
one time. His article of 1912 and his book of 1911, pp. 109-

promote national development without disruption. The liberal
position taken by these commissions was essentially the
point at which American mission theory came out with regard
to education.[7] Soon thereafter it had to face the gradual
supplanting of mission education by government schools.
(Latourette 1936: 165-167. Shafer 1944: 136-138.) But that
change was certainly not one calculated to alter the basic
philosophy of mission education. The contributions of the
remaining mission schools were seen by the governments, whether
colonial or independent, in very much the same terms as the
1922 commissions had seen them. It was all a far cry from
Rufus Anderson.[8]

II

We come now to the period 1890 to 1918, that amazing time
in the history of American missions and American mission
theory. Never have missions been so popular nor aroused so
much enthusiasm, both within the churches and with the public
generally, as they did during those years. Those were the
days when a President of the United States would speak to
a missions conference and an ex-President serve as conference
chairman. Large books dealing with mission theory which had
been no more than half a dozen in number during the previous
period of eighty years now poured forth in abundance, at
least forty-three of them in this period of only twenty-eight

----

112, emphasized the more liberal line of though mentioned
above but were also sympathetic to the conservative interests.

7
    The same position was taken regarding India and Korea by
McKee 1930 and Fisher 1928.

8
    The other major type of mission service besides education-
al, was medical. Much less was written about the basic philosophy for this kind of work, but what was said about it was
always parallel to what was said about the philosophy of
mission education, e.g. Speer 1902: 59-60. Speer 1919:
166-167.

years. The Student Volunteer Movement contributed much to this
enthusiasm but also was built upon it. The world was seen as
opening up for missions. There had never been "such a combination and concentration of world-wide signs. The whole horizon
is aflame," wrote one commentator (Pierson 1894: 26-27.)
There was talk now about going ahead and finishing the missionary task. (Barton 1908: 168-197.) This time was announced
as the "decisive hour of Christian missions"; the crucial work,
it was said, must be done in this day of opportunity just
as sowing must be done in the spring for there would be no
other time to do it. (Mott 1910. Pierson 1891: 115. Goucher
1911: 90.)

In the perspective of history it is evident that there was
much truth in these evaluations of that period. It was in
fact the time when the East was turning its back on old patterns
and structures and opening up most fully to the programs and
the persons coming from the West. Japan had been more open a
decade earlier and Africa was to be more open a decade or two
later. But for all of Asia other than Japan these years were
the time of the greatest receptivity to Christianity. The
analysts were right; what was not done then could not be done
later. Another perception which proved true was the realization at that time that the body of humanity had become in fact
a single body and that if healing were not brought to the dis-
eased parts at once the healthy parts would soon become in-
fected. (Todd 1890: 78.) The more recent spread of Eastern
religions in the West has borne out that insight though the
results need not be interpreted as negatively as they were
then.

The great increase in serious writing about missions
appeared primarily in the form of lecture series for academic
audiences. From the beginning of this period there seems to
have been a constantly increasing interest in establishing
special lectureships which were either limited to missions or
included missions among their concerns. The Student Lectureship on Missions at Princeton Seminary, the Cole Lectures in
Vanderbilt, the Fondren Lectures on Christian Missions at
Southern Methodist University, the Ely Foundation at Union
Seminary in New York and, most important, the Nathan Graves
lectureships established both at New Brunswick Seminary and
at Syracuse University, were the chief examples of this
development. The Duff Lectureship in Scotland was also used
as a platform by American authors (Person 1894. Speer 1910.)
and when, in 1894, the Barrows Lectureship was established
for   lectures in Asia it also became a valuable focus
for American missionary thought. These lectureships were the

forerunners of the professorships in missions which began to be
popular in the latter half of the period (Beaver 1976: 82-83.),
and which were also the product of the tremendous missionary
enthusiasm of the time.

Another reason for increased production in the field was
the larger number of denominations which showed an involvement
with mission scholarship. Prior to 1890 the writing on missions
in this country had been almost exclusively a Congregational
and Presbyterian preserve. The bibliography appended to this
paper provides a presumably representative listing of missiological monographs from the various periods. It includes
for the period before 1890, aside from sermons and the one
Reformed and one Unitarian tract which have been mentioned
(Scudder n.d., Tuckerman 1826), no writings by others than
Presbyterians and Congregationalists. During the period
1890-1918 the Baptists and Methodists began significant production, publishing nine and fifteen works respectively.
The Congregationalists published at about the same level as
these, while the Presbyterians with twenty-eight titles
continued to predominate. The same general situation prevailed
from 1920 to 1950.[9]   Other denominations continued to be
notably absent from this field of study. The Disciples of
Christ and the Reformed Church in America each had four or
five books on mission theory in the entire period from 1890 to
1950, but their small representation is not surprising since
they were smaller denominations. It is harder to explain the
fact that the Episcopalians and Lutherans were almost totally
unrepresented. Apparently, except for one valuable Lutheran
contribution, they were content to rely on their European
counterparts for their mission study. The American Catholics,
following the same pattern, did not do any serious writing
on missions till after the Second World War, (Considine 1945.
F. Voss 1946. Clark 1948.) though their promotional writing
as represented in their principal mission periodical, The
Shield, (1922-1969), was abundant.

----

[9]
     The Baptists produced twelve works, the Methodists four-
teen, the Congregationalists eight and the Presbyterians
thirty-one. Nearly half the Presbyterian production, however,
was from the pen of Daniel Johnson Fleming. Without his work
the Presbyterian contribution was only a little higher than
that of the others.

In the new enthusiasm following 1890 mission work was seen by its interpreters as the essential work of the church; no church could be healthy without it. Every Christian should be involved either as a worker or supporter. These ideas had been mentioned in the mid-nineteenth century (Hooker 1845: 14-17. Scudder n.d.: 6, 54, 70. Anderson 1967: 47.), but now they were stated more frequently and absolutely. (Speer 1902: 9-15. Henry Van Dyke in Varg 1958: 55. Baldwin 1900: 24-36. White 1915: 72-73.) There were statements made very similar to Emil Brunner's later dictum that the church exists by mission as fire exists by burning. "Air is not more necessary to the body than the missionary spirit is to a church of Christ," said one. (Baldwin 1900: 37.) The role of the lay person as distinct from the clergy was given greater importance by this emphasis. Laymen as well as ministers could be equal participants in mission activity and support. In fact we begin to hear from throughout the missionary movement those views of the centrality of the laity and the ancillary role of the clergy which were not generally advanced in the church until the 1950s and 1960s (Pierson 1891: 28-29, 124.)

As missions became more widely popular there burst forth an overwhelming emphasis on that side of their work which appealed to the general public, namely the social improvements accomplished by missionaries. Book after book on Sociological Progress in Mission Lands, The Social Aspects of Foreign Missions, The Service of Missions to Science and Society and similar subjects came from the presses. James S. Dennis' three-volume study of Christian Missions and Social Progress was only the most famous of these works. (Dennis 1897-1906. Capen 1914. Faunce 1914. Laurie 1881. Barton 1912. Keen 1906. Speer 1904.) Developments in the political order, economic productivity, scientific knowledge and social morality were rehearsed in detail and it is probably true, as one author noted, that missions had accomplished more in these lines than in the work of conversions to Christianity. (Peabody in Godard 1917: 33-35.) Josiah Strong who had, in his earlier years as a home missions worker, stirred the entire nation with his book on Our Country, now came forward with a two volume analysis of Our World in which he spoke almost entirely in terms of social questions and social progress. He saw a single world civilization emerging with common problems of urbanization, industrialization, concentrated wealth, racial divisions and war, and he saw a need for common solutions. The basic need, underlying other common solutions, was for a common religion which would unify the world, holding up the highest social and individual ideals, and bringing humanity to conscious cooperation with God in his plan for a better world.   He saw a socially conscious

Christianity as filling this need, but it would have to be
Christianity stripped of much of its ritual and doctrine
and exchanging its old individualism, which taught men how to
get to heaven, for a social-ism which would teach them how
to make a heaven. (Strong 1913-1915: II, 275-278, 362-376,
396.) Faced with this constant concentration on missions and
social problems some of the more traditional writers began
to fear that the secondary motives of missions were displacing
the primary religious ones and called for a recognition of
what was central in the faith. (Brown 1907: 22-28. Brown
1908: 2. Goddard 1917: 32-33.)

Interest in social change, which meant, in effect, Westernization, related naturally to interest in American national
power and imperialism. These years, particularly the
year 1898, marked the high point of nationalist and imperialist
feelings in American missions. In 1898, when America was
facing the decision about staying in the Philippines, church
journals were on the whole more in favor of than opposed to the
possibility. The mission boards by their promise to take
advantage of the possibility, should it materialize, carried
their influence in that same direction. (Anderson 1969: 283-
289, 292.) The more solid studies on mission over the period
as a whole, however, held more critical positions on imperialism. A Methodist minister, writing in 1890, pointed out some
of the beneficial social consequences which had followed on
European imperial conquests and said that "the fact that we
have no right to do evil that good may follow does not prevent
the Ruler of the universe from over-ruling the wicked passions
of men for the glory of his kingdom." This implied that
imperialism was part of human wickedness, even though some of
the consequences were good. (Todd 1890: 84. Goucher 1911:
168 makes the same point.) James Dennis advocated for America
"a watchful and forceful international position in Eastern
affairs," (Dennis 1913: 13.) but he also called on the church
to purify the conception of empire, seeking to eliminate the
ideas of conquest and exploitation and to check the tendencies
of military ambition and to condemn projects of political or
commercial greed (ibid., 160-161). Josiah Strong in his book
on Expansion took a very similar position, declaring that
American power should enter the world arena, not for the sake
of national aggrandizement but for the sake of justice and
benevolence. On these grounds he felt that Cuba should be
independent but that the Philippines should be ruled by
America until they were capable of self-rule. (Strong 1900:
162, 264-273, 287-292.) Robert E. Speer said frankly that
missions were not concerned "to turn independent states into
dependencies upon European or American governments." (Speer
1902: 28-29.) Speer and those associated with him did,

however, believe that missionaries in those independent states
should be provided with protection by their home governments
as other citizens were and supported action by the "enlightened nations" to secure the recognition of religious toleration
everywhere. (Speer 1910: 209-212, 219-230. Speer 1902:
95-108.) Thus, while in each of these writers imperial aggrandizement per se was condemned, the door was left open for
imperial domination with altruistic intention.

The growing interest in social change was accompanied,
not surprisingly, by some diminution in the absoluteness of
the religious demand in missions. Religious concerns were
still paramount but the final state of non-Christians was
not judged as negatively as it had been.[10] At the threshold
of this period the American Board passed through a bitter
controversy in which it moved from an unyielding belief in
the damnation of all who were not Christians to a willingness
to allow for belief in their possible salvation. (Varg
1958: 68-71.) In the succeeding years writers who stood
squarely in the main stream of American missions such as
James Buckley of the Methodists and Robert E. Speer, Arthur
Judson Brown and James Dennis in Presbyterian missions,
allowed for the possibility of salvation for those who had
never heard of Christ.[11] The Baptists, Henry Mabie and W.O.
Carver, spoke of the elements of value and of divine revelation in every religion, (Mabie 1908: 8. Carver 1910: 140.),
and the famous Methodist bishop from India, J.M. Thoburn,
recognized virtues in them, saying that Paul's description
of heathen immorality in ancient times could not be applied

10
There were, of course, exceptions, e.g. the missionary of
the Disciples of Christ, Charles Titus, (Titus 1906: 4-8,
65, 81.) and on the threshold of this period, the "Princeton
student" writing in The Missionary Review of the World, who
showed by Biblical arguments that people could not be saved
without explicit knowledge of Christ. (1887, pp. 125-131).

11
Buckley 1911: 29-32. Speer 1910: 33. Brown 1908: 8-9.
Dennis in Buckley 1911: 28-29. Buckley regards Dennis' concession of this point as entirely too hesitant, due to his
Calvinist background. An earlier Presbyterian who had believed in the salvation of non-Christians in their own
religion was Cornelius Duffie. Beaver 1968: 129 n.1.

to the major modern faiths.   (Thoburn 1895: 11-13.)

        All these men, however, combined their recognition of
values and virtues in other faiths with a firm belief in the
final truth and superiority of Christianity.   In Mabie's
thought the word, superiority, was hardly the correct one
to use since he saw Christianity as belonging to a different
order rather than being coordinate with the other religions.
It had a divine origin while they were human efforts using,
but in many ways misusing for human purposes, those hints
of nature which convey knowledge of God.   (Mabie: 77-84.)
His position has in it much to remind one of the later
teaching of Karl Barth.   Most authors, however, showed the
superiority of Christianity by means of ethical and religious
comparisons, not usually recognizing that they were simply
using standards derived from Christianity which would
inevitably cast it in a more favorable light.   Much of
Carver's work had this quality despite the fact that he was
also indebted to Mabie.   (Carver 1910:   119-170.)

        The method of comparing religions on Christian terms
was developed most fully by Frank Ellinwood, a secretary of
the Presbyterian Board, who wrote the first extensive treatment of non-Christian faiths to come out of American missions
since the somewhat mythological book by Sprague in 1837.   He
did not confine himself to unfavorable comparisons as Sprague
had done; he was prepared to provide whole chapters of
straight-forward description of other faiths.   But he referred to them constantly as "the false religions" and
following his descriptions proceeded to show their inferiority.
He argued for the superiority of Christianity because it
alone was built on a divine sacrifice for sin, saw God as
Father, bore the divine spirit which could transform human
character, and operated to bring men to penance and humility.
(Ellinwood 1892: 338-380.)   A closely parallel way of
presenting the superiority of Christianity was presented by
one of Ellinwood's colleagues, Samuel H. Kellogg, in his
Handbook of Comparative Religion (1899) and by his superior,
Robert E. Speer (Speer 1902: 109-129.   Speer 1910: 239-326.)
Even the more liberally oriented Robert E. Hume adopted the
same perspective when he took up the chair of comparative
religion at Union Seminary, New York.[12]

_____

    12
    Robert Earnest Hume 1914: 19-36.   Hume's father, a famous
Congregational missionary in India, followed an approach
much closer to that of Charles Cuthbert Hall bringing out
what Christianity could gain as well as give in the East.
Robert A. Hume 1905.   James Vernon's article of 1892 was of

There were some more appreciative views on other religions
beginning to be heard from the American mission movement in
this period. These emanated from two lecturers sent to Asia
at the turn of the century to present Christianity to Asian
intellectuals. John Henry Barrows, a prime organizer of the
Parliament of Religions at Chicago and later President of
Oberlin College, was one of the lecturers, and Charles
Cuthbert Hall, President of Union Seminary, New York, was the
other. Barrows portrayed first the good and then the bad
points in each of the religions and showed how they all
needed Christ. It was his view that Christianity included
what was best in all the other faiths and had further elements
which made it supreme, but he was careful to express the fullest appreciation for all that was best in the others and to
stress a universal rather than European quality in Christianity. (Barrows 1897: 15-12, passim.) Hall went further
in his appreciation of the Oriental consciousness, particularly
its sense of the contemplative life and aspiration toward
Ultimate Being. He felt that the West had much to learn from
the East and he was saddened at the condescension of many
missionaries and the contemptuousness of many other Westerners
toward the East. He wanted to see the mystical elements in
Christianity developed by an Eastern appropriation of the
faith. As he believed ever more deeply in the divinity of
Christ and Christ's inward correspondence with the essence
of the infinite, he appealed to the Oriental consciousness to
assimilate the Christian religion and to become the champion of a higher Christian thinking which would supplant
the aggressiveness, externalism and love of pleasure associated
with the West. (Hall 1909.) In reading Hall's lectures one
has the feeling, created by only one or two others in
American missiological literature, of being in touch with a
profound spirit and a great mind.

Thus far we have pursued a largely topical treatment of the
writing on missions during their heyday. We have not looked
at any of the major writers individually. Yet there were
giants in those days who deserve individual attention.

The earliest of them was Arthur T. Pierson, a Presbyterian minister who became so interested in missions that he
devoted his major time to writing about them. He served for

---

a piece with Ellinwood's more extended treatment.

many years as the editor of <u>The Missionary Review of the
World</u>, the principal interdenominational journal for American
missions, and produced a series of books, starting in the
1880's, on general mission questions. He had a vigorous and
original way of thinking and an extraordinary knowledge of
the whole missionary enterprise. He emphasized Biblical
thought about mission work, seeing it as a work of God as
well as a work with God, thus anticipating the more recent thought
on the <u>missio Dei</u>. (Pierson 1889. Pierson 1891: 103-109.
Pierson 1896.) He saw the church as called not to preach so
much as to witness, for preaching may just report a message
but witnessing must report an experience. If angels could
have witnessed, the gospel would surely have been spread to all
the world long ago, but this was impossible for

> "Never did angels taste above
> Redeeming grace and dying love."
>   (Pierson 1891: 44.)

Pierson, more than anyone else, has been regarded as
responsible for the great watchword of the Student Volunteer
Movement, "The evangelization of the world in this generation."
(Lotz 1970: 2-3.) He said the great question of the time was
how the church might "carry the good tidings round the world
during the lifetime of this generation." (Pierson 1891: 153.)
If all the truly committed Protestants were mobilized so
that each would be responsible for reaching personally or
through missionaries, three non-Christians a year, every person
in the world would be given an intelligent understanding of
the Christian gospel in twenty years time. (Pierson 1881,
1882.) This would not be done with the expectation that
all people would be converted but that there would be an
outgathering from the nations of those separated and con-
secrated to God. No more than that could be expected before
the eschaton. No Christianizing of the nations should be
thought of before the end of the age. (Pierson 1891: 65-73, 77,
96.) He protected himself against the charge of promoting
rapid, superficial evangelization by saying that we cannot
regard the gospel as presented when some preacher has merely
hurried through an area, but only when Christian homes and
schools and hospitals have established the example of
"the faith which works by love." (1891: 69-70.)

But despite these qualifications, there was criticism of
Pierson's view. Chalmers Martin of Princeton Seminary
declared that his emphasis on immediate world-wide evangelization did not do justice to Jesus' call to make disciples and
to teach them to observe all things. It did not follow the

practice of the apostles who baptized, organized, instructed
and edified their converts and ordained elders. Nor did it
fit with modern mission policy directed toward organizing
churches, giving them a competent ministry and conducting
them to the stage of independence and self-propagation.
(Martin 1895: 52-63.) Edward A. Lawrence, a promising young
Congregational minister who died at an early age after completing a trip around the world to study missions, maintained
in his book, Modern Missions in the East, that the aim of
world evangelization was inadequate because it ignored the
need for Christianizing the world which could best be done
by Christian institutions and a native ministry, and because
it was tied to certain pre-millennial views. (Lawrence 1895:
35-36.)

These objections did not dispel the popularity of world
evangelization as the aim of missions, though efforts to
answer the objections were not always satisfactory. John
R. Mott defended the watchword, in a book which used it as a
title, taking much the same line that Pierson had taken in
explaining that evangelization did not mean dashing through
an area preaching but meant repeated and intelligent presentation. (Mott 1900: 7-8.) Whether this included, as it had
in Pierson's thought, the presentation of all the social
benefits of Christianity, a requirement which destroyed the
precise quality of the aim, he did not at that point make clear,
Robert E. Speer, an avowed disciple of Rufus Anderson, tried
to defend the watchword against the charge that it neglected
Anderson's primary goal of organizing churches and helping
them develop strong leadership and self-support. Speer
replied that world evangelization was a true obligation but
that the purpose of foreign missions was just to establish
the churches which would release the power for this task.
(Speer 1910: 76-77.) Such a defense was really an admission
of the inadequacy of the original proposition. The direct
aim of missions was the establishment of churches and world
evangelization was relegated to a later time, not this
generation, and was to be achieved indirectly as far as
foreign missions were concerned.

This dispute brings to mind the two great innovators
in mission policy who were to be found among the American
foreign missionaries of that time. Though they did not contend
with each other explicitly, they stood on opposite sides of
this argument. Bishop William Taylor of the Methodists
advocated the spreading of missionaries widely and rapidly to
all lands, expecting them to find support through local employment.
As one of his backers explained, "where there is one missionary
there are a hundred needed," and self-supporting

missionaries were the only ones who could be sent in the
necessary numbers to blanket the earth with the gospel proclamation. (Todd 1890: 140-161.) This method paid little
attention to the steady, concentrated building up of the
local church but it fitted in well with the Methodist
penchant during the latter part of the nineteenth century for
rapidly expanding, minimally supported work. (Barclay
1949-1973: vol. III, pp. 156-158.)

The other American missionary who contributed a special
theory to mission work was John Nevius of the Presbyterian
mission in China. He went to the opposite extreme, believing
that mission work should be determined by consideration, not
of what would disperse missionaries most widely, but of what
would strengthen the local church for evangelism. There
should be no institutions of Christian service except those
that the local church might maintain. Careful training of
lay leaders by the development of Bible classes throughout
the church should be the principal concern of the mission.
Indigenous evangelists should be laymen supporting themselves
in their accustomed line of work, never employees of the mission, and ordained ministers should be educated only to the
extent and in the way that would keep them in touch with
local church thought and its level of support. (Nevius 1899.)
Nevius took an extreme stand and there were those who were
willing to support his main thrust but believed that it was
only sensible for the mission to pay local evangelists at
a level that, and until such time as, the national church
could support them. (Baldwin 1900: 71-76.) This modified
version of Nevius' view combined with a very un-Nevius-like
belief in foreign institutions of service proved to have great
survival power in American missions. Bishop Taylor's views
did not survive as long as he himself did.

We have yet to deal specifically with the two greatest
of the giants who bestrode the field of American mission
thought during this period and also the following period.
They are John R. Mott and Robert E. Speer. Both men came
out of the Student Volunteer Movement, which doubtless explains some of their defense of its watchword which we have
already noted. Both were primarily mission statesmen rather
than scholars, Mott leading the World Student Christian
Federation and other international and ecumenical agencies,
and Speer leading the Presbyterian Board of Foreign Missions.
Yet both wrote extensively, Speer with half-a-dozen large
scale books on the field of missions as a whole, Mott with a

somewhat smaller number of somewhat smaller books. Both of
them also wrote outside the field of mission studies giving
expression to their understanding of the Christian faith,
Speer especially producing a number of Biblical studies.

Mott was the more widely famous of the two. His books
were translated into numerous foreign languages and read all
over the world. His great strength lay in his ability to
survey the entire world situation facing the Christian mission
and his acumen in picking out those points which showed great
new opportunities and possibilities for the mission. This
he did in book form at the beginning of the new century, and
again after the Edinburgh conference of 1910, and once more
after the Jerusalem conference of 1928. (Mott 1900. Mott
1910. Mott 1931.) Always he could see a rising spiritual
tide in the non-Christian world (Mott 1910: 69-98.) and could
perceive that "the influence of Jesus Christ was never so
widespread and so penetrating and so transforming as it is
today." (Mott 1931: 49.) It has been said that he was one
of the last to maintain the nineteenth century missionary
interpretation of the times as showing the providential working of God assuring the rapid success of missions. (Beaver
1968: 129.) But he also introduced a new factor by his predominant emphasis on planning and strategy for the world as
a whole. Some earlier writers, especially Pierson, had
stressed the importance of an over-all plan and had worked
out idealistic schemes for covering the world. (Hall and
Newell 1818: 14-32. Pierson 1881. Pierson 1882. Pierson
1891: 156-158. Pierson 1894: 43-44. Lotz 1970: 2-3.
Thoburn 1895: 44-71.) Mott made the idea effective. His
conception of the Edinburgh conference was to develop through
it a plan which would recognize the unreached regions and the
untouched classes and would assign responsibility for each
class or area to a particular mission so that there would be
no over-lapping. (Mott 1910: 99-103.) His dream has been
constantly before Christian missions in all the succeeding
years, as may be witnessed in the recent program for Joint
Action in Mission, but it has never been more fully implemented
than it was by him at Edinburgh.

Speer has justly been regarded as the greatest leader
of American missions after Rufus Anderson. (R.P. Beaver
in Anderson 1967: 9.) His range of knowledge and his scale
of productivity, especially when his primary administrative
burden is remembered, must be seen as stupendous. He carried
the same kind of responsibilities as Anderson, yet produced
far more in the way of published studies of missions.[13]

He was not a profound or highly creative thinker but he had
a remarkably disciplined and clear mind. He took up problems
systematically showing both sides of them and explaining lucid-
ly why one side was finally to be preferred. He was forever in
debate with the various critics of foreign missions. To those
who pressed the needs within America he responded that foreign missions had never weakened the forces of the church at
home but rather had multiplied them. It was foreign missions,
he claimed, that had originated home mission activity in
this country. (Speer 1910: 48.) To those who doubted the
need for missions because of the unacknowledged, yet real,
activity of Christ among non-Christians he replied that "if
a hypothetical redemption through an unknown Christ wrought
by the grace of God in behalf of the unevangelized will suffice for them why will it not suffice for our own children?
. . . It has no effect upon their present lives." (Speer
1902: 11-12.)

     He combined effectively a sense of the need for individual
conversions and a recognition of the importance of building
the indigenous church, though it is noticeable that the
emphasis on the church became more and more marked in his
various restatements of the aim of missions. (Speer 1902:
59. Speer 1910: 75-76. Speer 1919: 203-224. Speer 1926:
272.) All of his writings gave much attention to the needs
of the national church, its right to organize in its own
way, to be the responsible evangelistic agent in its own
land, and to express the faith in its own style without any
imitation of the West or domination by foreign missionaries.
He was concerned that missionaries not take administrative
office in the church or control its financial resources, and
was likewise concerned about the fact that the younger churches
had not yet produced the independent theology which could be
expected from them. (Speer 1902: 63-64. Speer 1910: 73-75,

     13
     He did this by an extraordinary and even inhuman degree
of organization of life. Most missionaries who were invited
for dinner in the Speer home were surprised to find their
host would retire to his study as soon as the meal was
finished leaving further entertainment to his wife. Henry
Sloane Coffin in reminding his classes about the importance
of personal contacts in life used Speer as an example of what
to avoid since no one could meet Speer on a train and engage
him in conversation because he was always too involved with
a book.

113-176. Speer 1919: 203-224.) From the first he was conscious of the wider social scene in which Christian missions
operated and wrote much about their social effects, which he
saw as side-effects, but this emphasis on the "application
of the gospel to human solidarities" was another thing
that increased noticeably in some of his later books.
(Speer 1902: 28-30, 412-420. Speer 1904. Speer 1919: 225-
245.)

Speer's well-known colleague, Arthur Judson Brown, need
detain our attention only briefly, not because he was
unimportant but because his writings so closely parallel
Speer's in all their emphases and viewpoints. Brown produced
many works on missions; he had more time for this than most
people have since he lived to be 107. His most famous book,
often reprinted over several decades, was The Foreign
Missionary. This is the only full-length portrait of the
missionary which has appeared in America.[14] He departed
from earlier, conventional views in arguing that the
missionary should adapt to native ways of life including
possibly native dress.[15] On the other hand he defended
the economic standard adopted by the missionaries as necessary for their health and effectiveness. (Brown 1907:
91-103.)

Finally, in completing our survey of this period, we
should make note of the appearance on the American scene of

14
Another careful but brief examination of the missionary
appeared about the same time in Pfeiffer 1908: 44-77. A
short book displaying the great variety of work done by
missionaries and describing some of their desirable attitudes
is Thomas 1947. The nineteenth century's glorification of
missionaries is seen in one of Phillips Brooks' sermons.
Brooks 1881. None of these works, however, gave the full
treatment provided by Brown.

15
Brown 1907: 271-275. For the usual older view on ways
of life and dress Todd 1890: 98-99. It is important to realize that Todd was probably right in saying that the missionary should emphasize his Westernness as it could increase
his effectiveness. By Brown's time it was no longer so
true that Westernness increased effectiveness.

systematic studies of the science of missions. These did not
emerge from the major figures. Even those works by the famous writers which had the appearance of being full statements of their mission theory, such as Speer's Missionary
Principles and Practice or, from an earlier period, Rufus
Anderson's Foreign Missions: Their Relations and Claims,
turned out to be collections of wide-ranging ideas rather
than complete systems of understanding. However there were
two systematic studies, produced, not surprisingly, by professors, one of whom, even less surprisingly, was of German
background. Edward Pfeiffer, a professor of theology at the
Lutheran seminary in Columbus, deeply influenced by the work
of Gustav Warneck, published his Mission Studies in 1908.
In it he set out first the case for a separate development
of the science of missions since partial treatment in each
of the other realms of theology was necessarily so far short
of an understanding of the whole; and then he examined the
three divisions of this science: the aim, the basis
and the methods of missions. The aim was clearly the establishment of indigenous churches which would continue mission
work in their own countries. The basis was found first in
the missionary sections of the Bible which he analyzed,
and second in the Christian doctrines of God and Christ, of
justification and the eschaton. The methods appropriate to
missions were seen to be spiritual only, education and
medicine being seen as forms of indirect evangelism. He
presented a missionary understanding of the nature of the
church and a full statement of the ways in which the local
church in America could live as a missionary and mission-
supporting community. Here then emerged on the American
scene for the first time a fully elaborated statement of
all that the science of missions should include. It was
the only serious study of missions to come from American
Lutheranism prior to the 1950s.[16]

_____

16
     It is surprising that Lutherans in America did not
produce a vigorous missiology earlier since their missions
were developed in the tension between growing evangelical
sentiments absorbed from the environment and scholastic
conceptions of pure doctrine inherited from the past.
Missouri Synod mission magazines were especially conscious
of this tension but it was present in all of Lutheranism
in this land. Wentz 1955: 110. Lueking 1964: 126-129.

The second work of this type, appearing a year later, was <u>Missions in the Plan of the Ages</u> by W.O. Carver of the Louisville Baptist seminary, the first full-time missions professor in America, except for one three-year position held at Princeton in the 1830s. This work was not the full system that Pfeiffer provided but it did attempt to draw out a total Biblical understanding of the principles of missions. It covered the missionary message, plan, power, work and consummation, in terms of a series of selected texts from the Bible. With these two works American mission theory began to show some of the marks of a mature discipline, covering a wide range of phenomena and shaping them into a coherent whole. This maturity, however, was to be sharply tested in the next decades.

III

The years between the two world wars were years of criticism, crisis and confusion for world missions. The number of missionaries fluctuated widely. The purpose of the enterprise was severely questioned. Contributions dropped considerably, first because of demoralization and then because of the depression. Various new rationales and theories of missions or of opposition to missions were proposed. For all its difficulties, however, American missiology maintained the same high level of productivity it had achieved in the previous period.[17]

The immediate post-war years still carried much of the high idealism that had been preached during the war and interpreters of missions linked mission work to the current hopes for world-wide democracy and a new international order. A special committee of leading executives from the mission boards, chaired by Robert E. Speer, presented the case for missions as the necessary vehicle to carry forward the higher purposes of the war and as the undergirding for the new

---

[17]
The bibliography assembled for this paper lists 72 monographs which could be considered serious studies of missions in the thirty years before 1920, and 77 titles of this sort in the thirty years following.

internationalism. The committee argued that the rising democratic movement and the movement of missions would strengthen
each other. (Committee on the War 1920: xviii, 27, 38-50.)
Three further books in as many years and a fourth which
followed soon after presented missions in these same terms
as the basis and ally of the world movement toward democracy.
(Taylor and Luccock 1918. Patton 1919. Northern Baptist
Convention 1920. Love 1925.)

All the confident idealism regarding democracy and the
new internationalism, however, did not last long once
America began its return to normalcy. In reaction to idealism
came a wave of cynicism and in disillusionment with internationalism came a revival of isolationism. These new forces
were in their very nature antipathetic to foreign missions.
Exposés of the negative side of missionary activity then
began to appear in the general periodical literature. The
weaknesses of missionaries, the inadequacies of their services,
their lack of appreciation for other cultures and their domination of other peoples were held up to public scorn. The
Atlantic Monthly, Harpers, Current History and the Christian
Century carried articles deprecating missionary activity.
(Varg 1958: 160-166, 174. Buck n.d.) From the mission
board secretaries came in reply books bearing defensive
titles such as Foreign Missions Under Fire, Straight Talks
with the Critics of Missions, Are Foreign Missions Done For?,
and The Foreign Mission Enterprise and its Sincere Critics.
These books acknowledged the validity of many of the charges
but maintained that they did not affect the essential nature
of the missionary enterprise and envisaged a new kind of
mission free of such blemishes. (McAfee 1927. Patton 1928.
Speer 1928. McAfee 1932. McAfee 1935.) Much of what we
see in the mission theory of this period must be understood
as a response to the new atmosphere of doubt which had
appeared.

The emphasis on social action in missions became even
stronger than it had been in the pre-war literature. Reports
on new fields of social endeavor were now added, such as the
mass adult education movement initiated in China and later
developed in the mass literacy programs of Frank Laubach
(Laubach 1938, 1943). Books appeared on the programs for
family life (The Family and its Christian Fulfillment) and
on the whole new operation of agricultural missions working
to improve agricultural production and the quality of rural
life. (The Christian Mission among Rural People. Wiser 1930.
Hunnicutt and Reid 1931. Clark 1934.) Social problems were
now subjected to extensive research, especially through the

work of an American serving on the staff of the International
Missionary Council, J. Merle Davis. His studies centered on
the economic situation in which the younger churches found themselves and the implications of the economic base for the self-
support of the church. Social concerns filled the whole mission
horizon as he viewed it. "Evangelism," he said, "is cure of
sick bodies, of broken down, inefficient, and eroded farms, of
illiteracy, of insufficient and unbalanced diet, unsanitary
homes, impure drinking water." (Davis 1947: 233. The same
emphasis is found in Davis 1939, Moss 1930, Mott 1931: 51-52,
87-90, 96-97, and Davis 1946.) Much of Davis' work was done
in preparation for the Madras meeting of the International
Missionary Council in 1938. It is revealing that the American
preparatory volume for that meeting, edited by Samuel McCrea
Cavert, secretary of the Federal Council of Churches, was
at one with Davis' work in its total preoccupation with social
problems. A galaxy of the best known intellectuals of the
American churches prepared this volume so it did not represent a purely individual preoccupation. While the writer of
the principal study book for that conference, Hendrik Kraemer
from Europe, concentrated on strictly theological questions,
this group of leading Americans turned their attention
entirely to social issues. (Cavert 1939.)

   The concentration on societal matters involved an out-
spoken and continuing attack on the social evils of America.
This was a new element in mission thought. In the nineteenth
century there had been only appreication for American life and
the desire to reproduce it everywhere. In the early twentieth
century there had been occasional recognition of inadequacies
in American life and more frequent concern about the evils
which Western culture carried with it in its impact on the rest
of the world. But now those occasional references became
standard parts of most analyses of the missionary task. (e.g.
Speer 1919: 64-68. Committee on the War 1920: xvi, 43-44, 280-
288. Diffendorfer 1925: 300-303.) The ignominy of American
racial bigotry received the greatest denunciations. The most
radical criticisms of America came from the former missionary,
Sherwood Eddy, whose earlier writings on missions in other
lands gave way to streams of books dealing with the need for
change in America.

   With the recognition of evils in the West went a new
appreciation for the culture of the East and an emphasis on
emerging churches in Asia and Africa. This outlook had
appeared only occasionally before 1920; Arthur Judson Brown

had been the only one to write an entire book on the younger
churches. (Brown 1915a.)[18]   But in the 1920s and 1930s this
was a standard feature of missiology and numerous books and
articles either concentrated primarily on the younger
churches or made the development and indigenization of those
churches a major theme. (Calkins 1923. Rowland 1925. A Call
for Colleagues 1930. Miller 1926. Mott 1931: 149ff. Franklin
1933. McCorkel 1939. Doughty 1937: 116-117.) There was not a
little criticism of the missionaries of the past as having been
too ethnocentric and the call went out for a new kind of missionary who would appreciate other cultures and play a subordinate role in the development of indigenous churches.
(Committee on the War 1920: 317. Riggs 1923. Latourette 1932:
12. Franklin 1933: 182. Miller 1926: 66-68. Shafer 1944:
116-120.)

    Out of this emphasis grew a rationale for missions which
was almost entirely new. It may be characterized as the
rationale of ecumenical sharing. It emphasized the need for
churches around the world to help each other understand the
Christian faith and to bring to each other the riches and resources of their different cultures as they together learn to
follow Christ. The mission movement was presented as the vehicle for this new vision. Only Charles Cuthbert Hall, among all
the earlier writers, had made this an important element in
his picture of missions. Now it was seized on by some of the
most important apologists. As in cantilever bridge construction, said Mott, neither side can reach out beyond a certain
point but only as they meet at that point can they together
accomplish the common purpose, so only as Christ is jointly
known and presented to the world by the different churches
can his work be accomplished. (Mott 1931: 133-34. Latourette
in Miller 1926: 63-64. Cavert 1927. Fleming 1925: 23-47.
Wark 1929:99.) Under this new conception missions, which
had had a temporally limited task in the philosophy of
Anderson, Speer, Pfeiffer and their like, received a revised
mandate that would continue them forever.

    The appreciation for Eastern cultures naturally had an
effect on mission methods. Two American missionaries emerged
in this period, as there were two in the previous period, who

---

18

    The book by W.H. Wheeler on Self-Supporting Churches (1899)
was not a study of younger churches but of missionary methods,
taking a line very similar to that of John Nevius. Vinton 1910
is an example of articles which treated the work of particular
younger churches

may be regarded as important innovators in mission methodology
and contributors to mission theory, and the contributions
of both of them were in the direction of a greater adaptation
to the East. Both men were Methodist missionaries in India.
E. Stanley Jones was the most popular champion of peculiarly
Indian ways of carrying on mission work. He established
an ashram, or traditional religious devotional center and
school, and wrote about The Christ of the Indian Road and
Christ at the Round Table. At his round table the representatives of different religions could meet in mutual confidence
and equality to learn from each other, much in the style
developed all over Asia and Africa half a century later by
the movement for inter-religious dialogue. He looked for
new Asian interpretations of Christ, and believed that
much might be learned from them. (Jones 1929.)

The other of this pair of missionaries, J.W. Pickett,
did not so much initiate a new methodology as recognize one
that had already come into existence and become its analyst
and advocate. This was the method of mass conversions.
American missions had always been suspicious of mass movements.
In typical American style they thought of conversion as
an individual matter. Mission theorists like Arthur T.
Pierson had regarded any attempt to Christianize people in
masses as a great snare and as reflecting a "mad passion for
numbers" which was entirely contrary to Jesus' teaching.
(Pierson 1891: 89-90.) The American Methodists in India
had been among the first to move away from this position.
Their leader Bishop J.M. Thoburn in his Graves Lectures at
Syracuse had recommended approaching people in caste groups.
(Thoburn 1895: 138-141.) Pickett studied the mass movements
and provided the justification for them. He denied that mass
conversion was a heresy or that the motives of the converts
were materialistic. The desire for a better life and
hope of escape from oppression were themselves, he believed,
products of gospel preaching. John R. Mott and other
American leaders gave their blessing to this approach. (Pickett 1933: 5, 155-57. Latourette 1936: 159. Soper 1943:
242.)

The name which should be most closely associated
with the adaptation of Christianity to the ways of other
cultures and the appreciation of those cultures with their
new churches is that of Daniel Johnson Fleming. As professor
of missions for 26 years (1918-1944) at Union Seminary,
New York, he kept up a steady stream of books, all of
which in one way or another emphasized this theme. The
titles themselves, such as Bringing our World Together,

<u>Living as Comrades</u>, <u>Contacts with Non-Christian Cultures</u>,
and <u>Marks of a World Christian</u>, show his constant concern.
He was the world's pioneer, as far as Protestantism is concerned, in collecting and publishing examples of the new
forms of Christian art, architecture and liturgy which
were making their appearance in non-Western cultures. (Fleming 1937, 1938, 1942.) He wrote more books on mission
theory and method than any other American of any period.

        His favorite approach to his subject was to present
the reader with case studies of particular mission problems
involving cultural adaptation, religious accommodation or
the patterns of missionary life, and to let the reader work
out his own position after having his mind stretched by
various possible solutions. Sometimes his failure to state
his own position made his books appear exasperatingly in-
decisive. But he was prepared to take a stand where that
was appropriate to the nature of the book. He clearly
believed that God was working through all religions and cultures
and that all traces of a sense of Western superiority should
be eliminated. We should respect and love what is of God in
other religions and cultures. At the same time he was convinced
that the coming of Christ would enrich and fulfill much in
those religions and cultures. Already some crude and false
things had vanished through Christian contacts and we should
rejoice in this even though it means that converts would be
harder to win. It is not the adoption of the name of Christ
by others that should interest us in any case, but rather the
adoption of the spirit of Christ. Fleming did leave some place
for conversion, however, when he said that if the way is open
for those who hear of Christ to make him central in their lives
and to whorship God in him, that is the best thing to aim for.
(Fleming 1925: xi, 84-86, 88-91, 115-117. Fleming 1928: 161-
163. Fleming 1929: 136-142, 147-148.)

        It will be obvious that Fleming moved further in a liberal
direction than any missiologist we have looked at thus far.
But he was only the most prolific of a whole cluster of liberal
reinterpreters of missions in that period. His counterpart at
the University of Chicago, Archibald G. Baker, adopted a position of complete cultural relativism with regard to religions.
The task of the missionary should not be to secure the adoption of Christianity but to make improvements in society.
(Baker 1934) The Methodist editor, Roy L. Smith, maintained
that Jesus had not taught much about beliefs but taught us
rather a way of living and relating to people. He said that
the central concern of missions should be with converting
governments and with making people more open and kind and

and easier to live with. If Christians exhibited these qualities, the world would soon enough be ready to accept their beliefs. (Smith 1941: 152-156, 168, 206.) Oscar Buck, professor at Drew Theological Seminary, also stressed concern for
quality of life rather than numbers of converts. He believed
that Jesus' great insight had been that the ways of parents with
their children are the key to the inmost mystery of the universe. All else the non-Christian religions have, but this
they do not have. If we can persuade them to take this
as their center, it does not matter by what name they are called
(Buck 1934: 140-141, 160-161.).

A more widely known statement of the liberal position, not
as extreme as some of the others, came from Hugh Vernon White,
secretary of the American Board. He believed that Christ tea-
ches us to be concerned for humanity and therefore truly
Christian missions would not be concerned primarily for the
name of Christ or for his church but for the service of man.
Nevertheless, all religions are not alike or equally true.
There is a final truth which we have received through Christianity. In an oft-quoted passage, White expressed that final
truth:

> "that the life of active trust in
> God and love for all men is eternally
> right and represents the purpose of
> God for mankind; that such a life
> will be sustained by God despite all
> temporary defeat; and that such a
> life lived even in the face of en-
> mity and through sacrifice will be
> a force for the fulfillment of God's
> purpose to win men to himself and
> to create a society of persons who
> live that life together." (White
> 1937: 98-99.)

In two books issued in the late 1930s White propounded this
liberal creed and tried to break the association of missions
with all methods that had tended to violate the sanctity of
personality or had shown arrogance and insensitivity toward
others. (White 1937. White 1938.)

The climax in missiological discussion of this period came
in 1930 when a group of laymen, with Rockefeller funding, determined to launch a large-scale investigation of missions to decide the direction they should take and how the current criticisms should be met. The result of their decision was the creation of the Laymen's Commission of Appraisal and its subsequent report which stirred the greatest controversy on missions
that this country has ever seen.

The direction which the report would take could have been
inferred from the fact that the chairman of the Commission
was William Ernest Hocking, professor of philosophy at Harvard.
Hocking's view, as expressed more fully in his later writings,
was that Christianity and the other religions should grow together toward the final world faith that would unite all men.
This would happen as the religions cooperated and conversed and
thus made new discoveries about themselves and each other. Missionaries should involve themselves in that process. Hocking
believed that Christianity in its essence provided the ultimate
faith that humanity needed, but this essence would have to be
refined and developed through the challenge and contributions
of other faiths before it could ever be recognized as the final
religion. It would then be accepted spontaneously. (Hocking
1940. Beaver 1952: 8-10).

The Commission's report, entitled Rethinking Missions,
did indeed take a position similar to Hocking's. It recognized
in the life and teachings of Jesus a way to the knowledge of
God's love and holy will and an ethical outlook which can be
taken as final and should be communicated to the Orient. But
the way of communication should be that of mutually sharing
with other faiths all that each has to offer until all are
changed in substance and the separate names lose their divisive
meanings. (52-58) It was right for missions to have established
a Christian group in each land so that it could illustrate a
pure instance of Oriental Christianity and this group might now
enter into the efforts at mutual understanding. (50)   The
Commission's conception of missionary work combined in an interesting way something of the earlier, limited aim of church
planting with the later, unlimited one of ecumenical sharing,
but it did so in terms of a vision of inter-faith development
rather than inter-church development.

Regarding the service programs of missions, the Commission
marked a very sharp and very important break with what had been
the dominant philosophies. The predominant thinking, at least
prior to 1920, had tried to keep service functions ancillary to
evangelism, though sometimes recognizing that their support
could be given in a silent way rather than explicitly. The
Commission said that any form of subservience of service to
preaching destroyed the disinterested quality of the service
and so made it contrary to the spirit of Christ. Human service
should be done for its own sake and itself would be evangelism
in the true sense of the word. (67-69.) This attitude in mission service was one which was destined to grow steadily in the
years after 1950. The Laymen took a careful look at widespread
service institutions which missions had established and came to
the conclusion that their work needed to be done in more professionally competent ways even though this might mean closing

down some institutions to concentrate on the better ones. The
enormous fact-finding campaign which the Commission organized
to reach this conclusion provided the fullest documentation on
mission operations which has yet been made available, though it
also contained many inaccuracies as would be inevitable in a
work of such compass.

A storm of attack and some vigorous defense followed upon
the publication of the report. Church journals and also the
public press were full of it. (Varg 1958: 169-172.) Robert E.
Speer wrote the most extensive answer in a small book on the
subject. He criticized the report basically because it did
not recognize the divine revelation which was contained in the
Christian religion which set it apart from all the human inven-
tions of other faiths and made it necessary for all humanity.
(Speer 1933.) In general the reaction of mission boards showed
that the mission theory and theology of the Laymen's Commission
was not that of American missions.

Something more in touch with the total heritage of the
Christian faith was called for. The Commission and the liberal
missiologists we have examined were alike in reducing the missionary message to a bare minimum, often largely ethical, and
thereby losing much of the theological depth of the faith, the
understanding of the human condition and the work of Christ.
When we began to investigate the inter-war period we noted that
its crises would severely test the level of mature thought and
consensus which had apparently been achieved at the end of the
previous decades. The story we have traced of the '20s and
'30s suggests that missiology failed to meet that test. Instead of holding together and going deeper in response to many
new challenges, it seemed to become shallower and to wander off
into vague uncertainties or else to react defensively. Happily
that is not the end of the story. There were other thinkers
appearing who proved able to build on the previously established
consensus and to hold together a mediating yet challenging position in mission studies. But that was an achievement of the
next period.

IV

The first development which must claim our attention in
the new era, 1940-1952, is the appearance of a new, very conservative type of missiology which was far from occupying a
mediating position and was, in some of its representatives, far
from wanting to occupy it. It was a defensive reaction to
liberalism and the Laymen's Commission. In opposition to that

whole type of development there had been growing up a fresh
force in American missions which has in more recent years taken
the name of "conservative evangelicalism." Elements of this
force had been on the scene for a long time. Some non-denominational missions of a very conservative bent had been begun in
the nineteenth century, but in that period missionary thought
in general was sufficiently conservative to keep this group
from appearing to represent a markedly distinct missiology.
After 1920, however, the size of this group and its sense of
distance from the rest of mission thinking grew rapidly. It
developed in relation to the struggle over fundamentalism in
the denominations and as an expression of the suspicion that
the Bible was not being adequately held up as an infallible
authority in mission thought. A popular book by Augustus Hopkins Strong, the President of Rochester Theological Seminary
for forty years, entitled A Tour of Missions, attacked all
Biblical criticism that was not rooted in Christ because it led
to a change in the ultimate point of dependence in missionary
decisions. (Strong 1918.) The very liberal missiological
writings led to further reactions of this nature. The result
was a series of bitter controversies, some splits in mission
boards and the creation of splinter denominations and of more
non-denominational boards. (Lotz 1970: 91-97.)

But these conservative forces did not at first produce
much in the way of significant mission theory. That task was
left by them to the more conservative authors in the larger
missionary forces. There were a number of writers connected
with the major denominational missions who, in the years after
1940, produced vigorously conservative interpretations of missions which could be used by the conservative evangelicals and
some of these were quite widely accepted by them. One of these
was the Southern Baptist, William Own Carver, whose earlier
works we have already noted and who in 1942 published a new
work which made heavy use of the Bible for redefining the
church's mission. Another was Carver's successor in the
Louisville Baptist seminary, Henry C. Goerner, whose 1944 publication, "Thus it is Written." The Missionary Motif in the
Scriptures, was equally Biblocentric.

A third, who seemed peculiarly appreciated by the conservatives of the non-denominational missions, was Samuel M.
Zwemer of the Reformed Church mission in Arabia, later professor of missions at Princeton. He was a redoubtable warrior
who took up all the challenges to missions and dealt with them
thoroughly. He staunchly defended the authenticity of the
Great Commission in the Biblical text and the validity of that
command as a basis, though not the sole basis, for mission.
He called for bold preaching such as the apostles gave to the
world and a recognition of the coming judgement under which

the world stands. He was convinced of the finality of Jesus
Christ and adduced reasons for it, such as Christ's combination
of all human virtues and his wide outlook which included all
humanity. (Zwemer 1943: 25-39, 145-157, 185. Zwemer 1934.)
In some ways his point of view may seem like that of nineteenth
century missionaries, but when one compares his work with that
of another Reformed Church missionary of the earlier period,
John Scudder, it is obvious that Zwemer took his mission
theology much more seriously, studied widely and assembled all
the sources in scholarship which would support his views,
rather than being content with merely an emotional expression
of those views as Scudder was. Here was clear evidence of
growth and development in mission thinking.

   The self-consciously conservative evangelical movement in
missions, however, did begin to produce its own missiology
just at the end of the era covered in this paper. Robert Hall
Glover, who had worked with the Christian and Missionary
Alliance and then with the China Inland Mission and had written
one of the most popular histories of mission work (Glover 1924),
produced in 1946 The Bible Basis of Missions. The introduction
for the book was written by Samuel Zwemer and the thoroughly
Biblical emphasis of the work was very much in line with Zwemer's thought. Glover believed that there would be no general
conversion of humanity till after Christ's second coming and
that the mission of the Church in this era was to be a witness
to all and to gather the elect from every nation. (Glover
1946: 99-102.)

   Three years after Glover's work came Harold Lindsell's
A Christian Philosophy of Missions (later re-titled An Evangelical Theology of Missions) which was a much more extensive
work and which may be taken as the first example of a systematic mission study from the conservative evangelicals. It appeared just four years after the Evangelical Foreign Missions
Association was organized and reflected some of the reactive
stance present at the beginning of that group. It explicitly
tried to restore the old foundations lost in more recent years
and charged that unspiritual men had come to leadership in
missions. (Lindsell 1949: 196-203.) It referred to its own
position as "the final theology for Christian missions." (68)
The basic crisis revolved around the acceptance of the Bible
as the infallible word of God and the necessary ground for mission. (41) Here was the point where most denominational missions had gone astray. Lindsell affirmed that in cases where
it might appear as if data had demonstrated an error in scripture the believer would refuse to admit an error because his
faith told him that further data would inevitably demonstrate
the accuracy of the word of God. (54) He wished to restore
the old assurance that all who died without having heard of

Christ are lost forever and saw this, as Abeel had in 1838, as a
summons to help such people. (73-74.) The recognition of the state
of the lost could cause no delight but only distress for Christians.
The task of the divinely instituted church before the final day was
to preach the true faith, but if the church failed in this regard,
God might go outside the visible ecclesiastical structures to
complete the evangelization of the world. (115-116, 139.) Here
was a strongly stated and extreme view in opposition to the kind
of liberalism that had seemed to be regnant in missiological studies
if not in the actual missions.

But there were other voices beginning to be heard which were
more resonant to the whole of Christian faith than the liberals had
been yet were not as conservative as Zwewer and Lindsell. These
were the ones who proved able to express during the 1940s a strong,
moderate position which held mission thinking together as it had not
been held for the previous twenty years and even moved it to a new
stage of maturity as it grappled successfully with the challenges
to which it had been exposed. These writers were certainly in
touch with the neo-orthodox revival that was sweeping Europe and
were to some extent influenced by it, but they were none of them
markedly of that school. They all bore much more the stamp of
the American experience of evanglical missions, a warm piety, an
evident devotion, and a strong sense of the practical.

Most famous, though not most important, were the presidents of
two of America's leading theological institutions, Henry Pitney
Van Dusen of Union and John A. Mackay of Princeton. Both these
men, as well known theologians and outstanding leaders in the
national and international life of the church, contributed much
to strengthening world missions. They each wrote a number of
books about missions which, while hardly important contributions
to mission theory and theology, served to emphasize the central
importance of the church's missionary task. Van Dusen's work was
largely descriptive of the activities and accomplishments of
missions. Mackay's books were more analytical and theological
and provided, in one case, a deeper understanding of the Protestant
mission in Latin America, about which American missiology had
done almost no thinking. [19] Both men were active in the ecumenical

---

19
    Van Dusen 1939, 1940, 1943, 1945, 1947. MacKay 1932, 1950.
Other helpful statements on the reason for missions in Latin
America are provided in an appendix in Soper 1943 and in Buckley
1911: 122-123.

movement and linked mission to the concern for Christian unity. In
this they represented a major trend of their time. The connection
between mission and unity had been a recurrent theme in American
writing on missions from the earliest days, but it never played
so commanding a role in the understanding of missions as it did
in the fifth and sixth decades of the twentieth century.[20]

An excellent example of the central position in mission thinking
was provided by Kenneth Scott Latourette, professor of missions at
Yale. Of an evangelical stamp somewhat like Mackay, Latourette was
both closely related to the more liberal thinkers and widely acceptable among the conservative evangelicals. His chief work was in
mission history and thus falls outside our range of concern, but he
also published some in the field of mission theory and theology.
(Latourette 1936, 1938, 1948, 1949.) He was convinced of the eternal
validity of the Christian gospel for all men and of Christ as the
one way to God, the standard by which all religions and all human
life are to be judged. Other religions have much to admire, but
nothing which is not in Christianity. (Latourette 1936: 134-136.)
He made a place for Christian social action, but this did not
command much of his attention. (203-209) When it came to mission
methods, he was dismayed by the failure of Protestants to give adequate attention to the building of strong indigenous churches and
the training of a competent ministry. He regarded any emphasis on
evangelistic outreach to the largest possible numbers as short-
sighted and as partly responsible for the Protestant failures
(95-97, 158, 177.) He was supportive of all moves for indigenizing
Christianity in the mission lands and felt that any regular subsidies
for the churches of those lands should be ended in the interests of
establishing them more effectively in their environment. Foreign
missionaries, he felt, would still be needed to help those churches
carry their enormous missionary responsibilities for their homelands.
(138, 169 170, 172-175, 184-185.) With these emphases Latourette
provided a stabilizing and unifying perspective.[21]

The major achievement in the center of missiological thinking
came, however, from another source. This was Edmund D. Soper of
Garrett Biblical Institute. His Philosophy of the Christian World

---

[20]
    Stress on the unifying function of missions can be found all
through the years in American missiology. Beaver 1966: 245-246, 265.
Abeel 1838: 86-88. Baldwin 1900: 39-40. Speer 1902: 67. Speer 1910:
327ff. Fleming 1925: 142-153. Moss 1930. Mott 1935. Latourette
1938. Soper 1943: 269-280. Shafer 1944. Van Dusen 1947.
    [21]
    A view similar to Latourette's though with much greater

Mission, published in 1943, must be regarded as the epitome of the missionary thinking that was able to keep in contact with the great achievements reached prior to 1920 and at the same time to deal with the newer challenges which had caused so many to lose that contact. The work is also the most complete systematically-constructed exposition of the field of mission studies that America has yet produced. If certain comprehensive works of the early part of this century evidenced a stage of maturity in mission studies reached at that time, this work suggests a further stage of maturity reached in the new day.

The book examines the Biblical basis of missions and proceeds from there to an historical survey of the church's missionary activity. It then considers the reason for missions, giving attention in turn to each of the major religions, and ends with a consideration of missionary methods and the final missionary hope. Soper feels no call to attack the other religions of humanity. They are a reaching out after what is highest and best. He does not believe that God condemns those who have lived by the best they know. (46-53.) But at the same time he is overawed by the love of God in Christ and the precious gift which fills men and women with thanksgiving and moves them to share it in mission. (146) The missionary message is one of God known in Jesus Christ as our Father, just and righteous yet offering mercy to sinners. This is beyond all other religious conceptions. It is indeed good news and when people have lost all hope in themselves they may know that they have a share in God's love and receive forgiveness, healing and peace. The aim of mission should be conversion to Christ, for only as men take him as Lord will they grow in the life he brought. And beyond conversion. the aim must be the creation of the church, for without the committed community the gospel will cease to be made known. (138, 241.) With that community the gospel will increasingly permeate the life of society and Christian social action will appear. The church's effort should be concerned for whole human beings, body, mind and soul. (242-243) The church is not the final hope, however. The book ends with the expectation of the Kingdom of God, and because God is the living God we may have confidence that this great hope will be realized. (285-288).

With this comprehensive statement of Soper's we might well bring our survey to a conclusion. But there was one further and

_____

21 con't. attention to social action was the text book for Methodist church schools by another historian of missions Wade Crawford Barclay, 1934.

more all-encompassing development which took place just after the
mid-point of the century. An effort was made, as a preparation
for the 1952 meeting of the International Missionary Council in
Willingen, Germany, to gather together the whole ecumenically-
related missionary movement and the theological scholarship of this
country to formulate its theory and theology of missions. Fifty
papers were submitted by outstanding mission leaders and seminary
scholars from all over the country. These were discussed by appropriate commissions and a final report in five parts was presented
as the American contribution to the Willingen gathering. Nothing
so ambitious was ever attempted before--or since--in the way of
mission studies, and the product of that effort may well stand as
a landmark, an Ebenezer, for American missiology of 150 years.

The report saw the whole church as a missionary body sent into
the world. (National Council of Churches 1952: Commission V, 1)
The Great Commission, though often misused in narrow ways, does
express the aim and motivation which the church should possess.
That aim is "to make God as he is revealed in Jesus Christ so
known as to be faithfully served by all men." (I,2-3.) All kinds
of activity can appropriately be carried on toward that aim:
preaching, teaching, healing, suffering with the world and rejoicing in its anticipated joyous consummation. (I, 16-17.) Service
and preaching should be closely linked together rather than separated as the Laymen's Commission had recommended. (IV, 1, 11.)

All is to be done in the freedom given in Christ, rather than
under compulsion of self-love. In a crucial passage taken from
the paper submitted by H. Richard Niebuhr, the report says: "The
highest constructive service we know in the Christian community
is that of mediating to others, as best we can, this liberation
which comes to us in Christ." (I, 33) This freedom comes after
our natural interest and love, which point us toward mission but
which our sinfulness thwarts by twisting love back upon the self,
have been redeemed and released through Christ. In the missionary
movement there is manifest that deliverance from the fear of
death and concern for the self which allows the believer to turn
from self-defense to service of the neighbor, since he is persuaded
that his security and more than his security is provided by God.
Remorse is redirected so that it becomes repentance and restitution
rather than leading to further injury of others in fear of their
vengeance or to injury of the self in masochistic compensation.
(I, 32-33.) The report does say at one point that saving souls is
not central in the missionary task; the central thing is a "sensitive and total response of the church to what the triune God has
done and is doing in the world." (I, 6.) But when we are told in
the sentences just given above what it is that the triune God is

doing by way of a fundamental transformation of human existence, it is indeed something which could be labeled saving souls.

The report has much to say about the conduct as well as the basis of missions. Since the whole church is called to mission the authors approve the American pattern of mission agencies being created by the church as a whole rather than being independent societies. (III, 6.) Since all Christians are called to be missionaries in the generic sense, the report has to go further and define the role of missionaries in the specific sense. Some members of the total missionary community, the church, are selected and sent to work on particular frontiers where there would otherwise be no Christian witness. These are missionaries in the specific sense of the term. (II, 13.) In addition to the provision of missionaries everything should be done to strength the younger churches and to improve the training of their leaders, for the primary responsibility for mission in their lands belongs to them. (III, 13-14; V. 3, 8.)

A strain of humility runs through many parts of the report. The authors acknowledge that what they are saying about the younger churches has been said for twenty-five years without being adequately implemented, that the training of leadership is not keeping up with the growth of the churches. (III, 13-16.) They are concerned about the enormous American preponderance in Protestant missions and the way in which this may misrepresent the mission of the church (IV, 6-7.) they see that the American missionary's greatest problem is to identify, in his wealth, with the poverty of the world. And they recognize the harm being done by the division in America between the more conservative bodies and the majority of denominational missions and they admit they need to work for better relations in the spirit of penitence and charity. (V, 7, 9.) Most remarkable, they admit that in terms of the aim they have stated, the missionary task is not being overtaken. Rather than pointing to the great evidences of success everywhere, as had been the wont of the John R. Mott generation and also of the nineteenth century, they recognize the smallness of the achievement. (III, 16.)

Yet the report is full of hope. The authors see the mission as standing on the frontier between the two ages, the present evil age and the coming new age of God's rule. There are signs of God's final triumph appearing in many ways and there is everlasting assurance because this is God's world. (I, 14-15.)

V

The big, cooperative study of 1952 certainly did not bring
down the curtain on American missiology. Further work and many
changes have come since then. But that broadly conceived report
does provide a vantage point from which to look back over the
previous century and a half in order to see what has happened to
mission studies during that period.

The major impression they give is one that combines both
coherence and development. There is coherence in this sweep of
missiological work because it has been steadily dealing with the
same themes. What is said in one period has relevance for the
debates of another period. But at the same time there is development. What is said in one period is not the same as what is
said in another. There seems to be a growing understanding of
the range and complexity of the problems that have to be considered. Looking at the early period one is amazed at the absence
of any recognition of the range and complexity involved. But
that came gradually and was the clearest evidence that development
was taking place.

We have also noted the advance in maturity in this field of
studies. By maturity in scholarship we mean the recognition of
the full range and complexity of the issues and the ability to
hold them together in a well-constructed system of thought, not
allowing the different elements or the different points of view
to fall apart because of the increasing complexity of the questions and also not losing heart because of the more clearly recognized difficulties. In this understanding of the term it
would seem apparent that there has been some real maturity in
mission studies. Though at first they were certainly undeveloped
and later on there were times when they seemed to fall apart and
lose most of their structure as a coherent body of studies in
common conversation, they have on the whole dealt with ever wider
challenges and held together well, coming through the periods we
have covered in good spirits.

There have been four major themes that have run through the
whole pattern of thinkers whom we have considered. These have

been, the motive, the aim, the method and the hope
of Christian missions. In all of them there has been some development along with a large amount of constancy. The motive has
been expressed in varying ways as the great complexity of all
motivation has been recognized, but the ways have all been closely
inter-related. Love for Christ and loyalty to him have all along
been basic. Sometimes the loyalty has been expressed in terms that
savored of an almost mechanical obedience. This was particularly
true in some of the writers at the turn of the century. But in
general the inadequacy of any mechanical operation in relation to
missions has been recognized. This has been true in the case of
most treatments of the Great Commission as we have noted. The
charge that in the past proof texts like that one were used in a
cut-and-dried way is not, for the most part, true. Concern for
human beings has also been recognized as a strong motive and has
been kept in mutually strengthening and natural relationship with
love and obedience to Christ. The two sides are really inseparable and the attempt to separate them has seldom been made. One
pivotal development in the concern for human beings took place
around 1890 when the assumption of the necessary damnation of all
who had not heard of Christ was, for the most part, given up.
Concern thereafter was expressed more in terms of the need which
human beings have for Christ in life as we know it, leaving the
question of what happens after this life to the unfathomable wisdom of God.   This watershed in mission thought did not seem to
diminish missionary motivation, though some of the conservative
forces which held to the old formulation continued to fear that
it would. It may have been partly responsible for the great
increase in concern for the social evils under which people suffer,
though it must be recognized that that concern was present in the
very early expression of mission thought and grew, but was not
born, in the later years.

     The aim of missions was very loosely defined at first. Great
possibilities for a rapid conversion of the whole of the non-
Christian world were sometimes talked of. Often this was tied to
millennial expectations. But with the work of Rufus Anderson the
aim became much more precise and limited in the form of planting
the church in each land which would then be able to carry forward
the mission among its own people. That aim continued to be the
controlling one for most missions during the following years, but
it was frequently challenged by more grandiose alternatives that
swept many students of missions off their feet. The time of
greatest defection was from 1890 to about 1930. The first entic-
ing alternative was universal evangelization and we have seen
how widely that was accepted and how stubbornly and yet ineffect-
ively it was defended. The second alternative was that of
Christianizing the world in all its national and international

structures. Great visions were painted as to what would be done
especially around 1920, but failures and disillusionment took
their toll and by the end of the next decade the more limited
aim seemed reestablished. However, it was not entirely reestablished in its original, limited terms. By many it was now
linked to a new, unlimited aim which was the maintenance of a
continuing ecumenical conversation between the world's churches.
The American churches were seen as particularly in need of the
broadened outlook which such a conversation would supply. A
peripheral variation on this aim was that propounded by the
Laymen's Commission which suggested the continuing of a conversation between the world's religions, an idea which has become
more acceptable in missions in recent years.

The treatment of mission methodology is a prime example of
the way in which missiology has had to handle increasing
complexity. At the first the method advocated was always preaching, or those variations on preaching provided by Christian
tracts and Bible translation. "Civilizing" was only a secondary
and subordinate methodology in American thought. But by the end
of the nineteenth century the broad cultural impact of missions
received so much recognition that from then on it was often considered an independent and parallel methodology. There were
constantly new forms of social service created so that they
tended to dominate methodological thought. However, in the concluding, centripetal statements of mission theory which came in
the 1940s and early 1950s it is abundantly clear that service
programs and preaching were to be seen as a single whole and
kept in the closest relation to each other, the sharing of the
gospel being carried out in both. The politically and militarily
related methods which were so much in use in earlier centuries
and were not unknown in the nineteenth, were generally not approved by American writers, though this general stance was somewhat qualified at the turn of the century as we have seen. The
use of careful, global planning as a missionary method was a
recurrent theme in mission thought all through these years, but
it came to vigorous utility, rather than remaining an idealistic
hope, only after the beginning of the twentieth century.

Finally, we recall all the expressions of the missionary
hope which inspired American thinkers through the years. At
first it was a hope which anticipated rapid fulfillment. The
final age was about to dawn and Christ would soon be universally
and visibly triumphant and the missionary enterprise was the
harbinger of this fact. Echoes of this style of hope have continued in later times, most notably in the thinkers at the turn
of the century and some of the more conservative group we have
looked at in the last period. The other mode of hope was more

far-seeing, looking for a final triumph of Christ but not in
the near future or in direct correlation with the missionary
enterprise. This was the view of some of the men who wrote
after the early days but before the turn-of-the-century excite-
ment and also of most of the writers after 1930. In both groups
the final hope was a powerful element and this is shown nowhere
more clearly than in the 1952 report with which we have con-
cluded. In all mission thinking the church is seen as a body
consitituted for mission, living in hope and gathering a community of witnesses to that coming consummation.

Recognizing the fundamental continuities that have characterized mission thought it is surprising to find how little
there has been in the way of interchange of ideas between the
generations. Most students of missions have been in conversation with only fellow students of their own time. There is
scarcely ever a reference to previous masters of the field or
to their contributions which could be used by more recent
thought. Robert E. Speer's references to Rufus Anderson are
among the few exceptions on this point. The result is that
every author has given the impression that he was starting
from the beginning and the same ideas have recurred from time
to time as if they were fresh discoveries. The idea of global
planning around 1900 was an example of this. The conception
of the whole church as a missionary body, put forth in the
1952 study commissions, is another case in point. Obviously
those involved in mission studies have not normally studied
the history of mission studies.

But even so, there is no doubt about the fact that this
is a field which has grown--not because each generation knew
what the previous ones had thought and added new elements to
earlier constructions, but because each generation had to
face new challenges and deal with changing situations. In this
style of growing by alertness it is apparent that American
missiology has been quite adept. The recognition of new
challenges has, as we have noted, increased the complexity of
the field and led to a new level of maturity whenever the
complexity has been handled effectively and coherence has been
maintained. However, the absence of the historical background
has meant that this evident growth has taken place without any
strong sense of identity for the field itself. It is an
increasing sense of identity based on historical knowledge
which American missiology now requires.

BIBLIOGRAPHY

Abeel, David
      1838

            The Missionary Convention at Jerusalem: or an
            exhibition of the claims of the world to the
            Gospel. New York: John S. Taylor.

Alden, E. K.
      1890

            Missionary Motives. Boston: American Board
            of Commissioners for Foreign Missions.

Anderson, Gerald
      1969

            "Providence and Politics behind Protestant
            Missionary Beginnings in the Philippines,"
            in Gerald Anderson (ed.), Studies in Philippine
            Church History. Ithaca: Cornell University
            Press.

Anderson, Rufus
      1869

            Foreign Missions: Their Relations and Claims.
            New York: Charles Scribner.

      1967

            To Advance the Gospel. Selections from the
            Writings of Rufus Anderson edited with an intro-
            duction by R. Pierce Beaver. Grand Rapids:
            Eerdmans.

Anesaki, M.
      1913

            An Oriental View of Foreign Missions. Addresses
            at the First Unitarian Missionary Conference.
            Boston: American Unitarian Association.

Baird, Robert
      1844

            Religion in the United States of America. Glas-
            gow and Edinburgh: Blackie and Son.

Baker, Archibald G.
      1934

            Christian Missions and a New World Culture.
            Chicago and New York: Willett, Clark and
            Company.

Baldwin, Stephen L.
      1900

            Foreign Missions of the Protestant Churches.

New York: Eaton and Mains.

Barclay, Wade Crawford
1934
The World Mission of the Christian Religion.
Nashville: Cokesbury.

1949–
1973   History of Methodist Missions. New York:
Board of Missions of the Methodist Church.
3 vols.

Barrows, John Henry
1897
Christianity the World Religion. Lectures
Delivered in India and Japan. Chicago: A. C.
McClury.

1899
The Christian Conquest of Asia. Studies and
Personal Observations of Oriental Religions.
New York: Scribners.

Barton, James L.
1908
The Unfinished Task of the Christian Church.
New York: Student Volunteer Movement for
Foreign Missions.

1912
Human Progress through Missions. New York:
Fleming H. Revell Company.

1913
Educational Missions. New York: Student
Volunteer Movement for Foreign Missions.

Bashford, J. W.
1907
God's Missionary Plan for the World. New York:
Eaton and Mains.

Beach, Harlan P.
1899
New Testament Studies in Mission. New York:
International Committee of the YMCA.

Beaver, R. Pierce
1952
"North American Thought on the Fundamental

Principles of Missions during the Twentieth
Century (a survey article)," Church History
XXI, 4, pp. 3-22.

1959

"Eschatology in American Missions," in
Basileia, Walter Freytag zum 60. Geburtstag,
ed. J. Hermelink and H. J. Margul. Stuttgart:
Evang. Missionsverlag, pp. 60-75.

1966
(ed.)   Pioneers in Mission. The Early Missionary
Ordination Sermons, Charges, and Instructions.
A Source Book on the Rise of American Missions
to the Heathen. Grand Rapids: Eerdmans.

1968

"Missionary Motivation through Three Centuries,"
in Reinterpretation in American Church History,
vol. V of Essays in Divinity, ed. by J. C.
Brauer. Chicago: University of Chicago Press.

1976

"The American Protestant Theological Seminary
and Missions: An Historical Survey," Missiology
IV, 1, pp. 75-88.

Berg, Johannes van den
     1956

Constrained by Jesus' Love: An Inquiry into the
Motives of the Missionary Awakening in Great
Britain in the Period Between 1698 and 1815.
Kampen: J. H. Kok.

Berkhofer, Robert F. Jr.
     1965

Salvation and the Savage. Lexington, University
Kentucky Press.

Behrends, A. J. F.
     1896

The World for Christ. New York: Eaton and Mains.

Brooks, Phillips
     1881

"Heroism of Foreign Missions, Preached by Rev.
Phillips Brooks, D.D., in 1881" in T. B. Ray
(ed.), The Highway of Mission Thought, pp. 247-
270. Nashville: Southern Baptist Convention.
1907.

Brown, Arthur Judson
     1907
                    The Foreign Missionary; an Incarnation of a
                    World Movement. New York: Fleming H. Revell
                    Company.

     1908

                    The Why and How of Foreign Missions. New York:
                    Young People's Missionary Movement of the United
                    States and Canada.

     1915a

                    Rising Churches in Non-Christian Lands: Lectures
                    Delivered on the College of Missions Lectureship,
                    Indianapolis. New York: Missionary Education
                    Movement.

     1915b

                    Unity and Missions: Can a Divided Church Save
                    the World? New York: Fleming H. Revell
                    Company.

Buck, Pearl S.
     n.d.
                    Is there a Case for Foreign Missions? New York:
                    John Day Company.

Buck, Oscar MacMillan
     1932
                    "Self-Criticism of Missions Today," in Mission-
                    ary Review of the World, 55, pp. 209-212.

     1934

                    Christianity Tested. Its Significance for
                    Modern Missions. New York: Abingdon Press.

Buckley, James M.
     1911
                    Theory and Practice of Foreign Missions. New
                    York: Eaton and Mains.

Burkhart, I. E.
     1940
                    The World Goal of Bible Missions. Scottdale, Pa.
                    Menonite Publishing House.

Burton, Margaret E.
     1927
                    New Paths for Old Purposes. World Challenges
                    to Christianity in our Generation. New York:

Missionary Education Movement.

A Call for Colleagues from Leaders in the Younger Christian
        Churches. New York: Student Volunteer
        Movement for Foreign Missions, 1930.

Calkins, Harvey R.
    1923
                "Foundation Facts the Ground of Self-Support,"
                in International Review of Missions, 12, pp.
                421-433.

Campbell, David
    1827
                Duty and Privilege of Christians to Devote their
                All to Spreading the Gospel. Amherst, Massachu-
                setts: J. S. and C. Adams.

Capen, Edward Warren
    1914
                Sociological Progress in Mission Lands. New
                York: Fleming H. Revell Company.

Carver, William O.
    1909
                Missions in the Plan of the Ages. New York:
                Fleming H. Revell Company.

    1910
                Missions and Modern Thought. New York:
                Macmillan Company.

    1921
                The Bible a Missionary Message. A Study of
                Activities and Methods. New York: Fleming
                H. Revell Company.

    1942
                Christian Missions in Today's World. New York:
                Harper and Brothers.

Cavert, Samuel M.
    1927
                The Adventure of the Church. A Study of the
                Missionary Genius of Christianity. New York:
                Missionary Education Movement.

    1939
    (ed.)   The Church Faces the World. Studies in Prepara-
                tion for the Madras Conference of the Interna-

tional Missionary Council. New York: Round
Table Press.

Chaney, Charles L.
    1976
            The Birth of Missions in America. South
            Pasadena, Calif.: William Carey Library.

Christian Education in China. A Study made by an Educational
            Commission Representing the Mission Boards
            and Societies Conducting Work in China. New
            York: Foreign Missions Conference of North
            America, 1922.

The Christian Mission Among Rural People. New York: Foreign
            Missions Conference of North America, 1945.

Clark, Francis Xavier
    1948
            "The Purpose of Missions." A study of the
            mission documents of the Holy See, 1909-1946.
            New York: Missionary Union of the Clergy .

Clark, Edward
    1934
            The Other Half of Japan (a rural perspective).
            Harrisburg: Evangelical Press.

Clark, Nathaniel George
    n.d.
            ABCFM Higher Christian Education as Related
            to Foreign Missionary Work. n.p.

    1896
            A Century of Christian Progress. Boston: Ameri-
            can Board of Commissioners for Foreign Missions.

    1877
            Claims of the Unevangelized World on the Christi-
            an Church. Boston: American Board of Commis-
            sioners for Foreign Missions.

Committee on the War and the Religious Outlook. The Missionary
            Outlook in the Light of the War. New York:
            Association Press, 1920.

Cook, Edmund F.
    1924
            The Missionary Message of the Bible. Nashville:
            Publishing House of the Methodist Episcopal

Church, South.

Considine, John J.
1945

World Christianity. Milwaukee: Bruce Publishing Company.

Corey, Stephen J.
1937

Beyond Statistics. The Wider Range of World Missions. St. Louis: Bethany Press.

Davis, J. Merle
1939

The Economic and Social Environment of the Younger Churches. London: Edinburgh House Press.

1946

"Mission Strategy in the New Age," International Review of Missions, 35 (1946), 303-313.

1947

New Buildings on Old Foundations. New York: International Missionary Council.

Dennis, James A.
1893a

Foreign Missions after a Century. New York: Fleming H. Revell Company.

1893b

The Message of Christianity to Other Religions. Parliament of Religions. New York: Fleming H. Revell Company.

1897-
1906

Christian Missions and Social Progress; a Sociological Study of Foreign Missions. 3 vols. New York: Fleming H. Revell Company.

1908

The New Horoscope of Missions. New York: Fleming H. Revell Company.

1913

The Modern Call of Missions. Studies in Some of the Larger Aspects of a Great Enterprise. New York: Fleming H. Revell Company.

Diffendorfer, R. E.
     1925
               "What the Mission Boards Must Do," Missionary
               Review of the World, 48, pp. 299-303.

Doughty, William E.
     1937
               Christ and the World Today. New York: Methodist
               Book Concern.

Duffie, Cornelius R.
     1860
               The Salvability of the Heathen No Excuse for
               Neglect of Revealed Duty by the Christian.
               New York: David Dana, Jr.

Education in Africa. A study of West, South and Equatorial
               Africa by the African Education Commission under
               the Auspices of the Phelps-Stokes Fund and the
               Foreign Missionary Societies of North America
               and Europe. New York: Phelps-Stokes Fund, 1922.

Ellinwood, Frank F.
     1892
               Oriental Religions and Christianity. New York:
               Scribners.

     1899
               Questions and Phases of Modern Missions. New
               York: Dodd and Mead.

Elsbree, Oliver Wendell
     1928
               The Rise of the Missionary Spirit in America
               1790-1815. Williamsport, Pa.: Williamsport
               Printing and Binding Company.

The Family and its Christian Fulfillment. New York: Foreign
               Missions Conference of North America, 1945.

Faunce, William H. P.
     1914
               The Social Aspects of Foreign Missions. New
               York: Missionary Education Movement.

Fischer, Samuel W.
     1842
               The Obstacles and Encouragements to Missionary
               Effort, in the Ancient and Modern Church.
               Boston: Tappan and Dennett.

Fisher, James Ernest
    1928
                Democracy and Mission Education in Korea. New
                York: Teachers College, Columbia University.

Fleming, Daniel Johnson
    1916
                Revolution in Mission Administration as Exempli-
                fied by the Legislative History of Five American
                Missionary Societies in India. New York:
                Fleming H. Revell Company.

    1919
                Marks of a World Christian. New York:
                Association Press.

    1923
                Contacts with Non-Christian Cultures. A Case
                Book in the Christian Movement Abroad.   New
                York: George Doran Company.

    1925
                Whither Bound in Missions. New York: Associa-
                tion Press.

    1928
                Attitudes Toward Other Faiths. New York:
                Association Press.

    1929
                Ways of Sharing with Other Faiths. New York:
                Association Press.

    1933
                Ventures in Simpler Living. New York:
                International Missionary Council.

    1935
                Ethical Issues Confronting World Christians.
                New York: International Missionary Council.

    1937
                Heritage of Beauty; Pictorial Studies of Modern
                Christian Architecture in Asia and Africa. New
                York: Friendship Press.

    1938
                Each with his own Brush; Contemporary Christian
                Art in Asia and Africa. New York: Friendship
                Press.

1940

Christian Symbols in a World Community. New
York: Friendship Press.

1942

The World at One in Prayer. New York: Harper
and Brothers.

1945

Bringing Our World Together; a study in World
Community. New York: Scribners.

1949

What Would You Do? When Christian Ethics
Conflict with Standards of Non-Christian Cultures.
New York: Friendship Press.

1950

Living as Comrades; a Study of Factors Making
for "Community." New York: Foreign Missions
Conference of North America.

Franklin, James H.
    1933

The Never Failing Light. New York: Missionary
Movement.

Fowler, Charles H.
    1903

Missions and World Movements. New York: Eaton
and Mains.

Galloway, Charles B.
    1896

Modern Missions: Their Evidential Value (Cole
Lectures for 1896). Nashville: Publishing
House of the Methodist Episcopal Church, South.

Glover, Robert Hall
    1924

The Progress of World-Wide Missions. New York:
Doran.

1946

The Bible Basis of Missions. Los Angeles:
Bible House of Los Angeles.

Goddard, Dwight
    1917

The Divine Urge to Missionary Service. Ann

                              Arbor, Michigan.

Goerner, Henry Cornell
     1944

               "Thus it is Written." The Missionary Motif in
               in the Scriptures. Nashville: Broadman Press.

Gordon, A. J.
     1893

               The Holy Spirit in Missions. New York: Fleming
               H. Revell Company.

Goucher, John F.
     1911

               Growth of the Missionary Concept. New York:
               Eaton and Mains.

     1912

               "China and Education," International Review of
               Missions, I, pp. 125-139.

Hall, Charles Cuthbert
     1906

               Christ and the Human Soul or the Attitude of
               Jesus Christ Toward Foreign Races and Religions.
               Boston: Houghton Mifflin.

     1909

               Christ and the Eastern Soul. The Witness of
               the Oriental Consciousness to Jesus Christ.
               Chicago: University of Chicago.

Hall, Gordon
     1815

               Duty of the American Churches in Respect to
               Foreign Missions 2nd ed. Andover, Massachusetts:
               Flagg and Gould.

Happer, Andrew P.
     1880

               The Missionary Enterprise: Its Success in Other
               Lands and the Assurance of its Success in China.
               Shanghai: American Presbyterian Mission Press.

Headland, Isaac Taylor
     1912

               Some By-Products of Missions. New York: Eaton
               and Mains.

Hocking, William Ernest
    1940

        Living Religions and a World Faith. New York:
        Macmillan.

Hooker, E. W.
    1845

        The Cultivation of the Spirit of Missions in our
        Literary and Theological Institutions. Boston:
        T. R. Marvin.

Hopkins, Samuel
    1852

        The Works of Samuel Hopkins. Boston: Doctrinal
        Tract and Book Society. 3 vols.

Hume, Robert A.
    1905

        Missions from the Modern View. New York: Fleming
        H. Revell Company.

Hunnicutt, Benjamin and William Reid
    1931

        The Story of Agricultural Missions. New York:
        Missionary Education Movement.

Hume, Robert Ernest
    1914

        Will Jesus Christ Satisfy the Religious Needs of
        the World? Inaugural Adress. . . Union Theological
        Seminary. New York: Union Theological Seminary.

Irvin, William
    1866

        Our Lord's View of the World's Evangelization:
        an Address before the Synod of New York. New
        York: Presbyterian Mission House.

Jimeson, M. P.
    1855

        A Sermon on the Theory of Missions. Cincinnati:
        C. F. Bradley and Company.

Jones, E. Stanley
    1928a

        Christ at the Round Table. New York: Abingdon
        Press.

    1928b

        The Christ of the Indian Road. New York:

Abingdon Press.

1929

"Why I am a Missionary," Missions: An International Baptist Magazine, 20, pp. 135-136.

Jones, John P.
1910

The Modern Missionary Challenge. A Study of the
Present Day World Missionary Enterprise, Its
Problems and Results. New York: Fleming H.
Revell Company.

Jong, J. A. de
1970

As the Waters Cover the Sea; Millennial Expectations in the Rise of Anglo-American Missions
1640-1810. Kampen: J. H. Kok.

Keen, W. W.
1908

The Service of Missions to Science and Society.
The Presidential Address delivered before the
American Baptist Missionary Union. . . May 21,
1906. Boston: American Baptist Missionary
Union.

Kellogg, Samuel H.
1899

A Handbook of Comparative Religion. Philadelphia:
Westminster Press.

Latourette, Kenneth Scott
1932

"Modern Youth and the Missionary Appeal," The
Missionary Review of the World, 155, pp. 9-12.

1936

Missions Tomorrow. New York: Harper and
Brothers.

1938

Toward a World Christian Fellowship. New York:
Association Press.

1948

The Christian Outlook. New York: Harper and
Brothers.

1949

The Emergence of a World Christian Community. New Haven: Yale University Press.

Laubach, Frank C.
1938

Toward a Literate World. New York: Columbia University Press.

1943

The Silent Billion Speak. New York: Friendship Press.

Laurie, Thomas
1881

The Ely Volume; or the Contributions of Our Foreign Missions to Science and Human Well-Being. Boston: American Board of Commissioners for Foreign Missions.

Lawrence, Edward A.
1895

Modern Missions in the East; their Methods, Successes and Limitations. New York: Harper and Brothers.

Leber, Charles Tudor
1943

The Unconquerable; Concerning the Christian Mission in a World at War. New York: Fleming H. Revell Company.

Lindsell, Harold
1949

A Christian Philosophy of Missions. Van Kampen Press.

Lotz, Denton
1970

"The Evangelization of the World in this Generation": the Resurgence of a Missionary Idea among Conservative Evangelicals. Hamburg.

Love, James Franklin
1925

Today's Supreme Challenge to America. New York: George H. Doran Company.

Love, Julian Price
    1941

        <u>The Missionary Message of the Bible</u>. New York:
        Macmillan.

Lueking, F. D.
    1964

        <u>Mission in the Making</u>: <u>the Missionary Enterprise</u>
        <u>Among Missouri Synod Lutherans 1846-1963</u>. St.
        Louis: Concordia.

Mabie, Henry C.
    1906

        <u>The Meaning and Message of the Cross</u>. <u>A Contri-</u>
        <u>bution to Missionary Apologetics</u>. New York:
        Fleming H. Revell Company.

    1908

        <u>The Divine Right of Missions</u>. . . <u>a Study in</u>
        <u>Comparative Religion</u>. Philadelphia: American
        Baptist Publication Society.

    1910

        <u>The Task Worth While or the Divine Philosophy of</u>
        <u>Missions</u>. Seminary Lectures (1909-1910). Phila-
        delphia: Griffith and Rowland.

McAfee, Cleland B.
    1927

        <u>Changing Foreign Missions</u>. <u>A Revaluation of the</u>
        <u>Church's Greatest Enterprise</u>. New York: Fleming
        H. Revell Company.

    1932

        <u>The Uncut Nerve of Missions</u>. <u>An Inquiry and an</u>
        <u>Answer</u>. New York: Fleming H. Revell Company.

    1935

        <u>The Foreign Missionary Enterprise and its Sincere</u>
        <u>Critics</u>. New York: Fleming H. Revell Company.

McCash, Isaac Newton
    1913

        <u>Horizon of American Missions</u>. New York: Fleming
        H. Revell Company.

McCorkel, Roy J. (ed.)
    1939

        <u>Voices from the Younger Churches</u>. New York:
        Friendship Press.

Mackay, John A.
    1932
            The Other Spanish Christ: A Study in the
            Spiritual History of Spain and South America.
            New York: Macmillan.

    1950
            Christianity on the Frontier. New York:
            Macmillan.

McKee, William John
    1930
            New Schools for Young India. Chapel Hill:
            University of North Carolina Press.

MacKenzie, W. D.
    1897
            Christianity and the Progress of Man, as Illus-
            trated by Modern Missions. New York: Fleming
            H. Revell Company.

McLean, Archibald
    1907
            Where the Book Speaks, or Mission Studies in the
            Bible. New York: Fleming H. Revell Company.

Martin, Chalmers
    1898
            Apostolic and Modern Missions. New York:
            Fleming H. Revell Company.

Miller, Francis P. (ed.)
    1926
            The Church and the World. New York: Association
            Press.

A Missionary Offering, or Christian Sympathy, Personal Respon-
            sibility and the Present Crisis in Foreign
            Missions. Boston: Crocker and Brewster, 1843.

Moss, Leslie B.
    1930
            Adventures in Missionary Cooperation. New York:
            Foreign Missions Conference of North America.

Mott, John R.
    1900
            The Evangelization of the World in this Genera-
            tion. New York: Student Volunteer Movement for
            Foreign Missions.

1910

The Decisive Hour of Christian Missions. New
York: Student Volunteer Movement.

1931

The Present-Day Summons to the World Mission of
of Christianity. Nashville: Cokesbury Press.

1935

Cooperation and the World Mission. New York:
International Missionary Council.

1939

Five Decades and a Forward View. New York:
Harper and Brothers.

National Council of Churches of Christ in the U.S.A., Committee
on Research in Foreign Missions. North American
Report on . . . the Study of the Missionary
Obligation of the Church undertaken by the International Missionary Council. Five reports of
commissions on the 5 aims of the Study. Mimeographed, 1952.

Northern Baptist Convention, Department of Missionary Educa-
tion. The Triumph of the Missionary Motive.
Philadelphia: American Baptist Publication
Society, 1920.

Nevius, John L.
1899

The Planting and Development of Missionary
Churches. 3rd ed. New York: Foreign Mission
Library.

Patton, Cornelius H.
1919

World Facts and America's Responsibility. New
York: Association Press.

1928

Foreign Missions Under Fire. Straight Talks
with the Critics of Missions. Boston: Pilgrim
Press.

1931

God's World. New York: Richard H. Smith.

Pfeiffer, Edward
    1908

                Mission Studies. Outlines of Missionary Princi-
                ples and Practice. Columbus: Lutheran Book
                Concern.

Phillips, Clifton Jackson
    1969

                Protestant America and the Pagan World. The
                First Half Century of the American Board of
                Commissioners for Foreign Missions 1810-1860.
                Cambridge, Massachusetts: Harvard University
                Press.

Pickett, J. W.
    1933

                Christian Mass Movements in India; a Study with
                recommendations. Foreword by John R. Mott.
                New York: Abingdon Press.

Pickett, J. W., D. A. McGavran and G. H. Singh
    1938

                Christian Missions in Mid-India; a Study of
                Nine Areas with Special Reference to Mass
                Movements. Foreword by John R. Mott.
                Jubbulpore: The Mission Press.

Pierson, Arthur T.
    1881

                "Can This World Be Evangelized in Twenty Years?"
                The Missionary Review of the World, 4, pp. 437-
                441.

    1882

                Responses to 1881 article. The Missionary Review
                of the World, 5, passim.

    1889

                "The Mission and Commission of the Church,"
                Missionary Review of the World, new series, 2,
                pp. 321-332.

    1891

                The Divine Enterprise of Missions. Lectures. . .
                upon the Graves Foundation. New York: Baker
                and Taylor.

    1894

                The New Acts of the Apostles. The Duff Missionary
                Lectureship. New York: Baker and Taylor.

1896

"Christian Missions, the Peculiar Enterprise of God," Missionary Review of the World, 9, pp. 641–650.

1901

The Modern Mission Century Viewed as a Cycle of Divine Working; a Review of the Missions of the Nineteenth Century with Reference to the Superintending Providence of God. New York: Baker and Taylor.

Pomroy, S. L.
1853

The Grand Motive to Missionary Effort. Boston: American Board of Commissioners for Foreign Missions.

Price, Frank Wilson
1948

As the Lightning Flashes. Richmond: John Knox Press.

"Princeton Student"
1887

"The Theology of Missions," The Missionary Review of the World, 10, pp. 125–131.

Ray, T. B. (ed.)
1907

The Highway of Mission Thought. Eight of the Greatest Discourses on Missions. Nashville: Southern Baptist Convention.

Rethinking Missions. A Laymen's Inquiry after One Hundred Years by the Commission of Appraisal, William Ernest Hocking, Chairman. New York: Harper and Brothers, 1932.

Riggs, Ernest W.
1923

"The Missionary and the Native Church, " The Missionary Herald, 119, pp. 328–329.

Rowland, Henry Hosie
1925

Native Churches in Foreign Fields. New York: The Methodist Book Concern.

Scudder, John
      n.d.
                  The Redeemer's Last Command. New York: American
                  Tract Society.

Seelye, Julius
      1875
                  Christian Missions. New York: Dodd and Mead.

Shackford, John W.
      1917
                  The Program of the Christian Religion. New
                  York: Methodist Book Concern.

Shafer, Luman J.
      1940
                  The Christian Alternative to World Chaos. New
                  York: Round Table Press.

      1944
                  The Christian Mission in Our Day. New York:
                  Friendship Press.

Skinner, Thomas H.
      1843
                  Progress the Law of Missionary Work. Boston:
                  Crocker and Brewster.

Smith, Roy L.
      1941
                  The Revolution in Christian Missions. Nashville:
                  Abingdon-Cokesbury.

Soper, Edmund Davison
      1943
                  The Philosophy of the Christian World Mission.
                  New York: Abingdon-Cokesbury Press.

Speer, Robert E.
      1902
                  Missionary Principles and Practice. A Discussion
                  of Christian Missions and Some Criticisms upon
                  Them. New York: Fleming H. Revell Company.

      1910
                  Christianity and the Nations. New York: Fleming
                  H. Revell Company.

      1911
                  The Light of the World. A Brief Comparative

Study of Christianity and Non-Christian Religions. West Medford, Massachusetts: Central Committee on the United Study of Missions.

1918

What Constitutes a Missionary Call? New York: Association Press.

1919

The Gospel and the New World. New York: Fleming H. Revell Company.

1926

The Unfinished Task of Foreign Missions. New York: Fleming H. Revell Company.

1928

"Are Foreign Missions Done For?" New York: Board of Foreign Missions of the Presbyterian Church in the U.S.A.

1933

Rethinking Missions Examined. New York: Fleming H. Revell Company.

Sprague, William B.
1837

Lectures Illustrating the Contact Between True Christianity and Various Other Systems. New York: Daniel Appleton.

Stevenson, Richard
1905

The Missionary Interpretation of History. Cincinnati: Jennings and Graham.

1916

Missions vs. Militarism. New York: Abingdon Press.

Stow, Baron (ed.)
1846

The Missionary Enterprise: a Collection of Discourses on Christian Missions by American Authors. Boston: Gould, Kendall and Lincoln.

Strong, Augustus Hopkins
1918

A Tour of Missions. Philadelphia: Griffith and Rowland Press.

Strong, Josiah
    1885
                Our Country: Its Possible Future and Its
                Present Crisis. New York: Baker and Taylor.

    1900
                Expansion under New World Conditions. New York:
                Baker and Taylor.

    1913-
    1915   Our World. Garden City: Doubleday. 2 vols.

Taylor, Alva
    1912
                The Social Work of Christian Missions. Cincin-
                nati: The Foreign Christian Missionary
                Society.

Taylor, S. E. and Halford E. Luccock
    1918
                The Christian Crusade for World Democracy. New
                York: Methodist Book Concern.

Thoburn, J. M.
    1895
                The Christless Nations. New York: Hunt and
                Eaton.

Thomas, Winburn T.
    1947
                Look at the Missionary. New York: Friendship
                Press.

Thompson, Joseph P.
    1851
                John Foster on Missions with an Essay on the
                Skepticism of the Church. New York: Edward
                H. Fletcher.

Titus, Charles B.
    1906
                The Greatest Work in the World; or the Mission
                of Christ's Disciples. n.p.

Todd, Elbert S.
    1890
                Christian Missions in the Nineteenth Century.
                New York: Hunt and Eaton.

Trible, J. M.
    1892
                "The Authority for Missions," The Missionary
                Intelligencer, 5, pp. 2-8.

Tuckerman, Joseph
    1826
                Letter on the Principles of the Missionary
                Enterprise. Boston: I. Butts and Company
                for the American Unitarian Association.

Van Dusen, Henry Pitney
    1939
                Missions at Madras. Nashville: Abingdon Press.

    1940
                . . . For the Healing of the Nations; Impressions
                of Christianity Around the World. New York:
                C. Scribner's Sons.

    1943
                What Is the Church Doing? New York: C.
                Scribner's Sons.

    1945
                They Found the Church There; the Armed Forces
                Discover Christian Missions. New York: C.
                Scribner's Sons.

    1947
                World Christianity: Yesterday, Today, Tomorrow.
                Nashville: Abingdon-Cokesbury.

Varg, Paul A.
    1958
                Missionaries, Chinese and Diplomats. The
                American Protestant Missionary Movement in
                China, 1890-1952. Princeton University Press.

Vernon, James
    1892
                "The World Plan of the Gospel," The Missionary
                Intelligencer, 5, pp. 229-238.

Vinton, Sumner W.
    1910
                "Missionary Work of Native Churches," Missions.
                A Baptist Monthly Magazine, 1, pp. 647-651.

Voss, G.
    1946
            Missionary Accommodation: a study of its his-
            tory, theology and present need. New York:
            Society for the Propagation of the Faith.

Warburton, Stacy R.
    1943
            These Things Will Last. Philadelphia: Judson
            Press.

Wark, Homer E.
    1929
            A New Era in Missions. New York: Fleming
            H. Revell Company.

Warren, William
    1870
            These for Those, our Indebtedness to Foreign
            Missions; or What We Get for What We Give.
            Portland, Maine: Hoyt, Fogg and Breed.

Watson, Charles R.
    1911
            God's Plan for World Redemption. An Outline
            Study of the Bible and Missions. Philadelphia:
            Board of Foreign Missions of the United Presby-
            terian Church of North America.

Wayland, Francis
    1826
            The Moral Dignity of the Missionary Enterprise;
            a Sermon Delivered. . . 1824. 6th ed.
            Edinburgh: James Robertson and Company.

    1846
            "The Moral Dignity of the Missionary Enterprise
            . . . delivered. . . 1823," in Baron Stow (ed.),
            The Missionary Enterprise; a Collection of
            Discourses on Christian Missions by American
            Authors, pp. 1-21. Boston: Gould, Kendall,
            and Lincoln.

    1907
            "The Moral Dignity of the Missionary Enterprise"
            in T. B. Ray, (ed.), The Highway of Mission
            Thought. Eight of the Greatest Discourses on
            Missions. Nashville: Southern Baptist Con-
            vention.

Wheeler, W. H.
    1899

                Self-Supporting Churches and How to Plant Them.
                Grinnell, Iowa: Better Way Publishing Company.

Wherry, E. M.
    1912

                "Non-Christian Teachers in Mission Schools,"
                The Missionary Review of the World, 35, pp.
                913-915.

White, Hugh Vernon
    1937

                A Theology for Christian Missions. New York:
                Willett, Clark.

        1938

                A Working Faith for the World. New York:
                Harper and Brothers.

White, J. Campbell
    1915

                Missions and Leadership. Wooster: Collier
                Printing Company.

Wilder, Robert P.
    1925

                "Has the Missionary Motive Changed?" Missionary
                Review of the World, 48, pp. 931-935.

Williams, William R.
    1856

                Missions Needful to the Higher Blessedness of
                the Churches. A Discourse at. . . Union Theo-
                logical Seminary. New York: Robert Carter and
                Brothers.

Wiser, Charlotte V. and William H.
    1930

                Behind Mud Walls. New York: Friendship Press.

Zwemer, Samuel M.
    1934

                Thinking Missions with Christ. Some Basic As-
                pects of World Evangelism, Our Message, Our
                Motive and Our Goal. London: Marshall, Morgan
                and Scott.

1939

Dynamic Christianity and the World Today.
London: Inter-Varsity Fellowship.

1943

"Into All the World" The Great Commission: a
Vindication and an Interpretation. Grand
Rapids: Zondervan.

6

Response to
Professor Forman

James A. Scherer

This study of the history of foreign mission theory in America
by Charles W. Forman is comprehensive in scope and prodigious
in length. It runs to over one hundred pages (including bibliography). The study is done with thoroughness and care, and
certainly represents a labor of love as far as the task is concerned. Forman's study: a) surveys the field of American
missiological material beginning in 1810 and ending about 1952,
dividing it into four periods; b) enumerates major contributors
and trends in each period; c) comments on the missiological productivity of each period, based on the number of published
titles available; d) offers a summary evaluation of each period
according to the writer's own criteria; and e) not least, provides a comprehensive bibliography running to approximately 210
titles. This survey will surely make every future scholar's
journey over the terrain of missiological history easier. One
of the fine contributions made by the study is the author's re-
calling of the work of such distinguished missiological
predecessors as Rufus Anderson, A. T. Pierson, John R. Mott,
Robert E. Speer, J. Merle Davis, Hugh Vernon White, Edmund D.
Soper, The Willingen Conference Group, and countless others.

The criteria employed by Forman in his evaluation begin to
emerge at the end of section III where the author comments that
missiology in the 1920's and 1930's failed to meet the test of
maturity and consensus. He suggests the need for a "mediating
yet challenging position in mission studies", one steering a
course between tradition and new challenges, and between the
past and the future. The failure to develop such a mediating
position led, according to the author, to fragmentation and polarization in both mission theory and mission effort. On the
one hand, it triggered a defensive reaction among conservatives
which contributed nothing significant missiologically even

while intensifying disputation. On the other hand, it led liberal missiology to "wander off in many directions and into vague uncertainties". The author appears to find both alternatives unsatisfactory and unproductive, since both fail the test of maturity and consensus. Yet in the retrospective glance of 150 years Forman is able to discern coherence and development in the whole process. A great range of issues was uncovered, and some awareness of the complexity of those issues resulted. "Some real maturity has come", he notes. By 1950, American missiology has begun to come of age.

Forman's major criticism of American foreign mission theory is that up to now it has been conceived as an individualistic and fragmented discipline. There has been little in the way of interchange of ideas between the generations. Every author gives the impression of starting de novo. Lessons of earlier thinkers and periods have on the whole not been sifted and evaluated. The result is that missiology in America lacks "any strong sense of identity for the field itself". Not knowing our own history, we have in a sense been condemned to repeat it. Accordingly, concludes Forman, American missiology now requires "an increasing sense of identity based on historical knowledge" if it is to advance.

Forman's plea for a more collegial approach to missiology in future as a shared discipline of research and inquiry will surely meet with a positive response from ASM members. What the author refers to as a "mediating yet challenging position" would certainly be ecumenical in the true and correct sense of that term:

A. It would show respect for other traditions and concern for maintaining the unity of the church in mission. As far as possible it would seek to keep channels of communication open to all Christian groups, and draw on the strengths of various traditions.

B. It would reflect the concern that the whole body of Christ should witness to the whole gospel in the whole world. It would not exclude from missiological consideration any valid issue related to that witness, personal or corporate, secular or spiritual. It would see the task of mission holistically.

Perhaps the major contribution which the ASM can make to the future development of missiological studies in America is to provide the framework in which an "increasing sense of identity based on historical knowledge", and presupposing a more collegial approach to the discipline, can flourish.

And yet, while welcoming Forman's proposal to develop a more mature approach to missiology in America by giving it a clearer identity shaped by careful historical analysis, it is my view that this proposal does not go far enough. Good missiology is not simply the result of coherence and continuity in the interpretation of historical factors. Nor is it merely the search for a reasonable via media between extremes. The major shortcoming in Forman's analysis is, in my view, its apparent tendency to exclude theological factors in Christian mission and to deal on the whole descriptively with the history of foreign mission theory. Only in the final pages does Forman make reference to theological factors, and then only in terms of a summary reference without any detailed critique. Forman never makes his own theological criteria explicit. He wishes to have both "maturity" and "consensus" and suggests the need for a "mediating yet challenging position in mission studies". Still, we are not given the necessary theological criteria for measuring such efforts.

Maturity can never be simply a matter of greater historical depth and clarity, admirable though these may be. It also involves a "faith" component. Ultimate missiological wisdom would include an ability to discern and describe the ways in which the transcendent mystery of God's gracious revelation in Jesus Christ is reflected in the context of a particular milieu, along with the particular linguistic, social, cultural, economic and other materials for embodying that mystery in a concrete human society. How can earthen pots authentically hold divine treasure? (2 Cor. 4:7) That is the two-sided question which missiology must explore. In doing so, missiology can never escape its ultimately theological-anthropological frame of reference. It deals simultaneously with divine revelation and also with the materials of human history and culture. For this a merely descriptive analysis of past missiological theories will never suffice. We need a theological critique which probes the understanding of Jesus Christ, the promise of salvation, the nature of baptism and the church, the meaning of history and the kingdom of God in the light of Scripture and Tradition.

Let us be clear that missiology is not merely a kaleidoscope of changing historical forms influenced by or responsive to changing cultural patterns, political forces, or other determinants. It also has its given content forever fixed by God's sending of His Son into the world, an event which must be explicated in every generation in faithfulness to the Scriptures and in dialogue with culture. Without its Christological center, missiology would wander off into the vagaries of subjective speculation, a danger concerning which Forman has already warned us. How can one possibly explore the multitude of social, political, economic, cultural and religious contexts of mission

without first establishing the relevance and priority of the
center, Jesus Christ, crucified, risen, and reigning at the
right hand of God? How can one possibly decide for a position
between false alternatives unless one is guided by clear theological premises in making the choice? Missiology in the
ecumenical mainstream would not mean seeking unity or consensus
without reference to truth, or by avoiding the difficult search
for truth. Rather, it must point to a unity that can only be
found by taking a stand within the One who is "the way, the
truth, and the life". Forman's sound and admirably thorough
survey of historical factors in the development of American
mission theory would have been strengthened had he been able to
interweave it with an exploration of the underlying theological
issues in that development.

Let me conclude with several marginal reflections stimulated
by Professor Forman's paper. One has to do with the scope and
accuracy of the writers surveyed. Forman admits that he has
not included all missiological thinking of the period under
study. For example there is little or nothing from the Roman
Catholic, the Lutheran and the Episcopal traditions reflected.
It may be true that little formal missiology from these traditions was published, but there no doubt existed an implicit
missiology which could have been deduced from the reports and
resolutions of mission boards and committees, instructions to
missionaries, interpretation to supporting constituencies and
so on. Without question, this would have led the writer far
beyond the scope of a learned society paper. It may be necessary, however, for someone to fill in the missing gaps.

Even when it comes to the published writings of the mission
theorists of the churches and traditions chiefly represented in
Forman's study, those of the Congregational and Presbyterian
backgrounds, it is possible that these writings do not fully or
accurately reflect the missiological input of the churches and
mission boards to which they relate. We may note, for example,
that the American Board did not always take the advice of its
former leader and most famous missiologist, Rufus Anderson. We
may also keep in mind the fact that the report of the Laymen's
Inquiry (1932) did not have extensive grass roots support in
the churches to which the various commission members belonged.
The operational missiology of the churches and mission societies
may not always have corresponded to the opinions of scholars as
reflected in published works of missiology. The gulf between
the pew and the academic sanctuary is notorious, and we are
bound to ask whether the writers quoted always fully represented
the foreign mission theory of the churches to which they belonged. What is the real mission theory on which the American
foreign mission effort was based? Such questions remain for the
time being ineluctable, and it is to be hoped that some future

researcher will explore the relationship between the operational missiology of the "great century" and the theories set forth by famous missiologists of the period.

A second question has to do with the special character of American missiology when compared with the missiological product of other countries and regions. Does U.S. missiology have distinctive accents? What are some of its most enduring themes? What contribution has American missiology made to missiological understanding in the world? What can be projected from our missiological understanding of the past for the future development of missiology in America? These are tantalizing questions which deserve further reflection in the light of the valuable data which Forman has amassed.

A further reflection is that missiology prior to 1950, with minor exceptions, does not appear to have overly concerned itself with the burning issues of missiology in the 1970s. One misses from Forman's description of past missiological development much reference to the prophetic emphasis, matters of human rights, justice, and the tension between domination and dependence. Were these questions not raised by missiologists of the past? If not, why not? Is it only the voice of the "third world" which has introduced new dimensions into missiological thinking that do not appear to have been adequately represented until the recent past? Missionaries in the past had to cope with problems of power and justice. Is it possible that missiologists of the past did not regard these as prime material for their reflection? Here too it becomes the task of contemporary missiology to develop a continuity between the emerging issues and the concerns which preoccupied earlier generations.

7

Mission and Modernization:

A Preliminary Critical Analysis of Contemporary Understandings of Mission from a "Radical Evangelical" Perspective

Stephen C. Knapp

I Introduction

I have been asked to write a paper on the meaning of "mission" from an evangelical Protestant point of view. Whereas I am an evangelical, I speak from the perspective of a growing number of younger evangelicals who are not satisfied with the evangelical mainstream's approach to mission, as articulated for example by Billy Graham, the Fuller School of World Mission, or even the "Lausanne Covenant."[1] A number of us are seeking an alternative between the prioritizing of individual over corporate and structural salvation on the one hand, and the depreciation of the importance of personal conversion to Christ as Lord which has frequently characterized recent ecumenical Protestant missiology, on the other.

Along with others who are in the midst of this quest, my own positive approach is still in the process of formation. I look forward to this opportunity to share with all of you where my own pilgrimage has thus far led me. The critique of alternative positions as well as the articulation of a substitute suitable to my particular reading of the Bible and contemporary history which these reflections contain are provisional. I look forward to the opportunity for their correction and improvement by the wider Christian fellowship which this meeting of the A.S.M. will provide.

By way of further introduction, it should be said that at this stage the "radical evangelical" missiological ethos -- including my own attempts to speak from this perspective -- suffers from a great deal of provincialism. We are perhaps interacting too exclusively at this stage with ecumenical and evangelical Protestant missiology and insufficiently with Roman Catholic thought and experience. Perhaps this gathering will provide some opportunity for this particular form of provinciality to be corrected. Beyond this, "third world" leaders present will probably correctly discern that this "movement," (if one can call it such) is still largely a movement within Western theology and missiology. Even though radical evangelical perspectives on mission are certainly taking shape out of a depth of concern for the complicity of evangelical churches and missions in Western colonialism and neo-colonialism, those of us working out of a North Atlantic context are probably still pretty much trapped within the confines of the "grammar" of the North Atlantic theological and missiological debate. I look forward to the greater insight into the shape and depth of this provinciality that will come through the reflections on these comments from brothers and sisters from the so-called "third world."

It should also be said that even though I speak from an emerging perspective that has been variously called "young" or "radical" evangelical, I speak really for no one other than myself. There is a great diversity within this emerging perspective and just now considerable debate is taking place over the precise shape of a missiological "model," if you will, that does sufficient justice both to the teaching of Scripture and the demands of justice. To oversimplify somewhat, this debate is between three discernable trends or "models:" (1) an "Anabaptist" approach (the perspective that will be most visible in my own presentation), (2) a Reformed approach, and
(3) a social ethic modeled after the social reform movements emanating from the Wesleyan revivals.[2] These three approaches are not always clearly separate and distinct and are just now tending to meld together in varying degrees in various groups and people. Other more recent trends and movements, religious and political, add their distinctive contributions to the emerging ethos.[3] At the same time, expressions of what can be called a "radical evangelical" perspective are emerging in the third world, particularly in Latin America.[4] Here the struggle is to integrate in some way the central insights of liberation theology with some of the fundamental perspectives of an evangelical approach to mission.

II The Drama of Modernization as the Context
of Mission and Missiological Reflection

I would like to suggest that *perhaps the central factor which
divides contemporary missiological models from one another is
the varying answers (theoretical and practical) they give to
the question of how the Gospel relates to the contemporary
universal "civilizational process" of modernization.* I select
the term "modernization" purposely instead of what I would regard as narrower terms like "liberation," or "development."[5]
These narrower terms (and the realities they point to) will
certainly serve to point out the distinctiveness of some, but
not all, contemporary models. Those models (and especially
the conservative evangelical model) which reject the tendency
of liberation theology to equate mission with engagement in
the liberation struggle, for example, relate to the reality of
liberation only negatively or peripherally. On the other hand,
the larger dynamic of "modernization," I believe, serves to
give both evangelical social ethics and missiology and the
missiology of liberation theology much of their positive shape
and content, though in strikingly different ways.

In this paper I would like to define modernization as the
historical process which began in the 17th century with the
emergence of modern science and has moved through the successive stages of the emergence of modern capitalism, the industrial revolution and technology. The process entails a profound revolution in consciousness away from the dominance of
traditional religious world views over human thought and
action towards a recognition of man as an autonomous creator
of history.[6]   *I would like to suggest that this ongoing process is the primary, universal context or "drama" in which
contemporary mission (and missiological reflection) of all
stripes takes place.[7] The encroachment of this complex of
ideas, institutions, and processes onto both "traditional"
societies and less industrialized/modernized sectors of
"Western" societies, primarily through the vehicle of the expansive influence of Western capitalism, business, and technology is, I believe, what gives particular approaches to mission their distinctive shape.[8]* In what follows I will try to
defend this thesis by articulating some divergent models of
mission in terms of the particular shape of their normally unconscious "insertion" into the history of modernization as
well as their conscious theological interpretation of the
modernization process (or its particular components) as it relates to the overall goal of Christian mission. This approach
will perhaps reveal the distinctiveness of the particular
model of mission towards which I am moving, in contrast to

some of the other contemporary approaches, at the level of some very foundational assumptions and issues.

Jose Míguez Bonino in particular and liberation theology in general is forcefully reminding the missionary movement of the fact of its inevitable "insertion" into the historical processes of colonialism and neo-colonialism.[9] I would suggest that the fact of this insertion and the various forms it has taken in particular groups and at particular times, is the reality which deserves top priority in missiological reflection.

The initiative in the modernization process has been and continues to be with the West and North and has been maintained by an essentially colonialistic process of exploiting "pre-scientific" cultures, worldviews, and peoples in the name of scientific, technological and economic "progress." Modernization, Peter Berger reminds us, is inevitably "Westernization."[10]

In agreement with liberation theology (and in disagreement with mainstream evangelical missiology) I do not see how we can regard the central dynamics of the modernization process, particularly in its capitalistic form, as anything but oppressive. I suspect that the dynamics of oppression in modernization are more complex than a simplistic application of "oppressor"/"oppressed" categories reveals. But the inadequacy of our theories notwithstanding, the evidence of a fundamentally oppressive dynamic at work in the process of modernization seems ample enough.[11] This oppressive dynamic obviously carries with it significant implications for the crucial task of discerning acceptable models of missiological insertion into the history of modernization.

But the root causes of the oppressive dynamic of modernization cannot, I believe, be adequately discerned if we focus too single-mindedly on the contemporary symptoms and expressions of this oppression. The modernization process "began" with the scientific, industrial, and political revolutions of the 17th and 18th centuries, and probably even earlier with the "mercantile" revolution of the 15th and 16th centuries.[12] The particular expressions of the <u>present</u> stage of the drama cannot be understood without some grasp of the whole. Yet, it would appear that much contemporary missiological reflection attempts to do precisely this. In fact, it would appear that to a great extent we are caught up in the contemporary, surface expressions of modernization (or the dynamics of Eastern and Southern <u>counteractions</u> to capitalist, technological

modernization--the issues of liberation and indigenization)
without grasping sufficiently the larger historical context of
these expressions or the deeper theological meanings of the
process as a whole. This kind of narrowing of focus also
blinds us to the extent to which we ourselves are, in one degree or another, <u>victims</u> of the process, unable to transcend
a captivity to "modernity," and by the same degree unable to
challenge prophetically the process from the standpoint of
biblical faith.

We do not do justice to the drama of modernization either
if we regard it as anything except <u>universal</u> in its scope and
impact, however local cultural factors may shape its particular
effects, including the precise form of the "underdeveloped"
societies' response to the process.[13] It is a process that overtakes the vestiges   of "pre-scientific," pre-industrial, or
"traditional" modes of thinking, social and political organization, and technologies both in the West and the "third
world." The self-same process impacts defensive fundamentalism in upstate New York no less than an unsuspecting village
in the interior of Liberia.

Despite the great differences between rural New York and
the Liberian interior, some of the basic effects of the drama
of the encroaching scientific-industrial (and increasingly
technological) civilization are the same in both places.
These effects can perhaps be best summarized by the term
<u>secularization</u>. The process, of course, is uneven in its
effects in different places. Upstate New York (and even
fundamentalist Christian culture in upstate New York) has been
facing the challenge of modernization and secularization for
 50 years or more. Fundamentalism, in fact, is probably already a partially secularized counteraction to secularization.[14] But then, so are probably the many religious and
political movements in the "third world" which have emerged
in the face of the advancing scientific-technological civilization. The advancing scientific-industrial-technological
civilization is so potent in its impact that it normally evokes
critical concessions even in those most inclined to thwart its
advance. Anti-modern movements in the West and North, as well
as anti-Western movements of cultural and political affirmation in the East and South, are at fundamental levels modernized and Westernized reactions to Westernization and modern-
ization(!). They testify to the victory of the advancing
civilization in the very language of their protest.[15]

The word "secularization" warns us against focusing too single-mindedly on the institutional, technological, and political facets or results of modernization: the secularization and bureaucratization of the state, the declining control over culture of institutional religion, the breakup of the extended family structures through the process of urbanization, or the replacement of traditional technologies with modern ones. The drama of modernization/secularization is also, and perhaps even fundamentally, a drama of the alteration ("modernization") of <u>consciousness</u>. The alteration of social structure and consciousness go hand in hand, mutually influencing and reinforcing the changes in one another.[16]

There is also an inherent <u>totalitarianism</u> in the process, making it impossible to isolate the advance of a supposedly "neutral" technology from the advance of new modes of consciousness (and among the elite, scientific worldviews) which gave rise to the technology in the first place or the secularization of worldviews which will ultimately result from the technological advance. In the "third world" the secularization of consciousness occurs through the entrance of Western medicine and technology -- to the ultimate detriment of a consciousness of an effective supernatural order. The long-term (if not the immediate) effect of mere "technology" on <u>consciousness</u> in the "third world" is probably not qualitatively different from the effect, say, of Newtonian or Darwinian scientific theory on the consciousness of the elite in the West.[17] In both cases consciousness is altered in the direction of an increasing captivity to a practical materialism and "this worldliness" against which the traditional religious worldviews and eschatologies are decreasingly effective.[18]

I think that it is fair to say that it is axiomatic of most contemporary models of missiological reflection to regard this process of secularization as religiously neutral and perhaps even positive. Later on in the paper we shall try to document this assertion further by calling attention to the important shifts in ecumenical missiology that have taken place since the early 60s. But in our thinking this approach fails to take seriously enough the significant religious and spiritual contents and dynamics of the process of secularization.

Unfortunately, the transformation of consciousness effected by modernization is not merely a shift from a religious consciousness to a non-religious or a-religious one -- one which is equally or more well off than before in terms of responsiveness to the Gospel (McGavran, van Leeuwen and M.M. Thomas).[19]

   We would appeal to Langdon Gilkey (as well as to Peter
Berger) to support the hypothesis that secularization effects
a transition of consciousness of profound religious signii-
cance, a shift probably more negative than positive in terms
of the secularized person's willingness or ability to grasp
and live out of an authentically biblical consciousness. In
Gilkey's discussion of the theological significance of secularization he identifies the secular as "descriptive of the
spirit of our times, as referent to that fundamental attitude
toward existence characteristic of our age." "This spirit,"
continues Gilkey, "is by no means simply Biblical, nor does it
represent merely a neutral desacralizing of nonchurchly social
structures of which Christian faith might approve. On the
contrary, the present problem for faith and theology is precisely that the secular in this sense, as a basic spirit we
all share, tends to be subversive of any sort of faith and
discourse that might be called authentically Biblical."[20]

   The heart of my thesis, perhaps, is the contention that
*for the most part, Western missions and missiological reflec-
tions have heretofore and by and large been too uncritically
absorbed into this drama of the advance of scientific-
industrial-technological civilization and its secularizing
effects, too accommodating to the advancing civilization's
fundamental ideals and religious contents, and too inclined
to define the substance of the Gospel, the Kingdom of God,
and the church's mission in terms dictated by the process.* The
heart of the failure, it seems to me, is a failure to
recognize the secularized, functioning (and largely "pre-
theoretical") eschatology that is both the root of the modernizing process as well as its inexorable fruit, including
those secular movements of counter-modernization which it
spawns. Correspondingly, there has been a failure to allow
the biblical and particularly the New Testament documents to
be sufficiently determinative of the functioning eschatology
of the Church and its mission. The upshot of the failure is
an ongoing inability or unwillingness on the part of the
Church to be sufficiently prophetic in its involvement in
the history of modernization.

In my emerging perspective, this failure applies equally to most historical as well as contemporary, conservative evangelical as well as "ecumenical," capitalist as well as Marxist-oriented models of mission. In the rest of this paper, I will attempt an overview of this accommodation.

III
The History of Modern Missions in
the History of Modernization

From the very beginning and throughout its history the modern missionary movement has been an integral component of the whole "project" of modernization. This does not mean that its participation in the project was always accommodating in the extreme and never prophetic. There are examples enough of prophetic insertion on the part of missions and missionaries into the history of modernization.[21] In fact, however much missions were absorbed into the institutional processes which were the agents (and products) of modernization, the transcendent Gospel was also operative, often making missionaries more sensitive to modernization's dehumanizing manifestations than were other "carriers" of the process. In what follows I do not want to depreciate the plentitude of such instances. Neither do I want to demean the motives of mission boards and missionaries. The "insertion" and accommodation of which I speak was largely unconscious.

But a concern to do justice to the many instances of prophetic missionary resistance to the excesses of modernization cannot lead us to the other extreme of ignoring the obvious fact of the radical integrality of missions with the project considered as a whole. Nor can it relieve us of a responsibility to use contemporary insights and the greater objectivity that comes with historical distance to analyze this insertion critically so that we can be better equipped to discontinue whatever mistakes of the past continue into the present.[22]

The integrality of missions and modernization is a phenomenon much discussed and documented by both Christian and secular scholars.[23] Not all of these treatments are satisfactory however. There is a tendency, for example, to treat the issue too narrowly as simply a matter of the relation of missions to colonialism, as though colonialism (as a particular stage in the history of modernization or a particular socio-political arrangement between the more modern societies and the less modern ones) is coterminous with whatever there is about modern-

ization that deserves critical missiological reflection. Van
Leeuwen has correctly and forcefully pointed out that colonialization is but an aspect of a larger phenomenon -- the
advance of technological civilization ("modernization," in our
terms)- and that the larger project is the significant, universal context of Christian mission and missiological reflection.[24] Further, such a narrowness of perspective can fail to
do justice to the implications of neo-colonialism, as a subtler
and continuing form of Western and Northern dominance even
after the more overtly colonialistic arrangements have been
replaced by the political autonomy of third world nations. In
conservative evangelical Protestant circles one can detect a
tendency to precisely this form of narrowing, a tendency to
regard the critical issues of mission and modernization as
essentially behind us, now that the era of colonialism is
over.[25]

There is also a frequent tendency, especially in studies
that emphasize the integrality of missions and modernization,
to regard the modernization process and missions' various
accommodations to it as inexorable.[26] I have no quarrel with
the truth that Christian participation in history is unavoidable. This conviction is a fundamental element of my own
perspective. But the inexorability of modernity and its
correlate in the inevitability of missionary support of modernization is in fact itself a questionable ideology of modernity.
It too easily masks the fact that the processes of modernization
are moved by men and are subject to control and change by
human beings. One can detect in this deterministic approach
a mood that frequently traps the Church into forgetting that
prophetic options of human participation in any historical or
cultural movement are always open. Unfortunately, the desire
to be "respectable" (in this case by being "modern") overtakes
all of us, frequently at the expense of an authentically
prophetic insertion into the history of modernization.

There is also a tendency, less among scholars
perhaps than among the average missionary or layperson, to
regard the connections between missions and the modernization
process as merely coincidental, with the elements of accommodation viewed as merely necessary exceptions to the rule of
missionary practices grounded by-and-large in purely spiritual
and biblical motives. This attitude tends to accompany the
perspective which views the technological and civilizational

advances as empty of any specific theological or religious meanings or contents (i.e. "neutral") except insofar as they provide a providentially produced context for the advancement of an essentially spiritual and evangelistic mission. This approach is careful to challenge Western secular or third world Christian criticisms of missionary complicity in colonialism with carefully selected counter examples, weighted to prove the essential spirituality of the missionary enterprise.

Van Leeuwen, to my thinking, has successfully challenged this view, however one may disagree with his final approach.[27] Apart from the untenability of the spiritual/material distinction upon which this tendency seems to rest (along with the individualistic propensity to focus on "motives" as the really significant element in the question) such an approach does little justice to the obvious fact that the history of modern missions and the history of modernization weave in and through one another in quite a radical fashion. Warren has pointed out the striking reality of this integrality and interdependence, all the way from the role of Captain Cook in the missionary formation of William Carey through the virtual coalescence of British mission and colonial expansion in the 19th century.[28] We could add, in this respect, the coalescence of post-1945 American military and (conservative evangelical) missionary expansion in Asia.

This approach to the relationship of mission to modern-ization is closely related to another one: the tendency to see the relationship as one merely of collaboration and contact on the level of institutional processes and technologies conceived of as essentially free of religious contents and able to be utilized by missions for their own particular religious or spiritual purposes.[29] This view does not adequately perceive that modernization is a process in which institutions effect consciousness, and that both the institutions and forms of consciousness have their own latent religious contents, frequently (and we believe, normally) inimical to the very biblical faith which missions are intent on propagating.

It has not been sufficiently realized that this very idea of religiously neutral technologies and institutional structures (the business, corporation, state, and school) is itself the result of the impact of modernization on consciousness (and a correlate of the "privitization" of "religion"). All this leads to the conclusion that perhaps the critical failure in the history of modern missions has been the failure to perceive the extent to which the Church in its mission has been co-opted into a history alien to the history of Jesus Christ and His Kingdom, both at the level of institutional participation and consciousness formation.[30]

I suspect that those of us assembled here will find it easier to agree that the modern missionary movement has been co-opted into the history of modernization than to agree that such co-optation is into an essentially alien history vis a vis the history of the Kingdom. Convictions regarding the latter depend both on one's understanding of the biblical contents and dynamics of the Kingdom (or the relevance of these contents to a contemporary theology of history) and one's perceptions and valuations of the process of modernization.

However impossible it may be to build a decisive and convincing case for the negativity of the co-optation, the fact of the co-optation seems obvious enough. Besides the work of M.A.C. Warren to which we have already referred, Norman Goodall's Christian Missions and Social Ferment provides considerable additional evidence. With the possible exception of the mid-20th century interlude provided by Barth and Kraemer, the emphasis of missionary action and reflection from the beginning to the present has been one which closely associated the goal and process of mission with the institutions, processes, and values of various phases or facets of modernization. In the pre-1910 period which Goodall describes as "interfering with the secular" the integrality of missions with the processes of modernization is seen in the involvement of British and Swiss missions in the setting up of industry or as carriers of modernization through their introduction of Western legal concepts in Tahiti.[31] The close linkage of Christianity and the advance of commerce in the mind of David Livingstone is a much celebrated fact of missions history as is the close and explicit association of "civilization" and "Christianization" in the minds of missionary pioneers and patriarchs in the pre-World War I period.[32]

A deficiency in the analysis of the relation of the history of mission to the history of modernization more discernable in contemporary ecumenical (and Roman Catholic?) missiology is the tendency to regard the identification of mission with civilization as essentially a thing of the past--or, if of the present, something only conservative evangelicals trying to rejuvinate Edinburgh 1910 fall into!

Goodall's <u>Christian</u> <u>Missions</u> <u>and</u> <u>Social</u> <u>Ferment</u> documents
the "check to optimism" of the post-World War I period which is
reflected in the discovery of secularization and secularism at
Jerusalem in 1928, and in the Barthian critique of the natural
theology assumed in the earlier liberal identifications of the
Gospel with Western civilization.[33] This "neo-orthodox" interlude in missiological reflection may be to a great extent
responsible for the commonplace notion that however missionaries or missiologists of the past may have confused Christianization with civilization we are now relatively free from
committing the same mistake.

It is at this point however that the significant shifts
in ecumenical missiology in the 60s (with some roots, of
course, in the Barthian period) need to be scrutinized more
carefully. Johannes Aagaard has documented these shifts in an
article favorable to the general trends it records.[34] The
shift had roots in Willingen, 1952 and reached its climax perhaps in the Geneva Conference on Church and Society in 1966 or
in the Uppsala Assembly of 1968. Aagaard is correct, I
believe, in finding the roots of the current evangelical/
ecumenical polarization in the issues underlying these trends.
The <u>content</u> of the shift, to risk oversimplification, includes
the transition from the deductivist to an inductivist theological method (aided by the now commonplace critique of
Barth's theological "positivism") and from the church to the
world and history as the central <u>locus</u> of salvation history.
The latter shift implies a significant alteration, if not a
reversal, of the ecumenical watchword of the earlier, post-
Jerusalem period ("let the church be the church") and a
corresponding departure from the church-world distinction
implied in Barth's critique of liberalism.[35] As is particularly evident in the writings of M.M. Thomas, it also implies
a shift from Barth's critique of natural theology and the
missiological outworkings of this in the form of Kraemer's
position on the "point of contact." Thomas is explicit in
his concern that we are (or should be) now in a "post Kraemer
era."[36]

There are certainly cultural and political factors involved
(determinative?) in this shift. The most important one is
probably the emergence of the independent third world nation-
states and the growing concern of Christian intellectuals in
these situations to liberate their churches from the former
spiritual/material dualism (with its counterpart in institutional withdrawal from the world) towards a fuller participation (in community with non-Christians) in nation-building,

development, and (in the "pre-revolutionary" Latin American context) liberation. In the minds of third world leaders like M. M. Thomas, the German cultural situation which produced Karl Barth and Barmen can hardly be normative over the third world churches in the emerging nations. Whereas the message of withdrawal from the world was certainly appropriate to Germany in 1934 it is hardly what the already withdrawn and politically irrelevant churches of Asia, Africa, and Latin America need to hear in the midst of their nations' struggle towards development.[37]

What is perhaps not sufficiently realized in the contemporary missiological debate, however, is that insofar as these trends represent a significant shift from the Barthian period on the issue of mission and modernization, they also amount to a return on a fundamental level to the pre-World War I understandings on this issue.[38] To this same extent, the shifts evidence an ongoing captivity to modernity and its further advances on the part of the ecclesiastical and missionary establishment (first and third world alike) that carries with it the risk that its criticisms of the dehumanizing aspects of modernization will not go deeply enough, nor penetrate to its central religious and sociological structure and contents.

Admittedly the shift in ecumenical missiology since 1960 has been accompanied by a deeper appreciation for the oppressive facets of modernization and a greater resolve to stand in solidarity with its victims. But as we have already seen, the solidarity of missions with modernization's victims is not an entirely new phenomenon. The deeper continuity between the new trends and the earlier understandings is evident in the very cultural and political factors which have brought the new trends about. M.M. Thomas is quite explicit in his continuing commitment to the ideals of modernity, and, as we have seen from Peter Berger, the nation-building which so preoccupies Christian intellectuals in the third world today is in fact a strategy of modernization, albeit a post-colonial one.[39] Further, when van Leeuwen (to whom we would also appeal as a key participant in this trend) talks about the incognito presence of Christ in the advance of technological civilization, is he not in radical continuity with earlier emphases on the essential continuity between the advance of the Gospel and the advance of Western civilization, however the new fact of secularization may have removed the Church as the guiding and controlling factor in the process?[40]

Despite external appearances to the contrary, some of the expressions of liberation theology, at least, should probably be

viewed as examples of this return to pre-Barthian understandings. Gustavo Gutierrez, in fact, has provided an explicit theological justification for the merging of mission and the Kingdom with a particular stream of modernization history--the
history of liberation.[41] The more dependent liberation theology becomes on Marxist ideology the more it reveals on another
level its commitment to modernization, especially insofar as
Marxism itself can be seen as a variant expression of the
underlying ideology of modernization with its concurrent though
particular version of the myth of progress.[42]

In my emerging perspective, the missiology of Edinburgh and
the missiology of post-1960 ecumenical thought can be best
seen as missiologies of accommodation to modernization in its
two historically successive modes: first (and second) world
vs. third world "controlled" modernization. The significant
historical dividing point is the emergence of the independent
nation-states in the third world. The struggle between the
first and third world, which has its counterpart in the
struggle between first and third world churches, theologians,
and theologies, is a struggle rooted in the persistence of
first and second world efforts to control third world modernization (neo-colonialism) despite the acquisition of political
autonomy by third world nations and peoples.

The discernable contrast between Asian and African
theologies on the one hand and Latin American theologies on the
other, is perhaps best explained by the fact that unlike Asia
and Africa, Latin America gained political independence early
(and more under the influence of liberalism than of socialism),
is less euphoric, perhaps, about the supposed gains of such independence, and more realistic on the whole about the underlying
dynamics of neo-colonialism at work despite political independence.[43] The question this analysis puts to Latin American
theologies, however, is whether or not they have yet penetrated
deeply enough into the dynamics of which they are a part and
whether all of us who are concerned to align the mission of the
Church with the authentic liberation of man have yet escaped the
level of captivity to modernity which hinders us from being a
truly effective agent of liberation.

The discontinuities between recent ecumenical missiology and
the theology or missiology of the preceding ("neo-orthodox")
period (and the deeper level continuities with the still earlier
period) is also revealed in the shifts that have taken place

on the significance of secularization. I agree with Aagaard
that the post-60s shifts cannot be read as expressions of the
secularization of theology, purely and simply.[44] There are
important differences between the radical secular theologies
of Altizer, van Buren, etc., and the advocates of secularization that include Cox, van Leeuwen, Newbigen, West, and
Gutierrez.[45] But one should be careful also of underestimating
the continuities and in particular the very significant and
quite dramatic shift in missiological evaluations of the
secularization process between Jerusalem on the one hand and
post-60s ecumenical thought on the other.[46] The shift is
essentially one from viewing the liberation of modes of life
from ecclesiastical and metaphysical-theological control as a
process to be welcomed rather than opposed.[47]

Despite the use of the distinction between secularization
and secularism that has enabled this new valuation of secularization, there is reason to ask if this distinction does
justice to the real dynamic of secularization, its negative
impact on the church and its mission and its destructive
impact on third world peoples.[48] The ideal of an "open"
secular society free of ideologies (or of a Christian participation in the humanization process free of ultimate ideological
commitments) maintained by some advocates of this approach
seems to be unrealistic and may itself be a Christian theological expression of the liberal ideology
of a religiously and politically neutral secular sphere.[49] The
concern to rectify the Constantinian tendency in the Church's
earlier social and political efforts is laudible enough. But
does not the ideal of an open, secular sphere run the risk of
reinforcing the notion of modernized thought that religion is
limited to a private or specialized institutional sphere and
that the secular order is free from the demands of the Law and
the Gospel? In short, is this trend so much a rejection of the
Constantinian, theocratic ideal as an accommodation to
secularization?[50] Van Leeuwen and others correctly fear the
sacralizing of the secular order that was implicit in the
church-centered Constantinianism of an earlier day. But does
their solution run the risk of allowing the de-facto sacralizing of itself by the secular order to go not only unchal-
lenged, but blessed? In our concern to leave secular history
open, how do we serve as prophets in the midst of it? Doesn't
all prophecy challenge at some level, the supposed autonomy
of the secular sphere?[51]

This brings me to a major difficulty I currently have with
the tendency to identify the progress of the Kingdom with the
ongoing process of secular history from van Leeuwen on the one

hand to Gutierrez on the other. Perhaps incorrectly at this
stage, I see in these identifications (or moves toward identification) a tendency to sacralize one or another version of an
<u>abstracted</u> history. As I understand it, history is always a con-
crete history, and, given the universal, potent, and even
totalitarian character of the institutions and processes of
modernization, much of the "history" which we talk about is the
history of this process of modernization and its various modes
of counteraction. There can be no effective reading of the
"signs of the times" and no faithful discernment of where Christ
is or is not at work in history without first of all understanding this process sociologically and then bringing our theological
and biblical instincts to bear on these understandings as instruments of evaluation.[52] Much current reading of the "signs of
the times" show in my view too little sociological sophistication
as to just what precisely is going on in <u>concrete</u> history and
histories. What history are we talking about when we talk about
Christ working in it? How precisely is He working? With whom?
For what? Without this concretization we can too easily fall
into the trap of sacralizing the sociological forces of history
that are dominant at any particular time, regarding them as
inexorable works of providence and even of redemption.

Liberation theologies, of course, seek just this kind of concreteness. But do they take adequate account even so of the
totalitarian character of the modernization process which they
seek in their own way to retard or control? However much
revolutionary theorists may want to "fill in" the cognitive and
ethical contents of the "new man" through a radical critique of
unbridled materialism, isn't the "American Dream" so powerfully
and effectively communicated via the "revolution in rising
expectations" emanating from the North and West that the
revolution, when it comes, will be just another attempt to
incarnate the Dream, with all of its built-in tendencies towards
acquiring and living the "presence" of the Kingdom at the
expense of others? Is liberation theology free enough itself
from the ideals of modernity, or critical enough of these ideals,
to be prepared to offer a more authentically liberating substitute for the "eschatology" of capitalism? Is its own biblical
grounding <u>free</u> <u>enough</u> <u>from</u> <u>the</u> <u>encroachments</u> <u>of</u> <u>modernized</u> <u>con-</u>
<u>sciousness</u> <u>to</u> <u>allow</u> <u>it</u> <u>to</u> <u>discover</u> <u>in</u> N.T. <u>eschatological</u>
<u>perspectives</u> <u>such</u> <u>a</u> <u>substitute,</u> <u>in</u> <u>the</u> <u>form</u> <u>of</u> <u>a</u> <u>materialist</u> (<u>vs.</u>
<u>spiritualist</u>) <u>eschatology</u> which is nevertheless checked against
the perversion of materialism by its future, transcendent and
even "spiritualist" components?[53]

If liberation theology is insufficiently critical of modernization to check the encroachment of the materialist eschatology
of the American Dream in its totalitarian advance then ecumenical

theologies of "humanization" which are less sociologically self-
conscious than liberation theology all the more readily fall into
the trap of pinning abstract (and approving) theological labels on
the ethical and cognitive contents of modernization. Theologies
of "the human" currently in vogue seem to be filled with insufficient biblical content to counteract the contents of the
modernization processes, i.e. its own values, eschatology,
and worldview -- contents it also tends to impose on those
less modernized peoples whom it religiously "converts" as it
modernizes.[54]

IV.
Models of Insertion into the History of Modernization:
Towards a More Biblical Alternative

As we review the landscape of contemporary understandings and
practices of mission we can see various types of response to the
phenomenon of modernization at work, both on the level of theological analysis and missionary practice. Some of these models
may be more theoretical than practical--i.e. they are in varying
degrees determinative of what actually happens in mission
activity by one group or another at the concrete level. Those
that are concretely practiced serve as legitimations for such
practice and defenses against challenges from other models.
Those not yet concretized or extensively practiced are utopian
constructs--directed to motivate and legitimate change in the
direction which they specify and to solidify whatever change has
already taken place in such a direction.

Our goal in this final section is to outline some of the major
missiological approaches to the question of the relation of the
mission of the church to the dynamics of modernization that currently compete with one another for our commitment. This typological approach is fraught with all sorts of dangers. The
greatest risk, perhaps, is that I will set up the alternatives
to the one I prefer in a "straw man" kind of fashion, misrepre-
senting their advocates and making the case for my own all too
easily in the process. I doubt that any attempt at typology
escapes this hazard completely. I will welcome any criticisms
from those whose approach I subject to such a distortive analysis
and hope that my alertness to unperceived nuances, variations and
strenghts in these options will increase as a result.

A further and related weakness of this approach--which is
familiar enough to any of us who have seen ourselves placed in
somebody else's typology--is that typologies never do full
justice to the diversity of the concrete expressions they attempt
to embrace. At most, the typological approach can outline
"families" of theoretical systems and their corresponding

practices. They cannot hope to do justice to the infinite variants within the families. The typological approach which follows
will have served the outer limits of its purpose well if it succeeds in outlining correctly the general framework within which
the selected families' "members" think and act.[55]

I cannot hope within the limits of this paper or of my current understandings to include all of the major or relevant
types of missiological response to modernization. The obvious
omissions are the various Roman Catholic and Orthodox models.
Although I will refer in passing to some of these, I feel it
better at this stage to omit them than to treat them unsatis-
factorily.

At the same time, I suspect that the models which I do isolate
for treatment have some relevance to ongoing discussions within
Roman Catholic missiology in particular. The "dualist" option
I describe, for example, probably comes to expression in some
Roman Catholic missionary practice as well as in the practice of
conservative evangelical Protestantism. I suspect, too, that
the emphases of the model which I have labeled the "integrationist" option spans the Roman Catholic and Protestant divide
in contemporary missiology.

As I see it the major missiological models currently vying
for our attention and loyalty are divided essentially
between "integrationist" ones which self-consciously emphasize
the continuity between the mission of the church, the Kingdom of
God, and one or another version of modernization (development,
liberation, or humanization) and "dualist" models which tend to
regard salvation history and the history of modernization as
going along separate, parallel tracks.[56]

Roughly, I would place into the "integrationist" category
the theological advocates of the secularization process like
van Leeuwen and M.M. Thomas as well as liberation theologians
like Gustavo Gutierrez and Hugo Assmann and the less thoroughly
articulated theologies of "humanization." In its extreme form
this model tends to diminish the church/world distinction,
depreciate the place of proclamation for conversion and church
planting in mission, and operate with a history-oriented
hermeneutic of the "signs of the times" as over against the more
traditional church- tradition- and Bible-oriented hermeneutic.
Aagaard's article to which we have already referred documents
the trends which have brought this model and its variants to
the forefront in ecumenical missiology in the recent past.[57]

This model distinguishes itself from the dualistic model
which we will later describe in part through its positive assessment of the transition from medieval Christendom to a secular

society. This view tends to claim that secularization was what
the Bible had in mind all along and to find in the forces of
secularization (modernization) the ongoing work of providence
with its built-in "redemptive" process.[58] In the thinking of
M.M. Thomas and Arend Th. van Leeuwen, and to some extent in the
missiology of Leslie Newbigen, Hendrikus Berkhof and others, the
forces of secularization contain a kind of hidden presence of
Christ that forces a decision on non-Western peoples, analogous
perhaps to the intended result of the dualists' evangelism.
Advocates of this view tend to appeal to Bonhoeffer as the fore-
bearer of this assessment of secularization.[59]

The fact that some of the severest criticisms of van Leeuwen
come from the advocates of liberation theology should not be
allowed to mask the fact of the common underlying theological
structure shared by both. Both, in my current perception, par-
take of the shifts described by Aagaard, moving beyond the
church-centered mission of the earlier period to the notion of
the Missio Dei advancing through the forces of secular history.
In Gutierrez' terms, the shift is from a "quantative" to a
"qualitative" view of salvation. Gutierrez' and van Leeuwen's
readings of this secular history and the locus of its humanizing
dynamics are radically different, of course. Van Leeuwen views
the world-wide triumph of technology much more positively than
Gutierrez does and does not share Gutierrez' radical critique of
capitalism or his socialist revolutionary perspective. But both,
I think, should be classified as "signs of the times" theologies
or missiologies, however differently they read these signs or
localize the humanizing work of God in secular history and within
the modernization process.

My analysis of the trends in ecumenical discussion since 1960
have already revealed some of the points of my own discomfort with
this model. From the sociological side it is not enough, I believe, to talk about God's mission in history without a more concrete analysis of the dynamics of modernization and a more
biblically grounded theological assessment of these dynamics.
Contrary to humanization, secularization, and liberation
theologies I am inclined to think that technology and the modernization process has its own latent theological contents and meanings which compete with the consciousness implicit in biblical
faith. The church as a distinctive community within the world
with its institutional form uniquely rooted in biblical vs.
secular consciousness is essential to preserve the church from
secularization and to preserve its ability to participate
effectively in service to the world.[60]

In the model I am advocating mission is, at its heart,

disciple-making -- calling people to new loyalities and "out"
of the world so that they can be more effective servants in
and to the world.   In my view a secularized church has little
to offer the world. The various forms of the integrationist
model, in my judgment, really fail to come to grips with the
place of the church as a community distinctive enough to withstand and challenge the forces of secularization and the oppressive dynamics of modernization. In these models, an unchal-
lenged, secularized church and the "church outside the church"
in the form of action groups or liberation movements go too
much hand in hand.

Furthermore, these models really fail to take into account
the impact of secularization on their own assumptions as well as
the discontinuities between biblical and secular consciousness.[61]
By assessing the secularization process positively they tend to
accept the idea of secularized consciousness that the secular
sphere should be free of religious encroachments. But the retreat from the secular sphere of biblically rooted proclamation
and prophecy leaves a vacuum invariably filled by secular
ideologies and "Constantinianisms."[62]

The extent to which this model is itself a secularized option
is also revealed in its approach to biblical hermeneutics, where
the N.T. idea of a consciousness (i.e. a perspective on reality)
present in one's being "in Christ" is replaced by the post-
medieval idea of an unbridgeable "distance" between the biblical
text and the present. Again, this idea of distance, an integral
aspect of the modern philosophy of history latent in much
contemporary theological consciousness, contributes to the
depreciation of the relevance of biblical contents in social
ethics and forces us to look elsewhere for the decisive
components to concretize our theology and obedience.[63]

In distancing myself from the missiologies of humanization
which have been prominent in recent ecumenical Protestant and
Roman Catholic thought I am not advocating a retreat to the
spiritualistic dualist model of the "New Christendom" phase of
Roman Catholic thought or of the current evangelical mainstream.
In its contemporary evangelical expressions, at least, the
dualist model tends to regard the process of modernization as
religiously neutral (an idea that displays the depths of the
evangelicals' own secularity) and beyond this (in the tradition
of John Mott) as a providentially provided context for the
continuing expansion of the church snuggled within its womb.

Examples of this model are prevalent enough. The tendency
of some spokesmen from the School of World Mission at Fuller to
regard the modernization process with its technological advances
and dynamics of urbanization as an infinite provider of new

tools for evangelism and pockets of dislocated peoples receptive
to the Gospel is an expression of the dualist's positive assessment of modernization--and (implicity, at least) of capitalism
as its prime mover. This positive assessment of modernization
takes place despite the tendency of the option to make sharp
distinctions between discipling and perfecting, evangelism and
social action, and religion and politics.[64]

But the very rigidity with which these distinctions are made
reveals the extent to which evangelical consciousness has suc-
cumbed to modernization's dichotomization of life into public
and private spheres and its essential privitization of religion. [65]
Even though conservative evangelicals are quick to challenge the
ecumenical's tendency to merge mission with secular history or
evangelism with politics, it remains to be seen whether they
have done any differently in actual practice. The very rigidity
of the dualism tends to mask their de-facto political commitments and ideologies and leaves these commitments all the more
removed from the reach of critical, prophetic analysis. The
dualist model seems to thrive best in the societies and classes
that are the engineers of modernization in the capitalist mode,
which in the present seems to be in control of the whole
process. [66]

The tendency of dualism to regard technology and institutional
form as religiously neutral (and cognitively "empty") stems from
the impact of secularization on its own consciousness and
further contributes to the secularizing impact of modernization.
It has produced churches and mission boards modeled institutional-
ly after corporations and has thereby converted the church and
its missionary structures into even more effective carriers of
modernization and secularized consciousness.[67] It is likewise
insufficiently aware of the fact that its grounds for present
optimism regarding the prospects of church growth may be rooted
precisely in the closeness of its alliance with the modernizing
forces of capitalism and technology on traditional cultures.
Further, it seems virtually unaware of the likelihood that this
same alliance will eventually reap its full benefits in the
form of third world elites increasingly resistive to the dualist's
Gospel as well as the increased secularization of the very
churches which grew so rapidly during the preliminary stages of
modernization. [68]

The dualist model and its insistence on a politically neutral
Gospel is inconsistent at a fundamental level, for at its heart
it believes that the Gospel has enough politics and economics
within it to have provided the theological basis for the
American system and even the American dream. The "otherworldliness" of the dualism and even its concern to retain

a biblically futurist eschatology, tends to mask a de-facto, functioning, secularized eschatology (the affluent society = the presence of the Kingdom). It can even be asked if the dualist theological construction does not provide the critical legitimation for those very processes and institutions which are today the dominant carriers of modernization and secularization.[69]

The missiological responses to modernization I have thus far described are certainly oversimplifications of the actual diversity of responses and are not meant to be inclusive of all contemporary models of mission. The attempt has been, instead, to outline two dominant directions in contemporary thought and practice, particularly as these directions come to expression in the debate between "conservatives" and "progressives," "evangelicals" and "ecumenicals." In part the two options I have discussed have been isolated and described in ways that would help clarify a third (and in many respects mediating) altern- ative which many (including myself) are struggling to articulate and put into practice. As a "mediating option" this alternative is bound to be somewhat ambiguous in its relationship to the other ones. In some respects it is both "dualist" and "integrationist." I have thus far been unable to find a label for this model which would clearly set it off against the others and not, at the same time, be misleading with respect to its own intentions.

My own search for a more suitable alternative to either the evangelical dualist one into which I was initially socialized or the models now dominant in ecumenical missiology is being influenced especially by a couple of sources, including the Reformed heritage of Calvin and Kuyper and the Anabaptist heritage as it receives contemporary expression in the writings of John Howard Yoder. I have yet to resolve fully the conflicts between the Reformed and Anabaptist perspectives. My own emerging synthesis is also being influenced by the theologians of liberation as well as by the social scientific perspectives which inform their own work. Without having the time or space to describe this alternative completely I can perhaps summarize some of its major features.

Against the tendency in recent ecumenical missiology to re- place the church-centered mission with a mission and hermeneutic of history (which blunts, in my view, the church/world distinction), I am inclined to feel that it is the very blunting of this distinction that is perhaps the source of our problem. However difficult it may be to live out a fully Christian con- sciousness in secular society, I do not see how we can retain integrity in Christian profession if we don't try. In secular society this may very well mean some new form of sectarianism. But is this so bad? Doesn't the decline of Christendom provide

a unique opportunity to restore the church to its biblical
status as a prophetic minority within secular society?

The church as a prophetic, minority community is a far cry
from the "sectarianism" of fundamentalism or evangelicalism.
There is a persistent tendency, I believe, for theologians of
the ecclesiastical mainstream to regard the model of which I
speak as a new kind of "otherworldliness" or escapism, hope-
lessly out of touch with the demands of justice, humanization,
and nation-building.

At this point I can perhaps appeal to what I regard as the
decisive point of contrast between the model I am advocating
and the dualism of mainstream evangelicalism and fundamentalism.
Whereas the model here advocated is "dualistic" insofar as
it maintains the church/world distinction and disciple-making
and community-building as the central dynamic of mission, it
departs radically from the evangelical mainstream's tendency to
spiritualize, de-materialize, and de-politicize the Gospel.
In this respect, it carries within itself a radical critique of
the dichotomization of public and private spheres which Peter
Berger isolates as a major component of secularized consciousness.
Rejection of the docetism of the spiritualistic dualist option
implies a rethinking of a whole set of traditional theological
issues including biblical hermeneutics and the relation of
faith and works, evangelism and social action, and religion and
politics. This rethinking normally moves toward radically
integral (vs. dualistic) ways of understanding these things,
with corresponding shifts on the level of religious and societal
practice.

This model shares with liberation and secularization theologies
a concern to get beyond the reality of a ghetto church. But
from the perspective of this approach what makes a church a
ghetto is not the idea of a distinctive community as such, but
the tendency of communities to slip over into spiritualism,
into a de-materialization and de-politicization of the Gospel.
In my view, this tendency is normally the result of an
imperceptable breakdown of the real distinctiveness of the community. The tendency towards spiritualization--the move from a
distinctive community to a spiritualistic dualism--seems to
accompany the move into a de-facto cultural and political
captivity on the part of the community.[70]

This perspective shares with Miquez Bonino and liberation
theology generally the belief that a persistent heresy throughout the history of the church has been the tendency to
depreciate the historical-material (and "political") realm as the
only available context for the outworking of faith and obedience.
For this reason the option here advocated might be termed a

"materialistic dualism" in contrast to the "spiritualistic dualism" of the evangelical mainstream. It maintains the church/
world dualism without a corresponding dualism of body and spirit.
With this same conviction in view, it is suspicious of traditional theological constructions which have overly dichotomized faith
from works, law from Gospel, and regeneration from sanctification.
Commitment to Christ implies in its essence a transformation of
values as well as of the institutional forms which take shape in
dialectical relationship with these values. The community of
faith, in this construction, is itself a real though imperfect
example of the spiritual, cultural and political transformation
of the social and political order that will eventually encompass
the whole of creation. This model is likewise unsatisfied with
the evangelical's tendency to sharply distinguish evangelism from
political action. An evangelism that proclaims the Gospel of the
Kingdom and continually calls the hearer to radically new
loyalties -- to Christ over the nation-state and the ideals of
the Gospel over the ideals of modernity -- is itself a significant political action in the deepest sense of the term.

Whereas this model advocates a sharp dichotomy between the
loyalties and dynamics of the Kingdom and the dynamics of
modernization, it does not advocate a sharp distinction between
mission and the pursuit of <u>justice</u>. To be faithful to the Gospel
and their calling distinctive communities will have to stand in
solidarity with the victims of the injustices of modernization.
As understandings of the underlying dynamics of this injustice
unfold they will also be obliged to engage in prophetic evangelism of those most responsible for these dynamics. While this
model does not deny the possibility and cruciality of radical
changes in the system for the sake of greater justice (finding
alternatives to the institutional products and carriers of
modernization must be high on its agenda) it is careful to
distinguish the achievement of such radical changes from the
Kingdom which will finally come at the appearance of the Lord
Jesus Christ. In the meantime, it looks to the community itself
as the primary (though not exclusive) testing ground for the
kinds of institutional changes which will characterize the whole
society when the Kingdom is fully present.

NOTES

1. The phenomenon of "young" or "radical" evangelicalism is
    described in Richard Quebedeaux, The Young Evangelicals
    (New York: Harper, 1974), and comes to expression in the
    periodicals The Other Side (Savannah, Ohio) and Sojourners
    (Washington, D.C., formerly The Post American). The ethos
    is represented as well in the periodicals Right On
    (Berkley, California) and the "young Calvinist" Vanguard
    (Toronto, Canada). Key books from this perspective include:
    The Chicago Declaration, Ron Sider, ed. (Carol Stream, Ill:
    Creation House, 1974); Richard Mouw's Political Evangelism
    (Grand Rapids: Eerdmans, 1973) and Politics and the
    Biblical Drama (Grand Rapids: Eerdmans, 1976); Jim Wallis'
    Agenda for Biblical People (New York: Harper, 1976), Don
    Dayton's Discovering an Evangelical Heritage, (New York:
    Harper, 1976) and Ron Sider's Rich Christians in An Age of
    Hunger (Chicago: InterVarsity, 1977). See also The Other
    Side, March/April 1975 and The Post American, January 1975.

    The ethos addresses the feminism issue in All We're Meant
    to Be by Nancy Hardesty and Letha Scanzoni (Waco: Word, 1974);
    Man: Male and Female by Paul Jewett (Grand Rapids: Eerdmans,
    1975); and in a soon to be published book by Virgina Ramey
    Mollenkott, Women, Men, and the Bible (New York and
    Nashville: Abington, 1977).

    Radical "black evangelical" spokespersons have played a
    significant role in the emergence of radical evangelicals
    among whites. See for example the writings of Bill Pannell
    My Friend, the Enemy (Waco: Word, 1968) and Tom Skinner
    Words of Revolution (Grand Rapids: Zondervan, 1970). See
    also The Other Side, July/August 1975, for its special issue
    on "the new black evangelicals."

2. The Anabaptist approach comes to expression in Sojourners
    and to a lesser extent perhaps in The Other Side, as well
    as in The New Christian Revolutionary by Dale Brown (Grand
    Rapids: Eerdmans, 1971) and The New Left and Christian
    Radicalism by Arthur Gish (Grand Rapids: Eerdmans, 1970).
    Classifiable as "neo-Reformed" perhaps is the approach of
    Richard Mouw (Political Evangelism; "Weaving a Coherent
    Pattern of Discipleship," The Christian Century, Aug. 20-27,
    1975, pp. 728-31; and Politics and the Biblical Drama) and
    possibly Stephen Mott. Mott's thinking is apparently
    influenced considerably by a Niebuhrian "Christian realist"
    perspective (see his "'The Politics of Jesus' and Our
    Responsibilties," The Reformed Journal, Feb. 1976, pp. 7-10).
    The social-ethical perspective of pre-Civil War revivalism

and evangelicalism is making its impact on the movement
especially through the research and writing of Donald Dayton
(see his "The Holiness Churches: A Significant Ethical
Tradition," The Christian Century, Feb. 26, 1975, pp. 197-
200, and his "Recovering a Heritage" series in The Post
American [June/July 1974 through April 1975], now available
in book form [Discovering an Evangelical Heritage,
New York: Harpers, 1976]).

3. The radical-Anabaptist "wing" of the movement (Sojourners
    and to a lesser extent, The Other Side) is noticeably in-
    fluenced by the writings of John Howard Yoder (The Politics
    of Jesus, Eerdmans, 1972), Jacques Ellul (The Technological
    Society, The Presence of the Kingdom, The Political Illusion,
    etc.), William Stringfellow (An Ethic for Christians and
    Other Aliens in a Strange Land, etc.), and Dietrich
    Bonhoeffer (less his "world comes of age" theme than his
    emphases on costly discipleship, community, etc.). The neo-
    charismatic and"counter-cultural" community-formation
    movements have also influenced Sojourners.

4. See especially the writings of Orlando Costas (The Church
    and Its Mission [Wheaton, Ill: Tyndale, 1974] and his
    recently published Theology of the Crossroads in Contemporary
    Latin America [Amsterdam: Rodopi, 1975]), and Samuel
    Escobar and Rene Padilla (Let the Earth Hear His Voice
    [Minneapolis: World Wide Publications, 1975]pp. 116ff, 303ff).
    The missiological implications of this ethos come to expres-
    sion in the recently published The New Face of Evangelical-
    ism, Rene Padilla, ed. (Downers Grove, Ill: InterVarsity
    Press, 1976) as well as in the "Response to Lausanne"
    (International Review of Mission, LXIII, No. 252, Oct. 1974,
    pp. 574-76) and to some extent in John Stott's Christian
    Mission in the Modern World (London: Falcon, 1973). See
    also The Other Side,Nov.-Dec. 1975.

5. I select and prefer this term instead of some possible
    alternatives ("development," "liberation," "social change,"
    "economic growth," "progress") despite a strong measure of
    agreement with the liberation theologians who perceive a
    latent ideology behind the term's use. If such is possible
    I would like to disclaim such an ideological bias in my own
    selection of the term. "Modernization," I think, is the
    best term available for my particular purposes--to describe
    in sociologically and historically comprehensive terms the
    process with which we are all preoccupied as a basis for a
    comprehensive, radical critique. I agree with liberation
    theologians that whatever one wishes to call the process,
    it is in its essential components oppressive, and that
    the powerful societies and classes in the North and West are

primarily responsible for this oppression (see pp. 5-6, note 13, below).

On the other hand, I am inclined to ask if those who disclaim use of the term "modernization" are not in the process unconsciously masking their own commitment to the ideals and processes (ideology?) of modernization (see note 15, below). I think that it is only after we have analyzed the process in all of its breadth (a task helped, not hindered, by selection of the term "modernization") that we can subject the total process to a prophetic and root-penetrating critique from the perspective of biblical faith. Terms like "oppression" or "liberation" may well describe (in ethical terms) the core dynamics of modernization and demodernization. But they do not serve well the purpose of a broad and detailed descriptive analysis sufficient for a penetrating critique or the posing of radical alternatives.

The Marxist perspective, which I suspect lies behind the aversions to "modernization" terminology, may hinge too much of its critique of modernity on its critique of capitalism. To this same degree its critique of captialism (and modernization) may not be profound enough. However central capitalism may now be as an instrument of modernization and oppression, I am inclined to support Weber's contention that there were ideological, non-economic factors behind the emergence of capitalism, factors which themselves deserve analysis and criticism in any thorough-going critique of capitalism. Furthermore, it is not yet clear that existing Marxist models have themselves sufficiently overcome the dynamics of oppression which they initially set out to oppose--possibly because of a continuing, unreflective commitment (in common with capitalist societies) to the broader ideals and mechanisms of modernization. ization.
Though for somewhat different reasons, Peter Berger, Brigitte Berger, and Hansfried Kellner also select "modernization" over other possibilities (The Homeless Mind, Vintage, 1974). According to these authors modernization is understood as "the institutional concomitants of technologically induced economic growth" (p. 9). For them, "modernization" is preferable to terms like "development," "economic growth," and (we would presume) "liberation," because of the greater value-laden character of these alternatives. As may be apparent to readers of both this paper and The Homeless Mind, the analysis of modernization contained in this paper is dependent to a considerable extent on Berger's work.

6. Virtually all commentators on the modernization process, sociologists and theologians alike, point to this transition from a "static" and cosmological to a historical way of thinking as a crucial effect of the modernization process. Arend Th. van Leeuwen's understanding of secularization as the transmition from "ontocratic" to "theocratic" understandings of reality expresses this idea (Christianity in World History,[New York: Scribners, 1964]) as does Langdon Gilkey's contrast between the pre-modern "cyclical, cosmogonic myths" and the post-modern myths of temporal progress. (See his Religion and the Scientific Future [New York: Harper, 1970], pp. 67ff; see also Peter Berger, The Sacred Canopy, [Doubleday, 1967], pp. 105-125; Gustavo Gutierrez, A Theology of Liberation, [Orbis, 1973], p. 67; Friedrick Gogarten, Despair and Hope for Our Time [Phila.: Pilgrim Press, 1970], pp. 80-101 and Eric Voegelin, Israel and Revelation [Order and History, Vol. I, Baton Rouge: Louisiana State Univ. Press, 1956], pp. 126f).

7. In this I am in agreement with van Leeuwen even though, as will become evident, I am not able to accept his particular solution to the challenge of modernization and secularization for Christian mission.

8. I find Berger's concept of "carriers" of modernization very helpful. According to The Homeless Mind, the "primary" carriers of modernization are the institutions of technological production and political bureaucracy. "Secondary" carriers include among others, urbanization, mass communication and education (pp. 9,16,40,97-115, 121ff, 126 ff).

9. Doing Theology in a Revolutionary Situation (Phila: Fortress, 1975), pp. 2-20. The same inevitable "interdependence" of mission and the history of modernization and colonialization is the central theme of M.A.C. Warren's The Missionary Movement from Britain in Modern History (London: S.C.M., 1965) and is a central point made by J.C. Hoekendjik in his "Missiological Observations," Christopaganism or Indigenous Christianity, Tetsunao Yamamori and Charles Taber, eds. (Pasadena, Ca: Wm. Carey Publications, 1975), pp. 143-152. See also Enrique Dussel, History and the Theology of Liberation (Maryknoll: Orbis, 1976), pp. 75-109.

10. The Homeless Mind, p. 120; Pyramids of Sacrifice (New York: Basic Books, 1974), p. 122; Daniel Lerner, "International Communication and National Development," Communication and Change in the Developing Countries, Daniel Lerner and Wilbur Schramm, eds. (Honolulu: The University of Hawaii Press, 1967), pp.110-116. (See also note 13, below.)

11. See especially To Break the Chains of Oppression (Geneva:
     W.C.C.: C.C.P.D., 1976) and Charles Elliot, Patterns of
     Poverty in the Third World (New York: Praeger, 1975). (See
     also note 13, below.)

     The oppressive character of modernization in its various
     forms could also be approached through an analysis of the
     necessity of propaganda as an instrument of the process
     (see The Homeless Mind, p. 143). Illich's Deschooling
     Society successfully describes, in my view, the (religious-
     ly) propagandizing function of the school in the process of
     modernization.

     Victor Nazario, the "mentor" of Ivan Illich, faults the
     Theological Education Fund's "third mandate" emphasis on
     the dialectic of modern and traditional societies for an
     insufficient grasp of the inherently oppressive and Western
     character of the supposedly neutral, "universal" techno-
     logical civilization ("Theological Education for the Third
     World: Searching for Fundamental Issues," Learning in
     Context, The Search for Innovative Patterns in Theological
     Education, London, Theological Education Fund, 1973,
     pp. 18-26).

12. Accounts of the history of modernization in the West can be
     found in the following: Darcy Ribeiro, The Civilizational
     Process (New York: Harper, 1968); Talcott Parsons, The
     System of Modern Societies (Englewood Cliffs, N.J.:
     Prentice-Hall, Inc., 1971); Arend Th. van Leeuwen, Christ-
     ianity in World History (New York: Scribners, 1964), pp.
     271-348; Enrique Dussel, History and the Theology of
     Liberation (Maryknoll: Orbis, 1976); Max Weber, "Author's
     Introduction" to The Protestant Ethic and the Spirit of
     Capitalism (New York: Scribners, 1958), pp. 13-31; and
     Martin E. Marty, The Modern Schism (New York: Harper, 1969).

13. See Leslie Newbigin, Honest Religion for Secular Man (Phila:
     The Westminster Press, 1966), pp. 11-19.

     Berger points out both the continuity and the discontinuity
     between the modernization of the West and the modernization
     of the third world, focusing in particular on the fact that
     the dominant forces of the latter are from outside the soci-
     ety rather than from inside (as in the modernization of the
     West) (The Homeless Mind, p. 120). What is "modernization"
     for the West inevitably becomes "Westernization" for the
     East and an oppressive process of cultural imposition. I
     suspect that there were equally oppressive forces at work
     in the "modernization" of the West, however, and that the

dynamics of modernization are oppressive more as a function of the social location of the carriers and agents (vs. the targets and recipients) than of the cultural location. By focusing on the factor of the cultural externality of the carrier (i.e., modernization as Westernization) Berger may do insufficient justice to the oppressive dynamics of modernization internal to Western societies. Likewise, this particular focus can do insufficient justice to the fact that however the modernization impulse originated in the West and maintains its momentum by the exercise of powerful groups and interests in the West, it is now also "carried" by groups and structures internal to third world societies acting in a web of interdependence, of course, with the external, "Western" carriers.

The literature on the impact of Westernization/modernization on traditional, "third world" societies is voluminous. See for example, Arend Th. van Leeuwen, op. cit., 349–48; George M. Foster, Traditional Societies and Technological Change, 2nd 3d. (New York: Harper and Row, 1973); Peter Berger, et al., The Homeless Mind, pp. 138–58; M.A.C. Warren, The Missionary Movement From Britain in Modern History, pp. 78–99; Brian R. Wilson, Magic and the Millenium (New York: Harper & Row, 1973) and Contemporary Transformations of Religion, (New York: Oxford Univ. Press, 1976) pp. 46–60; Vittorio Lanternari, The Religions of the Oppressed (New York: Knopf, 1963); Daniel Lerner, The Passing of Traditional Society (Glencoe, Ill: Free Press, 1958); Bernard Meland, The Secularization of Modern Cultures (New York: Oxford U.P., 1966); K.M. Panikkar, Asia and Western Dominance (London: George Allen and Unwin, Ltd., 1953); Everett M. Rogers, Modernization Among Peasants: Impact of Communications (New York: Holt Rinehart, and Winston, 1969); and Arnold J. Toynebee, A Study of History (2 vol. abridged ed. by D.C. Somerwell), Vol. 2 (New York: Oxford University Press, 1957), pp. 151–188.

14. Later in the paper we will develop at greater length the thesis that evangelical Protestantism is a secularized phenomenon and (by implication) evangelical missiology a secularized/modernized missiology (see note 30ff, below).

15. Both Berger and Van Leeuwen point out the partially "Western" and "modern" character of most, if not all, third world responses or reactions to Westernization/modernization (see The Homeless Mind, pp. 133, 165,167,177 and 215). Berger's thesis that "collisions of consciousness" always cause some degree of contamination, even of the reactions against the collisions (nationalism, cultural revival, resurgent reli-

gions, etc.) is further supported by M.M. Thomas in his
The Christian Response to the Asian Revolution (London:
S.C.M., 1966), pp. 9-16. See also Daniel Lerner, op. cit.,
pp. 110-16.

16. I am dependent here particularly on Peter Berger's theory
(rooted in Max Weber) on the mutuality of influence between
consciousness and social structure. The Homeless Mind is
essentially an account of the effects of the institutions
of modernization (technology, bureaucracy, urbanization,
etc.) on pre-theoretical consciousness. See also Peter
Berger and Thomas Luckmann, The Social Construction of
Reality (Garden City: Doubleday, 1967).

17. As stated this may not be precisely correct. The difference
between pre-theoretical and theoretical consciousness may
be regarded as "qualitative." But following Berger I am
inclined to believe that the difference is better regarded
as one of degrees on a continuum, with people moving along
the continuum roughly proportionate to their position on
the "ladder" of worker-manager-engineer-scientist or
student-teacher-Ph.D. in the institutions of technological
production, education, etc. (See The Homeless Mind,
pp. 121ff). "Secularization" of consciousness to some degree
is involved at every "level" of the "ladder" and from the
point of the initial impact of Westernization on traditional
cultures.

Berger says that even for people working at low levels in
the institutions of technological production the whole
edifice of scientific and technological knowledge assumed by
the institution is latently present in consciousness.
Similarly the mere acquisition of a wrist watch and ball-
point pen by a person in a traditional society indicates
the beginning in a shift of consciousness towards bureau-
cratic conceptions of time (the watch) and the whole edifice
of scientific knowledge (the cognitive "background" of the
pen) (The Homeless Mind, p. 149).

18. The "this worldliness" of modern (secularized) vs. traditional consciousness is also a recurring theme in the historical
and sociological analyses of modernization and secularization. See Max Weber, The Protestant Ethic and the Spirit
of Capitalism (New York: Scribners, 1958) p. 182; Langdon
Gilkey, The Renewal of God Language (Indianapolis: Bobbs-
Merrill Co., Inc., 1969), pp. 31-71, especially 38-40, 53-57,
188, and Religion and the Scientific Future (New York:
Harper, 1970), pp. 67ff; Ernest Troeltsch, Protestantism
and Progress (Boston: Beacon Press, 1958), pp. 23-26; and H.
Richard Niebuhr, The Kingdom of God in America (New York:
Harper, Torchbook ed., 1959), pp. 151,182, 190ff.

I would regard this transition on the level of popular, pre-theoretical consciousness to be at the heart of the success of capitalism and an underlying dynamic of the "affluent society." It has its philosophical counterparts in the much documented contemporary theological and philosophical critique of "transcendence" and "metaphysics," as well as in the secularized eschatologies of both capitalism and Marxism (see Gilkey, RGL, pp. 55-56).

19. See pp. 24ff for documentation.

20. Op. cit., p. 33.

21. Many such examples can be cited, like the role of missions in the fight against the slave trade, the frequent opposition of missionaries to the development of colonial arrangements or to the oppressive facets of trade and commerce and the defense by missionaries of the natural rights of the "natives." All of the standard treatments of the relation between missions and modernization/colonialization—especially those written by people sympathetic to the missionary enterprise—are riddled with such examples (see note 23, below).

    That these examples do not alter the fact of a deeper level commitment to the process of modernization on the part of missions, however, can be seen in the fact that normally these oppositions were done in the name of a deeper commitment to the ideals of modernity, against their "deformations" on the part of slave traders, etc. (and, admittedly, in the name of those facets of modernity regarded as harmonious with biblical faith).

22. The simple fact is that we are in many respects better equipped now to critically analyze "modernization" and "modernity" than we have been heretofore. The social sciences have given us new tools for such analysis, however dependent they may be on the very modernization process we would critically analyze. We are seeing more visible evidence all the time of the long-term, negative effects of modernization (the ecology crisis, etc.), effects which were not yet visible (though invisibly in the making) during earlier periods. Furthermore, movements like liberation theology are helping us to see that even the highest ideals of modernization ("democracy," etc.) have a quality of mythology about them, and that their continual projection often serves as a legitimation for the continuation of oppression at a deeper level (see Miguez-Bonino op. cit., p. 15).

23. M.A.C. Warren's The Missionary Movement from Britain in Modern History documents this integrality. Other studies doing the same include Norman Goodall, Christian Missions and Social Ferment (London: Epworth, 1964); Stephen Neill, Colonialism and Christian Missions (New York: McGraw-Hill, 1966); K.M. Panikkar, Asia and Western Dominance; Bernard Semmel, The Methodist Revolution (New York: Basic Books, 1973), pp. 146-96; and James Dennis, Christian Missions and Social Progress: A Sociological Study of Foreign Mission (Edinburgh: Oliphant, Anderson and Ferrier, Vols. 1 and 2 [1897] and Vol. 3 [1906].

24. Christianity and World History, p. 14.

25. Though I have no specific references at hand at the moment, I believe Donald McGavran is inclined to share this perspective, contributing to the further impression (if not the reality) that the Fuller School of World Mission is insufficiently alert to the missiological implications of neo-colonialism and too one-sidedly preoccupied with the responsiveness of individual cultures treated in isolation from the universal, "civilizational" processes of modernization.

    In both ecumenical and evangelical Protestant circles such a narrowing of focus reveals a too selectively critical approach to modernization and probably masks a deeper, uncritical commitment to the aspects of modernization not thus isolated for special treatment. In other words, "colonialism" is correctly isolated as a negative facet or phase of modernization deserving a biblically rooted critique. But in the very process of highlighting this aspect discontinuities between biblical faith and other facets of modernization (or the "modernized consciousness" of the missionary or missiologist) are left beneath the surface. We are not advocating here a total discontinuity between the Gospel and every facet of modernization but are advocating an analysis of modernization comprehensive enough to expose its whole structure and process to prophetic scrutiny.

26. van Leeuwen, op. cit., pp. 331,333; Warren, op. cit., p.99.

27. Op. cit., pp. 267-70.

28. Warren, op. cit., pp. 21-24. See also the documentation of the confluence of British nationalist and Methodist missionary aspirations in the 19th century in Bernard Semmel, op. cit., pp. 146-69. The nation-state,

nationalism, and imperialistic nationalism need also
to be understood within the larger context of modernization.
In the history of modernization the idea of the state is
mythically projected (and often violently imposed and
concretized) as the privileged guardian and agent of the
benefits ("cargo") of modernity by both Western and
modernized non-Western purveyors of modernization. See
Berger, et. al., The Homeless Mind, pp. 167-68 and Daniel
Learner, op. cit., p. 109; Jacques Ellul's The Political
Illusion (New York: Alfred A. Knopf,1967) exposes some
of the dynamics of this dimension of the process, as
well as its religious, mythological components.

29. A quote from John R. Mott graphically typifies this approach:

"Why has God made the whole world known and accessible
to our generation? Why has he provided us with such
wonderful agencies? Not that the forces of evil might
utilize them. Not for us to waste or leave unused.
Such vast preparations must have been made to further
some mighty and beneficient purpose. Every one of
these wonderful facilities has been intended primarily
to serve as a handmaid to the sublime enterprise of
extending and building up the Kingdom of Jesus Christ
in all the world. The hand of God, in opening door
after door among the nations of mankind, in unlocking
the secrets of nature and in bringing to light invention after invention, is beckoning the Church in
our day to larger achievements. . . .Now steam and
electricity have brought the world together. The
Church of God is in the ascendent. She has well
within her control the power, the wealth, and the
learning of the world. She is like a strong and
well-appointed army in the presence of the foe. The
only thing she needs is the Spirit of her leader and
a willingness to obey His summons to go forward. The
victory may not be easy, but it is sure."

(John R. Mott, The Evangelization of the World in This
Generation, New York: SVM Press, [1900], pp. 130-31,
quoted by Charles West, The Power to Be Human, New York;
Macmillan, [1971], p. 169.) See also Donald McGavran,
"Technology and Mission," The Dictionary of the
Christian World Mission, Stephen Neill, Gerald Anderson,
and John Goodman, eds. (London: Lutterworth, 1970),
pp. 589-90. See note 64, below.

30. For material on the "worldview" or "symbolic universe" of
modernity and modernization see Peter Berger, et. al., The

Homeless Mind, pp. 23-40, 108-15, 147,168; Langdon Gilkey,
Naming the Whirlwind, The Renewal of God Language, pp.31-71;
Emil Brunner,"Secularism as Problem for the Church," Inter-
national Review of Mission, XX (1930), pp. 495-511; Ernst
Troeltsch, Protestantism and Progress, pp. 9-42; R.H. Tawney,
Religion and the Rise of Capitalism (Gloucester, Mass.:
Peter Smith, 1972), pp. 227-53; and Leslie Newbigin,
Honest Religion for Secular Man (Phila: Westminster, 1976),
pp. 30,34,37,42,43; 56-76.

The discontinuities between the elements of modernized and
biblical consciousness are many and over-ride, in my view,
the real elements of continuity. The basic meaning of
"secularization" in the Western context leads us, of course,
to look for both the elements of continuity and discontinuity. Many of the values and elements of the consciousness
of modernity are deformations of originally biblical ideas.
To this extent the Christian advocates of secularization
like van Leeuwen, Cox, Gogarten, M.M. Thomas and Gustavo
Gutierrez are correct to point out the continuities.
Neither can we deny that in some important respects modernization has produced an advance over pre-modern societies,
both in the West and in the third world. But, as will become more evident in the rest of this paper, I feel that
the advocates of secularization, dominant in the missiological reflection of the ecumenical movement since the
early 60s, are too euphoric over these advances, under-
estimate the discontinuities between the Gospel and the
fruits of secularization (and in the process tend to under-
rate the real significance of secularization), and too
readily associate the advance of mission with one or another
mode of advancement of modernization.

Without attempting at this point to develop a full, exeget-
ical case for the aspects of discontinuity from the biblical
side, I would like to outline a couple of the critical
disparities I perceive between modern and biblical consciousness: (1) the functioning eschatology of modernized
consciousness (the affluent society, the American Dream, or
the secular-Marxist "new society" as the presence of the
Kingdom) vs. the discontinuity between ultimate and pen-
ultimate hopes and sacrificial servanthood as the mode of
the Kingdom's presence in the New Testament view (see
Gilkey, op. cit., pp. 33,1888); (2) the dichotomization
of public from private, spiritual from material (and the
denial of the existence of a religious cosmic sphere) in
modern consciousness vs. the integrality of the individual,
communal, and cosmic in the New Testament perspective (see
John Howard Yoder, "The Message of the Bible on Its Own

Terms," Unpublished, and Berger, et.al., The Homeless Mind, pp. 29,47,65,105ff, 114,115,125,185-88).

For the idea of "insertion" into history I am to a considerable degree indebted to Jose Miguez Bonino, as well as for his idea of the alien character of insertion into cultural and national histories that is implicit in one's insertion into the history of Jesus Christ and His Church (see Doing Theology, p. 136; see also Oscar Cullmann, Salvation in History [New York: Harper and Row, 1967], pp. 324-25).

31. Goodall, op. cit., pp. 13-25.

32. Goodall, op. cit., pp. 25-26 (Livingstone) and 38-57 (mission as "enlightenment and uplight" in the period 1900-1918).

33. Goodall, op. cit., pp. 58-74. What is perhaps not sufficiently recognized is that Barth's critique of natural theology, particularly as it related to the missionary enterprise, extended to the kind of evangelicalism advocated by John R. Mott as well as to those more readily associated with the older liberalism and the social gospel. While Mott and others probably did not operate with a theologically formulated notion of natural theology, their tendency to link the program of mission with the advance of Western civilization clearly indicates that a pre-theoretical notion of natural theology, at least, was operative in their consciousness. This fact also reveals the underlying continuities between the social gospel and evangelicalism normally overlooked in contemporary evangelicals' (mythological) reconstructions of their past.

34. "Trends in Missiological Thinking During the Sixties," International Review of Mission, LXII, No1 245 (Jan. 1973), pp. 8-25. See also the excellent study recently translated and published by Dr. Anton Houtepen, Theology of the 'Saeculum,' A Study of the Concept of 'Saeculum' in the Documents of Vatican II and of the World Council of Churches, 1961-1973 (Kampen: J.H. Kok, 1976), especially pp. 62-63; 130 n. 302; 131, n.307.

35. The shifts in epistemology and the theological method during this period are evident in many current approaches towards contextual theology and especially in the liberation theologians' critique of the idealism of North Atlantic theology. (See Miguez Bonino, op. cit., pp. 86-105; Johannes Aagaard, op. cit., pp. 8-25; and Anton Houtepen, op. cit. pp. 149-50, 158-61. The impact of these same shifts on the

decline of "biblical theology" is documented in Brevard S.
Childs, Biblical Theology in Crisis (Phila.: Westminster
Press, 1970). See also Langdon Gilkey, Naming the
Whirlwind, pp. 78-106.

36. M.M. Thomas, The Christian Response to the Asian Revolution,
pp. 20-22 and "A Rewarding Correspondence with the late
Dr. Hendrik Kraemer," Religion and Society, XXIII, No. 2
(June 1966), pp. 5-14. See also Miguez Bonino (op. cit.,
p. 165) for his expressed concern to go beyond Barth on the
relationship of redemption to creation.

37. The relationship of these cultural and political factors to
the questions of epistemology and theological method (see
note 35, above) can be appreciated when we see the concern
for concreteness in theology that underlies liberation and
contextual theologies and the felt need to overcome the
deductivism of traditional theology to attain this concreteness (see Aharon Sapsezian, "Theology of Liberation-
Liberation of Theology," Theological Education IX, No. 4
(Summer 1973). The concern for concreteness in theology is
in part at least a concern to make theology more service-
able to the overall task of Christian participation in
nation-building, development, and especially, liberation.

It is also at this very point of concreteness that theolog-
ical advocates of the shifts in view feel a need to depart
from Barth and to identify with Bonhoeffer in his critique
of Barth over the same issue (see Paul L. Lehman, "The
Concreteness of Theology: Reflections on the Conversation
Between Barth and Bonhoeffer," Footnotes to a Theology, The
Karl Barth Colloquium of 1972, Martin Ramscheider, ed.,
Corporation for the Publication of Academic Studies in
Religion in Canada, 1974, pp. 53-76). For the relationship
of this question to the question of a "non-religious
communication of theological concepts" see Karl Barth,
The Humanity of God (Atlanta: John Knox Press, 1974),
pp. 58-59.

The question as to how this concreteness comes about,
particularly vis a vis the issue of the role of ideology
(and which ideology) in theology, is perhaps the major
point of contention between liberation theology and
European political theology (Moltmann, Metz, etc.). Both
of these movements, however, are probably best seen as
variant expressions of the single set of shifts here being
discussed. (See Jurgen Moltmann, "An Open Letter to Jose
Miguez Bonino," Christianity and Crisis, March 29, 1976,
pp. 57-63 and note 49, below.)

It is striking that however the emergence of the new nations may have been a factor in the shift from the neo-orthodox emphasis on the discontinuity between the Kingdom and cultural history and the current theological emphasis on the continuity, the shift has not been limited to third world theologians. It appears to be a universal trend, encouraged in the West perhaps by a post-war shift from cultural pessimism to cultural optimism, as well as by weaknesses inherrent in the neo-orthodox solution to the recurring and "modern" problem of faith and history. Increasingly this solution is interpreted as a de-historicization and (particularly in the case of Bultmann) a subjectivistic/individualistic reduction of the Gospel. The "Hartford Appeal" is perhaps best understood as a counteraction to this shift from transcendence to immanence thinking in post-1960's theology as well as an appeal to resurrect some of the Barthian instincts lost in the transition. (See Peter L. Berger and Richard John Neuhaus, Against the World for the World [New York: Seabury, 1976].)

38. At the same time it is important to see the continuities between the trends we are here discussing and theological emphases of the immediately prior period. Barth's critique of religion, for example, serves as a basis for van Leeuwen's affirmation of the process of secularization understood as the defeat of the claims of all religions to ontological status ("ontocracy," etc.).

39. See note 28, above.

40. Arend Th. van Leeuwen, op. cit., pp. 16,17,22,44. See also M.M. Thomas, op. cit. p. 31.

41. Gustavo Gutierrez, op. cit. pp. 69-72, 149ff. Gutierrez does not do away with all discontinuity between the Kingdom and liberation history culminating in a qualitatively new, socialist society. But on the surface at least it appears that whatever discontinuity is left is of the nature of the discontinuity between the perfection of a continually projected utopia and the imperfection of all of its historical manifestations (p. 177). For a critique of this "historical monism" from within the liberation theology movement see Miguez Bonino, op. cit., pp. 132-139. (See also notes 49 and 65. below.

42. For material on Marxism as a variant model of the single project of modernization see van Leeuwen, op. cit., p. 270; Peter Berger, Pyramids of Sacrifice, p. 122; Max Weber, The Protestant Ethic and the Spirit of Capitalism, p. 23. What applies to Marxism as a specific form of socialism also applies to other forms of socialism if one accepts Berger's

analysis that socialism is a compromise between the community of traditional society and the promised benefits
of modernity (The Homeless Mind, pp. 131,137,138).

43. The underlying commitment of Marxism, and we suspect of
many forms of liberation theology, to the continuing advancement of technological civilization is another evidence
of Marxism's underlying commitment to modernization. The
neo-Marxism of Marcuse is an exception to this, perhaps,
with its radical critique of very foundational structures and assumptions of modernity, including technology,
the ideology-free character of science, etc. (One Dimensional Man, Boston: Beacon Press, 1964).
Rubem Alves, more dependent on Marcuse than have been other
liberation theologians, is also a possible exception to this
generalization vis a vis liberation theology. (See his A
Theology of Human Hope [Washington, D.C.: Corpus Books,
1969] and his more recent Tomorrow's Child [New York:
Harper and Row, 1972]. See also Miguez Bonino, op. cit.,
p. 75.)

44. Aagaard, op. cit., p. 10.

45. See especially Langdon Gilkey's analysis in which he distinguishes Harvey Cox from the radical theologians van
Buren and Altizer (Naming the Whirlwind, pp. 25-27).

46. In "The Secularization Debate Foreshadowed, Jerusalem
1928," (The International Review of Mission, LVII, no. 277
[July, 1968], pp. 344-57), David Gill attempts to establish
that people at the Jerusalem Conference were not as uniformly against secularization as recent advocates of secularization have supposed. But that the climate regarding
secularization shifted significantly in the early '60s is
clear enough. With foreshadowings certainly in Bonhoeffer's
Letters and Papers from Prison, the significant turning
point is probably to be found in the writings of Friedrich
Gogarten and perhaps Dietrich von Oppen. Gogarten, in
particular, seems to be the first to have made the distinction between secularization (openness of the secular from
the encroachment of an absolutized religion or ideology)
and secularism (the absolutization of a religion or
ideology) on which the whole reassessment of secularization
seems to turn. See Friedrich Gogarten, Verhangnis und
Hoffnung der Neuzeit (Stuttgart: Friedrich Vorwerk Verlag,
1953, published in English in 1970 as Despair and Hope for
Our Time, (Phila.: United Church Press, 1970), and Dietrich
von Oppen, Das Personale Zeitalter (Stuttgart, 1960),
published in English as The Age of the Person (Phila:
Fortress Press, 1969).

47. See for example the influential (in ecumenical Protestant
    discussions) "Report on the Consultation of University
    Teachers on 'The Meaning of the Secular'" held at Bossey,
    Switzerland, Sept. 15-20, 1959, edited by Dr. Charles West.
    This definition of secularization also appears in the re-
    port on the Geneva Conference on the Church in Society,
    1966 (see Christians in the Technical and Social Revolutions
    of our Time, World Conference on Church and Society
    Official Report [Geneva, W.C.C., 1966], p. 158.)

    An underlying motive of the recent reassessment of secular-
    ization was apparently the concern to move beyond the
    dilemma posed by "two realms" dualism (with its tendency
    towards withdrawal from the world and/or implicit sacral-
    ization of the secular order) on the one hand and the
    explicit sacralism of either the Medieval synthesis of
    Aquinas or the theocratic social ethic of Calvin and the
    Puritans on the other. Houtepen feels that this dilemma was
    unresolved in the ecumenical debate through the mid-50s,
    and he sees it as a concern underlying the emergence of the
    ecumenical Protestant and Roman Catholic "theology of the
    saeculeum" of the 60s (op. cit., pp. 62-63; 82 n. 142;141).

    Ironically, successive and/or contracting theological
    appraisals of and counteractions to the German National
    Socialist experience may have been at work not only in the
    development of Barth's reaction against any integration of
    the Kingdom with cultural and political aspirations (with
    its correlative critique of natural theology) and of the
    earlier Bonhoeffer emphasis on costly discipleship (both
    implying the necessity of the church/world dualism) but
    also of the later openness of Bonhoeffer and Cogarten to
    secularization and the eventual flowering of this openness
    in the new, contextual, "natural theologies" of liberation
    and humanization (with their implied modifications, if not
    rejections, of the church/world dualism).

    Houtepen mentions that Barth himself solved the dilemma of
    dualism/theocracy by insisting on the character of the
    Church as an "event" never fully identifiable with the
    visible congregation (op. cit., p. 63). As Houtepen implies,
    this position of Barth may be itself a precursor of
    the current fading of the church/world demarcation. But
    that Barth still thought in terms of the dualism seems
    clear enough from Houtepen's own analysis of the trends in
    ecumenical theology. (See also Will Herberg, "The Social
    Philosophy of Karl Barth," in the introduction to Barth's
    Community, State and Church [Gloucester, Mass: Peter Smith,
    1968], pp. 36-37.) As will become evident, my own
    attempted solution to the dilemma, significantly dependent

on the insights of Anabaptism, is to avoid the sacralizing
option not by diminishing the church/world dualism but by
challenging a spiritualist construction of this dualism and
refusing the temptation to utilize secular power for the
enforcement of Gospel norms outside the church.

There seems to be a resolute failure on the part of social
ethicists of the Christian mainstream to consider the Anabaptist option as an alternative to theocracy on the one
hand or "two realms" theology on the other. This failure
is accompanied by a tendency to regard the radical option
as a spiritualist withdrawal and a failure to distinguish
between what I will later call "other worldly" and "this
worldly" constructions of the church/world dualism.

48. Langdon Gilkey rejects this distinction as distractive from
     the dominant "secular mood" of our time (and the signifi-
     cance of secularization as the process producing the mood).
     He identifices this mood as "this-worldliness" inimical
     to all religious faith, including biblical faith (Naming the
     Whirlwind, pp. 33f; see also note 20, above.).

49. For expressions of this ideal by some of the theological
     advocates of secularization see M.M. Thomas, op. cit., p.76
     (against the idea of a "Christian culture"); and Charles
     West, "Mission in East and West," The Missionary Church in
     East and West, Charles West and David M. Paton, eds.
     (London: S.C.M. Press, 1959) pp. 118,120,122. In his more
     recent writing Dr. West seems to show more openness to
     ideology at least in the sense of a temporary, heuristic
     device and vision (The Power to be Human, pp. 198ff).
     Does this represent a shift in response to the concern of
     liberation theologians for concreteness in theology or their
     insistence on the inevitablity of ideology?

     Even though we are arguing that liberation theologies are
     generally examples of these post-1960 theological shifts
     from church to world, transcendence to immanence, etc. (and
     fellow advocates of what we call the "integrationist" model
     of mission and modernization), we recognize the important
     fact that they are definitely opposed to the ideal of
     ideological neutrality in secular-historical engagements
     espoused by those theologies of humanization less attracted
     to Marxist social analysis. The issue of ideology and its
     role is perhaps the central issue of debate between liber-
     ation theologians and other types of humanization theology
     (see Jurgen Moltmann, "An Open Letter to Jose Miguez Bonino,"
     Christianity and Crisis, March 29, 1976, pp. 57-63).

The very substance and persistence of this debate should
lead to a re-opening of the question as to how successfully
the overall trend has overcome the older dilemma of dualism/
theocracy (note 47, above). From the viewpoint of liberation theologians, talk of humanization without a concretization through ideological commitments reveals an underlying commitment to a liberal ideology (and its ideal of a
neutral, secular sphere) if not a residual commitment to a
doctrine of the two realms. From the standpoint
of humanization theologies in the non-liberation
mode, liberation theology carries the risk of sacralizing
a secular Marxist ideology. Each "school" within the overall integrationist approach charges the other with a retreat
onto one or the other horns of the older dilemma,i.e.
dualism or theocracy.

One can detect a variety of stances within liberation
theology itself on the question of commitment to Marxist
ideology. While liberation theologians are united (against
other advocates of humanization theology) on the inevitability and necessity of ideological commitment, they are not
uniformly committed to the same level or depth of such a
commitment. None, to my knowledge, advocate a commitment
unaltered by the Gospel. Gutierrez and Assmann seem more
open to a fuller use of Marxist analysis than does Miguez
Bonino. An open but cautious utilization of ideology is
revealed in Julio De Santa Ana's account of the wrestling
with this issue in the Latin American Church and Society
movement (ISAL) (See "The Influence of Bonhoeffer on the
Theology of Liberation," The Ecumenical Review, VXXVII,
No. 2 [April, 1976], p. 192-94).

50. Rosemary Ruether, for example, challenges the idea advocat-
     ed by van Leeuwen that the Old Testament (vs. other Ancient
     Near Eastern) kingship was "secularized" in the sense that
     it was regarded as autonomous from the "cosmic totality"
     of a divine order. In Ruether's construction, the prophetic
     denunciations assumed the existence of an "ontocracy," not
     the freedom of the kingship from ontocracy ("Augustine and
     Christian Political Theology," Interpretation, XXIX, No. 3
     [July, 1975], p. 253). Ruether's analysis seems also to
     imply a criticism of the positions to which we now refer
     to the effect that they are variants of a liberal, "secular
     Augustinian," Constantinianism (in contrast to the "left-
     wing" Augustinianism of Ellul, Stringfellow, etc.). The
     position that advocates of secularization are continuing
     the conformity pattern of Constantinianism is also taken
     by Demosthenes Savramis, "Theology and Society, Ten Hypoth-
     ses," Technology and Social Justice, Ronald H. Preston, ed.
     (Valley Forge: Judson Press, 1971) pp. 398-421.

51. Few if any of those who advocate a positive theological
     appraisal of secularization are oblivious, of course, to
     this threat of a new sacralism. A concern to avoid a new,
     secular Constantinianism for example, lies behind their
     critique of those advocates of liberation theology who go
     beyond the positive appraisal of secularization to a
     positive (and absolute?) incorporation of a secular
     (Marxist) ideology into Christian theological reflection
     and social engagement.

     In some respects the emphasis on maintaining a neutral
     secular sphere takes on the appearance of a game in which
     Christian theologians begin by admitting that heretofore
     they have been guilty of breaking the rules (against
     absolutizing an ideology) and covenanting that henceforth
     they will not only cease from such rule-breaking but also
     serve as a referee to be sure that everyone else, inside
     and outside the church, abides by the rules as well. My
     difficulty with this approach is that it tends to restrict
     the encroachment upon the process by the authoritative
     Gospel as revealed in Scripture. As a result the
     games "players" have little more at their disposal than
     their individual instincts as to what it means to be human
     in concrete terms in the midst of the modernization process.
     This would appear to be an implication of Gogarten's
     critique of the Barthian emphasis on the biblical revelation
     to the effect that such an emphasis amounts to a "counter-
     ideological ideology." (See Theodore Runyan, "Secular-
     ization and Sacrament: Reflections on the Theology of
     Friedrich Gogarten," The Spirit and Power of Christian
     Secularity, Albert Schlitzer, S.C.S., ed.,[Notre Dame:
     University of Notre Dame Press, 1969], p. 135.)

     The maintenance of the church/world distinction appears to
     be an essential ingredient of the insistence on the unique-
     ness of God's revelation in Christ and through the Christian
     scriptures and Christian mission understood as the proclam-
     ation of this accessable, transcendent Gospel to the world.
     Reconstructions of the church-world distinction seem in-
     evitably to have hermeneutical implications (or presup-
     positions). They tend towards a new "natural theology"
     that diminishes the transcent uniqueness of the biblical
     revelation with its correlative commitment to the importance
     and possibility of a missionary message. These same
     hermeneutical implications work themselves out in the form
     of a social ethic minimally informed by biblical norm,
     precedent, or Weltenschaung with the resulting "gap" being
     filled by contextual and even secular ideological components.

I am some distance myself from having worked out a hermeneutical alternative that does justice to the humanity and
"contextuality" of Scripture and the interpreter of
Scripture. But in the midst of a quest for such an alternative I am unsatisfied with those options which, in an
accommodation to the consciousness of modernity, relegate
scriptural contents to a dead past minimally able to
speak prophetically and substantively to contemporary
society and its ongoing social processes (see John Howard
Yoder's The Politics of Jesus and "The Message of the Bible
on its Own Terms," unpublished, 1964. See also note 73,
below).

52. No rigid fact/value dichotomy is assumed here. Even in
the sociological aspects of our analysis we cannot totally
dissociate ourselves from the "symbolic universe" we
inhabit at the point of the beginning of our investigations
--provided in our case by the perspective on reality implicit in biblical faith. But neither does the persistence
of religious commitment throughout the analysis necessitate
falling into the extremes of subjectivity.

53. The deficiency of liberation theologies (and their Marxist
or neo-Marxist ideological underpinnings) of which I speak
is certainly not absolute or across-the-board. Adopting
Berger's idea of the dominant movement of modernization
and various movements of "counter-modernization" and the
inevitability of "modern" components in the counteractions
we are inclined to view even classical Marxism as in many
respects a movement of de-modernization, particularly vis·
a vis what Marx viewed as the primary instrument of the
demonic facets of modernization, i.e. capitalism. On the
other hand, Marxism was itself a post-Enlightenment
phenomenon, sharing and even advancing the Enlightenment's
critique of religion and traditional cultures as well as
capitalism's faith in progress via science, industrialization and technology (see Jose Miguez Bonino, Christians
and Marxists [Grand Rapids: Eerdmans, 1976], pp. 44,48,
50,61 and M.M. Thomas, Christian Response to the Asian
Revolution, pp. 14-16).

The neo-Marxism of Marcuse and others has departed radically from Marx's embracement of technology. A critique of
technology surfaces as well in liberation theology along
with an attempt to avoid a strictly materialistic notion of
liberation (see Hugo Assmann, A Theology for a Nomad Church,
[Maryknoll: Orbis, 1976], pp. 34,57, Gustavo Gutierrez,
A Theology of Liberation, p. 36). Miguez Bonino also
criticizes liberal theology for its tendency to allow the
bourgeois values of modernity to undercut biblical

authority (idem. p. 31).

At the same time I am inclined to agree with Paul Abrecht's
assessment that liberation theology has generally (or to
this point) yet to go far enough in its criticism of
modernization and technology. ("The U.S. Christian and the
World Struggle," Christianity and Crisis, Aug. 16, 1976,
pp. 186-91.) In an article which is also dependent on
Berger's analysis of modernization Van Harvey points out the
short-sightedness of third world theologies in general and
liberation theology in particular vis a vis the religious
challenge of modernization:

> "All the evidence indicates that the Third World is
> also rushing headlong toward modernization, of which
> the primary carriers are industrialization, technology,
> and bureaucratization. These structural monoliths,
> as have been shown, create distinctive modes of think-
> ing that, for the sake of simplicity, we call rational-
> istic. With modernization there will come those prob-
> lems the Westerner now faces: social mobility, rising
> educated classes, the dichotomy between the public and
> the private spheres, the hegemony of science and
> technology, the pluralization of life-worlds, and
> the "homelessness" of modern individualistic culture.
> What leads the Third World theoligians to think they
> can avoid this travail? Do they think that socialism,
> with its emphasis on the common good, will prove the
> the antidote to this rootlessness of capitalistic
> culture? One may be excused for having doubts about
> this. But even were it so, it should not be forgot-
> ten that socialism itself is a product of the Western
> (Faustian) will to truth. There is, therefore, some-
> thing ironical in the recent demand of Third World
> theologians to their colleagues in the West to become
> Marxist, if by that demand it is imagined that one
> could avoid the liberal problems of reconciling faith
> to the modern mind. Marxism has within it Western
> cognitive standards of truth. How, then, can any
> theologian adopting it long postpone dealing with the
> very questions this ideology raises for religious
> faith?"

Van A. Harvey, "The Pathos of Liberal Theology,"
The Journal of Religion, 56, no. 4 (Oct. 76) pp. 384-5.

54. This abstractness can only be effectively countered
     through biblically rooted <u>institutional</u> contents (counter-
     cultural models of community, etc.) that demonstrate human-
     izing alternatives to the dominant and dehumanizing insti-
     tutional aspects of modernization. The problem is not mere-
     ly one of countering the <u>cognitive</u> structures of modernity
     with ones derived from the biblical tradition but of work-
     ing these biblical contents outward (or "downward") into the
     institutional level. These institutional forms will not be
     mere replicas of N.T. patterns but will evolve out of a
     critical dialogue between biblical cognitive and institution-
     al contents on the one hand and an analysis of the dehuman-
     izing facets of modern society on the other. As much
     attention needs to be paid in this hermeneutical process to
     the elements of alien and dehumanizing consciousness-form-
     ation in the contemporary context as to the effort to re-
     incarnate the biblical contents "intact." The latter
     emphasis uncontrolled by the former can easily lead (as in
     mainstream evangelicalism and fundamentalism) to a selective
     hermeneutic unconsciously captive to modernity.

55. I assume here the dialectical relationship between cognitive
     models and their institutional outworkings or substructures
     argued by Peter Berger and Thomas Luckmann in <u>The</u> <u>Social</u>
     <u>Construction</u> <u>of</u> <u>Reality</u>. This approach need not and in fact
     does not assume that the theology behind the practice is al-
     ways explicitly worked-out or self-consciously held. The
     "theology" implicit in practice may be pre-theoretical in
     character.

56. In Gutierrez' critique of the "distinction of planes" model
     of the "New Christendom" phase in Roman Catholic missiology
     and his own alternative view of salvation history radically
     integrated with the history of liberation we have a good
     exposition of the two basic types of which I speak here.
     (See <u>A</u> <u>Theology</u> <u>of</u> <u>Liberation</u>, pp. 63-77, 149-187.)

57. See note 34, above.

58. See Friedrich Gogarten, <u>op</u>. <u>cit</u>., and Harvey Cox, <u>The</u> <u>Secular</u>
     <u>City</u> (New York: Macmillan, 1965) pp. 17-37. On the char-
     acter of the secular theologies emerging after World War II
     as legitimating of secularization (and a Christianity
     accommodated to secularization) see Peter Berger, <u>The</u> <u>Sacred</u>
     <u>Canopy</u>, pp. 155-171 and "A Sociological View of the Secular-
     ization of Theology," <u>Journal</u> <u>for</u> <u>the</u> <u>Scientific</u> <u>Study</u> <u>of</u>
     <u>Religion</u>, Vol. 6, no. 1 (Spring 1967), pp. 3-16. On the
     character of modernizing movements in the world religions
     generally as <u>ex</u> <u>post</u> <u>facto</u> legitimations of social change
     and secularization see Donald Eugene Smith, <u>Religion</u> <u>and</u>

Political Development,(Boston: Little, Brown, and Company,
1970), pp. 201-245. The more recent turn against the
optimism regarding modernization which underlay the secular
theology movement as well as the increased sensitivity to
the ideological character of secular theology comes to
expression in Rosemary Ruether, "A Second Look at Secular
Theology," Journal of Religion, Vol. 5, 1971, pp. 206-215.

59.   Themes from Bonhoeffer's Letters and Papers are commonly
referred to as the germ of the post-War theological rapprochement with secularization. That liberation theology is
a part of this rapprochement (though in a Marxist rather
than in a liberal mode) is in part demonstrated by the
formative influence of Bonhoeffer on the liberation theology
movement itself (see Julio De Santa Ana, "The Influence of
Bonhoeffer on the Theology of Liberation," The Ecumenical
Review, XXVIII, No. 2 [Apr. 1976], pp. 188-197. That
Bonhoeffer himself (and his works taken as a whole) retained
a higher emphasis on the distinctiveness of the church than
comes to expression in most post-War uses of his later
themes--and as legitimation of the general trend towards
cultural optimism after the war--is evident in the claim
Visser 'T Hooft makes for the influence of Bonhoeffer on the
"let the Church be the Church" emphasis in the ecumenical
movement prior to 1940 (see W.A. Visser 'T Hooft, op. cit.,
pp. 198-203).

60.   It is clear that I am here opting for the "defensive" and
sectarian (vs. the accommodating and non-sectarian) option
isolated as one of the two possible theological and institutional responses to secularization by Peter Berger (see
The Sacred Canopy, pp. 153,164). The defensive posture does
not in this case imply a "return" to the Christendom model
nor to the legitimation of oppressive political regimes
associated with medieval Christianity. Our vision instead
is for a prophetic witness enabled by an earnest attempt to
allow the N.T. vision of reality and the Kingdom (in contrast to its secularized version in capitalism or Marxism)
to provide our authoritative base-line. This will allow us
in turn to withstand more effectively the dehumanizing
facets of secular culture as well as to stand more
effectively in solidarity with its victims.

61.   It is surprising how little attention is given in contemporary
theological discussion to the problem of the secularization
of the Church. One of the few theologians to give the problem serious attention is Langdon Gilkey (see Naming the
Whirlwind, pp. 102,181 and his earlier work, How the Church
Can Minister to the World Without Loosing Itself [New York:
Harper & Row, 1964]). Despite the correctness of Gilkey's

charge that Barth and the "biblical theologians" recognized
insufficiently the impact of secularization on the church
itself (and hence the magnitude of the erosion of the
communicability of traditional Christian concepts to the
church as well as to the surrounding culture) the greater
emphasis on the transcendence of the Gospel over culture in
the "Barthian" period did yield sharp attacks on secular
influences in the church including the church's absorption
into capitalist culture. (See for example H. Richard
Niebuhr, Wilhelm Pauck, and Francis P. Miller, The Church
Against the World, [Chicago: Willett, Clark and Company,
1937].) The depths of the church's secularization was also
a latent concern behind H. Richard Niebuhr's Social Sources
of Denominationalism. See also E. Brunner, op. cit., Peter
Berger, The Noise of the Solemn Assemblies, (Garden City,
N.Y.: Doubleday, 1961); Gabriel Vahaman, The Death of God,
(New York: Braziller, 1961), pp. 3-78, and Jacques Ellul,
False Presence of the Kingdom, (New York: Seabury, 1972).

62.   On the threat of "secular Constantinianisms" see Leslie
      Newbigen, op. cit., p. 34ff. That the rise of secular
      culture is laden with religious conflict (between tradition-
      al and secular religions and "quasi-religions") is affirmed
      by Paul Tillich (Christianity and the Encounter of the World
      Religions, [New York: Columbia University Press, 1963]).
      Tillich's analysis is rich with insight into the profoundly
      religious character of the transition to modernity. While
      he generally affirmed the transition from medievalism as a
      step forward he was also acutely aware of the demonic
      features of modernization--features which in his mind
      clustered about the system of capitalism. Correspondingly,
      Tillich was less prone to posit the notion of a neutral
      secular sphere.

63.   It is one of the burdens of John Howard Yoder's The Politics
      of Jesus to challenge this notion and to affirm the ethical
      relevance of the N.T. Yoder's position carries hermeneutical
      implications in the areas of "worldview" or "consciousness"
      as well as in the areas of political and ethical stance.
      These former areas are brought out more directly in an un-
      published paper "Understanding the Bible on its Own Terms."
      An implication of our agrument is that without the possibil-
      ity of a biblical (vs. cultural) baseline for belief and
      action there can be no "insertion" into the history of
      modernization sufficient to withstand or challenge its
      totalitarian and dehumanizing impact on belief, values, and
      institutional forms. The decisive accommodation to modernity
      in the "integrationist" models is, therefore, the hermeneut-
      ical one--i.e. the concession to modernity's own relegation
      of the N.T. documents to a dead and unrepeatable past. The

"biblical theology" movement, now widely heralded as out-
dated if not defeated by the secularizing trend in theology
since 1960, sought to challenge modernity's hermeneutic at
precisely this point and to resurrect the biblical contents
to an authoritative, applicable status. In the period of
"neo-orthodoxy," however, this restoration of biblical contents was achieved most often by the adoption of a vertical-
ist "time/eternity" scheme (Barth, Tillich, Bultmann) which
depreciated in its own way the N.T. integration of cosmic
and horizontalist-eschatological outlooks.

Recently contemporary theology's hermeneutical accommodation
to modernity has been challenged by Robert Wink: "By de-
taching the text from the stream of my existence biblical
criticism has hurled it into the abyss of an objectified
past. Such a past is an infinite regress. No amount of
devoted study can bring it back. The biblical writers
themselves never treated their own past in such a manner.
Their past was a continual accosting, a question flung in
their paths, a challenge, and a confrontation. But because
the scholar has removed himself from view, no shadow from
the past can fall across his path. He has insulated himself from the Bible's own concerns. He examines the Bible,
but he himself is not examined--except by his colleague in
his own guild." (The Bible in Human Transformation,
[Philadelphia: Fortress Press, 1973], p. 4. See also
pp. 36,37 for Wink's view that biblical criticism is an
accommodation to the ideology of secularism and liberalism.)
In Salvation in History, pp. 324-325, Oscar Cullman expresses the conviction that solidarity with salvation history
reduces our solidarity with our national and cultural
history. This same conviction lies behind Miguez Bonino's
reservations with the more radical integrations of the
Kingdom and liberation history in theologies of liberation
(Doing Theology, p. 136).

64. In the article "Technology and Mission," (Stephen Neill,
The Dictionary of the Christian World Mission, [London:
Lutterworth, 1970], pp. 589-590) Donald McGavran displays
little sensitivity to the negative aspects of technology,
its possible religious contents, or its probably secularizing effects. I believe it is fair to say that by-and-
large the Church Growth School regards modernization in
positive terms and primarily in terms of the responsiveness
to the Gospel produced in its wake (via urbanization, etc.).
Correspondingly there is a paucity of reflection within the
School on the deeper theological and sociological meanings
of "conversions" to a "gospel" so radically encapsulated
in the advancing industrial civilization or presented as a
"cure" for industrialization's anomic effects.

There is likewise little in the Church Growth "arsenal" as
such that would offer those oppressed by modernization with
anything more than an opiate which discourages efforts towards radical change of the oppressive aspects of modernization.

The too facile equation of modernization with church growth
encouraged by McGavran's own emphases (if not advocated by
him in precisely these terms) appears in the title of an
article by a loyal Fuller alumnus William R. Read ("Church
Growth as Modernization," A.R. Tippett, ed., God, Man and
Church Growth, [Grand Rapids: Eerdmans, 1973], pp. 188-89).
Fuller's emphasis on modern technology as a neutral tool and
perhaps even a positive offshoot of the Gospel comes to expression in the writings and efforts of Ralph Winter as well
as in C. Peter Wagner's endorsement of Robert Schuller's
harnessing of technology and affluence for church
growth (see Wagner's Foreword to Robert Schuller, Your
Church Has Real Possibilities, [Glendale, Calif: Regal,
1974]).

On the other hand a more cautious and perhaps even critical
attitude towards technology and Westernization also comes
to expression in The School of World Mission. McGavran
himself has been a leader in the battle against ethnocentrism
in mission without apparently being conscious of the ethnocentrism latent in the technology and modernization he would
harness for church growth. In keeping perhaps with the
characteristic sensitivity of anthropology to the issue of
ethnocentrism Fuller anthropologists Tippett and Kraft tend
to moderate the overly optimistic (and ethnocentric?)
approach of their colleagues to technology, urbanization,
and modernization. Tippett's Solomon Islands Christianity
displays deep sensitivity to the tremendous cultural and
religious problems created by urbanization (London:
Lutterworth, 1967, pp. 94-99,330-341). Charles Kraft's
work in "ethotheology" potentially relativizes the cognitive
superiority of science and technology no less than that of
Western philosophy and theology.

65. Thomas Luckmann, The Invisible Religion, (New York:
     Macmillian, 1967.

66. For documentation relevant to the tendency of the evangel-
     ical missionary message to promote middle class values and
     status in Latin America see Charles Denton, "Protestantism
     and The Latin American Middle Class," Practical Anthropology,
     18, 1971, pp. 24-28. An urgent priority in missiological
     research is to determine the role of various models of
     missionary presence and proclamation (in terms of both their

theological and institutional contents) in the formation and
legitimation of classes exerting the power behind the opres-
sive dynamics of modernization. Such research would carry
forward into contemporary non-Western contexts (and with a
focus on the missionary enterprise as a "carrier" of sentiments fostering modernization) the work of Max Weber.
There is already an expanding body of research and literature on this general problem but little, to my knowledge,
with a particular focus on the role of the missionary
enterprise in this process. (See Robert Bellah, Religion
and Progress in Modern Asia, [New York: The Free Press,
1965] and S. N. Eisenstadt, The Protestant Ethic and
Modernization, A Comprative View, [New York: Basic Books,
1968].)

67.   "The Christianity which engaged in missionary action begin-
      ning in the eighteenth century was the Christianity of an
      already profoundly secularized society, that is to say, of
      a society where the churches had become societies differen-
      tiated in relation to the global society. They certainly
      exercised a large influence over this society, but the
      principal structures of this society were in the process of
      secularization. It was already possible to live in these
      societies without being Christian. Denominational member-
      ship had become a private affair or was on the way to be-
      coming it. The pietist overtones of many missionary
      societies were precisely a reflection of this situation,
      which can be characterized by a sort of dichotomy: on the
      one hand, existence in the global society, and on the other
      hand, more or less free and willing membership in a church."
      Roger Mehl, The Sociology of Protestantism, (Philadelphia:
      The Westminster Press, 1970, p. 173). See also Elmer S.
      Miller, "The Christian Missionary, Agent of Secularization,"
      Anthropological Quarterly, 43, 1970, pp. 14-22.

68.   The religionist Harold Turner has displayed unique sensi-
      tivity to this particular problem: "The Christian world
      has not yet reckoned with this striking fact, that its
      main expansion so far has been either into primal cultures
      or into those more sophisticated cultures that retained a
      primal form of religion. As a consequence Black Africa and
      Oceania represented only the second substantial expansion
      of faith into a major geographical and cultural area,
      comparable to the first extension into the Mediterranean
      and European peoples. And further: after the initial
      spread into the Mediterranean world, Christianity has de-
      pended in each of these advances upon alliance with a
      culture more sophisticated than that of the peoples it was
      winning." ("A Further Dimension for Missions: New
      Religious Movements in the Primal Societies," International

Review of Mission, LXII, No. 247 [July, 1973], p. 322.)

This insight of Turner's opens up the important question of pre-modern analogues to the alliance of Christianity with a "modernizing" society and the possible incongruities between the "conversions" produced in the wake of such alliances and those resulting from a missionary proclamation not so entwined with the ideology of a technically superior culture. Gregory Baum's recognition of the alliance between missionary proclamation and imperial ideology since the 4th Century leads him to despair entirely of recovering a distinctive missionary message in the present situation ("Is there A Missionary Message?" Mission Trends No. 1, Gerald Anderson and Thomas Stransky, eds. [Grand Rapids: Eerdmans, New York: Paulist Press, 1974], pp. 81-86). However much missiologists would like to retreat from Baum's radical conclusion neither the fact that he cites nor its missiological implications can be intelligently ignored.

69. This would seem to be the case especially if Martin Marty is correct in regarding evangelicalism as the new American mainstream and if the American mainstream is the crucial force behind the oppressive dynamics of world-encompassing modernization (see Martin Marty, "Tensions Within Contemporary Evangelicalism. A Critical Appraisal," The Evangelicals, David F. Wells and John D. Woodbridge, eds., [Nashville: Abingdon, 1976], pp. 176,178).

70. Advocates of the model I here promote should be realistic about its inherent instability from a historical and sociological point of view. John Yoder has pointed out that sects which combine radical political goals with a commitment to spiritual, non-violent means frequently dissolve either into violent revolutionary movements or spiritualistic monasticism. Sociologists tell us that sects in general tend towards greater adaptation to the dominant culture as they themselves face the problem of transmitting their values from one generation to the next. I see no ultimate, "packaged" solutions to these dilemmas. Neither do these dilemmas settle the theological or ethical question of the merits of this model. We are not here adovcating a total withdrawal from modernity and much less supposing that such a withdrawal is actually possible even if it were desirable. We are adovcating a counter-cultural stance that is sensitive to the integrality of modernity's values and institutions and struggles continually to counterpose them with the N.T. vision of the servant community (incarnating, imperfectly) the Kingdom's presence, actively seeking its relative incarnation in the larger cultural processes, and eagerly awaiting its full

arrival in God's consummation of history. In contrast to
liberation theology, we believe a focus on capitalism is
too short-sighted and narrow, and its tendency to exchange
the role of the Church with the role of the revolutionary
cadre unfaithful to the N.T. model of the Church in relation
to the coming of the Kingdom.

BIBLIOGRAPHY

Aagaard, Johannes, "Trends in Missiological Thinking During the Sixties," International Review of Mission, LXII, No. 245 (Jan., 1973), pp. 8-25

Albrecht, Paul, "The U.S. Christian and the World Struggle," Christianity and Crisis, August 16, 1976, pp. 186-92.

Alves, Rubem, A Theology of Human Hope, Washington, D.C.: Corpus Books, 1969.

_____, Tomorrow's Child: Imagination, Creativity and the Rebirth of Culture, New York: Harper and Row, 1972.

Barth, Karl, The Humanity of God, Atlanta: John Knox Press, 1974.

Baum, Gregory, "Is There A Missionary Message?" Missions Trends No. 1, Gerald Anderson and Thomas Stransky, eds. New York and Grand Rapids: Paulist Press and Eerdmans, 1974, pp. 81-86.

Bellah, Robert, ed., Religion and Progress in Modern Asia, New York: Free Press, 1965.

Berger, Peter, The Noise of the Solemn Assemblies, Garden City, N.Y.: Doubleday, 1961.

_____, Pyramids of Sacrifice: Political Ethics and Social Change, New York: Basic Books, 1974.

_____, The Sacred Canopy: Elements of A Sociological Theory of Religion, Garden City, N.Y.: Doubleday (Anchor), 1967.

_____, "A Sociological View of the Secularization of Theology," Journal for the Scientific Study of Religion, Vol. 6, no. 1 (Spring, 1967), pp. 3-16.

_____, Brigitte Berger and Hansfried Kellner, The Homeless Mind: The Modernization of Consciousness, New York: Random House, 1973.

_____ and Thomas Luckmann, The Social Construction of Reality: A Treatise in the Sociology of Knowledge, Garden City, N.Y.: Doubleday (Anchor), 1966.

_____ and Richard John Newhaus, Against the World for the World, The Hartford Appeal and the Future of American Religions, New York: Seabury, 1976.

Bonhoeffer, Dietrich, Letters and Papers from Prison, New York: Macmillan, 1967.

Brown, Dale, The New Christian Revolutionary, Grand Rapids: Eerdmans, 1971.

Brunner, Emil, "Secularism as a Problem for the Church," International Review of Mission, Oct. 1930, pp. 495-511.

Childs, Brevard S., Biblical Theology in Crisis, Philadelphia: The Westminster Press, 1970.

Costas, Orlando, The Church and its Mission, Wheaton, Ill: Tyndale, 1974.

_____, Theology of the Crossroads in Contemporary Latin America, Amsterdam: Rodopi, 1975.

Cox, Harvey, The Secular City, New York: Macmillan, 1965.

Cullman, Oscar, Salvation in History, New York: Harper & Row, 1967.

Dayton, Donald, Discovering an Evangelical Heritage, New York: Harper, 1976.

_____, "The Holiness Churches: A Significant Ethical Tradition," The Christian Century, Feb. 26, 1975, pp.197-200.

_____, "Recovering a Heritage," The Post American, June/July, 1974 through April, 1975.

Dennis, James, Christian Missions and Social Progress: A Sociological Study of Foreign Missions, Edinburgh: Oliphant, Anderson and Ferrier, Vols. I and II, 1897 and Vol.III,1906.

Denton, Charles, "Protestantism and the Latin American Middle Class," Practical Anthropology 18, 1971, pp. 24-28.

Dussel, Enrique, History and the Theology of Liberation, Maryknoll, N.Y.: Orbis, 1976.

Eisenstadt, S.N., ed., The Protestant Ethic and Modernization: A Comparative View, New York: Basic Books, 1968.

Elliot, Charles, Patterns of Poverty in the Third World: A Study of Social and Economic Stratification, New York: Praeger, 1975.

Ellul, Jacques, False Presence of the Kingdom, New York: Seabury, 1972.

_____, The Presence of the Kingdom, New York: Seabury, 1967.

_____, The Political Illusion, New York: Random House (Vintage), 1972.

_____, The Technological Society, New York: Random House (Vintage), 1964.

Escobar, Samuel, "Evangelism and Man's Search for Freedom, Justice, and Fulfillment," Let the Earth Hear His Voice, J.D. Douglass, ed., Minneapolis: World Wide Publications, 1975, pp. 303-26.

Foster, George M., Traditional Societies and Technological Change, New York: Harper and Row, 2nd ed., 1973.

Gilkey, Langdon, How the Church Can Minister to the World Without Loosing Itself, New York: Harper and Row, 1964.

_____, Naming the Whirlwind: The Renewal of God Language, Indianapolis: Bobbs-Merrill Co., Inc., 1969.

_____, Religion and the Scientific Future: Reflections on Myth, Science, and Theology, New York: Haper & Row, 1970.

Dill, David M., "The Secularization Debate Foreshadowed, Jerusalem, 1928," International Review of Mission, LVII, No. 227 (Jul. 1968), pp. 334-57.

Gish, Arthur, The New Left and Christian Radicalism, Grand Rapids: Eerdmans, 1970.

Gogarten, Friedrich, Despair and Hope for Our Time, Philadelphia: Pilgrim Press, 1970.

Goodall, Norman, Christian Missions and Social Ferment, London: Epworth Press, 1964.

Gutierrez, Gustavo, A Theology of Liberation, Maryknoll, N.Y.: Orbis, 1973.

Hallencreutz, Carl F., New Approaches to Men of Other Faiths, 1938-1968, Geneva: W.C.C., 1969.

Hardesty, Nancy and Letha Scanzoni, All We're Meant to Be, Waco, Texas: Word, 1974.

Harvey, Van A., "The Pathos of Liberal Theology," The Journal of Religion, Vol. 56, no. 4 (Oct. 1976), pp. 382-91.

Herberg, Will, "The Social Philosophy of Karl Barth," Karl Barth,
    Community, State, and Church, Gloucester, Mass: Peter
    Smith, 1968, pp. 11-67.

Hoekendijk, J.C., "Missiological Observations," Christopaganism
    or Indigenous Christianity, Tetsuano Yamamori and Charles
    Taber, eds., Pasadena: William Carey Library, 1975,
    pp. 143-52.

Houtepen, Anton, Theology of the 'Saeculum:' A Study of the
    Concept of 'Saeculum' in the Documents of Vatican II and
    of the World Council of Churches, 1961-1972, Kampen:
    J.H. Kok, 1976.

Illich, Ivan, Deschooling Society, New York: Harper, 1971.

Jewett, Paul K., Man: Male and Female, Grand Rapids: Eerdmans,
    1975.

Lanternari, Vittorio, The Religion of the Oppressed, New York:
    Knopf, 1963.

Lerner, Daniel, "International Cooperation and Communication in
    National Development," Communications and Change in the
    Developing Countries, Daniel Lerner and Wilbur Schramm, eds.,
    Honolulu: The University of Hawaii Press, 1967, pp. 103-25.

_____, The Passing of Traditional Society, Glencoe,
    Ill: Free Press, 1958.

van Leeuwen, Arend Th., Christianity and World History, New York:
    Charles Scribners Sons, 1964.

Lehman, Paul L., "The Concreteness of Theology: Reflections on
    the Conversation between Barth and Bonhoeffer," Footnotes
    to a Theology: The Karl Barth Colloquium of 1972, Martin
    Rumscheidt, ed., Corporation for the Publication of Academic
    Studies in Religion in Canada, 1974, pp. 53-76.

Luckmann, Thomas, The Invisible Religion, New York: Macmillan,
    1967.

Marcuse, Herbert, One Dimensional Man, Boston: Beacon Press,1964.

Marty, Martin, The Modern Schism: Three Paths to the Secular,
    New York: Harper, 1969.

_____, "Tensions Within Contemporary Evangelicalism, A
    Critical Appraisal" The Evangelicals, David F. Wells and
    John D. Woodbridge eds., Nashville: Abingdon,1975, pp.170-88.

McGavran, Donald, "Technology and Mission," The Dictionary of the Christian World Mission, Stephen Neill, Gerald Anderson, and John Goodman, eds., London: Lutterworth, 1970, pp. 589-90.

Mehl, Roger, The Sociology of Protestantism, Philadelphia: Westminster, 1970.

Meland, Bernard, The Secularization of Modern Cultures, New York: Oxford University Press, 1966.

Miguez Bonino, Jose, Christians and Marxists, Grand Rapids: Eerdmans, 1976.

_____, Doing Theology in a Revolutionary Situation, Philadelphia: Fortress, 1975.

Miller, Elmer S., "The Christian Missionary: Agent of Secularization," Anthropological Quarterly, 43 (1970), pp. 14-22.

Mollenkott, Virginia Ramey, Women, Men, and the Bible, New York and Nashville: Abingdon (upcoming).

Moltmann, Jurgen, "An Open Letter to Jose Miguez Bonino," Christianity and Crisis, March 29, 1976, pp. 57-63.

Mott, John R., The Decisive Hour of Christian Missions, New York: Educational Department of the Board of Foreign Missions of the Presbyterian Church in the U.S.A., 1910.

_____, The Evangelization of the World in This Generation, New York: S.V.M. Press, 1900.

Mott, Stephen, "The 'Politics of Jesus' and Our Responsibilities," The Reformed Journal, Feb. 1976, pp.7-10.

Mouw, Richard, Political Evangelism, Grand Rapids: Eerdmans,1973.

_____, Politics and the Biblical Drama, Grand Rapids: Eerdmans, 1976.

_____, "Weaving a Coherent Pattern of Discipleship," The Christian Century, August 20-27, 1975, pp. 728-31.

Nazario, Victor, "Theological Education for the Third World: Searching for Fundamental Issues," Learning in Context, The Search for Innovative Patterns in Theological Education, London: Theological Education Fund, 1973, pp. 18-26.

Neill, Stephen, Colonialism and Christian Missions, New York: McGraw-Hill, 1966.

_____, A History of Christian Missions, Baltimore:
     Penguin, 1964.

_____, "Secular, Secularism, Secularization," The
     Dictionary of the Christian World Mission, Stephen Neill,
     Gerald Anderson and John Goodman, eds., London: Lutterworth
     Press, 1970, pp. 545-47.

Newbigen, J.E. Leslie, "The Gathering up of History into Christ,"
     The Missionary Church in East and West, Charles West and
     David Paton, eds., London: S.C.M., 1959, pp. 81-90.

_____, Honest Religion for Secular Man,
     Philadelphia: Westminster, 1966.

_____ and M.M. Thomas, "Salvation and Human-
     ization, A Discussion," Mission Trends No. 1, Gerald
     Anderson and Thomas Stransky, eds., Grand Rapids: Eerdmans
     and New York: Paulist Press, 1974, pp. 217-29.

Niebuhr, H. Richard, The Kingdom of God in America, New York:
     Harper and Row, 1937.

_____, The Social Sources of Denominationalism,
     New York: Henry Holt and Co., 1929.

_____, Francis P. Miller and Wilhelm Pauck, The
     Church Against the World, Chicago: Willett Clarke and
     Co., 1935.

von Oppen, Dietrich, The Age of the Person, Philadelphia:
     Fortress Press, 1969.

The Other Side, Savannah, Ohio 44874

Padilla, Rene, "Christianity and the World," Let the Earth Hear
     His Voice, J.S. Douglass, ed., Minneapolis: World Wide
     Publications, 1975, pp. 116-46.

_____, The New Face of Evangelicalism, Downers Grove,
     Ill.: InterVarsity Press, 1976.

Pannell, William, My Friend, the Enemy, Waco: Word, 1968.

Panikkar, K.M., Asia and Western Dominance, London: George
     Allen and Unwin, Ltd., 1953.

Parsons, Talcott, The System of Modern Societies, Englewood
     Cliffs, N.J.: Prentice-Hall, 1971.

The Post American (Now Sojourners, 1029 Vermont Ave., N.W.,
    Washington, D.C. 20005.)

Preston, Ronald, ed., Technology and Social Justice, Valley
    Forge: Judson Press, 1971.

Quebedeaux, Richard, The Young Evangelicals, New York: Harper
    and Row, 1974.

Right On (Now Radix, Box 4307, Berkeley, Ca. 94704.)

Ramseyer, Robert, "The Anabaptist Vision and Our World Mission
    (I)," Mission-Focus, Vol. 4, No. 4 (March, 1976), pp. 1-6.

Read, William R., "Church Growth as Modernization," God, Man,
    and Church Growth, A.R. Tippett, ed., Grand Rapids:
    Eerdmans, 1973, pp. 188-98.

"Response to Lausanne," International Review of Mission,
    Vol. LXIII, No. 252 (Oct. 1974) pp. 547-76.

Ribeiro, Darcy, The Civilizational Process, New York: Harper,
    1968.

Rogers, Everett M., Modernization Among Peasants: Impact of
    Communications, New York: Holt, Rinehart, and Winston, 1969.

Rubingh, Eugene, "Missions and Secularization," International
    Reformed Bulletin, 56 (1974), pp. 24-35.

Ruether, Rosemary R., "Augustine and Christian Political
    Theology," Interpretation, XXIX, No. 3 (Jul. 1975),
    pp. 252-65.

_____, "Libertarianism and Newcolonialism: The
    Two Faces of America," Christianity and Crisis, Aug. 16,
    1976, pp. 180-83.

_____, A Second Look at Secular Theology,"
    The Journal of Religion, Vol. 51 (1971), pp. 206-15.

Runyan, Theodore, "Secularization and Sacrament: Reflections on
    the Theology of Friedrick Gogarten, The Spirit and Power
    of Christian Secularity, Albert Schlitzer C.S.C., ed.,
    Notre Dame: University of Notre Dame Press, 1967, pp.
    pp. 123-55.

Santa Ana, Julio De, "The Influence of Bonhoeffer on the Theology
    of Liberation," The Ecumenical Review, XXVIII, No. 2,
    (Apr. 1976), pp. 188-97.

Sapsezian, Aharon, "Theology of Liberation-Liberation of Theology," Theological Education, IX, No. 4 (Summer, 1973), pp. 254-67.

Savramis, Demosthenes, "Theology and Society: Ten Hypotheses," Technology and Social Justice, Ronald H. Preston, ed., Valley Forge: Judson Press, 1971.

Semmell, Bernard, The Methodist Revolution, London: Heinemann, 1973.

Shank, David, "Shape of Mission Strategy," Mission-Focus, Vol. 1, No. 3, (Jan. 1973).

Sider, Ronald, ed., The Chicago Declaration, Carol Stream, Ill.: Creation House, 1974.

_____, Rich Christians in an Age of Hunger, Downers Grove, Ill.: InterVarsity Press, forthcoming.

Sinai, I.R., The Challenge of Modernization: The West's Impact on the Non-Western World, New York: W.W. Norton, 1964.

Skinner, Tom, Words of Revolution, Grand Rapids: Zondervan, 1970.

Smith, Donald E., Religion and Political Development, Boston: Little, Brown, and Co., 1970.

_____, ed., Religion and Political Modernization, New Haven: Yale University Press, 1974.

Smith, R. Gregor, ed., World Come of Age, Philadelphia: Fortress Press, 1967.

Sojourners (1029 Vermont Ave., N.W., Washington, D.C. 20005).

Stott, John R., Christian Missions in the Modern World, London: Falcon, 1975.

Stringfellow, William, An Ethic for Christians and Other Aliens in a Strange Land, Waco: World, 1973.

Tawney, R.H., Religion and the Rise of Capitalism, A Historical Study, New York: Harcourt, Brace and World, 1926.

Thomas, M.M., The Acknowledged Christ of the Asian Renaissance, London: S.C.M., 1969.

_____, The Christian Response to the Asian Revolution,

London, S.C.M., 1966.

_____, "Modernization of Traditional Societies and the Struggle for a New Cultural Ethos," The Ecumenical Review, Vol. XVII, No. 4, (1966), pp. 426-39.

_____, "A Rewarding Correspondence with the Late Dr. Henrik Kraemer, Religion and Society, Vol. xiii, No. 2 (June 1966), pp. 5-15.

_____, "Christ's Promise within the Revolution: The Meaning of Evangelism and Service in the Post War World," Religion and Society, Vol. VIII, No. 1 (1961), pp. 15-25.

_____ and J.L. Newbigin, "Salvationand humanization, a Discussion," Mission Trends, No. 1, Gerald Anderson and Thomas Stransky, eds., Grand Rapids: Eerdmans, New York: Paulist Press, 1974, pp. 217-29.

Tillich, Paul, Christianity and the Encounter of the World Religions, New York: Columbia Uniersity Press, 1963.

_____, The Religious Situation, New York: Meridian, 1956.

Tippett, A.R., Solomon Islands Christianity, London: Lutterworth, 1967.

Toynbee, Arnold, America and World Revolution, New York: Oxford University Press, 1962.

_____, Civilization on Trial and The World and the West, New York: Meridian, 1958.

_____, A Study of History, 2 Vol. abridged edition, by D.C. Somervell, New York: Oxford University Press, 1947 (Vol. 1) and 1957 (Vol. II).

Troeltsch, Ernst, Protestantism and Progress: A Historical Study of the Relation of Protestantism to the Modern World, Boston: Beacon Press, 1958.

Turner, Harold, "A Further Dimension for Missions, New Religious Movements in Primal Societies, International Review of Mission, Vol. LXII, No. 247 (July, 1973), pp. 321-37.

Vahanian, Gabriel, The Death of God: The Culture of our Post Christian Era, New York: George Braziller, 1961.

Van Leeuwen, Arend Th., Christianity in World History, New York:
    Charles Scribner's Sons, 1964.

Vanguard (229 College St., Toronto, Ontario M5T 1R4, Canada).

Voegelin, Eric, Israel and Revelation (Order and History, Vol.1),
    Baton Rouge: Louisiana State University Press, 1956.

Visser 'T Hooft, W.A., "Dietrich Bonhoeffer and the Self-Under
    standing of the Ecumenical Movement, The Ecumenical Review,
    Vol. XXCIII, no. 2 (Apr., 1976), pp. 192-94.

Wagner, C. Peter, "Forward," Your Church Has Real Possibilities,
    Robert H. Schuller, Glendale, Calif: Regal, 1974.

Wallis, Jim, Agenda for Biblical People, New York: Harper and
    Row, 1976.

Warren, M.A.C., "The Christian World Mission in a Technological
    Era," The Ecumenical Review, Vol. 17, (1965), pp. 219-23.

_____, The Missionary Movement from Britain in Modern
    History, London: S.C.M. Press, 1965.

Weber, Max, The Protestant Ethic and the Spirit of Capitalism,
    New York: Charles Scribner's Sons, 1958.

West, Charles, "The Meaning of the Secular," (Report on the
    Consultation of University Teachers, The Ecumenical
    Institute, Bossey, Sept. 15-20, 1959.

_____, "Mission in East and West, Missionary Church in
    East and West, Charles West and David M. Paton, eds.,
    London: S.C.M. Press, 1959, pp. 117-31.

_____, The Power to be Human: Towards a Secular
    Theology, New York: Macmillan, 1971.

Wilson, Brian R., Contemporary Transformations of Religion,
    New York: Oxford University Press, 1976.

_____, Magic and the Millenium, A Sociological Study
    of Religious Movements of Protest Among Tribal and Third
    World Peoples, New York: Harper and Row, 1973.

_____, Religion in Secular Society: A Sociological
    Comment, Baltimore, Penguin Books, 1966.

Wink, Walter, The Bible in Human Transformation, Philadelphia:
    Fortress, 1973.

World Council of Churches, <u>Christians</u> <u>in</u> <u>the</u> <u>Technical</u> <u>and</u> <u>Social</u>
<u>Revolutions</u> <u>of</u> <u>our</u> <u>Time</u>, (World Conference on Church and
Society, 1966, Official Report), Geneva, W.C.C., 1966.

_____, <u>To</u> <u>Break</u> <u>the</u> <u>Chains</u> <u>of</u> <u>Oppression</u>,
Geneva, W.C.C., 1975.

Yoder, John Howard, "The Biblical Mandate," <u>The</u> <u>Chicago</u>
<u>Declaration</u>, Carol Stream, Ill.: Creation House, 1974,
pp. 88-116.

_____, <u>The</u> <u>Christian</u> <u>Witness</u> <u>to</u> <u>the</u> <u>State</u>,
Newton Kansas: Faith and Life Press, 1964.

_____,"The Otherness of the Church," <u>Concern</u>,
No. 8, pp. 19-29.

_____, <u>The</u> <u>Politics</u> <u>of</u> <u>Jesus</u>, Grand Rapids:
Eerdmans, 1972.

8

Contemporary Roman Catholic Understanding of Mission

Tim Ryan

Introduction:

A search for the contemporary view of mission in the Catholic
church puts one in contact with a bewildering variety of voices,
as often clashing with dissonance as blending harmoniously. To
do some measure of justice not only to the variety but also to
the relative strength and particular sources of the sounds one
hears is no simple task. I would be the first to admit that no
attempt at a single overview can do complete justice to such a
complex reality.

However, a particularly extraordinary opportunity to gain a
focus that is broad and serious has been presented to us over
the last three years. That opportunity was the Fourth International Bishops Synod on Evangelization. A representation of
bishops from Catholic churches throughout the world met in Rome
for the month of October, 1974. They represented opinions gathered by extensive consultations in their respective churches
over the period of the previous 18 months. And their discussions culminated one year later in an Apostolic Exhortation of
Pope Paul VI that was meant to represent the final fruits of
their discussions. The unfolding of this process gives us a
rare glimpse at how different areas and segments of the church
view a central, albeit diffusingly general theme. It seemed to
me an irresistibly interesting subject for a body such as this,
and also as valid a single focus as one could hope for in any
attempt to present a broad spectrum of contemporary Catholic
views on mission.

I. A Brief Delineation of the Process to be Examined and of the Material Available.

1)   The Document *"The Evangelization of the Modern World"*, prepared by the Vatican for the use of the Episcopal Conferences in preparation for the Synod. (mid 1973) *(1)*

2)   Documents prepared by various groups within the national churches for presentation to their conferences and the documents submitted by the National Conferences to the Secretariat for the preparation of the Synod in Rome. There is a mound of these documents available (mostly through private circulation unfortunately.) They are a tremendously fertile source of information about where national church Bishops conferences stood on the questions surrounding Evangelization. And many do the same for specific groupings within the national churches. *(2)*

3)   *"Working Paper for the Use of Members of the General Assembly"* *(3)* From the "abundant material" received in the replies of the Episcopal Conferences to the 1st Document *("The Evangelization of the Modern World")*, The Council of the Secretariat chose "certain questions, concerning which a deeper discussion could be had at the next Synod."

4)   The Proceedings of the Synod itself. Extracts from many of the speeches made by delegates during the Synod, the full texts of a good number of the speeches, the full texts of the Pope's opening and closing addresses, the Statements approved by the Synod, etc. are published for example in La Documentation Catholique, Nos. 1663 and 1664, of Nov. 8 and 17, 1974. The Declaration of the Synod Fathers and the Address of Philip Potter, Gen. Sec. of the WCC are published in the I.R.M., July, 1975.

5)   Reporting on the Synod. A particularly complete coverage is found in America (7 articles) with articles as well in Commonweal, Herder Korrespondenz, New York Times, etc. *(4)*

6)   Post Factum assessments of the Synod. (i.e. W. Marravee in Eglise et Theologie 6 (1975), Archbishop Carter in IRM, July, 1975).

7)   *"Pope Paul's Exhortation on Evangelization in the World"*, Vatican, Dec. 8, 1975 (Crux, Jan. 19, 1976.)

II. *"The Evangelization of the Modern World"*.

The first document prepared by the secretariat to stimulate discussion by the National Conferences opens with an attempt to settle on a common definition of evangelization for the purposes

of achieving some measure of common focus. Of the four possible
definitions listed, the Document opts for a middle ground: *"the
activity whereby the Church proclaims the Gospel so that faith
may be aroused, may unfold and may grow." (P. 6)* It thus attempts to avoid allowing the discussion to center on any activity
*"whereby the world is transformed in accordance with the will of
God"*; while not restricting it solely to *"the first proclamation
of the Gospel to non-Christians."*

The first section of the Document is dedicated to a *"Survey
of Evangelization in the Contemporary World Situation."* Certain
elements of the contemporary situation are assessed as favouring
evangelization -- for example, searchings for new life-styles
and meaning, for personal authenticity, and a common quest of
religions and ideologies for peace and justice. But other elements are possible hindrances -- secularization and atheism,
social change and the internationalization of influences in the
world; uncertainty, disagreement and institutional critique
within the church.

The second section of the document attempts a theological evaluation of the situation thus described. It reminds us that
the initiative for evangelization comes from God who chose to
reveal Himself in Christ and through his church. The response
of faith brings human personality to full development and is
meant for all persons. The authors then launch into an examination of the "fruit" of certain guidelines concerning evangelization put forward by the Second Vatican Council. Singled out
as sources of concern are teachings of the Council on the presence of the salvific influence of Christ outside the Church,
Freedom of Conscience, stress on the qualitative rather than
quantitative spread of the faith, the presence of genuine religious values in non-Christian religions, the humanity of
Christ, the importance of the 'signs of the times', and the
necessity to adapt the faith to all cultures.

The Theological evaluation ends with a list of apparent contradictions that must be eliminated by giving due weight to
complementary truths. The seeming contradictions are listed as
opposing: objective teaching to personal religious experience;
witness to proclamation; conversion as death to conversion as
new life; evangelization as a purely religious experience to
evangelization as merely human development; the building up of
the church to working for the salvation of humankind; internal
church reform to preaching the Gospel; promoting unity to calling
out of the world; ecumenism to proclamation of the whole truth
of the Gospel.

The final segment of this first document is devoted to a set
of guidelines and suggested practical applications. Their content

and exhortatory style suggest an unwillingness to allow that the troubling issues raised in the first two sections should have any significant effect on carrying on with present efforts.

III.   *Some of the Documents Submitted as Responses by the National Conferences.*

Although a careful analysis of all these documents would be extremely interesting and important for our purposes, it is obviously beyond the scope of the present paper to undertake anything nearly so ambitious. What can be done is a perhaps interesting representative comparison of the responses from the Americas, though in very brief form.

The Canadian reaction is a highly analytical response to the First Document in its language, form and content. Reactions to content in the Canadian church are "very varied and even contradictory." "There was a strong negative reaction to many of the questions." "Perspectives regarding the contemporary world are falsified by the fact that negative elements take up three times as much space in the document as positive ones." The Canadian church asks for a more positive use of the Theology of Creation and Redemption of the *Gaudium et Spes* document of Vatican II. "Secularization and changes in social conditions and values, to the extent that they are not fundamentally evil, neither assist nor impede evangelization. Rather they express new situations in which believers must find appropriate means for being present." *(5)*

The response to the First document prepared by the Latin American Bishops Conference takes a very different tack. While mentioning the Vatican document in the introduction, the response makes no further reference to it and is singularly uninfluenced by its approach. Rather, it attempts "to start from a particular, historical context" in order to "bring out important differences between the Church of Latin America and Churches in other continents." *(6)* A lengthy introduction to the history of evangelization in Latin America is followed by sections on the present socio-economic and political context. Then come two sections dealing with cultural qualities particularly marking the Latin American religious reality. Only in the last half of the forty-page study do we come to a study of the content, principles and agents of evangelization. The overall approach of the document is a concrete demonstration of the principle of evangelization enunciated on page 26: "The evangelizer is dealing with two poles that he must bring together: the revealed message and the present historical reality." "Medellin's apt formula was: 'Be faithful to the revealed word, incarnate in current happenings'."

When one picks up the reply of the U. S. bishops after reading through the Latin American document, he or she cannot help but be struck by the marked contrast in approaches. If we could term the Latin American approach "an examination of context", we would have to term the U. S. approach as "an examination of conscience." After a general confession of a "wide agreement that existing Catholic communities were not presently doing an effective job of evangelization," *(7)* the document proceeds to examine some specific failings. Over-concern with administration, lack of pastoral visitations, failure to effectively use the liturgy, weakness of parish structures, as yet ineffective pastoral councils and priests' Senates are singled out as structural weaknesses. With regard to content, there surfaces some disarming disagreement about effectiveness. "Many felt ...... that by preaching the 'social Gospel' evangelization was rendered far more effective than in the past," while an archbishop complained "that concern for social work has been exaggerated to the extent that the core teachings of the Church have been neglected. The practice of the Catholic faith is no longer seen as the challenge that it once was and this ...... has led to indifferentism." *(8)*

Just between these three National and Regional responses, there is ample material for an extensive analysis of differing views and approaches to the question of evangelization. We must content ourselves here with a single area of contrast that is striking and significant. There are clearly differing attitudes on how the world and human history relate to the process of evangelization. The U. S. document begins where the Roman schema did. It centers its attention immediately on the church's performance and looks to the world only for indications of significant areas of influence on that performance. The Canadian response begins from a similar immediate concentration on the church, but looks to the world as having a significant role in determining what type of evangelization is to be employed in any given place and time. It is the Latin American contribution that carries this emphasis the furthest. It begins with a lengthy discussion of the historical and social context before it even begins to define evangelization or interpret the church's performance. The revealed word to which we are called in faithfulness is "incarnate in current happenings." The world is no longer simply a conditioning influence on the effectiveness of evangelization. It is constituent element of that evangelization. Unless each place and time is properly understood and interpreted, no true discovery of the Gospel itself is possible.

IV.   *"Working Paper for the Use of Members of the General Assembly"*.

Having tried above to contrast but three contributions under a single standard of comparison, we can certainly sympathize

with the task of the General Secretariat of the Synod as it
attempted to synthesize 98 replies from all over the world. *(9)*
That attempt at synthesis was followed by an effort to choose
"certain questions concerning which a deeper discussion could be
had at the ... Synod." The result is a 27-page paper divided
into two parts.

Part I consists of an "exchange of experiences." Replies
from around the world indicate "a certain propensity for a more
intense interior life." "Everywhere today small communities
arise and spread spontaneously." *(10)* A series of questions
follows on the effectiveness of Pastoral and Presbyteral councils and on the role of the laity and the young in the life of
the churches. The existence of a great many Christians who
continue to believe but who maintain no regular relationship
with the church community is noted. A more positive assessment
of ecumenism appears than in the 1st Synod preparation document.
The important thing is "that all the churches, by a common
effort, lead the men of our time to Christ." *(11)* There follows
a discussion on experiences of dialogue with non-Christian religions and ideologies and of relationships between the "Churches
of ancient Christianity" and the "new churches." Finally a
subject is raised which will occupy much space in the second
part of the document: "What can be done to direct the effort
for human advancement toward the integral salvation of man,
without allowing the faithful, while building the terrestrial
city, to become alienated from the Christian vocation?" This
first section ends with mention of use of the Mass media and
the liturgy in evangelization.

In Part II ("Connected Theological Questions"), certain theological themes are raised that might do well to be treated explicitly by the Synod. The initiative of the Holy Spirit occu-
pies first place among the suggestions. It is seen as important
that the Divine initiative be stressed in order to remind us
that there are diffused in the world "seeds of the Word" and
that men's hearts are prepared before us. These pages focus
squarely on the particular theological element that we singled
out for comparison in the Canadian, U.S. and Latin American
documents. "In which manner can the authentic signs of God's
presence and purpose be deciphered in the happenings, needs and
desires of our times?" and "in non-Christian religions and
ideologies." *(13)* Surely a central question in regard to evangelization and one that will occupy much attention during the
Synod.

A second theological theme singled out for attention is the
word "evangelization", i.e. "the complex of activities by which
men are brought to share in the mystery of Christ." "Evangelization in its integrity cannot be understood, if the testimony

of charity does not shine; if the sacraments are not administered,
if institutions are not established ..... without the preaching
of the knowledge of Christ." *(14)* Evangelization is linked with
witness. "Nearly all the Replies of the Episcopal conferences
speak of witness, and affirm that witness belongs intrinsically
to the concept of preaching, so that even if preaching cannot be
replaced ordinarily by mutual witness, nevertheless the effectiveness of preaching depends in great part on the active testimony of life." Among all the ways in which testimony is given,
charity should stand out, not only in individual relations but
in struggling so that "social and political structures may be
transformed." *(15)*

A fourth theological discussion deals with the relationship
between evangelization and the church. While reiterating that
one can share in the life of Christ outside the church, it is
asserted that those within the church "enjoy greater benefit."
(16) It is because of this fact that calling others to the
church is not ecclesiastical self-seeking but "a manifestation
of love towards Christ and men." *(17)*

The paper ends with a brief section on the nature of conversion and one on Salvation as the goal of Evangelization. It is
this final topic that touches on another key area of theological
tension that receives a great deal of attention in all the preparatory documents and at the Synod itself. Simply put, what is
the relationship between salvation and liberation? The studied
attempt at a "both" ..... "and" relationship between the two
demonstrates the degree to which real consensus does exist in
the church. All are agreed that we cannot hold for a simple
opposition between the two realities, much less reject either
one or the other. Still the juxtaposing engaged in by this
document leaves one deeply uneasy that a facile synthesis is
being sought which will simply not hold together on a non-verbal
level. "Salvation on the one hand is essentially eschatological"
..... "on the other hand it throws a new light on the earthly
reality." "Salvation is intimately connected with human progress
and liberation." "Evangelization, even though it does not tend
directly to earthly progress moves the disciples of Christ to
cooperate ..... towards the edification of the world." *(18)*
Obviously the desire for consensus does not find here very satisfying expression. Much will be said at the synod on this subject.
It is in the interventions of the Latin American and French
bishops that we will come upon far more satisfying theological
syntheses of these respective emphases than we find anywhere
else in the process - including the final Apostolic Exhortation.

V. *The Synod Proceedings.*

The Work of the Synod followed a three-step agenda. First

came a sharing of experiences, with 88 different interventions being made by the participants. Secondly an attempt was made to clarify doctrinal concepts and principles. Finally, there followed a drafting of pastoral proposals for the Pope. A systematic analysis of the total input into this process is of course not feasible. What we can do however is run a rapid survey of the themes that surface repeatedly in the excerpts of the interventions that we have at our disposal. They provide a rare glimpse at what a broad cross-section of bishops throughout the world are most concerned about. Moreover, since many of the interventions were made explicitly in the name of the National Conferences that the delegates represented, we have a pretty fair view of what a number of whole hierarchies throughout the world are agreed upon among themselves.

The theological concern that surfaced in the preparatory documents regarding the relationship between the "seeds of the Word," the "preparation for the Gospel" and evangelization is proven to spring from a widespread and serious pastoral concern. Representatives from India and North Africa, from Japan, Black Africa and the International Orders rose to encourage "the recognition and promotion of the fruits of the Holy Spirit outside the limits of the visible church." *(19)* "In recognizing in the positive elements of these religions and ideologies the gifts of divine providence, we hope that the Grace of God will use these gifts for the salvation of the non-Christian." *(20)* Nor is this type of concern restricted to areas where contact with dominant non-Christian world religions is an unavoidable fact of life. A real appeal is heard from secularized Europe to have "the courage and serenity necessary to discern values that come from God and to insert oneself into an agnostic, hostile and even anti-humanist atmosphere." *(21)* "Living and speaking in a universe ..... fashioned by the scientific intelligence that reduces the unknown to the knowable and calculable, we must avoid speaking of God in terms that make him a travesty." *(22)*

A corollary to the recognition of fruits of the Spirit outside the Church is the necessity to receive those fruits within the Church when they are filled out and completed through conversion. "The Church must prove its openness to assimilate all the positive values of art, architecture, liturgy, etc." *(23)* The African bishops show themselves particularly sensitive to the question of allowing the church to shed the trappings of its missionary origins in favour of an authentic local cultural expression. Cardinal Malula of Kinshasa, speaking in the name of the 52 bishops of Zaire, recalls the legacy that the Church there bears for having been "one of the pillars of the tripartite Colonial regime of Government, the Church and Business." *(24)* "They were able to write here 'In Black Africa, Christ is the prisoner of White Christianity.'" *(25)*

Such an acceptance of local values and expressions means the establishment of a real universal pluralism: still an extremely troubling prospect for the predominantly monolithic structure of the Catholic church. A great deal was said at the Synod about the need for a growing acceptance of pluralism. "It is inevitable that the encounter of the Gospel with different cultures creates a diversity of expressions, for each culture has its signs, its symbols, its images, its language, its methodology. A certain pluralism in the liturgy, ecclesiastical discipline, in spiritual traditions and in some way in theology and catechetics is understandable. By theological pluralism we must understand co-existence - not of opposed theologies but of complementary theologies, in the sense that each one of them is a partial expression of the same integral truth. Pluralism deriving from diverse cultures ought to be considered a grace and an enrichment." *(26)* The concern for an acceptance of real pluralism is not the concern only of those engaged in new evangelization. It is also the obvious concern of those concerned with ecumenical dialogue. Cardinal Willebrands, President of the Vatican Secretariat for Christian Unity makes a similar plea: "The plurality of theological opinions and liberty of expression within the limits of the unity of the Catholic faith are of fundamental importance for dialogue. Theological pluralism damages neither the certitude nor the unity of the faith." *(27)* There are also strong appeals for "an audacious and dynamic decentralization," *(28)* and a relaxation of the domination of the Roman over the oriental rites within the Catholic church. *(29)*

Both the traditional "receiver" and "donor" countries under old mission relationships make an appeal for change. "The task of the missionary is not finished. But they must work within a new context, with a spirit of total availability to the local churches. The aid that they bring is not almsgiving that enriches the donor and humiliates the receiver. It is, on the contrary a sign of charity and humble service, an effective sign of caring for the universal church." *(30)* As the representative of the Belgian bishops puts it: "There is no denying that there is a certain disarray in the mission field ... The difficulties invite us to a new manner of mission cooperation between the different churches, beginning with a frank and open dialogue." *(31)*

A final theme attracting our attention in the Synod interventions is that of the relationship between Salvation and liberation - certainly one of the questions that most bedeviled the preparatory discussions. It is also one that we remarked did not seem to have found a very satisfying synthesis in the working paper provided for the delegates. It was predictable that the Latin American representatives would be the ones to address themselves most urgently to this question. Such in fact

was the case. As Cardinal Arns of Sao Paulo, Brazil, explains
in his written submission to the Synod: "The act of conversion
is the liberation from sin and the battle to efface its consequences ..... It is the liberation from evil but also the liberation for good, for living in the world a life of light, truth
and freedom. This encounter is a theological reality by which
man realizes his true humanity and integral liberation ......
Hope becomes the critique of all utopias and the demand to battle against the forces of death active in history." *(32)*

Two issues that were the subject of the last Synod are obviously still matters of great concern. African representatives
in particular point out the continued desire for an ordained
ministry more adapted to their needs. *(33)* One could only wish
that the connection between this appeal and the subsequent discussions and pronouncements on how evangelization can be advanced had been more seriously analyzed. And the issue of justice
in the world received some extremely stimulating structural analysis by two bishops at opposite ends of the present unbalanced
world order. *(34)*

The Declaration of the Synod.

Joseph Connors pointed out in the article he wrote before the
Synod opened that it was beginning without any schema of a final
text. Previous synods had had rough drafts. To begin without
one left it all dramatically up to the members of the synod to
produce something from scratch within the short four weeks at
their disposal. *(35)* A great deal of the discussion over the
relative success or failure of the Synod revolved around the
fact that it did in fact fail to produce any such comprehensive
final document. *(36)* The draft proposal of such a final statement prepared by a special Synod committee was completely rejected by the delegates on Tues., Oct. 22. This doomed any hope
of expressing real theological clarifications and presenting
concrete pastoral proposals before the ending of the Synod four
days later. *(37)* All that the Synod found it possible to do was
to issue a "Declaration" manifesting "some fundamental convictions and a few of the more urgent guidelines to further promote
and deepen the work we began." *(38)*

The document begins: "We wish to confirm anew that the mandate to evangelize all men constitutes the essential mission of
the church." (para. 4) The necessity is especially urgent for
those to whom the Good News has not yet been brought. It is a
mission that pertains to all members of the church and a grati-
fyingly humble appeal is made to the young "as particularly
suited to evangelize others." (5) The carrying out of this
mission demands "incessant interior conversion" and continual
community renewal. It requires an ability to discern the "signs

of the times" and to recognize the action of the Spirit at work
in all human history. Difficulties singled out for attention by
the document are secularization, atheism, lack of religious
liberty, the difficulty of "appropriate translations of the evangelical message" to different times and places and to the demands
of dialogue.

A final, relatively long segment of the short declaration
deals with the relationship between Liberation and Evangelization,
an indication of the importance accorded by the participants to
this question. It is asserted that the bishops "experienced
profound unity in reaffirming the intimate connection between
evangelization and ... liberation." (12) By evangelizing the
church "can do much to bring about the integral salvation or the
full liberation of men. She can draw from the gospel the most
profound reasons and ever new incentives to promote generous
dedication to the service of all men - the poor especially, the
weak and the oppressed - and to eliminate the social consequences
of sin which are translated into unjust social and political
structures." (12)

The declaration ends on a moving and sustained note of hope.
"While trying to be faithful to its mission in today's world,
the church commits itself completely to the service of the
future world ...... The time which occurs between Easter and the
Parousia is the time of tension and aspiration towards the world
which must come." (13)

The Closing Address of Paul VI.

The reporter for America in the fifth of his "Synod Jottings"
articles classified this speech as the "Yes ...... BUT" type
response that he sees as so much a part of the "Italian way."
(39) Certainly what leaps out at one after having read through
the enthusiastically positive assessment of the Synod with which
it begins is a section on "Points That Require Further Precision." The Pope points out that it was satisfying to hear so
much said with praiseworthy spontaneity and sincerity. But, it
cannot all be maintained without some qualification. Significantly, the first reservations deal with interventions that
address themselves to the relationship between the universal and
local churches. Local responsibility which is assumed must not
destroy solidarity with other churches and with the Pope. The
role of the Pope must not be reduced to certain extraordinary
circumstances. *(40)* Another area of concern over unity closely
related to this structural one is that which springs from adaptation of the gospel to different racial, cultural and social
contexts. It seems dangerous to the Pope to carry talk of this
plurality to the point of speaking of "diversified theologies."
Either the content of the faith is Catholic or it disappears."*(41)*

While human liberation has been rightly stressed, "the totality of salvation is never equivalent to one or the other liberation. The Good News will always retain its originality." *(42)*
Small communities must retain their links to ecclesiastical authority.

What is perhaps most instructive about the significance of
these reservations is the role in which the Pope casts himself
while making them. He does so, he says, "because our duty is
that of the sentinel who watches at the beginning of paths on
which the church embarks. ...... We cannot allow false directions to be taken." *(43)* Perhaps a great deal more light could
be shed on the particular type service that Papal pronouncements
and authority are meant to render to the church if that image
were kept in mind. The pilgrim band which is the church may
need sentinels at danger points from time to time on its journey.
But it will move nowhere if it has only sentinels to listen to.
Sentinels it must have, but also scouts and leaders and visionaries and guides.

The large number of bishops from all parts of the world who
took part in the Synod were called to function there as scouts,
leaders, visionaries and guides to the universal church. The
value of the Synod process rests in having given those path-
breaking services a systematic channel for communication with
the church at large and with the world. A Catholic who looks
back on this and other Synods cannot help but ask him or herself
quite urgently if establishing that type of communication in the
universal church only once every three years is anywhere like
enough. In other words is not some manner of universal voice
necessary in the church at all times to balance the warnings of
the "sentinel" with calls to travel on and directions to follow?
It is evident that Catholic church structure at the universal
level has a good distance yet to travel if it is to serve the
Church adequately in this regard.

A final reflection on the link between the functional role of
the Synod and that of the Pope is in order if we are to be in a
position to place the final document that we will study in its
proper perspective. When it was realized by the bishops that
they would be unable to produce a synthesis of their delibera-
tions before the end of their time together, they decided not
only on the brief declaration we summarized above. They also
resolved "to offer the integral fruits of our exchange to the
Holy Father with great confidence and simplicity, and to await
new impetus from him." *(44)* Joseph Connors in his final assessment of the Synod in <u>America</u> remarks that "one can only specul-
ate upon the major impact that may yet come indirectly from the
Synod. The theological clarifications and pastoral directives
that can give a new and long overdue impetus to evangelization

in the modern world may yet be offered to the church and to the
world in the form of a Papal encyclical." *(45)* Connors was a
good prophet! One year later such a Papal document did appear
and it will form the subject of the last chapter of this paper.

With that document in hand however, we cannot help but be
less sanguine than Connors about its possible value as the
"major impact" of the Synod. It was certainly true that: "Of all
the many Popes in this century who have written on this theme,
none has had the opportunity that Pope Paul now has of address-
ing himself to the task while the voices of leading bishops from
every part of the world are still echoing about him and their
reports and speeches are stacked before him." *(46)* But in view
of the role the Pope explicitly set out for himself in his closing discourse and the consequent tone that he felt called to
adopt, one should be little surprised that the "Apostolic Exhortation on Evangelization" is a disappointing mirror of the full
fruits of the Synod process. There is certainly a message in
this for future Synods. Comprehensive reports on an overall
process should not be left to those with significant responsibility to guard over a single facet of the process. If the
Synod is meant to speak to the Pope it should not be forced into
the position of having to do so through his voice. The implications of this assessment for the particular Synod that we have
been concerned with are also clear. We must take a systematic
look at the whole process and at all its stages in order to gain
the light that it has to shed on the subject of evangelization.
A dependence on the final document of the Pope alone would be a
mistaken and impoverishing use of valuable insights into central
concerns facing the church today.

VI. *Pope Paul's Apostolic Exhortation on Evangelization In
     The World.*

The exhortation begins with a reference to the action of the
Synod in remitting to the Pope the fruits of its labours and
awaiting from him a fresh forward impulse. (Para. 2) *(47)* "Our
words come from the wealth of the Synod and are meant to be a
meditation on evangelization." (3)

The message opens in fact on a strong note of exhortation:

> *"The Gospel message is not an optional contribution for
> the Church. It is a duty incumbent on her by the comm-
> and of the Lord Jesus, so that people can believe and
> be saved. This message is indeed necessary. It is
> unique. It cannot be replaced. It does not permit
> either indifference, syncretism or accommodation. It
> is a question of people's salvation. It is the beauty
> of the Revelation that it represents. It brings with*

it a wisdom that is not of this world. It is able to
stir up by itself faith - faith that rests on the
power of God. It is truth. It merits having the apos-
tle consecrate to it all his time and all his energies,
and to sacrifice for it, if necessary, his own life."
(5)

The presentation then proceeds to draw the link between Jesus'
proclamation of the Kingdom by word and sign to the vocation of
the church which "exists in order to evangelize." (14) The pre-
requisite for such a mission is that of "being evangelized herself", a demand including the call to "constant conversion and
renewal." (15) But however imperfect the church may be, they
are "certainly misguided" who claim "to love Christ but without
the church." (16) The Exhortation next moves on to a definition of evangelization, all of whose essential elements must be
kept in view. The church in evangelizing seeks to bring about
an "interior change" to convert "both the personal and collective
consciences of people." (17) She seeks this transformation not
only by reaching greater numbers by by "upsetting ...... mankind's criteria of judgment .... values .... thought .... and
models of life." (19) The gospel is capable of permeating all
cultures "without becoming subject to any one of them." (20)

"Above all the Gospel must be proclaimed by witness," but
this alone 'always remains insufficient.' (21) It must be "made
explicit by a clear and unequivocal proclamation." (22) But
proclamation in its turn is only fully developed when accompanied
by "adherence to a programme of life ..... to the Kingdom .....
the 'new world' ..... the new state of things ..... which the
Gospel inaugurates." (23)

The content of evangelization includes acceptance of God as
loving Father and Jesus as a salvation which is not merely "imm-
inent" but "transcendent and eschatological" and which includes
"the prophetic proclamation of a hereafter."(27-28) It embraces
the preaching of "brotherly love for all men" and of "the mystery of evil and of the active search for good." (28)

Moreover, "evangelization would not be complete if it did not
take account of the unceasing interplay of the Gospel and of
man's concrete life, both personal and social." (29) "Between
evangelization and human advancement - development and liberation - there are in fact profound links." These links are held
to be of an anthropological order - (a concrete socio-economi-
cally involved person is being evangelized) as well as of a
theological (the plan of creation and redemption are but one)
and evangelical order (the command of charity). (31)

This having been said, we must also not ignore the fact that
many generous and sensitive Christians are "frequently tempted
to reduce the mission (of the church) to the dimensions of a
simply temporal project." The salvation announced would be reduced to simple material well-being and the preoccupations of
the church would be merely initiatives of the political and social order. (32) The Church "reaffirms the primacy of her spiritual vocation and refuses to replace the proclamation of the
kingdom by the proclamation of forms of human liberation." (33)
"The church links human liberation and salvation in Jesus Christ
but she never identifies them." She is aware that "the most
idealized systems soon become inhuman if the inhuman inclina-
tions of the human heart are not made wholesome." (36) "The
church cannot accept violence." It is "uncontrollable" and moreover "sudden or violent changes of structures would be deceitful,in-
effective of themselves, and certainly not in conformity with the
dignity of the people." (37) "The church is becoming ever more
conscious of the proper manner and the strictly evangelical means
that she possesses in order to collaborate in the liberation of
the many." She does so by encouraging Christians to devote
themselves to liberation. The church's social teaching must be
the foundation of their wisdom "without confusion with tactical
attitudes or with the service of a political system." (38)

Next comes a section on "The Methods of Evangelization." Once
again the connection between witness and proclamation is stressed.
Proclamation must be not only verbal but consider modern insights
into the importance of images. Use of the liturgy, catechetics
and the mass media are stressed while the importance of personal
contact is not to be forgotten.

The reflection of a notable Synod concern is evident in a
section on "popular piety." It is seen as "rich in values" and
making people "capable of generosity", giving them "awareness of
profound attitudes of God" and "engendering interior attitudes."
"One must be sensitive to it" with a view of helping it "overcome its risks of deviation" and leading many to "a true encounter with God in Jesus Christ." (48)

The section on methods is followed by one on "The Beneficiaries of Evangelization." A "limitless universality" must be
the goal in spite of all obstacles from within and from without.
It includes those who can be as yet reached only by "pre-evan-
gelization" - "evangelization in the true sense although ....."
at its ..... still incomplete stage." (51) It extends also to
those "innumerable people who have been baptized but who live
quite outside Christian life." (52) It is addressed "to the
immense sections of mankind who practice non-Christian religions."
The Church "respects and esteems" those religions which "carry
within them the echo of thousands of years of searching for God"

and are all "impregnated with innumerable 'seeds of the Word'."
But the respect the church bears them and the complexity of
questions raised with regard to relating to them is not "an invitation to the church to withhold from these non-Christians the
proclamation of Jesus Christ," "which establishes with God an
authentic and living relationship which the other religions do
not succeed in doing." (53) Even those influenced by secularism,
"man-centered atheism" and "consumer society" must be addressed
and their world too is not without its "real stepping stones to
Christianity ..... at least in the form of a sense of emptiness
or nostalgia." (55)

A special sub-section is devoted to a discussion of the Ecc-
lesial "Communautes de Base" which were much discussed in the
preparations and proceedings of the Synod. They are described
as the spiritual and religious extension "of the small sociological community such as the village." Members may be linked
by age, culture or other characteristics or interests. There
is concern that such communities avoid engaging "in bitter criticism of the church," cutting themselves off from its outward
manifestations and "quickly falling victim to some political
option or current of thought ..... with all the attendant risks
of becoming its instrument." (58)

The final two sections of the Exhortation contain little
original material that would attract our particular interest.
The comments on "Workers For Evangelization" encourage all in
the church to engage in active evangelization, each according to
his or her own gift. All should do so in a spirit of unity with
the church. There is a particular appeal to the individual
churches to avoid withering isolationism in their relationship
to the universal church. Finally, "The Spirit of Evangelization"
should be fostered by a deep interior openness to the spirit, a
reverence for the truth, and a love for those to whom we address
ourselves. Proposing the truth of the Gospel should in no way
be considered "an attack on religious liberty" but rather a
clear commitment "fully to respect that liberty which is offered a choice of a way that even non-believers consider noble
and uplifting." (80)

The Apostolic Exhortation is a deadeningly long document. It
reminds one somewhat of those six-hour speeches by Party chair-
men to Communist Party Congresses that we hear so much about. It
tries too hard to speak of everything and to say all the essentials about everything.

But there are upsetting things about the document that go beyond its form. There is a numbing cautiousness about its approach, a blandness that seems to flow from an effort at absolutely tranquil motion. The structural problem we raised in the

introductory remarks to the document seem to me to be largely
responsible for this.

There is a widespread impression today that significant things
are happening in our world that call for dramatic initiatives by
the church. A clear reflection of that impression appears in
the preparations for the Synod and in many, if not most, of the
interventions of the delegates. It seems to me that it is that
spark which is the hope of the Gospel in our day. We must not
allow the cautious and calibrated tone of the final stage of the
process we have followed to smother it.

Moving beyond this discussion of general tone to a consideration of content, there is a very great deal in the exhortation
that we cannot help but rejoice at. There can be no doubt that
adaptation, pluralism, values in other religions and ideologies,
the relationship of salvation of liberation, etc. are vital
issues in the church's present search for how to live and spread
the spirit of Christ today. It is also clear that no significant segment of the church is interested in drawing back from
positions on these questions that have been steadily applied
since Vatican II.

However, there remains considerable malaise within the church
on these issues. The syntheses presented in the Apostolic Exhortation on these key points do not satisfactorily resolve the
points of contention. Conflicting assertions are simply juxta-
posed. We are told in par. 35 that "the church links human liberation and salvation in Jesus Christ but she never identifies
them."

Surely the eye of the storm that rages in the church over
this issue is concerned precisely with the existence and the
essence of any valid distinction between these two terms and of
the exact relationship between them - if a distinction is in
fact truly necessary. To simply assert that they are different
and yet related is to beg the whole issue.

The failure to achieve consensus on a greater depth of synthesis on these issues flows partly from limitations of the process, as we have seen. But I feel that there is another fundamental contributing factor. One of the facts-of-life demonstrated by the Synod was that context (socio-political, economic,
cultural) determines perspective - on theological as on other
levels. As long as our positions in the world remain as bewild-
eringly diverse and sometimes mutually opposed as they presently
are, we would seem to be most foolhardy to expect easy common
perspectives.

It is this truth on which Philip Potter ended his very fine overview of W.C.C. experience to the Synod fathers. Pluralism, he asserts, is not a danger to the uniqueness of the Gospel, but rather a condition of its universal expression. Thus evangelism is not a strategy that can be worked out by a universal body. "It takes place in a given place and with particular persons and groups. Therefore the base of evangelization is the local church. ..... What matters here is that there be a dialogue between local churches in mutual respect and correction." "Dialogue as a form of evangelization can be credible to those without faith only if the churches and Christians have learned to live this dialogue among themselves as a normal manner of existence." *(48)*

Evangelization is one thing to those whose hunger and thirst are "spiritual" and whose politico-economic structures are easily celebrated as the trouble-free gifts of God. It is another thing for those who are aware of actual human enslavement and whose bodies tremble with undernourishment and pain. Are we to wonder that Latin Americans speak differently of salvation than the North American or European? If the final assessment given of the Synod's search to define evangelization in our day is that we are agreed, then it will have been at the expense of truth. And it will have blunted the call to participate in the march of history where alone we can be saved.

Thus, ironically, Cardinal Felici's questions to Philip Potter, which were seen as an embarrassing confrontation *(49)* were in fact an unwittingly acute perception of the most vital message that the World Council had for the present Catholic church. The search for homogeneous analyses, definitions and strategy is illusory and idolatrous. It is a refusal to struggle with one another in search of the call to conversion that can come only through the discovery of the sin that separates us.

NOTES

1) *The Evangelization of the Modern World,* Vatican City, 1973.

2) By way of example: Evangelization in the Modern World, *Contribution of the Pontifical Commission Justice and Peace,* Canadian Catholic Conference, Feb. 1974 (mimeographed). *Report of the Canadian Canon Law Society,* C.C.C. 1974 (mimeo). *Report on Canadian Reaction to the Pre-Synodal Document,* (C.C.C., Feb. 28, 1974 (mimeo.) *The Reply of the U. S. Bishops,* Jan. 1974, C.C.C. (mimeo). *Certain Aspects of Evangelization in Latin America offered by CELAM to the Forthcoming Synod,* Apr.-May, 1974, C.C.C. (mimeo.)

3) *Working Instrument for the Use of the Members of the General Assembly,* Vatican City, June 7, 1974, Eng. Trans. C.C.C. (mimeo.)

4) Connors, J., "Agenda for Synod '74", *America,* Sept. 28, 1974, pp. 146-47; "Synod Jottings I," *America,* Oct. 12, 1974, pp. 186-87. "Synod Jottings II", *America,* Oct. 19, 1974, p. 205-206. "Synod Jottings III", *America,* Oct. 26, 1974, p. 225; "Synod Jottings IV", *America,* Nov. 24, 1974, p. 246-247; "Synod Jottings V", *America,* Nov. 9, 1974, p. 273; Connors, J. "Synod '74: Success or Failure?", *America,* Nov. 30, 1974, p. 346-348; "The Synod says No", *Commonweal,* Nov. 29, 1974, p. 204; D. A. Seeber, Realitaetsluecken in der Evangelisation, *Herder Korespondenz,* Nov. 1974, p. 553-557.

5) *Report on Canadian Reaction to the Pre-Synodal Document,* C.C.C., 1974, (mimeo.) p. 24.

6) *Certain Aspects of Evangelization in Latin America,* C.C.C., 1974 (mimeo.) p. 2.

7) *The Reply of the U.S. Bishops,* C.C.C., 1974 (mimeo.), p. 2.

8) Ibid, p. 7.

9) Relatio de responsionibus datis ad lineamenta de 'Evangelizatione Mundi huius temporis', C.C.C., 1974 (mimeo.)

10) *Working Instrument for the Use of the Members of the General Assembly,* C.C.C., 1974 (mimeo.), p. 4.

11) Ibid, p. 7.

12) Ibid, p. 8.

13) Ibid, p. 13

14) Ibid, p. 14.

15) Ibid, p. 19.

16) Ibid, p. 23.

17) Ibid, p. 23.

18) Ibid, p. 26.

19) Cardinal Duval, Archbishop of Algiers, Oct. 8, *La Document-ation Catholique,* 17 Novembre 1974, No. 1664, p. 970. (All translations from Doc. Cath. are my translations.)

20) Cardinal Taguchi, Archbishop of Osaka, Oct. 9, *Doc. Cath.* p. 972.

21) Cardinal Poma, Archbishop of Bologna, Oct. 9, *Doc. Cath.* p. 974.

22) Bishop Vial, Bishop of Nantes, Oct. 16, *Doc. Cath.* p. 983.

23) Cardinal Parecattil, Archbishop of Ernaculam, Sept. 30, *Doc. Cath.,* 3 Nov. 1974 - No. 1663, p. 905.

24) *Doc. Cath.,* p. 908.

25) Bishop Bayala, Bishop of Koudougou (Upper Volta), *Doc. Cath.,* p. 912.

26) Dom Weakland, Abbot-Primate of the Benedictine Confedera-tion, Oct. 9, *Doc. Cath.,* p. 971.

27) Oct. 11, *Doc. Cath.,* p. 975.

28) Bishop Carter, Bishop of London (Canada) Oct. 8, *Doc. Cath.* p. 970.

29) Bishop Hermaniuk, Archbishop of the Ukrainian Catholic Archdiocese of Winnipeg, Oct. 1, *Doc. Cath.,* p. 906. Patriarch Maximos Hakim, Patriarch of Antioch of the Mel-kites, Oct. 8, *Doc. Cath.,* p. 971.

30) Bishop Kabangi, Bishop of Luebo (Zaire), Oct. 11, *Doc. Cath.* p. 975.

31) Cardinal Suenens, Archbishop of Malines-Brussels, Oct. 2, *Doc. Cath.* p. 916.

32) *Doc. Cath.* p. 980.

33) Bishop Yago, Archbishop of Abidjan (Ivory Coast), Oct. 2, *Doc. Cath.* p. 907; Cardinal Malula, Archbishop of Kinshasa, Oct. 2, *Doc. Cath.* p. 907.

34) Bishop Kabangi, Bishop of Luebo (Zaire), Oct. 11, *Doc. Cath.* p. 975; Bishop Bernardin, Archbishop of Cincinatti, (written submission), *Doc. Cath.* p. 987-989.

35) J. Connors, "Agenda for Synod '74", *America,* Sept. 28, 1974, p. 147.

36) J. Connors, "Synod '74: Success or Failure?", *America,* Nov. 30, 1974, p. 346-348.

37) *America,* Nov. 9, 1974, p. 273; *America,* Nov. 30, p. 347, *Commonweal,* Nov. 29, 1974, p. 204; *N. Y. T.* Oct. 23, 1974, p. 9.

38) "A Declaration from the Synod", *International Review of Mission,* July, 1975, p. 311-314.

39) *America,* Nov. 9, 1974, p. 273.

40) *La Documentation Catholique,* 17 Nov. 1974, No. 1664, p.953.

41) Ibid

42) Ibid

43) Ibid

44) *I. R. M.,* July, 1975, p. 311.

45) *America,* Nov. 30, 1974, p. 348.

46) Ibid

47) *CRUX* Extra, Jan. 19, 1976, p. 2. All numbers in brackets throughout this section signify the paragraph numbering used in the *CRUX* edition of the Papal Exhortation.

48) *I. R. M.,* July, 1975, p. 318.

49) *America,* Nov. 2, 1974, p. 247; *Doc. Cath.* 3 Nov. 1974, No. 1663, p. 927.

BIBLIOGRAPHY

The Evangelization of the Modern World, Vatican City, 1973.

Evangelization In the Modern World, Contribution of the Pontifical Commission Justice and Peace, Canadian Catholic Conference, Feb. 1974 (mimeo).

Report of the Canadian Canon Law Society, C.C.C. 1974 (mimeo.).

Report on the Canadian Reaction to the Pre-Synodal Document, C.C.C., Feb. 28, 1974, (mimeo.).

The Reply of the U. S. Bishops, Jan. 1974, C.C.C. (mimeo.).

Certain Aspects of Evangelization in Latin America Offered by CELAM to the Forthcoming Synod, Apr.-May, 1974, C.C.C. (mimeo.)

Working Instrument for the Use of Members of the General Assembly, Vatican City, June 7, 1974, Eng. Trans. CCC (mimeo.).

Relatio de responsionibus datis ad lineamenta de 'Evangelizatione Mundi huius temporis', 1974, C.C.C. (mimeo.)

Pope Paul's Apostolic Exhortation on Evangelization in the World, *CRUX* Extra, Jan. 19, 1976; also printed in: *Christ to the World,* 1976, Vol. XXI, No. 1, pp. 2-29.

La Documentation Catholique, No. 1663, 3 Nov. 1974, p. 905-933; No. 1664, 17 Nov. 1974, p. 970-996.

America, Sept. 28, 1974, p. 146-147; Oct. 12, 1974, p. 186-187; Oct. 19, 1974, p. 205-206; Oct. 26, 1974, p. 225; Nov. 24, 1974, p. 246-247; Nov. 9, 1974, p. 273; Nov. 30, 1974, p. 346-348.

International Review of Mission, July, 1975, p. 295-301; p. 311-318.

9

U.S. Conciliar Protestant Concepts of Mission, 1950-1976

J. Walter Cason

It is as difficult to define an ecumenical Protestant as it is
to describe a concept of mission which would fit all the people
in this category.

U.S. ecumenical Protestant churches are separate denominations with somewhat eclectic interests outside themselves. They
form a set or group in the negative sense of not being Roman
Catholic and in not being opposed to some coordination and joint
action. They are generally those affiliated with the National
Council of Churches of Christ in the U.S.A. and with the World
Council of Churches. It should be noted however that less than
5% of their centralized budgets and 1% of their personnel are
allocated to ecumenical agencies. If the funding of interdenominational projects is calculated as a percentage of total
giving through local churches it would be less than 0.5%. These
agencies can be said to stimulate and "represent" one of the
facets of their constituent churches but ecumenical bodies have
never been delegated to make binding decisions for or speak
officially on behalf of these churches.

Ecumenical churches are sometimes called "mainline" or "historic" but these are ambiguous terms. If we are defined by our
leadership, in 1950 our elder statesman in mission was John R.
Mott, and on a world scale during this period we claim Hendrik
Kraemer, D. T. Niles, Stephen Neill and Lesslie Newbigin as well
as Philip Potter, John Gatu, M. M. Thomas and José Miguez-Bonino.
If we are classified by what we read, ecumenical Protestants are

more likely to appreciate the <u>Christian Century</u> rather than
<u>Christianity Today</u>. Many of us have a deep appreciation for
evangelical journals such as <u>Post-American</u> (now <u>Sojourner</u>) and
<u>The Other Side</u> -- in fact probably more enthusiasm than most
evangelicals display.

Although denominations are clearly the basic operational
units there is an interest in ideas from a wide variety of
sources including the World Council, the secular world, the
Roman Catholics, and the conservative Evangelicals. One example
of this is the claim that 60% of those attending the World
Evangelical conference at Lausanne in 1974 were members of
ecumenical protestant denominations.

WHAT IS OUR CONTEXT, 1950-1976?

In January, 1950, Russia had been an atomic power for five
months and Mao Tse-Tung had controlled China for twelve weeks.
India and Pakistan had been independent for three years,
Indonesia was just coming out of Dutch "police action", the
French had four more years in Indochina. Churchill was to serve
as British Prime Minister for five years and then resign saying:
"I decline to preside over the dissolution of Her Majesty's
Empire." Television was an experimental gadget, Sputnik was
seven years away. The Korean War began in the summer of 1950,
Senator Joe McCarthy's search for communists in American state,
society and church was yet to come.

American churches were entering into a period of unprecedented expansion and wealth in suburbia, with a sense of liberal
continuing progress which was not really shaken until the late
1960s. Mission budgets expanded but were not as large a percentage of general giving as in the 1920s, and the number of missionaries abroad was about 60% of that in 1925.

America in the third quarter of the twentieth century has
enjoyed a period of expansion comparable to that of Victorian
England. The transnational business and military thrust of the
U.S. continues to dominate wherever it can and by any means
available. For some Americans there has been a "failure of
nerve," for some a defensive call for isolation and self-suffi-
ciency, at least as an outcome of the Vietnam war. During the
past seven years some mission agencies have experienced a considerable change of orientation, sensing their own weakness to
create a new world and their own complicity in the cultural and
economic imperialism of their homeland.

In view of our national context such boards are moving
toward a greater emphasis on communicating in the U.S.A. both

the good and the evil aspects of American power abroad. There is
a growing awareness of our need for repentance. We also "have
this treasure in earthen vessels" (II Cor. 4:7).

HOW DO WE DETERMINE A CONCEPT OF MISSION?

What do we do?

One test of mission is in the expenditure of financial resources.
"Economic power is still the most crucial power factor in the
western missionary movement. It is still the most important way
that the western missionary expresses his concept of what it
means to 'preach the gospel'." (Quick: 52). An analysis of
funds allocated to projects and operating budgets could indicate
the relative interest in various types of mission if (a) it is
recognized that neither the number of grants or total dollar
value is an absolute gauge of interest, since some types of projects need more money than others, and some just come in smaller
units; and (b) there is some way to take into account the support from other sources to certain emotionally appealing aspects
of mission, such as leprosy work, printing Bibles, and sometimes
the expenses of local parishes. Even where calculations are
made there is an element of uncertainty in that classifications
of specific jobs into categories of work is a matter of personal
judgment. Thus, for instance, we still only have a quantifica-
tion of the opinions of some person or group when the functions
of the Board of World Missions of the Lutheran Church in America
are neatly divided as: 32.9% Communicating the Gospel; 1.1%
Helping Persons Mature; 26.8% Fostering Action in the World;
14.1% Ecumenical Relationships; 13.3% Supporting Personnel; and
11.8% Supporting Organization. (LCA, 1972: 639).

A numerical classification of personnel resources is also
interesting but extremely shaky for comparative purposes since
the methods of reporting vary so widely. United Presbyterians
include in their prayers, and presumably in some of their calculations, all active and retired missionaries (two persons in the
case of each married couple), administrative staff in the
national office, all home missionaries, chaplains, and national
personnel in leadership positions in each country where they
work. (Yearbook, 1972). The Lutheran Church in America, by contrast, provides data on a much smaller portion of their mission
personnel, i.e. foreign "Missionaries Classified By Type of
Service (Wives Excluded)", (LCA, 1972: 647).

In addition to calculations of assignment, a survey of the
attitudes of persons directly employed by a church in mission
should be an indicator as to what actually takes place on the
field. In a 1971 United Methodist survey, 96% of the group did

not think some races are naturally less intelligent than they are; 61% thought foreign imperialism was a major deterrent to development; and 67% would not agree with the statement: "Seeking to change social systems which dehumanize people is not a top priority function of a board of missions." (Davis: 112). Eleven percent disagreed with the theological implication in the questions posed and 8% commented on the inherent ideology of the survey. Revealing as it is, an instrument of this type should only be used for rough impressions and comparisons; it is certainly not possible to conclude, for instance that only 4% of the present missionaries are racists in any way. It would be helpful if comparable studies were available from other denominations and from the early 1950s. Quite apart from the tabulation of answers, the questions posed by a member of staff of the Board of Missions Department of Research and Survey give at least a quasi-official clue to the attitudinal issues considered important by one denomination in 1971.

The attitudes of national leaders in each country are increasingly important as mission boards seek to become more responsive and less directive. Are the present leaders compliant old "mission boys" educated according to the opportunities and ideologies of 30 years ago? Are they a modern intellectual elite? With what segments of their own society do these leaders, and the denominations they represent, identify? Data on such questions is unfortunately not available.

The attitudes and experience of mission board administrative personnel continue to be very crucial--probably more significant for what happens than is the attitude of the church at large or the person-in-the-pew. Has there been more than token utilization of diverse cross-cultural skills in appointing a person with U.S. missional experience to administer work in another part of the world? Are there many nationals from other countries as mission board executives in the U.S.? Are most executives those whose field experience was 20 years ago in the field they now administer? What opportunities for growth do they seem to have utilized? Again it can only be noted that data is not available.

What do we say we do?

The Education & Cultivation material from Boards of Missions should be a convenient source for determining present mission policy. This is true of some of the periodicals and study books which have a clearly educational purpose. It is not the case for the promotional materials which are designed for seeking funds. For example, the Field Representatives for Education & Cultivation of The United Methodist Board of Global Ministries

are a part of the "Advance Office" for raising designated gifts,
thus tending to give an unduly high priority to those stories
which will elicit funds rather than share the challenging story
of trying to be in mission in a difficult area. Some mission
boards consistently deal only with individual conversions,
others describe the same thing in promotional brochures but
detail a concern for social reconstruction and liberation in
other types of publications (such as: Stockwell, 1972; UMC,
1972; UMC, 1974).

Some comparisons can be made, for example, between the audio-
visual produced in 1962 by William F. Fore and the 1975 set produced by Friendship Press. The earlier series includes readings
from James K. Mathews, Charles W. Forman, Gerald H. Anderson,
Eugene L. Smith, Douglas Webster and Lesslie Newbigin. "The
gospel of Jesus Christ is the story of an event which makes all
the difference in history." "All the generations of all the
people of all the lands of all the world are dependent on
whether or not Christians today tell the story of this wonderful
deed God has done. The most important thing that a Christian
can do is to tell" (Fore: 18, 19). The motivation is quite
clear, the task of mission is to be effective in telling the
story.

The 1975 package acknowledges its indebtedness to the earlier
set and adds:

"But in the last quarter of the twentieth century many
things will be much different from the early 1960s. On
the international scene, the cold war has been cooled
by détente; Third World power has grown; indigenous
churches overseas have matured; space travelers have
landed on the moon; artificial communications satel-
lites have made the people of earth more aware of each
other; terms like assassination, equal rights, consciousness raising, world hunger, ICBM's and Indo-China have
gained new meanings in our minds. Our understanding of
the nature of the Christian mission has become more
clarified" (Eye: 1).

It would be an interesting exercise to go through this list,
underlining those items which make some real difference in the
theology and nature of mission. The list does not claim to be
exhaustive, so other items which really have changed the picture
should be added.

The more recent set quotes John 3:16 and Matthew 28:19-20 but
also states that "the church should recognize that God is creatively and redemptively at work in the religious life of

all mankind." There is more stress on dialogue and less on the
essential event of God in the incarnation. There is more on
mission as local action in the U.S. (giving someone a ride to
get their food stamps). Phrases such as "the despair of economic injustice" or working for "development and liberation"
appear but without sufficient analysis to show how we create and
perpetuate such injustices or how we can work to change structures embodying them.

A 1973 packet seeks to discuss the decisions required in supporting mission. A variety of difficult choices are included
but some of the choices related to more traditional evangelism
are expressed rather negatively, such as building a $300,000
church building, "Preaching the Gospel to the heathen," "Converting people to our way of life."

The most strikingly anti-evangelistic pieces which this writer has seen recently are the Friendship Press filmstrip "Mission Is..." and a sound-movie "Something More Than Rice." The
filmstrip of 96 frames is full of color and action with the notable exception of the one frame which says "Mission is preaching and teaching...telling about the Christian faith." This one
is illustrated by two weathered stone figures (Frame 85)! The
movie of the same vintage shows interesting work in Japan, the
U.S. and Nepal but the only reference to conversion is by an
American in Nepal who says that is the sort of thing missionaries formerly did, implying that it shouldn't happen now and
not stating why overt evangelism would be particularly difficult
in Nepal.

No brief filmstrip can be a complete treatise on the nature
of mission but sets of educational material which try to describe the mission of the church should say something compelling
about evangelism throughout the past 25 years, and certainly
today should illustrate vividly our concern for mission as liberation in a way these do not.

What do we say we ought to do?

Among the mission theoreticians are pastors, bishops, modera-
tors, professors and board secretaries. Although the last group
are in the best position to implement their ideas, the literature from all sources should be searched for changing emphases.
We always have regional studies providing background on the work
of mission. These are useful and generally positive tracts produced by denominational and interdenominational groups. A totally new emphasis is found in the series on The Future of the
Missionary Enterprise. These not only talk about the challenge

of nationalism and justice but are detailed dossiers of activist churches in oppressive situations such as Korea, the Philippines, Portugal, Bolivia and Kenya. Such literature may not be widely circulated in the churches now, but probably would not even have been sponsored by U.S. ecumenical Protestants in the 1950s. Another feature of this series - that of being a cooperative effort with the Vatican - would also have been unlikely before 1965.

Topics in missiological theory, expressed for a mass audience, included: the church and nation building (Forman, 1963); the missionary structure of the congregation (Williams; 1964); the reaction against Western missionaries (Scherer, 1964; Dodge, 1964).

In addition to these interpretive works, careful descriptive studies have given us a clearer picture of where and what the church is experienced as being. Among these special mention should be made of the sixteen volumes in the IMC/CWME "World Studies of Churches in Mission" as expressing with sometimes painful clarity what is the faith as practiced.

The interpretive and the descriptive works predominate over the visionary and the strategizing. Is this in any way an unusual feature of the times, or of ecumenical Protestant missions? Perhaps it says only indirectly what we ought to be doing.

How do we change, and how rapidly?

Theory, financial status, existing personnel and external events all help to create change but it is usually exceedingly slow. A basic means of change and growth as Christians is through prayer and worship as we seek the guidance of the Holy Spirit, but even this does not always cause us to move quickly or in the same direction. The Eastern Orthodox make this Trinitarian approach much more obvious than we do--and they are content to take a century in making a decision! Fads and key words (autonomy, interdependence, moratorium, indigenous) may come and go but a change in mission board policy requires the coordination of personnel in field, administration, and support groups. Even a major shift of budget allocations takes a year or two when funds are available. It is likely to take a decade or a generation to change the attitudes and orientation of donors, executives, and field personnel (expatriate and national) when their tradition and world view are expected to undergo a radical redirection. Ecumenical Protestant mission has changed considerably in the last quarter-century, with the attendant pain, anger and heart searching. Even in the more connectionally

oriented denominations, a policy change may mean that donor
churches simply change the agencies through which they work.
It is only when there has been an effective re-education campaign among field personnel and donors that the full effects of
a change in policy can be seen. In the education of donors, the
women's missionary societies have done excellent work while the
general church lags behind.

In employed personnel, in spite of some painful terminations
in the past decade the older "tenure" policy seems to apply on
the field and in administrative posts so that a significant portion of the leadership is in the hands of persons at work in the
same area for 10, 15 or 20 years. Missionaries have had fur-
lough opportunities for re-education and an average natural
attrition of about 5% per year as ways to bring in changes.
National leaders have no such attrition rate, nor is it appropriate to think that the mission boards would determine a policy
and then "educate" the national leaders to accept it! Thus for
many reasons it is unrealistic to think that the operation of a
church will jump around according to new emphases determined
every 3, 4 or 7 years in a meeting held abroad. Instead, a
national church will take up some changes, selectively and
usually slowly, deciding in their own way.

A CHRONOLOGY OF CHANGE

Having just described the imprecise and uneven nature of
change in mission it may be somewhat contradictory to attempt
any chronology of that change. This can only be an indication
of some of the interdenominational meetings and U.S. events which
signal change, without implying any particular speed or even
acceptance of a goal by a particular mission board or a national
church with which that board has historically been related.

1950 The post-World War II; post-China period. We were beyond
      "orphaned missions" but were building and expanding along
      lines familiar since the 1920s—which already had agricul-
      tural and vocational educational work as well as general
      education and medicine. Perhaps less stress was placed on
      evangelism than in the 1930s, but there was more stress on
      the implications of evangelism in society.

1950 Willingen meeting of the International Missionary Council:
      "Missions Under the Cross." Johannes C. Hoekendijk, true
      to his personal denominational heritage in the Netherlands,
      attacked the Church-centered view of missions which had
      been dominant since Tambaram (1938 IMC meeting) and thus
      began a divergence from the emphasis on "Church Growth"

which Dr. Donald A. McGavran developed so distinctively.
Work was begun, particularly by North Americans, to relate
the missionary task to the signs of Christ's sovereignty
in the secular world. (Newbigin, Fey: 179). Other emphases included: new forms of ministry; laypeople abroad in
mission; regional study centres; greater mobility for mission; and mission & unity.

1954   Second Assembly of the World Council of Churches, Evanston.
The movement toward uniting the IMC and the WCC, thus seeking to stress mission as one of the marks of the church--
but retaining the Willingen concepts of God working in the
secular and the avoidance of Church-centric mission.

1958   Ghana Assembly of the IMC. Regional organizations were
emerging such as the All Africa Conference of Churches (in
planning, Ibadan 1958; organized Kampala 1963) and the East
Asia Christian Conference (in planning, Prapat 1957, constituted at Kuala Lumpur, 1959).

1961   New Delhi, Third Assembly of the WCC. The integration of
IMC into WCC (as the Commission on World Mission and
Evangelism) was completed with the recognition that the
larger church-delegated assembly would influence the meeting of an organization of mission societies related through
national or regional mission board coalitions. In addition
to questions of structure, the "World Mission & Evangelism"
section of the WCC had to take note of the financial dominance of "Inter-Church Aid" within the Council. To a
lesser extent it was also forced to note the suspicion of
traditional mission work by the Orthodox Churches which
joined the WCC at New Delhi.

1963   Witness in Six Continents, the Mexico City meeting of the
Commission on World Mission and Evangelism. A theme of
mutuality and reciprocity in mission which was acclaimed
then, but had only produced a few "exchange" missionaries
to the U.S.A. by 1976. With the studies on "The Missionary
Structure of the Congregation": the missionary task was now
seen in the context of what God is doing in secular events.

1966   Church & Society Conference, Geneva. This was a symbol and
catalyst of church involvement for social change in society.
There was a mood of change which prevailed through the
Fourth Assembly of the WCC.

1968   Uppsala assembly of the WCC. The optimism of the people of
God in Exodus was apparent. There was a tactical confrontation by persons and parties concerning mission, with

social activist and traditional "salvation out of this
world" advocates speaking past each other.

In the U.S. we experienced activism, despair and self-
examination. The Urban Church movement of the 1950s had
moved to Civil Rights in the 60s, with emphasis on housing
and economic development and opposition to the Vietnam
war. The frank challenge of Black power after 1967,
showed that the Church's fight against racism had to
be within.

1970 There was a backlash against central structures, including church hierarchies, with less trust of bureaucracies,
more cynicism and an isolationist stance.

1971 Call for Moratorium of Missionaries and funds from abroad,
by John Gatu of Kenya. Following a proposal in South
India, 1947, and the action of Methodist missionaries in
Uruguay, 1967, the challenge to selfhood from Kenya (and
from Emerito Nacpil at Kuala Lumpur, 1971) began to be
considered.

1973 CWME Salvation Today, Bangkok conference. The diverse
multi-religious background papers and discussions emphasized varied experiences of salvation in many faiths and
ideologies. "Mission in Context" was discussed with sub-
topics on CWME within the WCC structure; the role of
Christians in changing institutions, Urban Industrial
Mission and rural agricultural mission. There were useful challenges but not adequate dialogue with advocates
of traditional evangelism (Samartha: 12).

1975 Nairobi, WCC Fifth Assembly. With a section on "Confessing
Christ Today" and a challenge by Mortimer Arias, a strong
evangelism-with-action statement was adopted and the
"Dialogue" section was redrafted to express more clearly
both the finality of Jesus and the reality of God's work
in each community (Samartha: 11-12).

AREAS OF SIGNIFICANT CHANGE

Military Personnel

Most missionaries were recruited for "lifetime" service in
1950 but for specific short-term assignments by 1975. There are
now less calls for pastor-evangelist or administrator; continuing requests come for special teachers and medical workers; more
technical specialists are called for. New workers include those

in Urban Industrial Mission and community organization (though
it was in 1839 that the American Board rejected a request for
someone trained in social organization/political science--
Phillips: 124).

Missionaries receive less training in their home countries
and (sometimes) more orientation in the area of service.   There
is less theological training of all missionaries--in some cases
even baptism and/or Christian faith are not required (UM
Reporter: 4).   Preparation now seems to include less study of the
history, culture and language of the area of service but more
ease of inter-personal communication through encounter groups.
There is, however, great diversity in missionary preparation and
most of the agencies have gone through several major changes in
goals, methods and institutions utilized during the period.

Changing Structures for Mission

Denominational Mergers: The numerous mergers during this period
increased the scope and complexity of mission boards and occupied their attention for several years before and after consummation.   When two churches formed the United Presbyterian Church,
USA in 1958, the Commission on Ecumenical Mission and Relations
united the work of five agencies (and COEMAR was dismantled in
1971, with proposals for a further restructuring again in 1976).
In 1961 the United Church of Christ brought together two denominations, within which four agencies became the United Church
Board for World Ministries.   A year later four Lutheran churches
formed the Lutheran Church in America, within which World
Mission was combined with Ecumenism in 1973 (though here "Ecumenism" seems to mean primarily relationships with the American
Lutheran Church and the Lutheran Church Missouri Synod).   The
Methodist Church consolidated the administration of General
Board and Women's Missions work in 1964; the church combined
with the Evangelical United Brethren four years later and by
1972 a total of seven agencies for home and foreign mission
worked through one mission agency.

Uniting Relief and General Mission Agencies: With the growth of
generously supported relief agencies since World War II, there
has been a move to coordinate this work with the general task of
mission.   General mission agencies have always been engaged in
tasks beyond evangelism but have been so heavily committed to
educational, medical, agricultural and industrial work as well
as evangelism that they could not respond to the sudden emer-
gencies of which we are now much better informed than in
previous eras.

The "uniting" of relief and mission has generally been at the top, with care taken to preserve the distinctive nature and appeal of the relief work for the cultivation of giving. This has meant that promotional literature was distinct, though not always contradictory in describing the nature of distress and its solution. Many of the relief agencies describe feeding programs but not land reform, militarism, or the collusion of local elites with transnational corporations.

Uniting Home and Foreign Work: The coordination of national and world divisions of mission boards has been accomplished by several U.S. protestant groups during this period; for many others it has not been attempted. Even in those which have "united" this is also a coordination at the top. Only a handful of individuals whose primary experience was within the U.S. have become workers or administrators of overseas work, and vice versa. Only a few "functional" secretaries have united National and World concerns. Those in Urban Industrial Mission have been better coordinated across all national boundaries—perhaps because urban culture is by nature more Western wherever it occurs.

Changing the Locus of Mission: For generations the Methodist Church stated a very broad "Aim" for their Board of Missions:

> "The supreme aim of missions is to make the Lord Jesus Christ known to all peoples in all lands as their divine Saviour, to persuade them to become his disciples, and to gather these disciples into Christian Churches; to enlist them in the building of the Kingdom of God; to co-operate with these churches; to promote world Christian fellowship; and to bring to bear on all human life the spirit and principles of Christ."   (Discipline 1964: 1176)

In 1972 the United Methodists stated that all of their agencies, including Publications, Pensions, Finance, etc. had Aims of Mission which include: "To witness in all the world, by word and deed, to the self-revelation of God in Jesus Christ and the acts of love by which God reconciles all people to himself...To bring God's people together into a Christian community....and to send them into the world as servants in the struggle for justice and meaning." (Discipline, 1972: 801).

Portions of the missionary task are then allocated to each group, including the Board of Global Ministries (Para. 1077-1078). Locating an "Aim of Mission" before all U.M.C. agencies does not necessarily make their employees burn with a new missionary zeal but it is at least a significant statement of purpose by those who vision the church as a whole.

Change in the National Council of Churches of Christ   It was
in 1950 that the Foreign Missions Conference of North America
became the Division of Foreign Missions of the National Council
(emphasis added) of Churches of Christ, U.S.A. In 1965 this was
combined with the relief agency, Church World Service, to form
the Division of Overseas Ministries. As was true of the denominational counterparts, Church World Service remained distinct
enough in operation and funding to attract particular donors.
The coordination with NCCC work in the U.S.A. is more distant
still but can theoretically occur.

New Theological Emphases

Evangelism/Dialogue   Through the centuries Christians have been
interested in religions, cultures and ideologies as the places
where people were and from which they might move to a Christian
faith. Whether regarded as an obstacle or a preparation for
evangelism they were (like a particular language) used as points
of contact for attaching a transplanted specimen of Christianity.
As symbolized by the Kandy, Ceylon (now Sri Lanka) consultation
of the WCC in 1967, the goal for some mission theorists may now
be: (a) a new contextualization of Christian faith which is significantly different from its incarnation in other places and
times; or (b) a strengthening of the existing complex of reli-
gion-culture so that people may realize their humanity more
fully and live according to God's logos present with all peoples.
These two further options are by no means identical as seen by
mission agencies. Option "b" is voiced primarily by abstract
theorists or by those with some orientation toward India. The
view is,however, held by some mission executives and a few
employed as missionaries and constitutes a current challenge comparable to Hocking's Rethinking Missions in the 1930s.

    It is always difficult to do justice to the question of faith-
ful dialogue. The Old Testament scholar, G. Ernest Wright, suggested that:

> "The Christian is (ideally) created by God as a humble
> person who faces another human being as a brother in
> need like himself, not as a subject to be proselytized.
> He knows that he cannot make converts; only God him-
> self can do that. Indeed, at a given moment in history
> it may not be God's will to enlarge the numbers of
> converts, but possibly instead to reform another reli-
> gion from within, and that especially where no commu-
> nity of Christians exists to replace an old one
> being broken." (Anderson: 30).

I suspect that some here would not accept that last sentence.

The clash of concepts was clearly stated recently when the
General Secretary of the World Council of Churches, Philip
Potter, lectured on "Faithful Witness and Dialogue." He had told
the story of Erik Nielsen's experience of sharing with a Hindu
(well told also in Sovik: 72-73). A pastor in the audience said:

> It would seem to me that possibly other living faiths do
> have an answer equally valid and I'm wondering if you are
> implying that Christians have the answer that indeed,
> ultimately the aim is still the same as when we sent out
> unselfconscious imperialistic missionaries, to
> convert everyone to be Christians?

Potter responded:

> We can never tell what's going to happen. We can only
> make the risk of love, knowing that God will do His
> own work. But if you ask my own personal conviction
> as a Christian, it would be to say, that I certainly
> do believe that God in Christ holds all things together
> and all people together, and I certainly believe with
> St. Paul that it is God's purpose to sum up all things
> in Christ. I equally believe that God is doing His work
> with all peoples of all the different faiths and in our
> intermingling in these days, and in the new and extra-
> ordinary possibilities we have to share with each other,
> to receive from one another, God is doing extraordinary
> things with us all. We can never take the credit for
> it and...the evangelist is never ourselves, it is God
> in Christ, through His Holy Spirit. Therefore it is
> wrong, both to claim that we should seek to make every-
> body Christians as it is wrong to claim that we should
> not. What is right is that we should all be faithful
> to that which we have received from God in Christ
> revealed in all His love for all human beings and his
> purpose for the fulfillment of their lives and of our
> lives.

Social Involvement

Refugee assistance is always popular with donors and is seen
by all as a legitimate form of service. Work for structural
changes, which was called "development" in the 1960s and with a
more radical analysis is called "liberation" in the 1970s, is
not done by the relief agencies but is at least among the goals
of some of the mission boards. In terms of projects and personnel it is a minor emphasis, but it is very important in question-
ing the way of life by which affluent nations benefit from the

oppression of the "third world." This is a clear move toward
"Witness in Six Continents" in that such work recognizes the
change and conversion needed within Western people and societies, and not just the molding of others after our Western
theological, cultural, economic and political image. If North
American churches really begin to hear the Gospel proclaimed to
our situation through Christians from other cultures this will
be a real revolution for our understanding of mission. It will
be far more radical than the fact that some of these Christian
missionaries use aspects of historical, social and economic
analysis developed by Karl Marx.

God's Action in History

The redemptive power of God in "secular" history and not just
in a parallel "Heilsgeschichte" is now affirmed not only in the
Secular City (Cox: 1965) in North America, but among the dis-
possessed in Latin America, the Philippines and Korea. This
opens the possibility of affirming in Christ their pre-missionary
history and the current action for humanization not under the
control of the churches.

When Christians find their calling through participation in
the secular processes of history, the Church becomes a sign but
not the shelter (see Frazier: 26). Christians form a support
community but not the ark of salvation; they are nourished by
the Word and Sacraments for current tasks building toward a
utopian hope. Mission in this orientation will be incarnate in
various histories, and will view traditional mission as using
cross-cultural methods to propagate a culture-bound version of
the Faith.

The challenge from the living God, active in our times and
places, calls us to pilgrimage with Him, which demands the sort
of committed mobility of ourselves and our organizations that
was seen in Abraham. Our work in mission--in our world--has
changed, we pray that these changes may be in obedience to Him.

BIBLIOGRAPHY

Commission on World Mission & Evangelism, WCC, "World Studies of
    Churches in Mission" London: Lutterworth, (N.Y.: Friendship),
    1958-1970. Includes studies of Buganda; Northern Rhodesia;
    Togo; India; Britain; Japan; Solomon Islands; Congo-Brazza-
    ville; Chile; Java; Michigan; and Hamburg.
Cox, Harvey, The Secular City, N.Y.: Macmillan, 1965.
Davis, James H., Cultural Attitudes of Missionaries, N.Y.: United
    Methodist Church, Board of Missions, 1971.

Dodge, Ralph E., The Unpopular Missionary, Westwood, N.J.: Fleming Revell, 1964.

Fore, William F., The Faith That Compels Us, N.Y.: Methodist Church, 1962.

Forman, Charles W., The Nation and the Kingdom, N.Y.: Friendship, 1963.

Frazier, William B., "Guidelines for a New Theology of Mission," in Gerald H. Anderson & Thomas F. Stransky, eds., Mission Trends No. 1, Grand Rapids: Eerdmans, 1974.

Friendship Press, Eye on Mission, N.Y.: 1975
                  Mission Impossible--Unless, N.Y.: 1973
                  Mission Is, N.Y.: 1973
                  Something More Than Rice, N.Y.: 1973

International Documentation on the Contemporary Church, The Future of the Missionary Enterprise, Rome: IDOC, 1973- Includes issues on: Mozambique White Fathers; Namibia; Philippines; Latin American Indians; South Korea; Ethiopia; European Migration; Bolivia; Portugal; Kenya; Women; Vietnam; Mission.

Lutheran Church in America, Minutes, Sixth Biennial Convention, 1972.

Hocking, W. Ernest, Rethinking Missions: A Layman's Enquiry after One Hundred Years, N.Y.: Harper's, 1932.

Hollenweger, Walter J., ed., The Church for Others, Two Reports on the Missionary Structure of the Congregation, Geneva: WCC, 1967.

The Methodist Church, Doctrines and Discipline, 1964, Nashville: Methodist Publishing House, 1964

Newbigin, Lesslie, "Mission to Six Continents," in Harold E. Fey, ed., Ecumenical Advance, London: S.P.C.K., 1970.

Phillips, Clifton Jackson, Protestant America and the Pagan World, Cambridge, Mass.: Harvard University Press, 1968.

Powles, Cyril, and Rob Nelson, "Mission Impossible--Unless," N.Y. Friendship, 1973.

Quick, Bernard E., He Who Pays the Piper, Trenton, N.J.: B. E. Quick, 1975.

Samartha, Stanley, "Courage for Dialogue: An Interpretation of the Nairobi Debate: mimeographed paper.

Scherer, James A., Missionary, Go Home!, Englewood Cliffs, N.J.: Prentice-Hall, 1964.

Sovik, Arne, Salvation Today, Minneapolis: Augsburg, 1973.

Speer, Robert E., Are Foreign Missions Done For?, N.Y.: Bd. Foreign Mission of Presbyterian Church U.S.A., 1928.

Stockwell, Eugene L., Latin American Self-Determination: Illusion or Reality?, N.Y. United Methodist Board of Global Ministries, 1972.

United Methodist Church, Board of Global Ministries, Latin America and the World Division, N.Y.: 1972.

United Methodist Church, Board of Global Ministries, Latin
    American Liberation, N.Y.: 1974.
United Methodist Church, Book of Discipline, 1972, Nashville:
    United Methodist Publishing House, 1973.
United Methodist Reporter, Dallas, February 27, 1976.
United Presbyterian Church, U.S.A., Mission Yearbook of Prayer,
    1972.
Williams, Colin W., What in the World?, N.Y.: National Council
    of Churches, 1964.
Williams, Colin W., Where in the World?, N.Y.: National Council
    of Churches, 1964.
Wright, G. Ernest, "The Old Testament Basis for the Christian
    Mission," in Gerald H. Anderson, ed., Theology of the
    Christian Mission, N.Y.: McGraw-Hill, 1961.

10

Black Christianity in America

Emmanuel L. McCall

The Program Committee for this session has requested a paper which notes the following concerns:

The development of Christianity among Black Americans
The question of African religious heritage
The distinctives of Black Christianity in America
The forms and origins for Black Christian Missions
What Black Christianity can offer America

The easier way of responding to these concerns is through a general survey. The following outline suggests the main items to be considered:

Introduction--Taking Black Christianity Seriously

I. The Question of African Origins
II. Early Negative Attitudes Towards Christianization of Blacks
III. God Moves in Mysterious Ways
IV. Black Christian Distinctives
V. Black Christian Missions
VI. A Suggested Agenda for White Christians

The reader should be prepared for two limitations in this paper. (1) Blacks are verbal communicators rather than writers. Some attribute this to the

African heritage which places a premium on physical
and verbal expression. Others suggest that the lack
of educational opportunities and media resources is
the reason. The limitation is that much statistial
and factual data will be absent because of the lack
of records or adequate archives. (2) The second
limitation is that the writer is more familiar with
Black Christianity as practiced by Baptists. Therefore, he brings that bias in discipline and choice of
illustrations.

For those sensitized to read further in this area,
a suggested bibliography concludes this paper.

Taking Black Christianity Seriously

Until the late 1950s black people were not taken
very seriously in America. The whole system of racial
segregation is testimony to that fact. If people are
not taken seriously, then the substances of their existence are not taken seriously. Consequently, little
value has been placed upon black Christianity. This
is evidenced by--

1. Racial segregation in religious practices.
2. The notion that "integration" even in re-
    ligion must be "into" white structures.
3. The entertainment value which the media
    places on black religious expressions.
4. The popularity of black religious cari-
    catures, especially by TV and night club
    entertainers.
5. The noticeable absence of black related
    issues in predominantely white religious
    and theological forums.
6. Negligible white involvement in forums
    designed to discuss issues of concern to
    black Christians.

In 1964, Joseph R. Washington authored a book entitled Black Religion. This came during the crest of
the Civil Rights Movement and at a time when white
Christians were positioning themselves either for or
against black people. Among his conclusions were--

1. The black church (he uses "Negro") is a
    "center for the disengaged." It has no
    sense of being historic, "no authentic
    roots in the Christian tradition," and
    no "meaningful theological frame of re-
    ference".

2. The only salvation for black Christians is ab-
    sorption into white church structures.

Unfortunately, this work was received by many
whites as authentic, and confirmed feelings of con-
tempt for black Christian structures in America. It
also gave a measure of comfort to some black Christians suffering from an identity crisis. There have
been and still are blacks who feel that anything
black is inferior and wrong, and everything white is
superior and right. Many black Christians have a
goal of making their churches, organizations and worship services as "white" as is possible. It is still
not a rarity to find churches scrambling to adjust
their worship if white visitors are present.

The most positive contribution of Joseph Washington's Black Religion was that it stimulated other
blacks to begin research and writing about black religion in America. Consequently, blacks are no longer
hanging their heads about their religious history or
their past. New agendas are continuing to be created
based on practical needs, theological issues, historical research, and opportunities for evaluative reflection.

The previous observations about whites not taking
the black church seriously is a generalization.
There are always exceptions to every generalization.
The fact that this discussion is in this conference
is an exception. The Black Church Studies department
at the Southern Baptist Theological Seminary, Louisville, Kentucky and its attendant activities are exceptions. If this gathering were polled, I am sure
other exceptions would be noted. This should not
siminish the impact of the generalization. The black
church must be taken more seriously by both white and
black Christians.

In reporting on the "Theology in the Americas" conference, a forum for the discussion of third world
theological movements, Beverly Harrison noted--

It was hoped originally that the unprecedented
opportunity to meet with and hear from this remarkable group would bring large numbers of
North American Theologians clamoring to participate. This did not happen: Numbers did not
accept the invitation, and a few well known

theologians scheduled to attend withdrew at
the last moment.[1]

It should be noted that Black Liberation Theology
was on the agenda for discussion.

It is this writer's contention that black Christianity has some positive contributions to make and
should not be taken lightly if the soul of America
is to be redeemed.

I. The question of African Origins

The attempt to link black American religious expressions to Africa is no new quest. As early as
1903 W.E.B. DuBois[2] identified five religious characteristics of African origin--

1. Religious feeling and fervor, rhythm
2. Mystical temperament vis-à-vis Baptism,
   the Lord's Supper, and moving of the
   Holy Spirit
3. Nature Worship
4. Notion of invisible influences for good
   or bad (voodoo)
5. Influence of the priests (shaman and
   witch doctors)

Russell Ames[3] suggests that while blacks and
whites influenced each other religiously during the
Great Awakening, their strains had previous independent development. His research determined that West
Africans were "skilled in singing--especially anti-
phonal choral singing where one group of voices answered another, interweaving and blending."[4]

In their African homeland the slaves had
been accustomed to singing in work, war,
love, and worship, and they also listened
to their professional entertainers and
musicians, some of whom were "living books,"
trained to preserve in song the history, laws
and customs of the people.[5]

Henry Mitchell's Black Beliefs[6] make a strong case
for African antecedents in black American Christianity, along with Gayraud Wilmore[7] and C. Eric Lincoln.[8] Among the emphases these men share are--

1. Despite the myth of Africa as a "dark"

continent Christianity was well established long before the arrival of European and American missionaries. Lincoln
cites the experience of Simon of Cyrene
(Mark 15:21), Day of Pentecost experience (Acts 2), Philip and the Ethiopian
eunuch (Acts 8:26-39) as biblical indications of contacts between Africans
and Christianity. He further suggests
that for 300 years (3rd-5th centuries)
nine of the prominent church leaders
were from Africa (Clement, Origen, Tertullian, Cyprian, Dionysius, Athanasius,
Didymus, Augustine and Cyril). The suggestion is not that they were black although they may have been), but that
they were African. It would be illog-
ical to assume that those referred to
both in the Bible and in church history
kept their faith a private affair, otherwise they would not have been noticed.

2. These men emphasize the fact that African
   religion was misunderstood by Europeans
   who defined Africans according to their
   norms. Osadolor Imasogie[9] has an excellent article on the extent of this mis-
   representation. He gives us African
   definitions of African religion.

Winthrop Jordan[10] suggests that most of the racial
myths related to blacks and Africans are rooted in--

1. The reports of voyagers who were uninformed
   and ill equipped to make value judgments
2. Slavers who distorted reality to justify
   their actions
3. Others profiting from the exploitation of
   slavery who also sought justifications
4. The romantic notions of William Shakes-
   peare who exalted the virtues of white-
   ness in order to win favor with Queen
   Elizabeth (while he maintained a black
   mistress)
5. Generalizations made about the whole
   African experience based on the limited
   exposure of tourists and slaveholders.

I would add a sixth myth making distorter-- the
carelessness of some American missionaries and

mission agencies who for a multitude of reasons dis-
tort realities. That multitude of reasons include
preconceived notions, cultural and racial prejudice,
the romanticization of their role, inadequate mission
philosophy, inadequate preparation, questionable motives and the application of double standards.

Having just returned from a seventeen day trip to
Ghana, I am grateful that I had read Mitchell's <u>Black
Beliefs</u> before going. Not only did it prepare me for
an open receptivity to learn from Africans, it also
equipped me to be prepared in noting parallels between American blacks and Africans. I am firmly convinced that we are kin. Among the most vivid impressions was the distinct difference in feeling and
spirit when the Ghanians sang the hymns and anthems
taught by the British and Americans, and those that
were native. They sang the English hymns with beautiful precision staying in canonized meters, standing
very still, expressionless except for their voices.
It was altogether different when they sang in Twi or
Ga. There was a radiance on their faces that reflected all they were feeling. The feeling took hold
of their whole being. They participated in worship
with all that they had, very much like many worship
services I have seen in black congregations across the
United States.

II. Early Negative Attitudes Towards Black
     Christianization

Winthrop Jordan,[11] H. Shelton Smith[12] and Samuel
Hill are among the writers documenting those reasons
offered against Christianizing the slaves of African
descent. Those reasons include--

1. Admitting recognition of "inner sameness
   of all men" (whether or not blacks had
   souls)
2. A loophole in English slave codes which
   permitted slavery, if it could be proven
   that the enslaved was subhuman
3. The question of whether freedom in Christ
   also meant freedom from slavery
4. The notion that Christian slaves would
   press for freedom and equality
5. The "Curse of Ham" (Hammitic Curse) was
   offered as justification for slavery on
   theological bases

6. The myth of lack of capacity among slaves. Related to this were certain theories of cranial structure, content and characteristics.

These excuses were offered by those who had vested interest in the economics of slavery. It would be amusing, if it were not so disgusting, to see the extent to which southern churchmen went in trying to justify the system of slavery and all of its attendant evils purely on biblical and theological grounds.

I digress for a moment to suggest that one of the agenda items for missions professors might be to become familiar with the origins of myths and notions that affect attitudes towards other peoples. Both secular and church histories must be re-examined in light of the bias with which they were written.

If you have difficulty in understanding black rejection now that many white structures have "opened the doors" consider among the reasons the distrust and suspicion by the errors of history, and the awareness among blacks of past realities.

III. God Moves in Mysterious Ways

One of the cliches of black hermeneutics is--

"God moves in mysterious ways,
His wonders to perform
He plants his footsteps on the seas
And rides on every storm."

While white churchmen were debating whether or not blacks had souls or should be evangelized, God was moving in the religious movements called the Great Awakenings, the first coming in the 1740s and 50s. In addition to the blacks purposely evangelised by men like George Whitefield and Samuel Davies, others responded while attending the needs of their masters in the protracted meetings. Once it was discovered that the slaves were caught up in the religious phenomena of conversion, shouting, barking, religious laughing, etc., there was no longer a question of whether or not the slave had a soul. The question which slavers were confronted with was "what do we do with them?" Three distinct patterns emerged--

1. Absorption. Some converted slaves became

members of their masters' churches. In most
instances their privileges were limited.
Sections of the building were reserved for
them. Special slave sermons or teachings
were directed towards them. Especially
were they enjoined to be obedient, tem-
perate, submissive and moral. (Again notice the double standard.)

2. <u>Separation</u>. The second pattern was to allow
   the slaves to worship to themselves in facilities provided by the master(s). The
   white pastor was often in charge of the
   worship as every caution was observed to
   prevent religious gatherings from turning
   into freedom rallies. The fear was real
   for the champions of black liberation have
   most often been preachers, i.e. Nat. Turner,
   Denmark Vessey, Martin Luther King, and
   many others in the more recent and present
   struggles.

   Some slaves were permitted to preach, but
   only in the presence of white superiors.

   Some slaves were exhorters used to prepare the crowds for the white preacher or
   to make additional comments after his sermon.

   These services were most often held in
   the afternoon, thus beginning a tradition
   of afternoon worship still observed in
   black churches. The current use of the
   afternoon worship is for special occasions,
   congregational exchange, or musical worship.

3. <u>Secret meetings</u>. Some masters refused to
   allow their slaves to be Christianized.
   Those slaves so inclined often held secret
   worship in the woods or other obscure
   places. Hollow logs or tubs became the
   drums with which they beat out rhythms for
   their music. Dearing King, a Chicago pastor recalls having heard his grandmother
   state the origin of certain spirituals.
   "Steal Away" was a secret coded message
   sung by slaves in the presence of their
   masters, indicating a secret worship
   meeting that night. "I Couldn't Hear

Nobody Praying" was often sung by a house
servant to the field slave indicating that
their services were not heard up at the
"big house."

Out of these three separate experiences emerged
three basic kinds of worship among blacks--

1. Worship that is high churched, formal, comparable to Episcopal, Lutheran, Presbyterian, some Methodist white churches
2. Worship that is a synthesis of black and
   white stylizations
3. Worship unaffected by white standards,
   closely akin to services that I discovered
   in Ghana when I was on my own (unaccom-
   panied by missionaries).

The three distinct forms may be found all over the
United States. While number 3 was basically a rural,
southern expression, out migration has disseminated
this style nationally. It is most often found among
Baptist, Pentecostal, Church of God, some Methodists,
and independent congregations.

IV. Black Church Distinctives

Black distinctives are more visible in worship and
outreach. Each of these will be considered.

Worship

Black worship may be characteristically described
as "celebration." We gather to celebrate what God
has done, what He is doing, and in confidence that He
will continue to be and do that which has been previously experienced. There is vicarious identification with biblical personalities and situations which
reflect divine deliverance. When a black choir sings-

> "O Mary, don't you weep,
> Pharoahs army drowned in the Red Sea
> O Mary, don't you weep,"

there is both a "you are there" attitude about the
event, but also celebration because of what this now
means to the worshiper. From that celebration comes
hope that whatever situation one faces deliverance
will come.

Black worship is a participatory event. The choir
is there to lead the singing for the congregation,
not to do it for them. Black preaching is a dialog-
ical experience with God, the preacher, and the congregation. Without that dialogue participation, it
would be bland. Even those who neither sing, nor respond in the sermon find other ways of involvement;
rhythmically patting their feet, nodding affirmations,
smiling assent, or doing the variety of extras that
are a part of the worship experience.

Black worship is not governed by a printed order
of service or a clock. While both are present,
neither is essential. Blacks come to the experience
to experience, not to fill a commitment. In every
worship there must be a happening--some call it
"moving of the Spirit," or some spiritual assurance
that "God is in this place." A preacher may not be
well trained and he may be a poor sermonizer, but if
he can lead the congregation in celebration he need
not fear.

The Preacher

Essential to black worship is the preaching.
Everything builds up to that dramatic moment when
"the man of God" takes his place. It remains a truism
that a black congregation will forgive their pastor
for almost any shortcoming except his inability "to
say it." Until recently the choice preacher was he
who could move the congregation to emotional ecstasy.
Since the life and ministry of Martin Luther King, Jr.
the emphases has shifted to one who can combine intellect with charisma.

Therein lies one of the conflicts in black church
circles. The men who have college and seminary
training are in a minority. Men lacking these resources are often defensive. Some denominational
conflicts are more sociological as men with academic
credentials assert themselves, and men without academic credentials determine to maintain control.

The pastor is the dominant person in the leadership
of black churches. Men of position or wealth in the
congregation know that they must come by him. Their
position or money means nothing in the congregation
if "Brother Pastor" decides against them. Skillful
black pastors, however, have learned how to use men

of wealth or position to achieve desired goals.

The dominant role of the black pastor may come
from two sources: (1) the continuing influence of the
African religious tradition which allows unusual prestige and influence for the witch doctor, priest,
shaman or medicine man. These are considered inter-
mediaries between the divine and man, and are ordained
with special powers. Black Americans still have this
kind of regard for the preacher. (2) The second
source is biblical. As Moses, Joshua, Gideon, David,
etc. were men divinely appointed by God to be followed
by men, so is the black preacher. Quite often a congregation may refer to the pastor as "Our Moses,"
"Our Joshua," "the one standing in John's shoes." As
children we were taught to reverence the preacher
even if we didn't like him. Biblical references to
divine judgment upon those who opposed or disparaged
the preacher were engrained into us.

In former years the preacher fulfilled a variety
of roles for his congregation and community. He gave
legal advice, counseled, offered his version of clin-
ical resources, supported business ventures, offered
agricultural extension information, etc. Some few
were professional teachers, lawyers and M.D.'s. The
black preacher has and can still assemble the greatest
audience of black people. He does so every Sunday.

There is a wind of change blowing. The previous
paragraph refers to years when blacks had limited
opportunities to education, training and the professions. Now that there are people in every congregation with a variety of educational and professional
skills, the wider influence of the preacher is being
diminished. For some enamored with the former model,
great anxieties, tensions and fears abound. There are
forums at work attempting to help such persons learn
the skills of team work thereby enhancing their ministries.

Black preaching is an art to itself. It makes
great use of what is now called narrative theology.
But, narrative theology is not a new innovation to the
black pulpit. For generations we've been "telling the
story." The black preacher is a great storyteller.
He knows the essential ingredients in communicating.
These include[14]--

1. Allowing time for the sermon to be enjoyed

(lulling over it as one does delicious
food)
2. Giving enough details to keep the action
moving, yet not moving beyond the listeners. The people want to hear it again,
even if they know the story. The idea is
to relive the experience and resolve the
conflict. The listener also wants to
hear the story as another tells it to
ascertain any variations on the theme
3. The speaker cannot break out of sequence
by skipping to the middle or the end
4. The sermon must build to a climax which
takes a variety of expressions. Some
move immediately to music. The variations are abundant
5. Throughout the entire process spontaneity
is maintained by avoiding the need for a
manuscript, and continuing a dialogue
with the audience. The preacher is communicating with them, not to them.
Black preaching makes full use of extem-
poraneous styles.

Black Music

Black music provides another basic distinctive in
black worship. The expression "soul" is a contemporary way of saying, "express yourself". This
blacks do unreservedly. Some expressions are accul-
turated, some are mimicked. Those that are genuine
continue.

Black musicians can run the gamut in church music.
They can sing the great anthems and hymns of the
church in either the original or in black stylization.
They are more comfortable in the music that expresses
the black "Sitz in Leben," the spirituals and gospel
songs.

Improvision is a commonplace event in black music.
The singer sings as he feels. He does not feel the
same way at all times. Last Christmas I attended a
concert featuring Handel's "Messiah." Sitting near
the front of the auditorium, I was able to see the
astonished looks on the faces of both the conductor
and organist as the contralto soloist improvised, yet
without causing chaos to the instrumentalists. That
became the high point in a well done presentation,

for the audience came alive to familiar sounds from
the improvision.

The genius of black church music is that it comes
from the gut level experiences of the people that
create it. It is not fashioned by a mystic detached
from the routine of life, nor the academician trained
in music theory. A song may be sung one way in Georgia, a different way in Mississippi, still differently in Chicago or New York. No one will be upset
when others sing as they feel. This makes possible
other adaptations which often occur when one sings to
himself or for himself. Black people can often be
heard singing while working. To do so is to nourish
one's own being. Thus, black music is not intended
for the cathedral, but in the bosom of ones own pilgrimage, whenever and wherever that takes him.

It is unfortunate that black church music has been
secularized and commercialized by black musicians,
who got their start singing in churches, and by entertainment concerns that have demanded certain stylizations for "show biz." This is unfortunate because it
has profaned legitimate expression, it has had a cor-
rupting influence on others undisciplined in church
music, and it has provided false caricatures to the
general public.

Outreach

The other major distinctive which I wish to emphasize is the holistic approach which the black church
takes toward life. The lines between "secular" and
"sacred" are not as closely observed. Politics, economics, education, community actions and events are
legitimate concerns of the church. No one can tell
the preacher that these are off limits in his preaching or active participation. He can discuss or participate in any movement as freely as he pleases. He
is held in disdain if he neglects to do so.

When black churchmen use "liberation," the word
includes the whole person, not just "soul." That
liberation concerns itself with those movements that
might affect one's wholeness or well being.

Before the local, state and federal governments
began to be serious about black education, black
churches and church judicatories were sponsoring both
elementary, secondary and college education. This

was often done by the meager earnings of domestics and gardners.

When no other forums for the performing arts and community expression were available, the black church house was there responding to that need.

Without the benefit of news media, black people were kept informed by black churches.

The civil rights rallies of the late 50s and 60s were not held in municipal auditoriums or cathedrals, but in black church houses. That's why so many were destroyed.

Despite the popularity of a few non-clergymen during the movements of the 60s, the major thrusts and sustained accomplishments were achieved by the leadership of black clergymen.

Black churches are still in there fighting to achieve equality in job opportunities, housing and justice before the law; providing remedial education for young people trying to make it; retraining for the underdeveloped and unskilled; day care and nursery facilities for multitudes of women who must work; leisure time activities for idle youth; services for senior citizens left to fend for themselves by a "success minded" youth oriented culture; fighting the influence and wrecked lives of the drug pusher and his addicts; doing battle against those who capitalize off of base motives. The campaign against black exploitation films and clothing styles has largely been fought by black churchmen.

Black actors and actresses joined the fight after the outcome became evident, but the real credit belongs to black churches who consistently expressed themselves in a variety of ways.

Perhaps the concept of human totality in mission, ministry and life needs to be rethought by white churchmen. It is evident that a cultural religion has silenced the prophetic voice that must be sounded if our nation is to find its rightful place in the purposes of God.

V. Black Christian Missions

Again, I apologize to the non-Baptist reader for

the lack of reference to missions other than as expressed by Black Baptists. I prefer to speak about
that with which I am familiar.

Home Missions

Home missions has had the greatest emphases among
black Baptists. Everything that our churches and denominational structures have done have been home missions. Here is where the needs were. No sense of
adventure, no pangs of guilt, nor misguided notions
of martyrdom drew mass attention of blacks to foreign
fields. This is not to deny black American mission
activity in other lands. It is to affirm that the
needs have always been massive here. When you consider the following, the reasons become apparent:

1. Black churches provided educational opportunities for black youth prior to the 1950s.
   Municipal, state and federal governments
   did not become really interested in black
   education until it became apparent that
   the Supreme Court might rule as it did
   in 1954.
   Since 1954, the sudden availability of
   public funds created a "Town-Gown" conflict
   between the church and academic communities. Denominational structures originally
   created for the correlation of educational
   resources were suddenly left without a
   reason for being. Some are trying to restructure for new ministries. Others are
   dissipating or marking time.

2. Until the 1950s most black people facing
   various physical needs were assisted by
   churches, not welfare organizations. Most
   churches had "mission funds," "Poor Saint"
   funds or resources under similar designa-
   tions for human relief. Most churches
   still receive a separate special offering
   for these purposes.
   Poverty has always been a reality to
   black Americans. Churches committed themselves to benevolent organizations,
   offerings or the support of special
   efforts to resolve these needs.

3. The meager resources which black people
   had were also used in local fights for

Justice, community betterment, response to situations not otherwise
provided for or ignored by those in
authority. There are still many
communities in America where public
services supported by tax dollars
end where the black community begins.
That is to say that paved streets,
street lights, water and sewer services are denied certain sections
where minorities live. Before public
accommodation laws were enacted,
blacks had to provide and maintain
their own community recreational
services. The black church was the
agency through which these needs
were supplied, or the agency doing
battle with the power structure.

In addition to resources for relief gathered
through church offerings, missionary societies in
black churches have assisted in support of such ministries. Their efforts have been meager, since their
resources and activities were subject to church control.

The reality is that black churches have done mission work, unorganized and with minimal structure
from larger denominational structures.

There are three national conventions of black Baptists comprising total memberships of about 10½
million people. (There are many black Baptist
churches that have no structural denominational relationships. Others have membership in the American
Baptist Convention (ABC)--about 11 percent; some 375
churches are members of the Southern Baptist Convention (SBC).)

The Progressive National Baptist Convention, has a
well defined, organized home mission structure which
is three years old. The full time executive director,
Dr. Joseph O. Bass, has done a yeoman's job of developing structures for concern, support and ministry.
The PNBC is also cooperating with the ABC in a project called Fund of Renewal (FOR) which is attempting
to raise 7 million dollars for special mission projects for Black, Hispanic and Indian ministries.

All three conventions have limited resources for

church pastoral aid, emergency assistance, some church loans, and endorsement of chaplaincy programs. Christian education programs are handled under Christian education boards. Black Baptists continue to support educational institutions of all academic levels, even though the "Town-Gown" conflict exists.

Foreign Missions

All three conventions of black Baptists have foreign mission programs. The National Baptist Convention, Inc. has work in Sierra Leone, Liberia and Ghana, West Africa; Malawi in Central East Africa; the Republics of South Africa and Lasotho; and Bahama Islands.

The National Baptist Convention of America (Unincorporated) has work in Africa, Jamaica and Panama.

The Progressive National Baptist Convention through the Baptist Foreign Mission Bureau has work in Nigeria, Bahama, and Haiti. The Foreign Mission Bureau was organized in 1960 as an attempt to keep the foreign mission program alive at the impending split in the NBC, Inc. This split did occur in 1961 resulting in the formation of the PNBC. After several years of cooperative support, the PNBC accepted full sponsorship of the Baptist Foreign Mission Bureau.

All three of these conventions have similar foreign ministries that include primary, secondary, and college education; hospital ministries, agricultural ministries, evangelism and church development ministries.

Lott Carey Baptist Foreign Mission Convention

Another organization that deserves special mention is the Lott Carey Baptist Foreign Mission Convention. This is not the first black American foreign mission convention, but it has had a long, admirable, continuous history. Black Baptists between 1840 and 1895 formed a number of mission conventions. Among these were The Northwestern Convention, The New England Convention, African Mission Convention, Tri Party Convention, Western States and Territories Convention, and Consolidated American Baptist Missionary Convention.

In November 1880, at Montgomery, Alabama the

Foreign Mission Convention was organized in response
to a call from W. W. Colley. Colley had been sent as
a foreign missionary to Africa by the Southern Baptist
Convention's Foreign Mission Board from 1875-79. After
this term, he returned inspired with the desire to
get blacks involved in African missions. Southern
Baptists encouraged his attempts in 1879 and '80 resulting in the above mentioned organization.

In 1885 the American National Baptist Convention
was organized in Louisville, Kentucky for home mission
purposes.

In 1893, The Baptist National Educational Convention was organized for the support of educational
ventures.

Because these three (The Foreign Mission Convention, The American National Baptist Convention, and
The Baptist National Education Convention), all
appealed to support from the same churches a consoli-
dation meeting was called. The intention was to mini-
mize conflicts of interests, uncontrolled promotions,
and duplicate travel. The call meeting was held in
Montgomery, Alabama in 1894. The new convention held
its first annual meeting in Atlanta, Georgia in 1895.
Its name was The National Baptist Convention of
America.

Although organized with a Home Missions Board,
Foreign Missions Board, and Education Board, the
first split occurred in 1897 over the issue of foreign missions. There were those led by Lott Carey,
a former missionary to Africa sponsored by Southern
Baptists, who felt that foreign missions was not receiving its proportionate share of attention. In
1897, they pulled out and organized the Lott Carey
Baptist Foreign Missions Convention. The strength of
this organization is on the east coast particularly
in New York, Pennsylvania, District of Columbia, Virginia, Maryland and the Carolinas. The headquarters
are in Washington, D.C.

The Lott Carey Convention remains solely a foreign
mission convention, but its member churches are members of one of the three National Baptist Conventions,
American Baptist Churches, and Southern Baptist Convention.

New Models

Black Baptists are now seeking new models for fulfilling mission tasks. At present there is a search
for meaningful organization. Until 1954 Black Baptists organizational strength majored on black education. With the Supreme Court decision in 1954, and
the subsequent "town-gown" conflict many denominational structures lost their reason for being. By
1958 the challenge of the Civil Rights struggle captured the attention and monetary support of most black
Baptist organized efforts. Since its climactic years,
mid-1960s, black Baptist units have been left without
detailed organizational structures for doing missions.
A valiant attempt is being made by the Progressive
National Baptist Convention. Dialogues and forums
continue to be held all over the nation by black ministers concerned for viable alternatives.

Anyone interested in these forums might want to
attend either of the National Baptist Conventions,
the C. D. Hubert Lecture Series at Morehouse School
of Religion, Atlanta, Georgia, or any of the other
forums sponsored by the Interdenominational Theological Center, Atlanta.

Bishop College, Dallas, Texas, sponsors the L. K.
Williams Institute each April. The United Theological Seminary, Monroe, Louisiana has a missions forum
each fall, as does Virginia Union School of Theology,
Hampton Institute, Benedict, Shaw and Morris Colleges.
The Southern Baptist Theological Seminary in Louisville has had and will continue to sponsor such
forums.

What will emerge from these forums is still in process. There are some things that could be expected--

1. Mission organizations will be small
   and manageable covering no more than
   a state or area, with the obvious exceptions of National Baptist Conventions.
2. Mission tasks will be holistic responding to such needs as right relationship with God and man; remedial
   services of every description; methods
   for challenging social, economic and
   political ills; equipping church constituencies to be sensitive and

responsive to the multiplicity of
needs.

3. Liberation theology will continue to
be constructive in black mission concerns. For an excellent treatise one
should read Cecil Cone's The Identity
Crisis in Black Theology. A statement on Third World Theologies of
Liberation appears in the Review and
Expositor, Summer, 1976, Southern
Baptist Theological Seminary, Louisville, Kentucky.

4. Lay persons and youth will have more
significant roles in shaping the
strategies in response to #2.

5. White denominations will be relegated
to supportive roles where they are involved in mission projects with blacks.
Those persons closer to the actual situations will need to be free to assume
leadership in mission content and
strategies.

A case in point is the CHANCE program in Harlem,
New York. For years Southern Baptists had been chan-
neling money through missionaries to various ethnic
groups in New York with only mediocre results. In
1969, a group of blacks pastoring storefront churches
formed the Central Harlem Association of Neighborhood
Church Endeavors. All they asked of Southern Baptists was some seed money and some technical assistance when requested. Not only has CHANCE developed
indigenous leadership, but they have been far more
effective than all of our previous efforts on their
behalf.

CHANCE includes a wide range of ministries--a theological institute for storefront pastors; leadership
training for lay persons; remedial and after school
activities for youth; summer religious and cultural
activities; image building programs; recreation, arts
and skills programs; nutritional and mother's aid
service (home economics). Rather than applying band-
aids, CHANCE seeks to remove the cancer.

The point is, we must revise our philosophy of
missions. Equipping and facilitating roles must replace paternal instincts and notions. This moves me
to my final observations.

VI. Some Suggestions for White Christians

Perhaps the one question most often asked me by
sincere Christians who happen to be white is "How can
we help?" The more expedient question is how can
whites relate to blacks. I conclude this paper with
some suggestions as to how white Christians may respond to black mission concerns.
1. Do not consider blacks as objects of missions.
Blacks are persons to be reached as any other person
in America. Special categorization is offensive since
it establishes perimeters based on history, class or
race. An awareness of history, racial distinctives
or class norms should be essential only in helping us
develop sensitivity and strategies. I personally reject the notion that only persons within a certain
race, class or culture can effectively communicate to
their fellows. Such a notion is a convenient cop-out
leading to the same kind of isolationism that now has
us polarized. The real challenge for us is to take
the time to develop those sensitivities that will enable us to relate to groups within our communities.

Ethnic studies in our colleges and seminaries is
one approach to this kind of equipping ministry.
Again, I refer to a program that is succeeding at the
Southern Baptist Theological Seminary. In January
1970, we piloted a class in Black Church Studies.
This class was not intended for the 8 or 10 black
students on this campus of more than 1800 religious
vocational students. Rather, it was designed to inform and equip the white students to minister to the
whole community. The success of the first class led
to it being repeated in the next two January terms.
The continued demand for the class led us to expand
to a department of Black Church Studies. Since 1973,
five courses have been rotated in the three J-terms
(January, June, July); (1) "Interdisciplinary" (a
comprehensive course of all the following courses);
(2) "The Black Church and Social Justice;" (3) "Black
Hermeneutics;" (4) "Black Church History;" (5) "Liberation and Reconciliation" (Liberation Theology and
community practicum).

We will continue to rotate these courses in the J-
terms using distinguished blacks as visiting professors. Others having taught are George Kelsey, J.
Deotis Roberts, Edward L. Wheeler, Thomas Kilgore and
Benjamin S. Baker.

Because of continuing requests the Interdisciplinary course will be offered each regular semester beginning in September. Students in our schools of theology, religious education, church music and social work who have taken some of these courses and are now functioning ministers, continue to express appreciation for the contribution of these studies to their ministries.

2. A second suggestion to white Christians is the repeat of something said earlier. Theological professors would do well to familiarize themselves with the way attitudes towards various minority groups in America were formed. Most of us are informed by myths originated more than 300 years ago by persons with unchristian motives. In addition to the bibliography included at the end of this paper, I call attention to the revision of my doctoral dissertation, "Brothering My Brother," which is to be published late in 1977.

3. Black church structures are continuing to search for models that can be improvised in response to mission needs. Whites have had time to develop those organizational structures that facilitate mission action. Ways must continue to be devised that will allow blacks to become familiar with these structures. The Home Mission Board, SBC, provides six internships designed to allow black seminarians to participate in white organizational structures. These students are encouraged to improvise models that may be used in black church units.

4. Perhaps the most significant contribution which whites can make to black mission concerns is to find ways of developing an American theology that addresses itself to America's dilemma. I agree with C. Eric Lincoln in saying that it is futile to continue our ego mania of studying in Europe or importing European theologians when our problems are more peculiar to America. If Christianity were thriving in Europe, there might be validity to such a quest. If the various reports are accurate, that Christianity is a dying force in Europe, why go to the dying to seek life?

We need an American theology and mission strategy that makes Christianity creditable--both at home and abroad. American missions suffer from the creditability gap of a faith that proclaims a living,

loving Lord, whose adherents participate in inhumane
ventures, exploitation, hate, and death. We need a
theology that challenges the inconsistencies of civil
religion; that challenges socio-economic sins operating in the name of free enterprise; that address
those substantive issues of human existence; that considers man in Hebraic wholeness, rather than dichoto-
mies alienating body and soul.

Such a theology will discard some phrases, positions and words now commonly used. Missiologists,
likewise, need to question phrases, positions and
words held sacred. Such words as "heathen," "pagan,"
"evangelize," "minister," "Christianize" all need re-
evaluation both in light of their historic deriva-
tions and applications, and their current implications. The existence of double standards must be
analyzed and exorcised.

In all of the above, and more, Third World liberation theologies have a word to share if we are willing to hear. The disturbing question is, "Who Is
Listening?"

BIBLIOGRAPHY

The following bibliography is suggested for those who wish to read more on the subject.

Ames, Russell. The Story of American Folk Song. New York: Grosset and Dunlap, Inc., 1960.

Boye, R.H. National Baptist Convention of America. Nashville: National Baptist Convention Publishing House.

Cone, Cecil. The Identity Crisis in Black Theology. Nashville: African Methodist Episcopal Church, 1975.

Cone, James H. The Spirituals and the Blues. New York: Seabury Press, 1972.

DuBois, W.E.B. The Souls of Black Folk. Connecticut: Fawcett Publications, Inc., 1973.

Eighmy, John Lee. Churches in Cultural Captivity. Knoxville: University of Tennessee Press, 1972.

George, Carol V.R. Segregated Sabbaths (Black Methodism). New York: Oxford University Press, 1973.

Heilbut, Tony. The Gospel Sound: Good News and Bad Times. New York: Simon and Schuster Publishing Co., 1972.

Hill, Samuel, Jr. Religion and the Solid South. Nashville: Abingdon Press, 1972.

Johnson, Joseph. Soul of the Black Preacher. Philadelphia: Pilgrim Press, 1971.

Jordan, Winthrop. White Over Black. Baltimore: Pelican Books, Inc., 1969.

Jones, Major J. Christian Ethics For Black Theology. Nashville: Abingdon Press, 1974.

Lincoln, C. Eric. The Black Experience in Religion. New York: Doubleday Publishing Company, 1973.

Mbiti, John. African Religions and Philosophy. Garden City, New York: Doubleday, 1970.

McCall, Emmanuel L. The Black Christian Experience. Nashville: Broadman Press, 1972. (Baptist Book Stores)

Mitchell, Henry. <u>Black Beliefs</u>. New York: Harper and Row, 1975.

Mitchell, Henry. <u>Black Preaching</u>. New York: J. B. Lippincott Co., 1970.

Pelt, Owen and Smith, R.L. <u>The Story of National Baptists</u>. New York: Vantage Press, 1960.

<u>Review and Expositor</u>, "The Black Experience and the Church", Vol. LXX, No. 3, Summer 1973. Louisville: Southern Baptist Theological Seminary.

Roberts, J. Deotis. <u>Liberation and Reconciliation: A Black Theology</u>. Philadelphia: Westminster Press, 1971.

Washington, Joseph R. <u>Black Sects and Cults</u>. New York: Doubleday and Company, 1972.

Wilmore, Gayraud S. <u>Black Religion and Black Radicalism</u>. New York: Doubleday and Company, 1972.

Woodson, Carter G. <u>The History of the Negro Church</u>. New York: Associated Publications, 1921.

A more extensive bibliography may be obtained from--

Emmanuel L. McCall
Home Mission Board, SBC
1350 Spring St., N.W.
Atlanta, Georgia 30309

NOTES

[1]Beverly Harrison, "The 'Theology in the Americas' Conference," Christianity and Crisis (New York: Christianity and Crisis, Inc., October 27, 1975), p. 251.

[2]W.E.B. DuBois, The Souls of Black Folk (Connecticut: Fawcett Publications, Inc., 1973), p. 128 ff.

[3]Russell Ames, The Story of American Folk Song (New York: Grosset and Dunlap, Inc., 1960), pp. 116-131.

[4]Ibid., p. 128.

[5]Ibid., pp. 128-129.

[6]Henry Mitchell, Black Beliefs (New York: Harper and Row, 1965).

[7]Gayraud Wilmore, Black Religion and Black Radicalism (New York: Doubleday and Company, 1972).

[8]"The Black Experience and the Church," Review and Expositor, Vol. LXX, No. 3 (Louisville: Southern Baptist Theological Seminary, Summer, 1973).

[9]Ibid., pp. 283-293.

[10]Winthrop Jordan, White Over Black--American Attitudes Toward the Negro (Baltimore: Pelican Books, Inc., 1969).

[11]Ibid.

[12]Shelton Smith, In His Image (Durham: Duke University Press, 1972).

[13]Samuel Hill, Jr., Religion in the Solid South (Nashville: Abingdon Press, 1972).

[14]These elements are suggested by Henry Mitchell's Black Preaching, Chapter V, op. cit.

11

The Churches and the Indians: Consequences of 350 Years of Missions

R. Pierce Beaver

Roman Catholic and Protestant Churches have been engaged in missions to the American Indians within the bounds of the United States about an equal length of time, namely, some four hundred years,--the Catholics a little longer and the Protestants a little less. The Catholic missions in the southeast and southwest were outposts of the Spanish missions in Latin America, and those on the Canadian border, the Great Lakes, and the Mississippi Valley were extensions of the French action in Canada. Until the last half-century Catholic missions in the vast interior formed much more a foreign mission of the European Catholics than a "home mission" of the Church in America. Belgians appear to have been especially active. Protestant missions began with British financial assistance, but have always been confined to American personnel, and they have been continuous since the 1640's.

Both Catholic and Protestant missions in America were, along with the lesser impact of action in the Orient, the means of calling Christians in Europe to a renewal of mission. The Latin America missions were also responsible for stimulating the development of missiology, and because of the legalism pervading the Spanish conquest it was cast in the mold of canon law. The more spontaneous French missions were a source of spiritual renewal in the Church in France. The Protestant missions to the Indians form the fountainhead of Protestant worldwide evangelization and provided a much nore powerful dynamic than did the efforts of the chaplains of the Dutch East Indies Company. Out of the Indian missions came both the global evangelistic enterprise of all Protestantism and American "home missions." Inspiration, theory and models were important gifts to the global mission.

All the missionaries and their directors were creatures of their own cultures, and until very recently few could see in Indian cultures anything but barbarism. Moreover, they completely identified the gospel with their own particular varieties of Christianity and with the segment of American or European civilization out of which they came. Consequently the missions, while intent on protecting and preserving the Indians from injustice and exploitation, have nevertheless been among the most destructive forces in the disintegration of Indian society. The early missionaries in Latin America tried to turn the aborigines into red Catholic Spaniards, while Protestants sought to make them red WASPS. The French were the least destructive. Their early missioners, too, wanted to settle the Indians in towns where they could live according to models of French civilization and Catholic liturgical piety, but the policy of the government prevented that. Canada was intended to yield to France the products of the forest--furs, naval stores, and timber--and to attain that economic goal it was essential that Indian civilization should be disturbed just as little as possible. From Bartolome de las Casas to Issac McCoy to C. H. Cook the missionaries were devoted to protecting and preserving the Indians from destruction, and whenever they seemed to fail in their larger social objectives they rejoiced in the eternal salvation of individual souls, which they considered to be their main business. Those persons engaged in the contemporary debate about the meaning of salvation should gain illumination from a study of the missions to the Indians.

ROMAN CATHOLIC MISSIONS

This paper deals primarily with Protestant missions, but a short overview of the course of Catholic missions is provided. That story began in Florida with the martyrdom of Luis Cancer and companions in 1549. Simultaneously with the founding of St. Augustine in 1565 Fr. Pedro Martinez and two other Jesuits began evangelization. He was soon killed on the Georgia Coast. Ten more Jesuits arrived in 1568 and established mission stations along the coast as far north as North Carolina. Father Juan Baptista Segura led a group to Virginia, where six were murdered, and the remaining two were withdrawn. The Franciscans made an abortive attempt in 1573, and returned under Fr. Alonzo de Reynoso in the 1580's. A century later they had a staff of more than fifty at thirty doctrinas or stations. However, the British were given Florida by the Peace of Paris in 1763 and the Catholic missionaries were expelled, cancelling out a tremendous investment of faith and work.

The missions in the southwest were the northernmost extensions of the work of evangelization in Mexico. After the Indians of the Caribbean had been killed off by enslavement and
exploitation and there had been a tremendous effort by Bartolome
de las Casas and other missionaries to protect the rights of the
Indians, the Spanish crown assigned to the missions the gover-
nance of the Indians as well as their conversion and civilizing.
A magnificent job of acculturating the people to Spanish civilization was done by the Franciscans and others who followed them,
whatever one may think of the legitimacy of that goal. (Bolton
1960B; Kino 1948; Spicer 1962, 288-298, 504-516; Spicer 1975,
7-93) However, when the authorities of the state decided that
the missions had completed their job, those missions were secularized and the people subjected to the civil government and to
diocesan clergy. The suppression of the Jesuits was an additional calamity. Many tribes lacked adequate pastoral oversight
and nurture for as much as a century and a half. Some tribes,
such as the Yaquis, made their own effective adjustment to
social organization and Catholic religion; while others reverted
to paganism, and many revived pagan ideas and practice under a
veneer of Spanish Catholicism. Father Eusebio Francisco Kino,
the heroic and creative pioneer of the Primeria Alta founded
Tumacacari and San Xavier del Bac in southern Arizona in 1691
and 1696. The Franciscans eventually succeeded the Jesuits, and
the Papagos became a Christian people. San Xavier del Bac still
serves them. (Geiger 1939) Spicer notes with regard to all the
Spanish missions in the southwest that the missionaries overex-
tended themselves and that they were unable everywhere to establish the mission communities where indoctrination under constant
missionary tutelage became the basis of new behavior. (Spicer
1962, 504-5).

The Jesuits had been the pioneers in Baja California and from
there penetrated Alta California. When their Society was dissolved, the Dominicans took over the peninsula and the Franciscans were sent to the northern region. When Spain decided to
colonize and missionize Alta California in the 1760's, Friar
Junipero Serra was the spiritual general of the operation. San
Diego de Alcala was established in 1769, and San Francisco in
1776. Altogether twenty missions were founded. They flourished
in the usual form and manner until the Mexican government secularized them. Then a decline was rapid and only a tiny remnant
of Christians remained after the influx of Americans in the
Gold Rush of 1849. A revival of ministry was begun near the
close of the century. Ten priests were engaged in the work in
the mid-1960's, caring for twenty-eight churches and chapels,
and about 5,000 Catholics. (Engelhart 1908; Palou 1926;

Chapman 1916, 1921; Richman 1911; Sullivan 1971)

East of the Jesuits in the Primeria Alta the Franciscans
moved through Chihuahua into New Mexico. Missionaries accompanied the early military expeditions, but the first church was
not built until 1598, San Juan de los Cabelleros. Missions
were established among the Zuni, Hopi, and Navajo peoples.
There were twenty-five stations with fifty missionaries in 1620.
There were schools, and 60,000 converts were claimed by 1630.
The usual Mexican mission town pattern was introduced. However,
decline set in, and the Pueblo revolt of 1680, due to cultural
and religious tensions, swept away the entire mission structure.
Twenty-one missionaries were killed. Diego de Vargas recon-
quered the region between 1692 and 1696, and missionaries returned to the Zuni and Navajo. The Hopis henceforth were impervious to Christianity, while it was little more than nominal
among the other Pueblos, a mere veneer covering Indian belief
and practice. Secularization in 1767 really ended the mission.
The American invasion brought further disintegration. Archbishop Lamy after annexation attempted to improve ministry to
Indians and many of the nominal missions were incorporated into
the diocesan structure. A vigorous new mission effort did not
begin until after 1900. Statistics for 1965 were thirteen
priests serving twenty-four villages, three day schools, two
boarding schools. (Spicer 1962, 152-214; Dozier 1975; Horgan
1975; New Catholic Encyclopedia I, 404) After the independence
and then annexation of Texas no fruits of twenty-five years of
Franciscan missions remained there. (Bolton, 1916, 348-423;
Bolton 1915).

Spicer notes that there were two great Catholic missionary
campaigns, one an integral part of the conquest from 1600 to
1750, and another from 1900 to 1950. (Spicer 1962, 504) The
coercion practiced in the first created grave problems for the
second. Coercion was far more brutal and intense in New Mexico
than in Arizona and California. Sunday Mass was prescribed and
native rites proscribed. Ceremonial objects were confiscated
by raiders. Participants, particularly leaders, were beaten to
death and even by priests; some were enslaved. Punative expeditions destroyed villages and crops. Ceremonies were then
held secretely and cult objects carefully hidden. Punishment
simply revived the old religion. After secularation and after
American rule, the Indians were free to determine their own
cultural and religious choices. Generally among most of the
Pueblos the old religion revived in strength, with nominal alle-
giance being given to Christianity by allowing children to be
baptized and incorporating into ritual a patron saint for each
pueblo village.

French missions, largely Jesuit, extended westward through
the Great Lakes region and into the Mississippi Valley, leaving
some small remnants here and there except in Louisiana. (Jesuit
Relations; Delanglex 1935; Garraghan 1938; Shea 1899) The
martyrdom of some missionaries stimulated support in France.
(O'Brien 1960; Talbot 1935, 1949) The missions in what became
the United States were but a holding operation after British
conquest. The national government about 1795 encouraged Catholics to renew the work at Vincennes and Kaskaskia. The Great
Lakes missions received more attention. Spring Hill Academy
near Detroit was founded in 1809. Fr. (later Bishop) Frederick
Baraga led a revival in Michigan, beginning in 1829, and established the model town of La Anse. However, intense pressure led
to the removal of Indians to lands west of the Mississippi, constantly disrupting and destroying the mission. A noteable instance of conservation was the move of 700 Catholic Pottawa-
tomies in 1836-1838 to eastern Kansas, where they became the
base for the substantial community, St. Mary's, under Fr. J. B.
Duernick. Dominicans and later Franciscans evangelized in Wisconsin with meager results until a revival occurred in the present century. Farther westward Fr. Augustin Ravoux began a
mission to the Dakotas near St. Paul, and left a vernacular cat-
echism and prayer book. A permanent missionary presence came
to the Chippewas after 1874, and Benedictines created communities at Red Lake and White Lake. There were nineteen churches
with 5,000 Catholics in north Minnesota in 1965.

The northwest was the great area of Jesuit effort, and the
memory of Fr. Pierre Jean De Smet is associated with it.
(Chittenden & Richardson 1905; Lavielle 1915; Margaret 1940)
Missionaries ranged over the plains and the Rocky Mountains from
the Indian Seminary of St. Regis at Florissant near St. Louis to
the Oregon country. (Garraghan 1938; Burnes 1966; Duratschek
1947) Father De Smet originally responded to an appeal from
Flatheads, and from 1840's through the 1870's made journeys,
founded missions, supervised them, promoted the cause, and
lobbied with government agencies. He served as a government
agent on occasions, even while attending to mission matters.
His publications were influential: *Letters and Sketches*, 1843;
Oregon Missions and Travels, 1847; *Western Missions and Missionaries*, 1863; *New Indian Sketches*, 1865. The Oblates of Mary
Immaculate entered the Oregon Country at Walla Walla in 1848
under Rev. John Brouillet; but the Jesuits took over from them.
The Missionaries were mostly Europeans, especially Belgians and
Germans. They tried hard to destroy the Indian religion, cultural customs, polygamy, and all that they regarded as superstitions. Reservation policies and Protestant competition prevented creation of tightly controlled communities. The Indians
generally thought of the sacraments and rites as sources of

power, and judged them by their apparent success or failure.
Liturgical piety seems to have been more effective than boarding
school education, and it was more likely than Protestant emphases on preaching, individualism and biblicism to offer Indians
identity and cohesion as society crumbled under white aggression.
(See accounts of the two missions to the Blackfeet in Harrod
1971.)

Just as with Protestant missions, President Ulysses S. Grant's
"Peace Policy"gave a tremendous impetus to Catholic missions.
(Rahill 1954; Beaver 1966A, 123-176) When invited by Secretary
of the Interior Cox to participate in the supervision of agencies, Catholics made a grave mistake in claiming thirty-eight out
of about seventy reservations. They were awarded seven and
accepted them, but, considering this an injustice, refused to
cooperate with either the Board of Indian Commissioners or the
Bureau of Indian Affairs. General Charles Ewing as Catholic
Commissioner of Indian Affairs contended with government and
with Protestants. The Bureau of Catholic Indian Missions was
founded in 1874 with J. B. A. Brouillet as executive director
from 1874 to 1883 and William H. Ketcham from 1901 to 1912.
They expanded and promoted the missions, sought to counteract
Protestant influence, and won much aid from the government. The
Third Plenary Council of Baltimore created the Commission for
Catholic Missions among the Colored People and the Indians to
take a collection in every church on the first Sunday in Lent
and to dispense it to the missions. Roman Catholic missionaries
in 1873 were working only with nine tribes. There were then
sixteen missionaries, fourteen schools, and 2,250 communicants
on four of the locations. (Report of Board of Commissioners of
Indian Affairs, 1873, 332-347) Soon, however 100 sites for
missions were secured. Schools had increased to fifty-nine by
1896. After government aid was terminated in 1899, Ketcham developed a system of contract schools, various tribes assigning
funds from federal subsidies. By 1965 there were as the fruit
of tremendous development during the previous fifty years Catholic missions on forty reservations, fifty-three schools with
8,637 pupils, 401 churches and chapels, and 130,122 Catholic
Indians. (New Catholic Encyclopedia I 407; II, 889).

Bishops now have juridiction over missions in their dioceses
and in many Indian churches have been incorporated into the
diocesan structure. The work is more pastoral than evangelistic,
but in 1974 converts numbered 747. Rev. J. B. Tennelly, executive director of the Bureau of Catholic Indian Missions reports
that in 1976 the personnel of congregations and orders engaged
in Indian ministry is as follows: "The Jesuits have 82 priests
and 19 scholastics and brothers engaged in 39 Indian missions
and five schools. The Franciscans have about 62 priests and

16 brothers who serve 124 large and small missions and conduct
two schools. Eleven Capuchin friars are in charge of 11 missions and three schools. Ten other religious communities of
men are engaged on 15 missions altogether and supervise several
schools. Diocesan priests are in charge of the remainder.
About 300 nuns of some twenty sisterhoods teach in 38 schools
and maintain two small hospitals. About 200 lay teachers are
employed in our schools." *Our Negro and Indian Missions, 1975*,
the Annual Report of the Secretary of the Commission for the
Catholic Missions among the Colored People and the Indians,
page 33, reports that in 1974 there were in forty-three dioceses
155,600 Catholic Indians in 398 churches. There are 265 priests
assigned to Indian work, of whom 196 are engaged full time in
pastoral service on reservations, thirty-four in education and
administration, and thirty are pastors of white parishes who
also serve small Indian missions. There are thirty-nine schools
with 6,538 pupils. 3,680 infants were baptized in comparison
with 747 adults.

PROTESTANT MISSIONS:

THE COLONIAL PERIOD

(Beaver 1948, 1962A, 1966A 7-52, 1966B, 1968, 1969; Chaney 1976;
Gray 1956; Hare 1932; Kellaway 1962; Tracy 1840; Vaughan 1965,
235-308)

Both the narrators of voyages and their editor, the Rev.
Richard Hakluyt, stoutly avowed that evangelization of the
Indians was a major, and even the chief, purpose of British exploration and colonization. (Lucas 1930; Williamson 1931;
Wright 1943; Beaver 1966A, 7ff; Parks 1928) The Virginia, Plymouth, Massachusetts, and Connecticut Charters all made the
same professions. (Brown, *Genius of the United States*,I, 53,
67-68, 236, 337, 463; *Records of the Govenor and Company of
Massachusetts Bay*, I, 17; *Charter of the Colony of Connecticut.*,
II, 8) The great seal of Massachusetts even showed an Indian
shouting the Macedonian cry, "Come over and help us!" The last
mention of evangelization in a charter occurred in the case of
Pennsylvania. (*Minutes of the Provincial Council of Pennsylvania*, 17) Despite the charters, neither Virginians nor New
Englanders began evangelization until they were militarily
strong enough not to fear the tribes. A genuine mission never
was launched in Virginia because of the reaction to the massacre
of 1622, although attention was given to education of Indian
youths. (Land 1938; Robinson 1952) However, in Massachusetts
Thomas Mayhew, Jr., began personal evangelism in 1642 and public
preaching in 1646, the same year in which John Eliot began public services on the mainland. (Hare 1932; Kelaway 1962;

Vaughan 1965, 245-252, 286-7; Mather, *Magnalia* III, 111; Winslow 1968; Beals 1957) By 1674 there were fourteen towns of "Praying Indians" with 4,000 inhabitants in Massachusetts and Plymouth.

The mission villages were destroyed or seriously injured by King Philip's War in 1675-1676, and they never fully recovered. The decline in eastern Massachusetts was eventually offset by an abortive effort to the north in 1730 and a successful one to the west in 1734. (Beaver 1966B, 33-73, 75-105) John Sergeant, a tutor at Yale College, was ordained as missionary to the Housatonic Mohegans at a great council of the tribes held by Governor Belcher at Deerfield. As in the case of the earlier towns of Praying Indians, the General Court set aside the town of Stockbridge for the converts. Its fatal flaw was the inclusion of four white families who were supposed to be examples to the Indians. When Sergeant died in 1759 he left a church with forty-three communicants, a day school, and a boarding school. The missionary had baptized 182 persons, of whom 129 were living in the village at his death. Those away from the village were often spontaneous evangelists. The Christians were recognized as a separate Stockbridge nation. Jonathan Edwards succeeded from 1749 to 1758. When the next pastor, Stephen West arrived, the Indians and whites were divided into separate congregations, and the Indians entrusted to the care of John Sergeant. After the Revolution the Stockbridges moved to New Stockbridge, New York, and then by stage to the region of Green Bay, Wisconsin, where a remnant remains.

A short distance from Stockbridge on both sides of the New York-Connecticut border there was a Moravian mission established directly from Germany. It was begun by Christian Heinrich Rauch at Shekomeko in Dutchess County in 1740. A main station was soon developed at Wedquadnach or Gnadensee (now Indian Pond), bisected by the border line, and an out-station at Scaticook on the Housatonic. Well laid-out, prosperous villages quickly arose, the inhabitants maintaining themselves by farming and crafts and living according to Moravian communal liturgical piety. The white settlers destroyed this mission by personal interference and legal suppression. Some of the Christian Mohegans joined a mission to the Delawares near the Wind Gap in the Blue Mountain in Pennsylvania. (For this and the following narrative, see: Gray 1952, Beaver 1966A, 20-24, 58-59).

The unhappy story repeated itself. Settlers forced a move from the Wind Gap to another site where allies of the French killed a number of the inhabitants. All were interned at Philadelphia in 1763 when they barely escaped death at the hands of a mob. Communities of converts at several new sites were forced to withdraw ever westward across Pennsylvania, until missionaries David Zeisberger and John Heckwelder led the people to the Muskingum country of eastern Ohio, supposedly far beyond white interference. There peaceful and prosperous Moravian towns arose

again, only to be destroyed and ninety Christians of all
ages to be murdered by American militiamen at Gnadenhutten on
March 8, 1782. Migration continued by stages through northern
Ohio, Michigan, and Ontario until the final site of New Fair-
field, Ontario, was given to the Methodist Church of Canada in
1902.

Contemporary with Stockbridge and Gnadensee was the mission
of David Brainerd, a Connecticut man, who was commissioned by
the New York-New Jersey Board of Commissioners of the Society
in Scotland for Propagating Christian Knowledge on November 22,
1742. (This Board also supported Azariah Horton among the
Montauks of Long Island.) Brainerd began work a few miles
southeast of Albany, moved to the Forks of the Delaware, and
itinerated on the Susquehanna. Then through a mighty working
of the Holy Spirit in the spring of 1745 among Indians in the
neighborhood of Cranbury, New Jersey, the young missionary
gathered a congregation and community. Still another settled
Christian town developed. Unfortunately Brainerd's short life
was terminated by tuberculosis at the home of Jonathan Edwards
on October 9, 1747. His example and his *Memoirs* inspired
hundreds of missionary vocations during the nineteenth century.
His brother John was his successor, but before many decades the
state of New Jersey confiscated the land and sent the inhabitants to Brothertown, New York. (Brainerd, ed. by Edwards
1749; Beaver 1966B, 105-124).

The Iroquois of the Susquehanna, especially at Onohoquaga,
and the Finger Lakes were the targets of Massachusetts misson-
aries, including Elihu Spencer (1747), Gideon Hawley (1753-56),
and Joseph Bowman (1762); but all failed. (Beaver 1966B, 185-
209) The Mohawks were the exception. Wheelock, when pastor at
Lebanon Crank, Connecticut, had tutored the Mohegan youth, Samson Occum, and that experience inspired his scheme of mission.
(Wheelock 1763 and 1765; Sprague, *Annals*, I, 493-499; McClure
and Parish 1811; McCallum 1932; Beaver 1966B, 211-234) No other
New England strategist approaches Wheelock in creativity, but he
was too often at odds with his supporters and staff. He was
authoritarian, uncooperative, and did not sufficiently trust his
missionaries and allow them initiative, especially the Indians.
Consequently there were frequent financial and morale problems.
Wheelock established Moor's Indian Charity School at Lebanon
Crank, where he educated together both Indian and white youths
for missionary service. The Indians were expected to learn
true piety from the whites, and the whites the Indian languages
and customs from the red students. Girls were enrolled, especially to be prepared to be wives to the evangelists. Graduates
were sent into the Iroquois country. Wheelock in 1770 moved
his school to Hanover, New Hampshire, when he established Dart-

mouth College. However, the school soon declined.

The most renowned graduates of Wheelock were Samson Occum and Samuel Kirkland. Occum was sent by Wheelock to England and Scotland to raise funds and was lionized there. He was thwarted in fulfilling his first assignment to the Cherokees and in a much later one to the Oneidas. All his adult life he was pastor and evangelist to the Mohegans, Niantics, and Montauks. Coming to an agreement with the Oneidas in 1773-1775, he led most of his people in 1784 to Brothertown in central New York. Occum's life was hard and not the least because Wheelock and the white parsons always expected a much higher quality of performance from him than from themselves. (Blodgett 1935; Richardson 1933; Beaver 1966B, 153-183).

Samuel Kirkland, after leaving Wheelock's school, studied at the College of New Jersey (Princeton), and then in 1766 began his mission to the Oneidas. During the Revolution he kept them friendly to the Americans, and Congress supported him as missonary, chaplain to the army, and Indian agent. The academy which he founded later became Hamilton College. (Lennox 1932).

One mission of the period was in stark contrast to the New England missions, and that was the Anglican mission to the Mohawks. It came into being though the influence of two royal governors of New York, the Earl of Bellomont and Lord Conbury, with the support of Queen Anne and the Archbishop of Canterbury, who prevailed upon the newly formed Society for the Propagation of the Gospel in Foreign Parts to undertake it. The Rev. Thoroughgood Moore was sent to Albany in 1704, but Henry Barclay, appointed in 1737, was the first effective missionary. The incumbants at Albany doubled as pastors to the whites and as missionaries to the Indians, but the Indians got too little attention. The first fulltime appointee, the Rev. John Stuart, arrived at the outbreak of the Revolution, just in time to be interned. The mass movement into the Church of England was fostered by the principal war chief, Thayendanegea or Joseph Brant, and the Superintendent of Indian Affairs, Sir William Johnson. They detested the New England Puritans and they believed that Indians could become Christians and remain thoroughly Indian. Most of the nation became Christians. Remaining loyal to Great Britain, most of the Mohawks moved to Ontario after the Revolution. (Klingberg 1940; Lydekker 1938; Flexner 1865; Buell 1903; Pound 1930; Chalmers 1955; Wood 1922).

THEOLOGY, MOTIVATION, AIMS, AND METHODS IN THE COLONIAL PERIOD

It is difficult to estimate the amount of popular support of
the missions in the early period. Societies were founded in
Great Britain to sustain the work. The very first of all Protestant mission agencies was chartered by Parliament on July 27,
1649: the Society for the Propagation of the Gospel in New
England. Rechartered after the Restoration as the Company for
the Propagation of the Gospel in New England and Parts Adjacent
in North America, it was popularly known as the New England
Company. Its local agents were the Commissioners of the United
Colonies of New England until their dissolution in 1684, after
which local divines and laymen were appointed to a Board of Commissioners. This company made grants to Eliot, his colleagues,
the Mayhews, and others. (Kellaway 1962; Chaney 1976, 106-108)
Its Boston board overlapped with the Indian Commissioners of the
Society in Scotland for Propagating Christian Knowledge. This
Scottish Society had also a New York-New Jersey Board, the functions of which were eventually turned over to the Trustees of
the College of New Jersey at Princeton, and briefly a Connecticut Board related to Wheelock's work. This Society was founded
in 1701 for work in the Scottish Highlands, was chartered in
1709, and got into support of the Indian missions in 1730 because of a bequest made for that purpose. Harvard College got
an Indian Fund in the same manner. The Edinburgh Society supported Stockbridge and missions to the Iroquois country. There
were also three Anglican societies which Dr. Thomas Bray established after spending some time in Maryland as commissary of the
Bishop of London: The Society for Promoting Christian Knowledge, 1699 (for literature for Anglican priests), the Society
for the Propagation of the Gospel in Foreign Parts, 1701 (for
the provision of Anglican ministers in the colonies), and Dr.
Bray's Associates (for education of African slaves). The Mohawk mission was the first effort of evangelization undertaken
by the S. P. G. (Thompson 1951; Klingberg 1940) These several
societies fixed the pattern of organization for mission by
Protestants with the exception of the Moravians, whose entire
denominational structure existed for mission. The Moravians
did organize societies, however, for raising funds among non-
Moravians.

The first local missionary society in America was organized
in Boston in 1747 in support of the mission at Onohoquaga
through the influence of David Brainerd. Wishing to continue
the outreach to the Iroquois and to cooperate with the Society
in Scotland, persons in the vicinity of Boston in 1762 secured
from the legislature a charter for a Society for Propagating
Christian Knowledge, but the King in Council disallowed it.
(Kellaway 1962, 194-196) The legislatures of the several col-

onies, especially Massachusetts, gave land and money to the missions; and Congress made grants during the Revolution to Kirkland, Wheelock, John Sergeant, Jr., and some of the Indian preachers. Samuel Hopkins and Ezra Stiles, Congregationalist pastors in Newport, Rhode Island in 1773 founded a society to send freedmen to Africa as missionaries, received good support, and had two men in training when the outbreak of the Revolution ended that venture. How much direct giving was done by individuals and churches cannot be discovered. John Eliot, who once wrote that all the churches made collections, would never respond to that question put by the officers of the New England Company. Cotton Mather reported that all the good people were glad for Eliot's work and that the ministers supported him. (Magnalia I, 503) Support was surely greater in Massachusetts than elsewhere. During the Revolution it dwindled to practically nothing.

   Action and support in mission were forthcoming because the impulse to evangelization was theological much more than humanitarian or prudential. Charles Chaney in *The Birth of Missions in America* states:

> Reformed theology from all of its varied sources
> molded the thought of those who returned to lead
> the English Church after the Marian Exile. Those
> ideas that related mission work to God and his
> Church, that dignified the mission by locating it
> in the fabric of history, and that provided mis-
> sionary motive and zeal were generally common to
> all of English Protestantism in the Elizabethan
> period. In reality, the English Reformation
> rather than distinctively Puritan thought provided
> the frame of colonial missionary theology. (p. 6)

But it was the Puritans who were most influential and who first took action. The main dynamic for mission was eschatology. The settlers of Massachusetts (and New England generally) viewed their occupation of the new continent as "an errand into the wilderness" to make it blossom as the rose through these servants of God entering into his purpose to bring history to its grand fulfillment in his Kingdom. Bringing the lost Indians home to God was seen in this context. (Chaney 1976, 30-40; Rooy 1965; Beaver 1959).

   The mission was "the work of the Lord amongst the Indians for forwarding of publishing of the glad tydings of peace." (Commissioners to Governor of the N. E. Company in Forde 1896, 18) Consequently the greatest motive for mission was *gloria Dei*, the giving of glory to God. (Mather, Magnalia, I, 524;

Chaney 1976, 17-19; Beaver 1968B, 23-29) It remained first until a quarter century after the Revolution. Coupled with that
motive was compassion for the spiritual fate of the perishing
heathen and pity for his miserable physical and intellectual
state of barbarism. Cotton Mather put it succinctly thus:
"... God has caused us to desire his *Glory* in your salvation;
and our hearts have bled with *pity* over you, when we see how
horribly the Devil *oppressed* you in this, and *destroyed* you in
another world." (Mather, Magnalia I, 524-525).

Other motives in New England missions were the obligation of
carrying out the missionary objectives of the charters, being
coworkers with God in the furtherance of the Kingdom, love of
Christ, submission to the will of God, discerning the signs of
the times (prophecy), emulation of the Roman Catholic missionaries, and blocking further advance by France and French missions. (Beaver 1962, 1966B; Chaney 1976, 48-84) The Moravians
and David Brainerd were primarily moved by the love of Christ.
Indebtedness to the Indians was a theme of sermons in London,
but the Americans had no such idea. As Solomon Stoddard put it:
the British had come to the Indians' market and paid their asking price for the land, even though the King's patent had made
that legally unnecessary. (Stoddard 1722) Samuel Hopkins
brought together the glory of God, compassion for souls, and
obedience into the doctrine of "disinterested benevolence," a
powerful motive to vocation and support for three-quarters of a
century. Missions best glorify God, save others, and bring the
least personal honor and reward to an individual. (Chaney 1976,
81-83, note references in Hopkins' Works.) Eleazer Wheelock in
1763, like Solomon Stoddard forty years earlier, regarded the
depredations by hostile Indians as the scourage of God's wrath
because of disobedience to the missionary purpose of God and to
the charters. One must participate in mission to absolve himself from the common guilt. Moreover missions were an economi-
cal means of defense. If only half the money spent on fortifi-
cations and military campaigns were invested in missions to the
Indians, converted Indians would provide a much more effective
defense for the settlers, and the resulting profit to the Crown
would have paid all the expense of the missions. (Wheelock
1763; Beaver 1966B, 229; McCallum 1932, 12) The Rev. Charles
Chauncy told Joseph Bowman at his ordination that his ministry
would serve both God and Country, and Joseph Sewall asserted
through the missions "the presence of Christ will be like a
wall of fire" on the frontiers. (Beaver 1966B, 62, 206, 207).

The mission was possible because the Indians were regarded as genuinely human, if not humane, persons created spiritually in the image of god, although utterly depraved through the power of Satan. They were naturally endowed with reasonable minds, which could comprehend and respond to the gospel. They could be saved and must be saved, although they were the very dregs and ruins of mankind, slaves of the Devil, as their barbarism proved. (See Chaney 1976 for documentation, 19-21; Pearce 1952) The Puritan exclaimed: "We cannot but adore the kindeness of God towards poore lost souls, his great compassion in seeking and searching out his sheepe, among the poore naked natives of the wilderness, so far removed from the sound of his glorious Gospell, and the wisdome of his unsearchable Counsells appearing in his providences that have been very wonderful for handling the word of life unto them." (Forde 1896, 35) Responding to the gospel with faith the Indians could be redeemed from sin and everlasting death, and from barbarism to civilization. The question was answered once and for all, and no later American missionaries ever questioned the basic humanity, the possession of souls, and the reasonableness of mind of any primitive people, no matter how frequently and vehemently other whites might call them beasts.

Evangelization and civilization were inseparable. Transformation from damnation to salvation and growth in Christian faith would be demonstrated in the progressive conformity of the converts to English civilization. Puritan man represented the very flowering of the gospel. The gospel was powerful enough to make the Indian Christian into one. He need not be a second class Christian. The Indian had no choice. The only dissenters were Johnson and Brant among the Mohawks and Charles Chauncy in Boston, who held that Indians could be Christians and remain Indian culturally. (Beaver 1966B, 200) The Moravians were told by Count Zinzendorf not to apply the Herrnhut "yardstick," yet they made the converts Herrnhuters. (Schattschneider 1975, Hamilton 1951) Eliot told the Indians that:

> ...they and wee were already all one save in two
> things .... First, we know, serve, and pray unto
> God and they doe not: Secondly, we labour and
> work in building, planting, clothing ourselves,
> and they doe not ... I told them that if they would
> learn to know God I would teach them. (Shepard
> quoted by Chaney 1976, 22)

All the missionaries undertook that dual task.

The above propositions about the purpose of missions and the nature of the Indian determined methods. (For a more detailed account of methods see Beaver 1969) Heavily doctrinal preaching (Brainerd and the Moravians were exceptions) was the means employed above all else, although Thomas Mayhew, Jr., began with personal conversation and "spent more time after sermon in reasoning with them than in sermon." (Mather, Magnalia II, 371) Catechization intensified the impact of the preaching, and the first book printed in any Indian language was Eliot's *Indian Cathechism*. Fearful of the influence of bad whites, on the one hand, and of pagan Indians, on the other, the converts, inquirers, and their families were collected into villages of "Praying Indians." The church and the school built by the colonial government, in the case of the Puritans, were at the center of the common life. The organization of churches was at first long delayed, but by the second century was effected as soon as there were baptized converts. Farming, carpentry, blacksmithing, spinning, weaving, and other crafts were taught in school along with reading, writing, and religious subjects. There were more red than white teachers. Few white ministers other than Eliot, the two Sergeants, Brainerd, and Kirkland were able to preach and teach in the vernacular languages. But it was the expectation that native pastors, evangelists, and teachers would be raised up adequate in numbers. The first Indian ordained was Hiacoomes on Martha's Vineyard in 1670. There were thirty-seven Indian ministers in Massachusetts in 1700 (Forde 1896, 83-88) John Sergeant sought to improve over the day school by establishing a boarding school, where the youths would be separated from home influence. (Sergeant 1743, 3-4) This set a precedent that would be followed in later missions to the Indians and in all missions overseas. For a time more advanced students for the ministry were sent to the Boston Latin School and to Harvard College, but that experiment was abandoned. Vernacular literature was seen necessary for education and religious nurture, and John Eliot took the lead in producing an "Indian library" including a full translation of the Bible in the Massachusetts language. Vernacular preaching and literature, organized churches, Bible translation, education for civilization including the boarding school, and the recruitment and training of indigenous ministers and other agents were methods that were passed on to Protestant overseas missions.

THE MISSION BOOM AFTER THE REVOLUTION

The revival known as the Great Awakening produced a new concern for nominal Christians and unchurched persons, those who
had not been "born again" or received the second baptism of the
Spirit. While there were many such individuals throughout the
older regions they were thought to comprise the majority in the
cabins and settlements of the frontier. Therefore, a new kind
of mission arose alongside the mission to the Indians. During
the quarter century before the Revolution and immediately after-
wards various associations, presbyteries, and synods appointed
missionaries to the frontier peoples. They must not be allowed
to become utterly heathen. (Chaney 1976, 115-128) Meanwhile
during the War the Indian missions were reduced to the vanishing
point. When the War ended the Mohegans, Niantics, Montauks
and Stockbridges removed to land ceded by the Oneidas in central
New York, only to encounter once more the forces of aggression
and attrition. Samuel Kirkland returned to the Oneidas. Suddenly enthusiasm for mission erupted with tremendous vigor.
Boston men in 1787 organized the Society for the Propagation of
the Gospel among the Indians and Others in North America, while
in the same year the Moravians revived an earlier agency now
named the Society for Propagating the Gospel among the Heathen,
intended to receive any compensation that Congress might give
for war losses and to accept gifts from persons not Moravians.
(Chaney 1976, 138-140; Weiss, n.d., appendix; Elsbree 1928, 49-
51; Hamilton, K. G., 1940, 114-124) Others followed rapidly.

The Connecticut Missionary Society was established by the
state Congregationalist body in 1789, and the Massachusetts Missionary Society came into being the following year. Both made
efforts but failed to maintain continuing missions to the Indians. (*Panoplist* XI (1815), 222-224; Chaney 1976, 140-141) The
Friends' Aborigines Committee of Philadelphia of 1795 (Kelsey
1917, 92) sent an educational mission to Chief Cornplanter's
Seneca. (Wallace 1970) The examples of the new Baptist Missionary Society (1792) and especially of the union London Missionary Society (1795) had immediate impact across the Atlantic
Ocean. The New York Missionary Society was organized in 1795
and the Northern Missionary Society in the State of New York in
1796. (New York Missionary Magazine 1800, 5-15, 89-109; Chaney
1976, 158-160) These two agencies sent missionaries to the
Tuscaroras and other Iroquois in New York. By 1820 there were
twenty or thirty similar societies, almost all of them having
the world in view and mentioning specifically as the objects of
mission the Indians, the frontiersmen, and the heathen to the
ends of the earth.(Chaney 1976, 154-174; Elsbree 1928) However,
the frontier was moving so rapidly that it absorbed nearly all
the men and money, leaving only a small supply for the Indian

mission and none for overseas. The women began organizing in financial and prayer support of these societies beginning with the Boston Female Society for Missionary Purposes in 1800 and the Boston Female Cent Society in 1802. (Beaver 1968, 13-34)

The Federal government's responsibility for Indian affairs after the inauguration of the Constitution rested in the War Department. General Henry Knox, first Secretary of War, decided that civilization was the only alternative to extermination of the red men. He believed that Christian missionaries, or persons so motivated, were best able to undertake such a program as he recommended to President Washington in 1789. (*American State Papers*, Class 2/1, IV, 52-54) Resident missionaries, who would never be involved in trade or land acquisition, would be supplied with farm machinery and implements and with stock. They would teach religion and morality and inculcate friendship for the United States. (*Ibid.*, 65-66) The Iroquois in a council in 1792 requested on Samuel Kirkland's behalf an annual grant of $1,500, since Kirkland was aiming at transforming his little school into an advanced academic-agricultural academy. That sum was authorized for twenty-one years, but it could not be used because Knox thwarted his own plan by a decree that such funds could not be used to teach Christianity to persons who were not already converted. (*Ibid.*, Class 2/1, IV, 167-170, 225, 235; Lennox 1932, 171ff; Ibbotson 1922, 27-31) Kirkland found other resources, and his Hamilton Oneida Academy was chartered in 1793. Knox did stimulate new interest in the missions to the missionaries.

The New York Missionary Society devised a new plan which would be developed in approaches to the Southern tribes and the Plains Indians across the Mississippi River during a third of a century. It was based on the earlier New England models, Knox's concept, Kirkland's school, and the mission of the London Missionary Society to Tahiti. During the spring of 1799 the Rev. Joseph Bullen and Deacon Ebenezer Rice were commissioned as missionaries to the Chickasaws in western Georgia. They were given letters of commendation and assistance to the War Department. Rice was to be both catechist and general mechanic in charge of construction. Both men were expected to teach farming and crafts. Bullen's son would be schoolmaster. The wives and daughters in both families would instruct girls and women. A blacksmith was hired. Here then was "the mission family" which would comprise a team for evangelization and education and be the nucleus of a church. A "settlement" was to be made as soon as possible, but the timing was to be left to the Indians. Un-

fortunately after reports of a good beginning, the mission disintegrated, and was terminated in 1803. (Beaver 1966B, 235-248;
N. Y. Missionary Society, *Annual Report*, 1800, 1801, 1802, 1803,
1804).

However, in that very same year the Standing Committee of the
General Assembly of the Presbyterian Church in the U. S. A. appointed Gideon Blackburn missionary to the Cherokees with the
understanding that: "The preaching of the word is not the immediate object of the present mission but to prepare the way
for its reception at a future and . . . not too distant day."
(Chaney 1976, 165-166) He established an academy which operated
for seven years. The War Department gave a small grant and in
1810 it began to give a small annual subsidy to the Moravian
school for Cherokees at Springplace. (Schwarze 1923, 101, 107)
The mission was being renewed with an emphasis on education or
civilization and in another phase of the church-state partnership in missions.

THE FOREIGN MISSION BOARDS AND THE INDIANS:

THE CIVILIZATION FUND

The long delay in sending missionaries overseas was broken
through a student movement which originated at Williams College
and Andover Theological Seminary when the American Board of
Commissioners for Foreign Missions was organized in 1810. The
first missionaries were sent to India in 1812. The General
Convention of the Baptist Denomination for Foreign Missions was
founded in 1814. Through action of the highest judicatories of
the Presbyterian Church in the U. S. A., the Associate Reformed
Church, and the Dutch Reformed Church there was founded in 1817
the United Foreign Missionary Society for the middle Atlantic
States; and it eventually took over the missions of the New
York and Northern New York Societies. (Chaney 1976, 188-203 for
documentation) The U. F. M. S. had financial difficulties, and
it merged with the American Board in 1826. That merger brought
Presbyterians, Dutch Reformed, and others into the A. B. C. F.
M. The Methodist Episcopal Church organized its Missionary
Society in 1819 and the Episcopal Church its Domestic and
Foreign Missionary Society in 1821. The Presbyterian Church
divided into New and Old School branches. The New School people
remained with the American Board, but in 1836 the Old School
General Assembly took over the recently established Western
Foreign Missionary Society of the Pittsburg Synod and made it
its Board of Foreign Missions. Denominationalism was becoming
rampant and characteristic of American Christianity largely
because of religious liberty and competition for support. One
after another throughout the nineteenth century the denomina-

tions organized their boards for foreign missions. Since they
were concerned with evangelization of the heathen speaking languages other than English they naturally assumed responsibility
for the missions to the Indians and most of them retained it
until after the Civil War. While the Methodist national organization nominally had control, actually the Indian missions were
largely managed by the local conferences and districts. National organizations could treat with government much more effectively than small local or regional societies.

It was in each case an impetus given by the federal government which stimulated the two great advances in Protestant missions to the Indians during the nineteenth century; but it was
the American Board's first Indian mission which resulted in the
establishment of the Civilization Fund. Cyrus Kingsbury was
dispatched to the Cherokees in 1816. He stopped in Washington
en route for conversations with the President, the Secretary of
War, and other officials. He recalled the deleterious effects
of white aggression on the tribes and argued that Americans
should share their blessings with the red men through schools,
and thus bloody and costly wars would be avoided. He asked for
buildings and farm tools. President Madison heartily endorsed
the plan, and the Secretary of War ordered the agent for the
Cherokees to build a school house and a home for the teacher
where the pupils might board. (*American State Papers*, Class 2,
II, 477-478; Walker 1931) Kingsbury established the Brainerd
Station at Chickamauga, and then left it to others and went on
to found the Eliot Mission among the Choctaws. (A. B. C. F. M.,
Annual Report, 1816-1822; Strong 1910, 35-46).

The House of Representatives responding to President Madison's annual message to Congress in 1818, recommended that the
Indians be "moralized" rather than exterminated and established
a permanent "Civilization Fund," by an act of March 1819. It
provided a meagre appropriation of $10,000, but it worked won-
ders in calling the churches to action. The subsidy was available for schools of agriculture and mechanical and domestic
crafts in tribes near the borders of settlements. The government provided two-thirds the cost of buildings. Until its
termination in 1873 the Fund stimulated mission action. (Beaver
1966A, 67-79) The United Foreign Missionary Society was at the
time scouting for a location west of the Mississippi, and was
awarded assistance in establishing the Harmony and Union Stations among the Osages. A year later (1820-21) grants were
awarded to the U. F. M. S. Osage schools, the A. B. C. F. M.
Brainerd and Eliot schools along with the Foreign Mission
School at Cornwall, Connecticut, the Baptist General Convention's Cherokee schools at Great Crossings and Valley Towns, the
New York Missionary Society's Tuscarora and Seneca schools, a

Presbyterian Chickasaw school, Issac McCoy's Baptist School at
Ft. Wayne, and to the Hamilton Baptist Missionary Society for
the Oneida school. (*American State Papers*, Class 2/II, 271-273)
Schools numbered twenty-one in 1824 and thirty-eight with 281
teachers and 1,159 pupils in 1826. (*Ibid.*, 457-459, 674, 825)
In addition to the societies just mentioned Episcopalians, the
Roman Catholics the Cumberland Missionary Society, the Western
(Presbyterian) Missionary Society, and the Society for the
Propagation of the Gospel Among the Indians were participating.
In the year 1825 the government gave $13,620, while $11,700 was
applied from tribal annuities and the mission agencies invested
$176,700 in private funds. (*Ibid.*, 669) The government sub-
sidy was serving as seed money for the enterprise. Without that
incentive the churches would have done far less in the Indian
missions.

Most of the church/school stations were small affairs, but
the ideal was a station with an adequate "mission Family," such
as the Brainerd and Eliot Stations and the U. F. M. S. stations
at Harmony and Union among the Osages. The U. F. M. S. states
its policy thus:

> Besides the branches of learning taught in common
> schools and Christianity, the boys will be instruct-
> ed in agriculture, and the mechanic arts,--and the
> girls in spinning, weaving, sewing, knitting, and
> household business. ...in every establishment there
> shall be a superintendent and an assistant, who shall
> be Ministers of the Gospel, a schoolmaster, a farmer,
> a blacksmith, a carpenter and such other mechanics
> as shall be found necessary, all of which come under
> the general denomination of *Missionary*. This number
> may be increased as occasion shall require, and at
> every station there shall be a Physician, by profes-
> sion; or a person acquainted with the practice of
> physic. (UFMS, *3rd Annual Report*, 1820, 18-19)

The wives are not mentioned, but they were expected to teach,
and single women were appointed also. Such a station involved
not only much personnel, but also a large financial investment
in land, buildings, and equipment. The system worked well among
the settled Cherokees and Choctaws, but it was not adapted to
the nomadic life of Osages and other Plains Indians. The Indians would move far from the station. Only a few children could
be brought back to the boarding schools.

There were day schools as well as the boarding schools, but
attendance was likely to be poor in them. Boarding schools
took the children and youths away from parental control. Some
of them, mostly in the South, were academies with ambitious
curricula, including Latin. The Presbyterian Spencer Academy
for Choctaws was most advanced, according to Robert F. Berkhofer, Jr. Most of the schools used the Lancastrian system,
borrowed from the usuage of the British disenters in their missions. This method employed the more able pupils to tutor
others. English was generally the language of instruction,
largely because it was thought that its use introduced the students to American ways of thinking, attitudes, and civilization
generally. (Berkhofer 1965, 16-43).

Because civilization was the point at which the churches and
government joined in partnership, education appears to be the
main activity of the missions. Nevertheless the missionaries
were equally concerned with saving souls, and churches were
planted and nurtured. (See Berkhofer 1965, 44-69 for description of the character of the churches.) Rufus Anderson, the
American Board administrator and theoretician who dominated
American mission thought, called for putting evangelization a-
head of civilization, and intended this principle to apply to
Indian as well as overseas schools. (Anderson in Beaver 1967,
147-172) But in the Indian work the schools continued to get
equal stress with evangelization throughout the nineteenth century. A native ministry was still the ideal as in the colonial
period, but not many Indians were ordained. A few, along with
nationals from overseas, were educated in the Foreign Missions
School at Cornwall, Connecticut. (Strong 1910, 144-145) In
church life, as in literature for both church and school, English was primarily used, and the vernaculars were employed very
little. Consequently the press did not have the important place
which it held in overseas missions. The American Board, the
Presbyterian Iowa, and the Baptist Shawnee presses were the notable exceptions. (Berkhofer 1965, 49 note 26) The American
Board Cherokee press was turned over to the Cherokee nation.
Bible translation and publishing were of very small volume compared with overseas. Congregational and Presbyterian rigorous
standards for church membership kept their congregations small,
even among the Five Civilized Tribes of the South, while the
less rigorous, more informal Baptist and Methodist churches with
their camp meetings grew more rapidly. The success of the combined civilization-evangelization program was greatest among
those five nations, and that enabled them to survive the horrors
of removal across the Mississippi and to reestablish themselves.
The American Board relinquished the Choctaw, Cherokee, and
Tuscarora missions in 1859 and 1860 because the churches were
considered mature and self-reliant.

The several mission boards followed their people into Kansas, Arkansas, the later Indian Territory, and westward along and beyond the Great Lakes, but attrition and decline were severe. The important new ventures were into the Oregon country of the Northwest and to the Dakotas or Sioux. Dr. Marcus Whitman and Samuel Parker sought mission sites for the American Board in the Oregon country in 1835 and Whitman in 1836 founded a station among the Cayuses near Walla Walla. Henry S. Spalding went at the same time to the Nez Perces at Lapwai in Idaho. (Drury 1936, 1937, 1958, 1963-66; Eels 1882, 1886; Josephy 1965, 206-207, 216, 247-252, 253-259; Hinman 1933, 65-66, 69-70; Burns 1966, 30-36, 174-177) The massacre of 1847 destroyed fourteen whites including the Whitman family. Little of the mission survived. Spalding was expelled by an Indian Bureau agent just when his work was thriving, but some of his flock remained faithful. (Josephy 1965, 281, 289-290) It was not until 1871 that Spalding was able to return as both a Presbyterian missionary and government teacher, and he arrived when a band of Christian Yakimas initiated a revival which caused the church to grow rapidly. (Josephy 1965, 432-433; Drury 1936; Hinman 1933, 69ff; McBeth 1908) The first native minister was ordained in 1879, and twenty years later there were seven of them serving six churches. (McBeth 1902, 242).

The Mission to the Dakotas was the last undertaken by the American Board and its only genuinely vigorous one after 1850. Dr. Thomas S. Williamson, Samuel Pond, and his brother Gideon established stations at Lake Harriet and Lacquirparle in 1834, from which they reached out to the nomadic Dakotas. Stephen Riggs joined them, and the half-Dakota Joseph Renville was their advisor and interpreter. Two churches were founded before 1850. (Bartlett 1876; Riggs 1869, 1887; Pond n. d.) The Episcopalians were also attracted to the Sioux. Bishop Henry B. Whipple of the Minnesota Missionary District assigned missionaries to the Oneidas, who had moved from central New York already members of that denomination. Then in 1860 he began work with the Dakotas. (Whipple 1912) There was an uprising of the Dakotas in 1862 brought on by unbelievable stupidity and grave injustices inflicted on the nation by the Indian Bureau, the suppliers, the Army, and the settlers. Since between six and seven hundred whites were killed and others captured, the popular outcry for extermination of the Sioux was loud and fierce. Those Indians most responsible fled to Canada, while thirty-eight men were hanged and the rest of the people interned under terrible conditions. (Riggs 1869; Hinman 1933, 77ff) Stephen Riggs was appointed chaplain and interpreter, while Thomas E. Williamson, J. S. Williamson, and other missionaries gave unstinted service to the prisoners at Mankato, Minnesota, and internees in a concentration camp near Fort Snelling. An elder, Robert Hopkins,

ministered to his fellow victims, and he was instrumental in the
development of a great revival. There was practically a mass
movement into the church. The elder Williamson and Gideon Pond
in a single service baptized 274 persons. Their total eventually reached 306 converts baptized. An Episcopal Church missionary baptized nine others. This baptism marked a capitula-
tion to a certain stage of acculturation. The condemned men
were moved to Davenport for three more years of prison, while
the internees were taken to Crow Creek; and at these places the
missionary ministry continued. A new edition of the Dakota
hymnal was printed and parts of the Bible were translated. All
the prisoners and internees were released and placed on the
Santee Reservation in Nebraska, where a very strong church
emerged. From it as a base Dakota pastors and evangelists evangelized other bands of the nation. The Episcopal mission also
flourished. Both the American Board and Episcopal missions emphasized the vernacular language.

When the New School Presbyterians withdrew from the American
Board in 1870 in order to unite with the Old School, the A. B.
C. F. M. turned over the larger part of the churches to the
Home Mission Board of the reunited General Assembly, and soon
entrusted the others to the American Missionary Association.
(Strong 1910, 186-195; See Walker, D. E.., 1968, 39-73, 91-123
on cultural impact.) Before this time the Baptist and Methodist
churches and missions had been transferred to the Home Mission
agencies.

Missions and government together sought persistently to force
the Indian to acculturate to the white model. Robert F. Berkhofer, Jr., in *Salvation and the Savage: An Analysis of Protestant Missions and American Response, 1787-1862* (Berkhofer 1965)
demonstrates that in the seventy-five years after the Revolution
the aim of missions was what it had been previously, namely, to
transform what was considered to be a barbarous, uncivilized,
cruel, untrustworthy, and lazy savage into an honest, humble,
trustworthy, industrious and pious counterpart of the white
American. Church, school, and the example of the missionaries
were meant to be the instruments of change. Model farms and
settlements were laid out and the Indians encouraged to conform
to them. Sex roles were to be reversed, and in particular farming and gardening were supposed to become the work of men. The
community was expected to live under law, and move gradually towards United States citizenship. Equally important as agents of
change were neighboring white settlers, Indian agents and their
employees, and the Army. They were all forces of disintegration
of Indian civilization and the missionaries were hostile to
most of them because their influence was bad and not conducive
to the high level of white civilization which the missionaries

had in view. Each party confronted the other's culture as a
totality. The Indian resisted all change, and the white man
thought him to be ignorant, stupid, and lazy. But change came
inexorably through all the various forms of white aggression,
and the longer the missionary contact lasted the more likely
there was to be change. Mixed bloods accepted Christianity
more rapidly. Adoption of the clothing of the whites was taken
to be the symbol of conversion to the white man's religion.
Progress in Christian faith was measured by the degree of visible acculturation. Invariably the conversion of a group of
Indians set them against their fellows and strife led to division or at least to the presence of two contending parties.
Berkhofer examines several varying patterns of Christian and
pagan interaction and the results thereof. With few exceptions
Christian missions tended to produce fragmentation which grew
more marked with the years. With very few exceptions acculturation fell so far short of the mark set, that few missionaries
believed that they had come even near to success.

Motivation to Indian missions during the period of seventy-
five years after the War for Independence shared in the general
motivation to world-wide mission. (Beaver 1968) The call in
the beginning struck the old notes. In its *Address to the Public* the Northern Missionary Society exclaimed: "Surely, not
only a concern for the glory of God, and gratitude for that redemption which he hath purchased with his own blood; but compassion for the souls of those savages, should arouse from indifference and prompt us to action." (*N. Y. Missionary Magazine*,
I, no. 2, 104). But by 1810 *gloria Dei* had almost entirely disappeared, and had been replaced by obedience to the Great Commission of Christ. Compassion had combined with a perversion of
eschatology in the form of millenial speculation to produce a
frantic "plucking of brands from the burning" or saving perishing souls from the everlasting fires of hell. Hopkinsian "disinterested benevolence" had been transformed into a consequence
of love of God, -- a happy working for the grace of God in the
lives of men, for if all men love God and do right in his sight
they will be saved by his grace. Nationalism had produced a
spiritual sense of manifest destiny as companion to the political notion: God in his providence was forging in America a new
man and a new nation peculiarly fitted and destined to occupy
this vast continent and to be the premier evangelist of the gospel and of democracy to the whole world.

Only a small minority of churchmen were concerned with the
Indians, and they were additionally motived by a specific feeling of indebtedness to the Indians for the wrong done them in
breaking treaties, grabbing their land, and generally defrauding
and exploiting them. "I know not what account we have yet to

settle for the manner in which we have dealt with them; but sure
I am that we can never make them better recompense than by sending them the Gospel. We have not only taken possession of their
lands, but we have sent forth among them a stream of disguised
poison: and how can we ever better make amends, either for the
cruelty or the wrong, than by sending after it the river of the
water of life with its healing virtues?" (Van Vechten 1822)
Again and again it is said that the wrongs can be righted only
by the giving of the gospel and Christian civilization. These
alone can keep the Indian from Extermination and give him the
character required to share American civilization and citizenship with the white man.

REMOVAL AND AFTERMATH

That which the federal government built up in cooperation
with the missions through the Civilization Fund it simultaneously destroyed by its policy of removing tribes to the west of
the Mississippi River and locating both eastern and western nations on fixed reservations. Many a missionary deluded himself
into thinking that the Indians could be permanently removed from
contact with, and influence by, "bad" whites. Isaac McCoy, a
Baptist missionary at the Carey Station near Niles, Michigan,
was a leader of, and spokesman for, those holding such views.
(McCoy 1840 and 1970 reprint with intro. by Berkhofer; Schultz
1972; Beaver 1966A, 95-11) A representative of anti-removal
views is James B. Finley, Methodist missionary to the Wyandots
at Upper Sandusky, Ohio. (Finley 1840, 1854, 1855, and ca.
1855; Beaver 1966A, 91-94) McCoy was a typical frontier Baptist with a very jaundiced view of the secretaries and directors
of the Baptist Board in Boston, whom he thought to be too easily
influenced by the American Board personnel. They were too ignorant and idealistic about Indians. He really believed that his
flock would be saved by removal. He lobbied with the President,
Congress, and the Baptist Convention. Across the Mississippi he
often served as government agent and surveyor; and he labored
mightily to keep whites out of Indian territory.

The eastern tribes were being pressed by federal and state
action to go westward, and one after another all or part of numerous tribes made the move, usually with suffering and death.
The land exchanged was of a much poorer nature, and the fixed
boundaries of the reservation put an end forever to freedom for
hunting and change of habitation. The drive for a national
policy of removal extended from President Monroe's special message to the Senate on January 27, 1825 to the enactment of Andrew Jackson's Indian Removal Bill on May 28, 1830. (*Addresses*

and Messages of the Presidents, I, 536-538; *Public Statutes* 1854, IV, 411)　McCoy states that Jackson offered him the post of administrator of the Civilization Fund as a reward for his services in getting the bill passed.

Removal was required even of the Five Civilized Tribes of the south, despite the fact that they had generally attained the acculturation which was the declared aim of both the federal government and the missions.　(Foreman 1953)　It was Georgia's attack on the Cherokees and their defense by the American Board and its secretary Jermiah Evarts which brought removal to the attention of the entire American public.　Georgia disregarded the treaties, extended state law over the Cherokees, and confiscated the land including mission property.　A suit brought to the Supreme Court by the tribe was dismissed for want of jurisdiction, since the Cherokees were legally "a foreign nation."　Evarts and senators who were members of the American Board then mounted a vigorous campaign in Congress and the press.　Missionaries on the spot defied the state of Georgia.　When two were imprisoned for four years at hard labor the Board took their case to the Supreme Court and fought for the Cherokees under their names.　The Court handed down a decision favorable to the missionaries and the Indians in February, 1832.　But President Jackson and Georgia ignored it, and Jackson sent the Army to remove first the Cherokees and then other tribes.　(Beaver 1966A, 103-115 for the story and documentation)

The missions generally suffered attrition under removal and were often difficult to reestablish at new sites.　Consequently they weakened steadily, and the disruption of the Civil War reduced them to a very low ebb.　The effect of the growing sectionalism and then of the War was to remove the large southern tribes from the orbit of the "northern" mission boards to that of the Southern Baptist, Presbyterian, and Methodist Churches.

PRESIDENT GRANT'S PEACE POLICY AND NEW MISSION ACTION

The second large increase in mission activity during the nineteenth century was caused by President Ulysses S. Grant's "Peace Policy."

Once the Civil War had ended and the slaves had been freed, benevolent and philanthropically inclined persons took a look at the Indians and were horrified by what they saw.　(Mardock 1971) Missionary motivation arose more than ever out of the concern for "restitution."　There was likewise a revival of the prudential motive of saving the cost of cruel and futile wars by investing in the less expensive preventive measure of conversion.

Two missionaries can be maintained at the cost of one soldier. (*Missionary Herald* LXXIV, no. 2, 38 (Feb. 1877) It is far cheaper to Christianize than to exterminate. (*American Missionary* XVI, no. 11, 254; XX, no. 3, 64; American Miss. Assoc., *Annual Report*, 1875, 17).

The Bureau of Indian Affairs had become corrupt at every level of administration. Agents and suppliers made fortunes out of jobs and contracts. Concerned persons called for a reformation and suggested bringing in the churches. The Friends had protected the Senecas in a legal land grab a generation earlier, and William Penn's friendship with the Indians was recalled. (Society of Friends 1840, 1841; Kelsey 1917) Then an editorial in the Washington *Weekly Chronicle* of September 14, 1867 suggested that the Friends be asked to save the Bureau from corrupt politics. Three organizations of Friends responded positively. The Rt. Rev. Henry B. Whipple, Bishop of the Episcopal Church in Minnesota, lobbied effectively for reform. William Welsh, an Episcopal layman, took a delegation to Washington to interview the President-elect Grant. Grant in his inaugural address said that he favored a course that would bring civilization and citizenship to the Indians. He appointed a Seneca Indian, General Ely S. Parker, as Commissioner of Indian Affairs and appointed Army officers to the several superintendencies of the Bureau. However, the Northern and Central Superintendencies in Nebraska and Kansas-Indian Territory were assigned to the Liberal and Orthodox Friends respectively. They were requested to nominate agents for the reservations. But Congress, angry at the loss of lucrative patronage, forbade Army officers to hold civilian posts. (See Beaver 1966A, 125-130 for documentation.) Following the report of an Indian Peace Commission, Congress in an Act of April 10, 1869 authorized a special fund of $2,000,000 "to enable the President to maintain peace among and with the various tribes, bands, and parties of Indians, and to promote civilization among said Indians, bring them where practicable upon reservations, relieve their necessities, and encourage their self-support." The Act further authorized the appointment of a Board of Indian Commissioners composed of ten philanthropists who would serve without financial compensation and exercise joint control with the Secretary of the Interior. However, that official, Jacob Cox, saw to it that the Board would have no real power and could only inspect and advise. There was no organic relationship of the Board to the Bureau. This is the origin of "The Peace Policy." (See Beaver 1966A, 123-176; Fritz 1963; Keller 1968; Priest 1942; Rahill 1953; Rushmore 1914; and Whitener 1959) The Board of Indian Commissioners was called a "church board," and its members were said to represent certain denominations, but none were nominated by denominational agencies. After tremendous exertions and unhappiness over utter

inattention to their recommendations the entire membership of
the Board, with one exception, resigned in 1874, but the board
continued an ineffective existence until 1933.

President Grant answered Congress' barring of Army officers
by asking mission boards to nominate all superintendents and the
agents under them and to supervise them. The boards were expected to procure administrative personnel and to engage in evangelization. The mission boards asked to participate were the
American Missionary Association (Congregationalist), the Domestic and Foreign Missionary Society of the Episcopal Church, the
American Church Missionary Society (another Episcopal agency,
but without a mission program), the Missionary Society of the
Methodist Episcopal Church, the Board of Foreign Missions of the
Presbyterian Church in the U. S. A., the Board of Foreign Missions of the Reformed Church in America, and the American Unitarian Association. Completely ignored were the three churches
with the most Indian members,--the Southern Baptist, Presbyterian, and Methodist Churches, and the two Protestant agencies
with the longest experience of work with Indians, that is, the
American Board of Commissioners for Foreign Missions and the
Moravian Church. The American Board was eventually offered one
agency, and later small agencies were given to the United Presbyterian Church in North America, the Christian Church (Disciples), and the Evangelical Lutheran Church. The boards made
valiant efforts to secure men of ability, integrity, and genuine concern for the Indians, but the salaries (formerly multiplied by graft) were far too small to provide for families, and
politicians and high officials of the Indian Bureau learned how
to circumvent the boards in their good intentions. While gentle
as doves, their secretaries were certainly not as wise as ser-
pents. Gradually, the boards were bypassed in appointments.
The situation became so intolerable that the Reformed Church and
the Orthodox Friends withdrew in 1880. The Garfield administration ignored the boards, and the Secretary of the Interior under
President Arthur, H. M. Teller, said flatly that there was no
such thing as a "Peace Policy," and terminated the connection
with the mission boards. (Beaver 1966A, 141-152 for documentation).

Evangelization was given a great boost by the "Peace Policy,"
and this continued even after its termination. The Episcopal
Church became the most active of all, entering nationally upon
Indian mission with tremendous enthusiasm. The work was supervised by an Indian Commission of the denominational Missionary
Society; the (Indian) Missionary District of Niobara was created
with William Hobart Hare as Bishop; and numerous local societies
were formed both to provide the needs of the missions and to
labor for Indian rights. Other boards also increased their ef-

forts. Missionaries increased from fifteen in 1869 to 74 in 1873, schools from ten to sixty-nine, teachers from seventeen to eighty-six, and pupils from 594 to 2,690. There were ninety churches. The annual conference of mission board executives held under the auspices of the Board of Indian Commissioners allowed for the discussion and resolution of common problems and policy.

The boards were in this period as zealous for the futherance of Indian rights as evangelization. They tried to hold Indian Territory exclusively for Indians, but failed. However, there was still lacking any sense of there being spiritual and cultural values in the Indian heritage which should be conserved in a Christian context. All the talk about religious liberty for the Indian really meant liberty of action by church agencies. The period of the Peace Policy was a time of positive action by missions, but it was all still directed towards turning the Indian into a citizen and farmer on his own individually possessed land, and conforming to white civilization. (Beaver 1966A, 152-201) The goal was integration. There was great satisfaction over passage of the Dawes Act granting Indians the right to hold land in severalty.

There was furor in some Protestant circles and among the public over the charge that the Roman Catholics were taking over the Indian schools as the first step in capturing the entire public school system. The charge was made by the Rev. Dr. Thomas P. Morgan, first as Commissioner of Indian Affairs and then as secretary of the Baptist Home Missionary Society, and by the American Protective Association, a rabid nativist organization. They blackmailed the mission boards into repudiating subsidies for their schools. Congress by stages from 1895 to 1899 reduced and cut off all subsidies for sectarian schools. This put an end to the partnership in missions to the Indians between the Protestant Churches and government which had existed from the very beginning of British colonization. Thereafter some agencies made contracts with certain tribes for schools which would receive portions of funds due the tribes from the government under the terms of treaties.

THE MISSIONS IN THE TWENTIETH CENTURY

Secretary of the Interior Karl Schurz in 1881 opened all reservations to any church or society wanting to open work, provided that sectarian competition did not disrupt the public order. This brought a few more agencies onto certain reservations. Each addition further fragmented the social structure. There was a gradual increase in the work of the older mission boards and some new ones entered upon Indian evangelization, with the greatest increase being in the southwest. A comprehen-

sive survey in 1921 revealed that twenty-three, but actually
twenty-six, denominations carried on missions to the Indians.
(Lindquist 1923, 428-429) All of them together had a total of
597 churches in 175 tribes, 268 ordained Indian ministers and 550
other Indian church workers, and 32, 164 communicants with some
80,000 additional constituents. The same survey stated that
there were forty reservations where there was neither a Roman
Catholic or Protestant church or mission. A similar survey made
in 1950 for the National Home Missions Congress indicated that
the churches or societies engaged in mission to the Indians had
grown to thirty-six, the increase being largely due to the entrance of conservative Evangelical denominations and societies.
(Lindquist 1951, 31ff) The communicant membership was only
39,200 and the constituency 140,000. There were 213 Indian
workers out of a staff of 833, showing that missionary personnel
was overwhelmingly white. The survey revealed that the ministry
was inadequate, that youth were being lost, and that there was
still very little concern about conserving the Native American
culture.

The inadequacy of the ministry noted in that 1950 survey had
just then been confirmed by a 1948 study made by an Indian minister, Dr. Frank F. Belvin. He found 232 Indian ministers, of
whom 71% responded to his questionnaire. Seventy per cent were
ordained; about 71% of all were in Oklahoma, 50% of those serving the peoples formerly called "The Five Civilized Tribes."
About 36% were Southern Baptist ministers. There were few
young men, the average age being fifty years; and those already
above sixty years of age were the largest group. More than 60%
supplemented meagre incomes by farming and stock raising. Only
31% of the ministers had finished high school, while 11% had
graduated from college and 5.5% from both college and theological seminary. Belvin himself was the only Indian minister who
had undertaken graduate study. The largest local church had
500 members, while the average membership was sixty-five. (Belvin 1942).

Unhappily there is still today a crisis in the Native
American Christian ministry. The most recent study was issued
in 1974 by the Native American Consulting Committee of the Unit-
ed Presbyterian Church in the U. S. A. The Report is entitled
*Mending the Hoop: A Comprehensive Report of the Indian Church
Career Research and Planning Project*, by Dr. Cecil Corbett and
Rev. Gary Kush of Cook Christian Training School at Tempe,
Arizona. (Corbett and Kush 1974) This survey covers the Indi-
an ministry of seven churches which cooperate in Cook School:
United Presbyterian Church, Reformed Church in America, Chris-
tian Reformed Church, American Baptist Churches, Episcopal
Church, United Church of Christ, and the United Methodist

Church. These seven denominations have 452 Indian parishes, as follows: United Presbyterian 112, Reformed Church in America 8, Christian Reformed 8, American Baptist 16, Episcopal 156, United Church of Christ 29, and United Methodist 113. They are served by 128 Indian and 49 non-Indian ministers. The Episcopal Church reported 28 priests. (Since then the first Navajo priest was ordained in August 1976.) The United Presbyterian Church has fifteen ordained pastors. The average age of the ordained clergy is fifty-two years. The ministers entered on church careers at an average age of thirty-four. Only four Indians were enrolled as students in theological seminaries in the spring of 1974. The desperate need of further education for Indian ministers is being met principally by Cook Christian Training School through programs in the School and through extension courses. 56% of ordained and 65% of fulltime lay workers were involved in such programs 1974. *Mending the Hoop* has resulted in a new emphasis on Theological Education by Extension. Between February 1975 and August 1976 Cook School's Extension Program has enrolled 286 students from nine tribes, nine states, at nineteen sites, sponsored by four denominations. (Cook Christian Training School, *Theological Education by Extension Report*, August 1976) The Episcopal Church was already engaged in its Dakota Leadership Program, and in 1975 it was offering extension courses at nine centers. (*Dakota Leadership Program Newsletter*, October 1975)

No overall survey of Indian and Inuit missions and ministries have been made since 1950, but the writer of this paper is now engaged in making a comprehensive survey of all the activities of Protestant and Roman Catholic Churches in the United States and Canada.

The secretaries of the mission boards lost their annual conference sponsored by the Board of Commissioners for Indian Affairs. Those associated with the mainline denominations then attended the Lake Mohonk Conference annually, but its concern was rights, not missions. The Home Missions Council was organized in 1908 and the following year it created its Committee on Indian Affairs. Committee membership comprised fourteen denominations, the American Bible Society, the national Y. M. and Y. W. C. As, and the Indian Rights Association. However the increasing numbers of Evangelical missions were not members. When the H. M. C. combined with twelve other agencies to form the National Council of Churches in the U. S. A. in 1950, the Committee became a department of the Division of Home Missions of the N. C. C. Now and again the National Council of Churches has undergone structural reorganization and eventually the special office for Indian Affairs disappeared. It had had the leadership of two able secretaries, first Dr. G. E. E. Lindquist

and then Rev. E. Russell Carter. During the half-century of its
existence under several names the Committee brought together representative of the member agencies for study and consultation,
developed cooperative ministries, coordinated activities, promoted comity and the establishment of new missions, improved education in government and mission schools, secured better health
service, fostered better education of ministers, and persistently
championed Indian rights. Of course the judgment of the white
secretaries determined what rights were to be protected and furthered. The Committee persistently fought the Peyote cult. It
kept the Indian Service under constant scrutiny and repeatedly
intervened with government over cases of injustice, land grabs,
and other violations of the rights of the Native Americans.
This agency was generally in friendly and cooperative relations
with the Bureau of Indian Affairs, excepting when John Collier
was Commissioner under Franklin D. Roosevelt, because they
thought him to be the enemy of the goals which the churches had
sought since the beginning of the nation. Through the influence
of the Committee a National Fellowship of Indian Workers was organized in 1936. (Handy 1956, 54-58, 74, 89-91, 149, 167-168,
199; Lindquist 1923, 1951) In recent years the Fellowship became somewhat inactive, but there has now been a revival with
the staff of the Cook Christian Training School taking leadership.

Important developments in recent years include forms of ministry to Indians in urban-industrial situations, the entrance of
more Evangelical mission agencies, the development of Mormon
missions, the coming of the Indian activist or Red Power Movement, and a changing attitude towards Indian culture.

Neither the churches nor the public have been very responsive
to the Indian Power movement, yet some notice had to be taken of
the Wounded Knee episodes, the Trail of Broken Treaties, the
occupation of the Washington headquarters of the Bureau of Indian
Affairs, the seizure of Alcatraz, of the dormitories of Augustana
College at Sioux Falls and of the Alexian Brothers' Novitiate
at Gresham, Wisconsin, as well as the protests over policy at
the Presbyterian Ganado mission. There has been no funding of
Indian projects by churches similar to that invested in certain
Black enterprises. There has been only token appointment of
Indian Personnel, such as an Indian president of Ganado College
and of a Muno woman to be director of Indian ministries for the
American Baptists. The *Christian Century* continues to give considerable news about Indian matters, and Evangelical agencies
now have a news vehicle in *Indian Life*, published by Christian
Hope Indian Eskimo Fellowship (CHIEF) every two months.

Early Mormon missions had failed for various reasons. New efforts began with the creation of the Southwest Indian Mission at Gallup, New Mexico, 1943 and the Northern Indian Mission at Rapid City, South Dakota, soon thereafter. The suffering of Indians in the terrible winter of 1948-1949 led to a still continuing program in which youths of the Church of Latter Day Saints help in farming, business, education, and recreation. Brigham Young University recruits and supports numerous Indian students. The most unusual service is the Voluntary Indian Placement Program, involving thousands of Mormon lay persons. Approximately 4,500 young Mormon Amerindians are placed in homes of church members who agree to pay the full expense of their support during the school year. (Arrington 1974, 21ff; Rappoport 1964).

Indians during the past quarter-century have left reservations and migrated to the cities, hoping to share in the affluence of the white population and to fashion a life of their own choosing. Denied their fair share of that affluence, they have been forced to adjust to a style of life very different from that on the reservations. The plight of the city Indian lay heavily on the consciences of those Christians who had done little to prepare him for that collosal change. By 1958 14% of Protestant mission personnel were in the cities. (Lively 1958, 7) Current information awaits the completion of the writer's survey. The Committee on Indian Work of the National Council of Churches created in Rapid City a pilot cooperative project sponsored by the local city and county Councils of Churches as well as itself. (Lindquist, 1951, 54-67) An Indian Service Center was established at Phoenix. (*Ibid.*, 68-69) Another important pilot project was undertaken in St. Paul and Minneapolis in 1952 by the local United Church Committee on Indian Work, offering assistance in housing, public relations, and various social services. (*United Church Committee on Indian Work* 1957).

Anne Lively's study in 1958 revealed that apparently rather suddenly there had come a surprising change in the attitudes towards Indian culture and religion. Thirty-five percent of the Protestant mission staff and 44% of Catholics still held to the traditional goal of assimilation, but 9% of Protestants and 11% of Catholics now valued Indian culture highly and advocated conservation, while 57% of Protestants and 37% of Catholics desired retention of cultural values in partial assimilation. Moreover, 81% of Episcopalians, 75% of Congregational-Christians, 74% of Roman Catholics, and 53% of Methodists regarded Indian religions as either entirely or largely reconcilable with Christianity. (Lively 1958).

Recent annual meetings of the Fellowship of Indian Workers
have been concerned with Indian religious and cultural tradition
and values and their adaptation in Christian life and worship.
The Episcopal Church has been in the forefront of the movement
for indigenization. A Navajo Episcopal Council under Navajo
leadership has been established, bringing together the parishes
in three dioceses, and the 1976 General Convention of the
Church went a step farther in creating a Navajo Mission District
for the parishes in Arizona and Utah, which will eventually have
its own bishop. The first priest was ordained in 1976. Navajo
medicine men have joined the Church and are encouraged to use
ancient prayers in private and public worship. The Dakota
Leadership Program also encourages acculturation in the Sioux
Episcopal churches. Native Americans are at last venturing into
theological discussion and writing. Discussions in the 1972 and
1974 conferences of the N. F. I. W. contributed to several chapters in Benjamin A. Reist's book, *Theology in Red, White, and
Black* (Reist 1975) and stimulated the writing of *God is Red* and
articles by the Dakota author Vine Deloria, Jr. (Deloria 1973A
and 1973B).

GENERAL EFFECT OF THE MISSIONARY IMPACT

Missionaries have ministered to the Native Americans with
great devotion and often with heroism. They sought first the
saving of souls and the planting of churches. No price can be
put upon the worth of a single soul, but many critics believe
that the tremendous investment of lives, time, and money has produced such small numerical results as to make the venture highly
questionable. Thousands of Indians and a few tribes did become
Christians, and if the total could be calculated over the three
and a half centuries the number would be impressive. A major
reason for the numerically small community of believers is that
the missionaries sought to "civilize" as well as convert and
assimilation to the white pattern was usually considered to reveal the reality of conversion. Minds did not meet. White missionaries asked white questions and answered them in white fashion. The prior work of God among the Indians was seldom recognized. Points of correspondence and identity in the two faiths
were not sought, recognized, and employed in the communication
of the gospel and in fostering the growth of an indigenous
church.

The Christian missionaries were the ardent champions of the
Indians against many forces of white aggression. They consistently fought for Indian rights as they saw them, not for what
the Native Americans wanted as their rights. Few understood
that the mission has been one of the most destructive forces in
the disintegration of Indian society and culture for two rea-

sons: There was a persistent effort to root out customs and religious ideas and practices as "barbarism" and "superstition,"
and the Christian presence was destructive of tribal structure
unless an entire tribe was converted as in case of the Mohawks
or Cherokees. As many separate parties were created as were
missions present, and they were often hostile to each other as
well as to the portion of the tribe thay called "pagan." The
mission was, of course, only one of the many forces of disintegration. They include the Indian policy of the U. S. government,
the actual practices of the Indian service and the corruption
which so long characterized it, the system of treaties made only
to be broken, the exploitation and robbing of the people by contract suppliers, the rape of the land by settlers and government,
the destruction of the hunting economy of the forest dwellers and
the killing off of the buffalo on the plains, the popular regard
of the Indian as a wild beast fit only for extermination, the
butchery and brutality of war, the internment of once free people
on reservations of poor land in a state of neglect and pauperism.
The missionaries and their supporting constituency in the churches tried to protect the Indians against many of these evils and
they championed the rights of the Indians, but usually in the
context of the ultimate goal of assimilation. One wonders what
might have happened in regard to culture and religion if the conviction about the compatibility of the gospel and Indian culture
held by Charles Chauncy, Sir William Johnson, and Joseph Brant
had been more widely accepted.

Contemporary mission theory stresses the indigenization of the
faith in any culture, an awareness by missionaries of cultural
and religious values, and the closest partnership of national
leaders and missionaries in the acculturation process. Culture
and faith interact and produce something new. By a selective
synthesis that avoids syncretism the people are offered a viable
alternative to maintenance of an obsolete order and to adoption
of the model which the intruding and dominant force is seeking
to impose. Governments everywhere attempt to produce complete
conformity of minorities to the "national" model, just as did
the United States government and the missions with respect to
the Indians. It was the five great southern tribes which best
fulfilled the expectation of the government and missionaries.
Consequently the American Board terminated its missions to Cherokees and Choctaws as having succeeded. Here and there where a
large enough portion of a people had become practicing Christians
the Christian faith did become an effective integrating force in
individual and tribal life. The case of the Pimas through the
ministry of C. H. Cook is an excellent example of what was some-

times achieved.   Edward H. Spicer (Spicer 1962, 149-150, 519-520) states: "Considered from the tribal point of view, there is no other example of constructive transformation through Protestant mission work remotely comparable to that of the Pimas."

C. H. Cook spent ten years from 1868 on the Pima reservation as a teacher invited by the headman of the tribe. He began full-time action as an evangelistic missionary in 1879, and the next year the Christian Reformed Church transferred its mission to the Presbyterian Church in the U. S. A., and Missionary Cook then had full control of the field. Within a single decade he baptized 1,800 Pimas or half the tribe. He gave reintegration and stabilization to a sadly disintegrated tribal society by reorganizing it through bringing traditional structural elements into church polity. The key to his success may have been his selection of former headmen to serve as elders of the local churches and fusing into one the church session and village council. Deacons assisted the elders in district matters as well as purely congregational matters. Annual revival meetings replaced traditional cermonies. Pima ministers led worship and preached. Teachers in government schools cooperated with the missionary. Two-thirds of the people on the reservation were members of reservation churches by the time that Cook retired in 1911. Spicer states: "The total effect of Cook's activities, which emphasized so strongly the development of leadership through their own organizations, was a strong movement towards cultural assimilation of the Pimas and the regeneration of a dying community organization." Cook's insistence on English baptismal names, short hair, and rejection of certain customs did not lead to rejection of his leadership. (Cook 1976. On camp meetings see George Walker 1969.)

THE EFFECT OF MISSIONS ON INDIAN RELIGIONS

There is today throughout the Christian world mission a general acceptance of the necessity of the accommodation, acculturation, or indigenization of the Christian faith to the specific culture of each people. The newest term for this is contextualization, which stresses theological reformulation. However, this position has come late in mission history, and the missionaries usually transplanted doctrine, polity, piety, and cultus from their homelands and churches and reproduced the models familiar to them. Nationals were until very recent times discouraged from attempts to make cultural adaptation and the autonomy of churches was long delayed. One consequence has been the rise of what westerners call independent or separatist churches. They are a universal phenomenon but most numerous in Africa where there are more than 6,000, ranging in size from a single congregation to the huge Church of Jesus Christ on Earth through the Prophet Simon Kimbangu, which claims 4,000,000 members. (Examples: Barrett 1968; Daneel 1971-74; Martin 1976) Some have broken off from mission churches over the question of indigenous leadership and others have arisen spontaneously out of the desire to express Christianity in indigenous cultural form. Some are syncretistic forms of indigenous religion with Christian aspects. They tend to practice faith healing, and they arise in greatest numbers where the prophet is an important figure in society and where missionaries have been present for a long span of years. Given the general repression of Indian culture and religion, the slowness of missionaries to raise up an adequate Indian ministry, the practice of curing in Indian religion, and the place of the prophet in tribal societies, it might be expected that the impact of missions would have resulted in numerous indigenous religious movements. However, they have been relatively few.

Syncretism or even legitimate adaptation was not possible in Christian cultus whenever the missionary held all of church life firmly in a paternalistic hand and completely controlled the community. There were numerous places in the southwest where missionaries and officers of state had ruthlessly suppressed indigenous religions and coerced conformity to Christianity. Following a revolt or secularization, when there was inadequate pastoral care for a long period, the native religion had revived, but often wore a thin veneer of Catholicism or added a few items of Catholic practice to the indigenous system. Prophetic movements were numerous in some areas, but not enduring. (Spicer 1962, 527ff) The more important new religions were revival movements, some aimed mostly at restoration, some at elimination of the whites, and others attempting to provide the means of coexistence. (Underhill 1965, ch. 23) Certain new religions were spontaneous attempts to appropriate the gospel by Indians in ways relevant to Indians.

The Ghost Dance Religion was one that was generally hostile to whites and sought a restoration of the prewhite situation. The Paiute founder or messiah, Wovoka or Jack Wilson, had "died" and returned to life in 1886 with a message and ceremonial that would achieve the desired goals. Dances would bring back the Indian dead and the wild game. A certain amount of Christian terminology, including the name Jesus, was used, but the content was not Christian. Wovoka was a restorationist, but he did not seek to kill off the whites. The religion spread rapidly and did in most instances aim at eliminating the whites. The Dakotas or Sioux espoused it in that form, but Ghost Dance shirts did not deflect bullets as hoped when the Army in 1890 brutally suppressed the movement. (Mooney 1896, reprint 1965; LaBarre 1972) The religion survived among the Pawnee as a na-

tionalistic revival, and was transformed into some local cults
in the northwest. (Wallace in Intro. to Mooney reprint 1965, x)
It made some headway among the Indians of the southwest, excepting the Navajo, who feared the dead. (Spicer 1962, 272-273,
527-529).

The Peyote Religion, organized and incorporated as the Native
American Church and including other cults, is the best known of
the Indian religions, and there is a voluminous literature.
(Aberle 1966, LaBarre 1969, Petrullo 1934, Slotkin 1956, Stewart
1944, 1948, 1952, Spicer 1962, 530-537) Peyote is a mildly hal-
lucinatory cactus button, long used as an aid to securing visions, a very important aspect of Indian religions. It spread
northward from Mexico. There are a few tribes among whom the
cult has no Christian features, but generally it is highly syncretistic. Its adherents call themselves Christian, but the
missionaries and the Indian Work Committee of the Home Missions
Council/National Council of Churches fought it. It is never
listed by Protestants in a directory of churches. Indian religious concepts are combined with Christian doctrine. There is
belief in the Trinity and in the traditional spirits. Its ethical teaching is much the same as that taught by the Protestant
missionaries, and there is stress on brotherly love, devoted
nurture of the family, and on that cardinal Protestant virtue of
industry. The religion succeeds in that goal so persistently
sought by the missionaries, namely, abstinence from alcohol.
The weekly worship is held from about eight o'clock on Saturday
night to eight o'clock on Sunday morning, and takes place
around a sacred fire. There is ceremonial smoking of tobacco
and the sacramental eating of the peyote. After the eating the
worshipers enter into contemplation and await a vision. The
worshipers seek power. The religion has been a constructive
force in Indian society. Organization began with the Oto Church
of the First-born, developed by Jack Koshiway with the help of
White Horn, who had brought peyotism to the Oto. The First-born
Church of Christ was incorporated in Oklahoma in December, 1914.
Others who were propagating peyotism followed Kashiway's example
with his cooperation, and several groups united in incorporating
the Native American Church in Oklahoma City on October 10, 1918.
There are other incorporated groups also. Incorporation brought
protection and recognition. (LaBarre 1969, 167-174).

The earliest and still continuing new religion to arise from
Protestant missionary impact was the Religion of Handsome Lake
or Ganiodayo among the Senecas of the Allegheny. It is variously
called Handsome Lake Church, the New Religion, the Good Message,
and the Long House Religion. The Friends of Philadelphia established their Aborigines Committee in 1795, and their first mission was to Chief Cornplanter's people on the Allegheny River.

They had been friends with Cornplanter for some years and had
educated two of his sons. Five Quakers arrived in 1799 to begin an educational mission. Conversions were not sought. One
writer says that Handsome Lake's religion was born of miscegena-
tion of Quaker and Seneca stock; but it was an equal and fruitful mating. The founder combined Quaker and Iroquoian virtues
and produced power for personal and community living. He propagated his new religion for sixteen years until his death in
1815, leaving it well established. A later revival gave it additional stability and vigor. Handsome Lake taught that the
end of the world was near, he denounced sin, and called for repentance that would lead to salvation. He taught temperance,
mutual helpfulness, the sacredness of the family bond, and co-
existence with whites. The religion brought renewal to the
Seneca people. (Wallace 1970, 239-337; Deardorf 1951).

The Shaker Religion and the Feather Cult of the northwest
coast are other indigenous adaptations of Christianity. Initial
knowledge of Christianity came through contacts with the American Board and Methodist missions into the Oregon country in the
1840s. Christianity was then largely rejected because it did
not appear to confer the power that was expected. There was a
complex of rites and practices involving singing, dancing and
prophecy current in the region during the nineteenth century.
(Dubois 1938, Frank 1975, 393) Stimulus to development was
given by the prophet Smohalla about 1870. He had "died" and
returned to life with a revelation. He was militantly anti-
white at first, but became more moderate. His cult merged with
other prophet-dance religions into the Long House Religion, so-
called because of the traditional type of building where the
rites were held. It was out of this background that the Shaker
Church arose.

The founder of the Shaker Religion or Church was John Slocum,
who "died" at Shelton, Washington, 1881, and returned to life
while relatives had gone to the city to buy a coffin. He reported that he had been denied entrance into heaven because of
his sins, and that he had been sent back to be reborn. He was
given a mission to tell others to repent and find salvation.
A second dying and resurrection brought additional illumination.
This church combined shamanism and Christian faith healing, but
it turned vehemently against shamanism as it had been tradition-
ally practiced. Shaking is a rite employed in worship and in
a healing ceremony in the home of a patient. No fees may be
received for healing. The church buildings are like simple
Protestant churches and always have a bell. There is an altar
or prayer table. Everything about the church is kept scrubbed
clean. Barnett states (p 243): "The most important rites are
those of healing, worship, thanksgiving, divination, and burial,

in approximately that order of significance. Less consistently observed are the rituals of conversion, ordination, dedication, confession, and baptism." The Lord's Supper is not practiced. Shakerism is highly individualistic, but group worship is essential. There is obsession with sin, and the individual is alone responsible for seeking his salvation. Power from God comes after proper humility and submission. Doctrine is weak. The church provides identity and cohesion. It is not anti-white, but it is for Indians only. (Barnett 1957; Frank 1975, 394ff; Gunther 1949).

The Feather Religion, founded by a Klickitat, Jack Hunt, about 1904, is another variety of the Long House Religion. (Dubois 1938) Ruth M. Underhill states that it is a reaction to the Shakers with more Indian features. (Underhill, 1965, 262).

The Holy Ground Religion, propagated by Silas John among the Apaches beginning about 1920 and still practiced, is apparently the youngest of the new religions. A petition to the superintendent of the San Carlos Agency in 1921 asking for permission to hold "Indian Prayer Service" every Sunday concludes with this paragraph:

> Believing that it will not be well to force
> civilized church work on our people, who have for
> past unknown ages, been untouched by such proceed-
> ings; we desire to take step by step, and if fate
> does not interfere hope to induce our Apache Indians
> to live a pure Christian life, such as they never
> dreamed of. Those who come and help along with our
> work are all expressing a feeling of Brotherly Love
> and cooperation,...

The missionaries openly opposed the new religion. There is an annual ceremony as well as weekly worship. Its development was not deterred by Silas John's imprisonment for thirty years. Edward H. Spicer describes the religion as "a combination of concepts, rituals, and moral rules from Protestant and Catholic Christianity and the old Apache religious system, with the latter predominating." Traditional medicine men practice their ritual as part of the Sunday worship within the "Holy Ground." (Spicer 1962, 532-536).

There are phenomena common to all these new religious movements. The prophet, the vision, and faith healing are very similar to the new churches in Africa. Given the rise of Indian consciousness and the activist movement, on the one hand, and the powerful Charismatic Movement sweeping through Protestantism

and Roman Catholicism, on the other, the time seems ripe for
the advent of a prophet with charismatic power to lead a movement on a continental scale.

Just as the separatist churches in Africa are a challenge to
the mission-planted churches, so the several new forms are a
challenge to American Indian mission Christianity. They reveal
the genuine spiritual concerns of the Indians, the questions
which they ask, and some indication of directions in which acculturation must move. Vine Deloria, Jr., has pioneered with a theological apologetic for the Indian cause with his book *God is
Red*. (Deloria 1973; see also 1973B) A missionary to the Navajos
writes to the author of this paper that he and his people are
seeking illumination to move away from the paternalism of their
ancestors in the mission. A new day in the American Indian
Church is inevitably dawning.

BIBLIOGRAPHY OF WORKS CITED

Aberle, David F.   1966.   The Peyote Religion Among the Nava-
                                ho. Chicago: University of Chicago
                                Press

Addresses and Messages of the Presidents of the United States,
                                Inaugural, Annual, and Special,...
                                1789 to 1846, comp. by Edwin Wil-
                                liams, 2 v. N. Y.: E. Walker, 1846

American Board of Commissioners for Foreign Missions. Annual
                                Report, from 1810

American Missionary   Organ of the American Missionary
                                Association. Indian affairs begin-
                                ning in 1870

American State Papers, Documents, Legislative and Administrative,
                                of the Congress of the United
                                States, 38 v. Washington, D.C.:
                                Gales & Seaton, 1832-1861

Arrington, Leonard J. 1974.   "The Mormons and the Indians."
                                Mimeo. paper presented at Florida
                                State University, 1974

Barrett, David B.   1968.   Schism and Renewal in Africa. Nai-
                                robi: Oxford University Press.

Bartlett, S. C.   1876.   Historical Sketch of the Missions
                                of the American Board among the
                                North American Indians. Boston:
                                American Board of Commissioners for
                                Foreign Missions

Beals, Carleton.   1957.   John Eliot, the Man Who Loved the
                                Indians. N. Y.: Julian Messner

Beaver, R. Pierce   1948.   "The Concert of Prayer for Mis-
                                sions." *Ecumenical Review*, July
                                1948, 420-427

                        1959.   "Eschatology in American Missions."
                                Basileia. Walter Freytag zum 60.
                                Geburtstag. Stuttgart: Evang.
                                Missionsverlag

Beaver, R. Pierce.   1962A. "American Missionary Motivation Be-
                             fore the Revolution." *Church His-
                             tory*, XXXI, 2 (June 1962)

                      1962B. Ecumenical Beginnings in Protestant
                             World Mission. The History of
                             Comity. N. Y.: Thomas Nelson & Sons

                      1966A. Church, State, and the American In-
                             dians. St. Louis: Concordia Pub-
                             lishing House

                      1966B. Pioneers in Mission. Grand Rapids:
                             Eerdmans

                      1967. To Advance the Gospel: Selections
                             from the Writings of Rufus Anderson,
                             ed. with an introduction by R. P. B.
                             Grand Rapids: Eerdmans.

                      1968A. All Loves Excelling. American Prot-
                             estant Women in World Mission.
                             Grand Rapids: Eerdmans.

                      1968B. "Missionary Motivation through
                             Three Centuries." Reinterpretation
                             in American Church History, ed. by
                             Jerald C. Brauer. v. V of Essays
                             in Divinity. Chicago: University
                             of Chicago Press, 1968

                      1969. "Methods in American Missions to the
                             Indians in the Seventeenth and
                             Eighteenth Centuries." *Journal of
                             Presbyterian History*, 47, no. 2
                             (June 1969), 124-148

Berkhofer, Robert F.,Jr. 1965. *Salvation and the Savage*. Lexing-
                             ton: University of Kentucky Press.

Belvin, B. Frank.   1949. The Status of the Indian Ministry.
                             Shawnee: Oklahoma Baptist University

Blodgett, Harold.   1935. Samson Occum. Hanover, N. H.: Dart-
                             mouth College

Bolton, Herbert E.   1915.   Texas in the Middle Eighteenth
                                Century. Berkeley: University of
                                California Press

                        1916.   Spanish Exploration in the South-
                                west, 1542-1706. N. Y.: Scribner

                        1960A. The Mission As a Frontier Institu-
                                tion. El Paso: Academic Reprints,
                                (reprint of a classic)

                        1960B. The Rim of Christendom, A Biography
                                of Eusebio Francisco Kino, Pacific
                                Coast Pioneer. N. Y.: Russell &
                                Russell (originally 1936)

Brainerd, David.   1793.   Mirabili Dei inter Indicos: Or the
                                Rise and Progress of a Remarkable
                                Work of Grace ... Worcester, Mass.:
                                Leonard Worcester

Brown, Alexander.   1897.   The Genius of the United States ...
                                a Series of Historical Manuscripts.
                                2 v. Boston: Houghton, Mifflin.

Buell, August C.   1903.   Sir William Johnson. N. Y.: Appleton

Burns, Robert I.   1966.   The Jesuits and the Indian Wars of
                                the Northwest. New Haven: Yale
                                University Press

Chalmers, Harvey.   1955.   Joseph Brant, Mohawk. East Lansing:
                                Michigan State University Press

Chapman, C. E.   1916.   Founding of Spanish California,
                                1687-1783.
                        1972.   Reprint: N. Y. Octagon Books

                        1921.   History of California: The Spanish
                                Period.
                        1971.   Reprint: East St. Clair Shores,
                                Michigan: Scholarly Press

Chaney, Charles   1976.   The Birth of Missions in America.
                                S. Pasadena: William Carey Library

Chittenden, Hiram M. and
Alfred T. Richardson. 1905. Life, Letters, and Travels of
                            Father Pierre Jean De Smet, S. J.,
                            1801-1873. 4 v. N. Y.: Harper.
                       1969. Reprint: N. Y.: Arno Press

Cook, Minnie.   1976. Apostle to the Pimas. The Story of
                            Charles H. Cook. Tiburon, CA.:
                            Omega Books

Corbett, Cecil, and
Gary Kush.   1974. Mending the Hoop. Report of the
                            Indian Church Career Project. Ob-
                            tainable: Tempe AZ.: Cook Chris-
                            tian Training School

Daneel, M. L.   1971. Old and New in Southern Shona
                            Churches. The Hague: Mouton. 2 v.
                            v. 1, 1971, v. 2, 1974

Deardorff, Merle H.   1951. "The Religion of Handsome Lake." in
                            Fenton, Willian N., ed. Symposium
                            on Local Diversity in Iroquois Cul-
                            ture. Smithsonian Institution,
                            Bureau of American Ethnology, Bulle-
                            tin 149. Washington: U. S. Govern-
                            ment Printing Office

Delanglez, Jean.   1939. Frontenac and the Jesuits. Chicago:
                            Institute of Jesuit History.

Deloria, Vine, Jr.   1973A. God is Red. N. Y.: Grossett &
                            Dunlap.

                      1973B. "The Theological Dimensions of the
                            Indian Protest Movement." *Chris-
                            tian Century*, XC, no. 33 (Sept.),
                            912-14

                       1974. The Indian Affair. NY: Friendship
                            Press.

De Smet, Pierre-Jean, S. J. 1847. Oregon Missions and Travels,
                                 N. Y.: Edward Dunigan

                            1863. Western Missions and Mission-
                                 aries. N.Y.: James B. Kirker

Dozier, Edward P.　　1975.　"Rio Grande Pueblos."　Spicer Edward
　　　　　　　　　　　　　　　H., ed. Perspectives in American
　　　　　　　　　　　　　　　Indian Culture Change.　Chicago:
　　　　　　　　　　　　　　　University of Chicago Press

Drury, Clifford M.　　1937.　Marcus Whitman, M. D., Pioneer and
　　　　　　　　　　　　　　　Martyr.　Caldwell, Idaho:　Caxton
　　　　　　　　　　　　　　　Printers

　　　　　　　　　　　　1936.　Henry Harmon Spalding, Pioneer of
　　　　　　　　　　　　　　　Old Oregon.

　　　　　　　　　　　　1940.　Mary and Elkanah Walker, Pioneers
　　　　　　　　　　　　　　　among the Spokanes. Caldwell, Idaho:
　　　　　　　　　　　　　　　Caxton

　　　　　　　　　　　　1952.　Presbyterian Panorama.　Phila.:
　　　　　　　　　　　　　　　Westminster

　　　　　　　　　　　　1958.　The Diaries and Letters of Henry H.
　　　　　　　　　　　　　　　Spalding and Asa Brown Smith.　Glen-
　　　　　　　　　　　　　　　dale, CA.: A. H. Clark

　　　　　　　　　　　　1963.　The First White Women Over the Rock-
　　　　　　　　　　　　　　　ies. 3 v. Glendale, CA.: A. H. Clark,
　　　　　　　　　　　　　　　1963-1966

　　　　　　　　　　　　1973.　Marcus and Narcissa Whitman and the
　　　　　　　　　　　　　　　Opening of Old Oregon.　Glendale,
　　　　　　　　　　　　　　　CA.:　A. H. Clark.

Dubois, Cora.　　　　　1938.　The Feather Cult of the Middle Co-
　　　　　　　　　　　　　　　lumbia.　General Series in Anthro-
　　　　　　　　　　　　　　　pology, No. 7, ed. Leslie Spier.
　　　　　　　　　　　　　　　Menasha, Wisc.:　Banta Pub. Co.

Duratschek, C.　　　　1947.　Crusading Along Sioux Trails:　A
　　　　　　　　　　　　　　　History of the Catholic Indian Mis-
　　　　　　　　　　　　　　　sions of South Dakota.　St. Mein-
　　　　　　　　　　　　　　　rad, Indiana:　St. Meinrad Abbey

Edwards, Jonathan　　1749.　An Account of the Life of the Late
　　　　　　　　　　　　　　　Mr. David Brainerd ... Chiefly
　　　　　　　　　　　　　　　taken from his own Diary... Boston:
　　　　　　　　　　　　　　　D. Hinchman

Eels, Myron.   1882.   The History of Indian Missions on
                                    the Pacific Coast, Oregon, Washing-
                                    ton, and Idaho. Phila.: American
                                    Sunday School Union, 1882

                            1886.   Ten Years Among the Indians at
                                    Skokomish, Washington Territory,
                                    1874-1884. Boston: Congregational
                                    Sunday School & Publication Soc.

Elsbree, Oliver W.   1928.   The Rise of the Missionary Spirit
                                    in America. Williamsport, Pa.:
                                    Williamsport Printing and Binding Co.

Engelhardt, Zephyrin. 1908.   The Missions and Missionaries in
                                    California. 4 v. Santa Barbara,
                                    CA.: Santa Barbara Mission, 1908-
                                    1915. 2nd ed., 2 v., 1929-1930; re-
                                    cent reprint by Boston: Milford
                                    House

Finley, James B.   1840.   History of the Wyandot Mission at
                                    Upper Sandusky, Ohio, Under the Di-
                                    rection of the Methodist Episcopal
                                    Church. Cincinnati: Wright &
                                    Swormstedt. Recent reprint, ed. by
                                    D. W. Clark. Plainview, NY: Books
                                    for Libraries

                            1855A. Autobiography of Rev. James B. Fin-
                                    ley. Cincinnati: Methodist Book
                                    Concern

                            1855B. Life Among the Indians. Cincinnati:
                                    Curts & Jennings ca. 1855

Flexner, James T.   1959.   Mohawk Baronet: Sir William Johnson
                                    of New York. N. Y.: Harper

Ford, John W., ed.   1896.   Some Correspondence Between the Gov-
                                    ernors and Treasurers of the New
                                    England Company in London and the
                                    Commissioners of the United Colonies
                                    in America. London: Spottiswode

Foreman, Grant.   1913. Indian Removal: Emigration of the
                                 Five Civilized Tribes of Indians.
                                 Norman: University of Oklahoma
                                 Press

Frank, David.   1975. "Wasco-Wishram." Spicer, Edward H.
                                 Editor, Perspectives in American
                                 Indian Culture Change. Chicago:
                                 University of Chicago Press

Fritz, Henry E.   1963. The Movement for Indian Assimila-
                                 tion, 1860-1890. Phila.: Univer-
                                 sity of Pennsylvania Press

Garraghan, Gilvert J. 1938. The Jesuits of the Middle of the
                                 United States. 3 v. N. Y.: Amer-
                                 ica Press

Garraghan, W. B. Bischoff 1945. The Jesuits in Old Oregon. Cald-
                                 well, Idaho: Caxton Printers

Geiger, Maynard.   1939. The Kingdom of St. Francis in Ari-
                                 zona, 1839-1939. Santa Barbara,
                                 CA.: Santa Barbara Mission

Gray, Elma E.   1956. Wilderness Christians: The Moravian
                                 Missions to the Delaware Indians.
                                 Ithaca, N. Y.: Cornell University
                                 Press

Gunther, Erna.   1949. The Shaker Religion of the North-
                                 west. N. Y.: Smith, Marian W., ed.
                                 Indians of the Urban Northwest. N.
                                 Y.: Columbia University Press

Hamilton, John T.   1967. History of the Moravian Church: The
and Kenneth G.   Renewed Unitas Fratrum, 1722-1957.
                                 Bethlehem, Pa.: The Moravian
                                 Church in America

Hamilton, Kenneth G. 1940. John Etwein and the Moravian Church.
                                 Bethlehem, Pa.: Times Publishing Co.

                          1951. "Cultural Contributions of Moravian
                                 Missionaries Among the Indians."
                                 Pennsylvania History XVIII (Jan.)

Handy, Robert T.   1956.   We Witness Together. N. Y.: Friend-
                                ship Press (Home Missions Council
                                of N. A.)

Hare, Lloyd C. M.   1932.   Thomas Mayhew, Patriarch to the In-
                                dians (1593-1682). N. Y.: Appleton

Harrod, Howard L.   1971.   Mission Among the Blackfeet. Nor-
                                man, Okla.: University of Oklahoma
                                Press

Hinman, George W.   1933.   The American Indian and Christian
                                Missions. N. Y.: Fleming H. Revell

Hopkins, Samuel.   1854.   Works of Samuel Hopkins, D. D., ed.
                                with a Memoir by Edward A. Park.
                                3 v. Boston: Doctrinal Tact & Book
                                Society

Horgan, Paul.   1975.   Lamy of Santa Fe. N. Y.: Farrar,
                                Straus, & Giroux

Ibbotson, Joseph D.   1922.   Documentary History of Hamilton
                                College. Clinton, N. Y.: Hamilton
                                College

Josephy, Alvin M., Jr. 1965.   The Nez Perce Indians and the Open-
                                ing of the Northwest. New Haven:
                                Yale University Press

Kellaway, William.   1962.   The New England Company, 1649-1776.
                                N. Y.: Barnes & Noble

Keller, Robert H.   1965.   The Churches and Grant's Peace Pol-
                                icy. Unpublished Ph. D. Disserta-
                                tion, University of Chicago

Kelsey, Rayner.   1917.   Friends and the Indians. Phila.:
                                Associated Executive Committee of
                                Friends on Indian Affairs

Kenton, Edna.   1956.   Black Gown and Redskins. Adventures
                                and Travels of Early Jesuit Mission-
                                aries in North America (1610-1791).
                                London, Toronto, N. Y.: Longmans,
                                Green, 1956 ed.

Kino, Eusebio F.   1948.   Historical Memoir of Primeria Alta,
                                1683-1711, ed. and annotated by
                                Herbert E. Bolton. Berkeley: Uni-
                                versity of California Press. 2 v.
                                in 1

Labarre, Weston.   1969.   The Peyote Cult. Revised. N. Y.:
                                Schoken. Originally New Haven:
                                Yale University Publications in
                                Anthropology, No. 19

                        1972.   Ghost Dance. N. Y.: Dell

Land, Robert H.   1938.   "Henrico and Its College." *William
                                and Mary Quarterly*, 2nd Seried, 18
                                (1938), 453-498

Lennox, Herbert J.   1932.   Samuel Kirkland's Mission to the
                                Iroquois. Unpublished Ph. D. dis-
                                sertation, University of Chicago

Lindquist, G. E. E.   1923.   The Red Man in the United States.
                                N. Y.: Doran

                        1944.   The Indian in American Life. N. Y.:
                                Friendship Press

Lindquist, G. E. E.   1951.   Indians in Transition. New York:
  with collab. E.   National Council of Churches of
  Russell Carter   Christ in the U. S. A., Division of
                                Home Missions

Lively, Anne O.   1958.   A survey of Mission Workers in the
                                Indian Field. A study Conducted for
                                the Committee on Indian Work of the
                                Division of Home Missions. N. Y.:
                                National Council of Churches of
                                Christ in the U. S. A.

Lucas, Charles.   1930.   Religion, Colonizing, and Trade, the
                                Driving Forces of the Old Empire.
                                London: SPCK

Lydekker, John W.   1938.   The Faithful Mohawks. N. Y.: Mac-
                                millan, 1938

Mardock, Robert W.   1971. The Reformers and the American
                               Indians. Columbia, Mo.: Uni-
                               versity of Missouri Press

Martin, Marie-Louise. 1976. Kimbangu, An African Prophet.
                               Grand Rapids: Eerdmans

Mather, Cotton.   1820. Magnalia Ghristi Americana, or the
                               Ecclesiastical History of New Eng-
                               land, 2 v. 1st American ed. from
                               London ed. of 1702. Hartford:
                               Andrus, Roberts, and Burr. 1820

McCallum, James D.   1932. The Letters of Eleazer Wheelock's
                               Indians. Hanover, N. H.: Dart-
                               mouth College Publications

McClure, David, and   1811. Memoirs of the Rev. Eleazer Wheel-
Elijah Parish.   lock, D. D. Newburyport, Mass.:
                               Edmund Little

McCoy, Isaac.   1840. History of Baptist Indian Missions
                               Washington: William N. Morrison.
                               Reprint by Johnson Reprint Co'., ed.
                               with intro. by Robert F. Berkhofer,
                               Jr. 1971

Missionary Herald.   Organ of American Board of Com-
                               missioners for Foreign Missions,
                               succeeding *Panoplist* in 1821

Mooney, James.   1896. The Ghost Dance Religion and the
                               Sioux Outbreak of 1890. 14th
                               Annual Report, Bureau of American
                               Ethnology, 1892-1893, Pt. 2.
                               Washington: Smithsonian Insti-
                               tution. Reprint: Anthony F.
                               Wallace, ed. University of Chica-
                               go Press, 1965

New York Missionary Magazine, 1-4, 1800-1803

New York Missionary Society. Annual Report of the Board of Di-
                               rectors, 1799 to 1815, usually
                               appended to annual sermon

O'Brien, John A.   1960. The First Martyrs of North Ameri-
                              ca: The Story of the Eight Jesuit
                              Martyrs. Notre Dame, Ind.: Uni-
                              versity of Notre Dame Press

Palou, Francisco.   1926. Historical Memoir of New Califor-
                              nia translated into English from
                              the Manuscript in the Archives of
                              Mexico, ed. by Herbert E. Bolton.
                              4 v. Berkeley: University of
                              California Press

Panoplist.   vs. 1-3 1805-1808; *Panoplist &*
                              Missionary Magazine. vs. 4-13;
                              Panoplist & Missionary Herald, vs.
                              13-17, 1817-1821; *Thereafter Mis-*
                              sionary Herald

Parks, George B.   1928. Richard Hakluyt and the English
                              Voyages, ed, by James A. William-
                              son. N. Y.: American Geograph-
                              ical Society

Pearce, Roy Harvey.   1952. "The 'Ruines of Mankind;' the In-
                              dian and the Puritan Mind." *Jour-*
                              nal of the History of Ideas, 13
                              (1952), 200-217

Petrullo, Vincenzo.   1934. The Diabolic Root. Philadelphia:
                              Oxford

Pond, S. W., Jr.   n. d. Two Volunteer Missionaries and the
                              Dakotas, or the Story of the Labors
                              of Samuel W. and Gideon Pond. Bos-
                              ton: Congregational Sunday School
                              & Publication Society

Priest, Loring B.   1942. Uncle Sam's Stepchildren, the Refor-
                              mation of United States Indian Pol-
                              icy, 1865-1887. New Brunswick, N.
                              J.: Rutgers University Press

Public Statutes at Large of the United States ... 1798 to March 3,
                              1845. 5 v. Boston: Little, Brown,
                              1948

Rahill, Peter J.   1953.   Catholic Indian Missions and Grant's Peace Policy, 1870 to 1884. Washington: Catholic University of America Press

Richardson, Leon B.   1933.   An Indian Preacher in England. Hanover, N. H.: Dartmouth College. (Samson Occum)

Richman, I. B.   1911.   California under Spain and Mexico, 1535-1847. Reprint: N. Y.: Cooper Square Books

Riggs, Stephen R.   1869.   Tah-Koo Wah-Kan, or the Gospel among the Dakotas. Boston: Congretional Sunday School & Publication Society

                                         1887.   Mary and I: Forty Years with the Sioux. Boston: Congregational Sunday School & Publication Society

Robinson, W. Stitt.   1952.   "Indian Education and Missions in Colonial Virginia." *Journal of Southern History* 18 (1952), 153ff

Rooy, Sidney H.   1965.   The Theology of Missions in the Puritan Tradition. Grand Rapids: Eerdmans, 1965

Rushmore, Elsie M.   1914.   The Indian Policy During Grant's Administration. Jamaica, N. Y.: Marion Press

Schattschneider, David A. 1975.   "The Missionary Theories of Zinzendorf and Spangenberg." *Transactions of the Moravian Historical Society*, XXLL, Part III, 213-233. Nazareth, Pa.: Whitefield House

Schultz, George A.   1972.   An Indian Caanan, Isaac McCoy and the Vision of an Indian State. Norman, Okla.: University of Oklahoma Press

Schwarze, Edmund.　　1923.　History of the Moravian Missions among the Southern Tribes of the United States. Bethlehem, Pa.: Times Publishing Co.

Sergeant, John.　　1743.　A Letter from the Rev. Mr. Sergeant of Stockbridge to Dr. Colman of Boston; Containing Mr. Sergeant's Proposal of a more Effectual Method for the Education of Indian Children ... Boston: 1743

Shea, John G.　　1899.　History of the Catholic Missions Among the Indian Tribes in the Unites States, 1529-1854. N. Y.: P. J. Kennedy (originally 1855)

Slotkin, J. S.　　1955.　"Peyotism," 1521-1891." *American Anthropologist*, v. 57, 202-230; v. 58, 184

　　　　　　　　　　1956.　The Peyote Religion. Glencoe, Ill.: Free Press, 1956. Reprint: N. Y.: Octogon, 1975

Society of Friends.　　1840.　The Case of the Seneca Indians in the State of New York. Phila.: Merrihew & Thompson

　　　　　　　　　　1841.　Appeal to the Christian Community. N. Y.: 1841

Spicer, Edward H.　　1962.　Cycles of Conquest. The Impact of Spain, Mexico, and the United States on the Indians of the Southwest, 1533-1960. Tucson: University of Arizona Press

　　　　　　　ed.　1975.　Perspective in American Indian Culture Change. University of Chicago Press. See his: "Yaqui" on pp. 7-93.

Sprague, William B.　　1858.　Annals of the American Pulpit, or Commemorative Notices of Distinguished American Clergymen. 9 v. N. Y.: Carter, 1858-1869

Stewart, O. C.   1944. Washo-Northern Paiute Peyotism.
                              Berkley: University of Califor-
                              nia Press

                       1948. Ute Peyotism. Boulder: Univer-
                              sity of Colorado Press

                       1952. Menomini Peytoism. Philadelphia:

Stoddard, Solomon.   1722. An Answer to Some Questions of Con-
                              science Respecting the Country.
                              Boston: B. Green

Strong, William E.   1910. The Story of the American Board.
                              Boston: Pilgrim Press

Talbot, Francis X.   1935. Saint Among the Savages. N. Y.:
                              Harper (Jogues)

                       1949. Saint Among the Hurons. N. Y.: Har-
                              per (Brébeuf)

Thompson, H. P.   1951. Into All Lands: History of the
                              Society for the Propagation of the
                              Gospel, 1701-1950. London: SPG,
                              1951

Tracey, Joseph, ed.   1840. History of American Missions to the
                              Heathen from Their First Commence-
                              ment to the Present Time. Worces-
                              ter, Mass.: Spooner & Howland

Underhill, Ruth M.   1965. Red Man's Religion. Chicago: Un-
                              iversity of Chicago Press

United Church Commit- 1957. A Mission to the Indian American in
tee on Indian Work,   the City. Summary Report of a Sur-
Minneapolis, St. Paul   vey by A. Z. Mann. n. p.: n. pub.

Van Vechten.   1822. The Duty of Christians Towards the
                              Heathen, Taught by the Example of
                              Christ. A Sermon ... Schechnetady,
                              N. Y.: Cabinet Printing House

Vaughan, Albert T.   1965. New England Frontier: Indians and
                              Puritans, 1620-1675. Boston: Lit-
                              tle, Brown

Walker, Deward E., Jr.   1964.   A Survey of Nez Perce Religion,
                                   .. Jan. 1964. Philadelphia: Pres-
                                   byterian Church in U. S. A., Board
                                   of National Missions

Walker, Robert S.   1931.   Torchlights to the Cherokees, The
                                   Brainerd Mission. N. Y.: Macmil-
                                   lan, 1931

Wall, James M.   1973.   "Indian Theology and the White
                                   Man's Laws." *Christian Century*,
                                   XC, no. 33 (Sept. 19), 907-908

Wallace, Anthony C.   1970.   The Death and Rebirth of the Sen-
                                   eca. N. Y.: Knopf

Weiss, F. L.   n. d.   The Society for the Propagation
                                   of the Gospel Among Indians and
                                   Others in North America. Dublin,
                                   N. H.: privately printed, n. d.

Wheelock, Eleazer.   1763.   A Plain and Faithful Narrative of
                                   the Original Design, Rise, Pro-
                                   gress, and present State of the
                                   Indian Charity-School at Lebanon,
                                   in Connecticut. Boston: Richard
                                   and Samuel Draper

                          1765.   A Continuation of the State, etc.
                                   ... of the Indian Charity-School
                                   ... 1762-1765. Boston: Draper.
                                   Further continuations were pub-
                                   lished in London by Wheelock's
                                   agent, Whitaker.

Whipple, Henry B.   1912.   Lights and Shadows of a Long Epis-
                                   copate, Being Reminiscences and
                                   Recollections. N. Y.: Macmillan

Whitner, Robert L.   1959.   The Methodist Episcopal Church and
                                   Grant's Peace Policy, 1870-1882.
                                   Microfilm dissertation, University
                                   of Minnesota

Williamson, James A.   1931.   A short History of British Expan-
                                   sion, 2nd ed. N. Y.: Macmillan

Winslow, Ola E.   1962. John Eliot, "Apostle to the Indi-
                                 ans." Boston: Houghton, Mifflin

Wood, Louis A.   1922. The War Chief of the Six Nations:
                                 A Chronicle of Joseph Brant. Tor-
                                 onto & Glasgow: Brook

Wright, Louis B.   1943. Religion and Empire: The Alliance
                                 Between Piety and Commerce in Bri-
                                 tish Exploration, 1538-1625. Chapel
                                 Hill: University of North Carolina
                                 Press

12

Two Centuries of Cultural Adaptation in American Church Action: Praise, Censure, or Challenge?

Louis J. Luzbetak, S.V.D.

During the last two centuries, in varying forms and degrees, we have observed three major directions taken by Christian missionary action: (1) an ethnocentric direction, (2) an incipient adaptational direction, and (3) an incarnational direction. The progression is from less and less ethnocentrism to more and more genuine cross-cultural sensitivity. These three directions have at times been described in slightly different terms: from dependence, to independence, to interdependence; from subjugation, to liberation, to mutuality. Personally, I prefer "mutual enrichment" to "mutuality" because the former term tells me much more about the nature of the interdependence we have in mind--not mutuality for its own sake but mutuality for mutual enrichment.

But before going any further, I wish to emphasize that we are not so much concerned about blaming the past as about learning from it, especially about learning from the past two centuries, which happen to be the theme of this year's American Society of Missiology meeting. One of the easiest mistakes to make is to look back a generation or two, or a century or two, and then to pass judgment on that generation or century in light of our present-day knowledge, opportunities, and general cultural and social context, forgetting that, a generation or a century from now, it will be our turn to be judged quite unfairly on the basis of what is impossible for us to understand, appreciate, or do today. Missionaries have always been, and always will be, children of their age. Like everyone else in the world around them, to a large extent missionaries are molded by their culture and society. We are to chide, and we deserve to be chided, only for what could and should have been understood, appreciated, and done in the given circumstances.

*1976 ASM Presidential Address

I.   ETHNOCENTRISM

A.   Anthropological Reasons For Missionary Ethnocentrism

That the missionary approach of the last two hundred years, at least in practice if not in theory, has been largely ethnocentric can hardly be denied. So that we might view this missionary ethnocentrism in a somewhat more objective light, it might be well for us briefly to recall the nature of ethnocentrism.

Social living presupposes agreement among the members of a social group on what the "rules of the game" of life should be. A society has no choice in the matter: if it is to survive as a society it must adopt for itself a set of standards and expectations ("culture") which will tell the interacting members of the particular society or sub-society what is to be regarded as normal, correct, right, proper, good, just, and beautiful. Such a socially-shared set of norms covers all aspects of life, i.e., all the "proper" ways of coping with a society's physical, social, and ideational environment. The "rules" pertain not only to the various forms (the *what, when, how, when* and *where*) but also to the *why* (to the meanings of forms and to the underlying premises, values, and goals of a particular way of life), and how all these elements relate to one another. Such agreement makes communication and the necessary predictability of behavior of interacting individuals possible. Confidence and pride in one's ways and values encourages cooperation, group loyalty and solidarity. From the point of view of *intra*-group relations, therefore, enculturation (the process of learning one's culture) is useful and, in fact, necessary.

Because the "rules of the game" are essential for survival, the individual learns such "rules" well. In fact, he generally masters them to such an extent that they become a "second nature" to him. The result is that, for any normal individual, of any society, to think, feel, or act in any way other than the "normal" requires great effort and, at times, violence to self (Luzbetak, 1976c:73-79).

On the other hand, since the individuals of all societies without exception learn to regard their specific ways and values as normal, enculturation may become dysfunctional, rather than functional, in *inter*-group relations. On the *inter*-group level, enculturation may become "ethnocentrism," the more or less unconscious tendency to regard as applicable to all societies the standards of one's own. One's own culture tends to be regarded as the superior and objective norm for judging what is right or wrong, good or bad, just or unjust, beautiful or ugly, holy or

unholy in any society. Thus enculturation, useful and necessary
especially at the *intra*-group level, may become a source of
countless misunderstandings, mistakes, and tensions at the *inter*-
group level.

Missionary work is by its very nature an inter-group rather
than an intra-group activity. It is a constant challenge to the
churches to keep ethnocentrism under control. In fact, depend-
ing on the degree of control, or lack of it, ethnocentrism may
be an inclination, an imperfection, a vice, a form of imperialism, or even madness, e.g., xenophobia, Nazism, Mau Mau terror-
ism.

Ethnocentrism is, therefore, by no means a monopoly of Christian missionaries or of Americans. It has always plagued poor
mortals, and I venture to say that it exists even here in our
midst at this moment as we protest against it. I venture to say
that it will continue among us until the end of time--hopefully
in ever-diminishing degree. Some of the most vocal newer
churches aspiring for liberation, while rightfully condemning
Western ethnocentrism , fail to recognize how deeply ethnocentric
they themselves may be both in relation to other cultures (including the cultures of the West) as well as in relation to sub-
cultural behavior within their own societies. In any case, "Let
him who is without sin cast the first stone" (Jn 8:7). I am not
condoning ethnocentrism: I am merely suggesting that, while we
struggle to bring ethnocentrism under control, we try to understand it and, as objectively and as effectively as possible,
deal with what is a very human and universal fact of life.

B.   Theology and Ethnocentrism

1. Basic Principle. Whenever there is a conflict between
man's culturological needs on the one hand and the essentials of
faith on the other, the demands of faith must be given the preference. Although some may regard such a stance as being itself
ethnocentric,[1] the Christian to whom faith is a reality recognizes that this theological position is hardly more ethnocentric
or imperialistic than a physician's insistence on the basic
principles of medicine when such principles are in conflict with
a particular culture.

2.   Scripture and Ethnocentrism. The Old Testament was, no
doubt, particularistic in approach. On the other hand, it was
unquestionably universalistic in design and intent. The promise
of the protevangelium (Gen 3:15), the covenant between God and
Noah (Gen 9:8-17, 25-27), the promises to Abraham (Gen 12:3),
the prelude to the covenant with God's People (Ex 19:3-6), many
prophetic pronouncements (e.g., Is 40:5; 42:1, 4,6,10; 45:15-25;
49:6; 51:4-5; 52:10,15; 66:18-21; Am 9:12; Hab 2:20) and numerous other references in the Old Testament, especially in the

Psalms (e.g., Ps 2; 33:8-11; 47; 66; 67; 72:17; 86; 96; 98), all
speak of Yahweh's universalistic intent. The real meaning of
Israel can be found, in fact, only in its *world* mission. God in
His inscrutible wisdom decided to make Himself known to the world
through a very unique Revelation to a very distinct people "so
that all the peoples of the earth may come to know your name and,
like your people Israel, revere you ..." (words taken from the
dedication of the temple, 1 Ki 8:43).

Israel, therefore, enjoyed a unique position with God, sealed
by a "covenant" (e.g., Gen 6:18; 9:9, 11, 16: Ex 2:24; 34:10;
Le 26:42; 2 Chr 2:11; Ps 3:8; Is 5:25; 63:8; Jer 31:31-34; Joe
2:17; Mic 6:3, 5; Acts 3:25; Heb 8:10): "You are my people and I
am your God" (e.g., Lev 26:11-12; 2 Chr 35:4; Ps 81:8-16; 95:7;
Jer 7:23; 24:7; 32:38; Eze 37:24; 2 Cor 6:16; Heb 8:10). Yahweh
is depicted as a "jealous" God (e.g., Ex 20:5; 34:14; De 4:24;
5:9; 6:15; Jos 24:19; Is 9:7; Joe 2:18; Na 1:2; Zec 1:15; 8:2;
1 Cor 10:22; 2 Cor 11:2), Who does not tolerate fraternization
with idolaters. In turn, Israel expresses its abhorence of idolatry and its unique relationship with Yahweh in very human
terms, albeit, at times, in very ethnocentric terms (Loiskandl
1975:106).

The New Testament follows a centrifugal approach, a "sending-
out," rather than the centripetal or "drawing-in" approach of
the Old Testament. The Messiah, "the Anointed," is "the Sent-
One," while His closest collaborators are "apostles," i.e.,
"those sent on a mission."

The New Covenant is by its very nature supranational in its
method as well as in its intent and as such is incompatible with
ethnocentrism. "God loved the *world* so much that He gave up His
only Son (Jn 3:16). Christ is the light of the world (Jn 1:4;
9:5; 12:46). All mankind has a common Father in heaven (Lk 11:2;
Rom 8:15; Eph 4:6). All men are neighbors to one another (Lk
11:29-37). Although the Jews of Christ's time had little use
for Samaritans, Jesus saw no contradiction in speaking of "good"
Samaritans (Lk 11:29-37: 17:16). Nor did He find anything wrong
in conversing with a Samaritan woman and in extending to her the
same invitation to the Kingdom that He extended to his fellow-
Jews (Jn 4:1-42). When He gave His command, it was to go and
"make disciples of *all* nations" (Mt 28:19). The outwardly ethnocentric character of God's People of the Old Covenant, therefore,
no longer makes sense in the New. The Council of Jerusalem in
49 A.D. condemns Judaizing (Acts 15:1-30; Gal 2:1-10. Paul,
the apostle to the Gentiles, withstands Peter to his face, in-
sisting that God makes no distinction between Jew and Gentile
(Gal 2:11-14). Circumcision is no longer to be regarded as of
divine law (Acts 15:1-30; Gal 2:1-14). Unclean foods are no
longer to be regarded as unclean (Acts 11:1-18; 1 Cor 10:23-30).

Openness to local social structures becomes a basic policy of
the apostolic Church: native Cretans, for instance, are ordained
to lead the local Cretan Christian community (Tit 1:5).   Very
pertinent here is Peter's address in the house of Cornelius
(Acts 10:34-36): "...God does not have favorites, but...anybody
of any nationality who fears God and does what is right is acceptable to him.   It is true, God sent his word to the people of
Israel, and it was to them that the good news of peace was
brought by Jesus Christ—but Jesus Christ is Lord of *all* men."
Ethnocentrism is definitely an unchristian attitude.

C.   Ethnocentrism in Historical Perspective

Three major types of ethnocentrism, in varying degrees, have
been conspicuous throughout the last two hundred years of American history: (1) paternalism, (2) triumphalism, and (3) racism.

1. Paternalism. Perhaps the most common form of missionary
ethnocentrism has been "paternalism," an attitude based on good
intentions and on what may have at the time seemed to be Christian virtue.   However, paternalism is neither true charity nor
true virtue.   Rather, paternalism is "charity" and "compassion"
that *humiliate* and make the beneficiary *dependent* on the donor.

During the two centuries under discussion, for many missionaries the main object of mission action was to save souls.   The
Great Commission and love for Christ and the glory of god were
also generally among the missionary's motives.   But whatever
motives there may have been, such motives, perhaps more often
than not, were more or less colored by paternalism.   The new
Christians were regarded as not being able to take care of their
own souls even in small matters—so "dependent" were they on
missionaries.   The very strong emphasis on social betterment of
peoples was frequently paternalistic, that is, aiming to give
direct assistance to the suffering individual, with relatively
little understanding of the need for changing social institutions
and providing socio-economic opportunities, a concept of charity
that is of rather recent missiological vintage.   One of the
common reasons given for the shortage of Spanish-speaking clergy
in the U.S. Catholic Church, for instance, is the feeling among
the people themselves, engendered over several centuries by the
dominant group, that the padre must come from the "outside,"
that is, from the "superior" outside.   Although there may be as
many as 250,000 Catholic Chicanos in the Diocese of Brownsville,
the Diocese, it is believed, has not had more than five Chicano
ordinations to the priesthood in the past one hundred years.
Generally speaking, such a feeling of inferiority and dependence
is so deeply ingrained in the Hispano-American Catholic that,
despite the openness of the Catholic Church today and despite
the efforts made to encourage Hispano-American vocations to the
priesthood, such vocations are very rare indeed.[2]

2. *Triumphalism.* Another form of ethnocentrism very common during the two hundred years under consideration was triumphalism. Until toward the end of the Vietnam War, Americans have generally been very proud of their form of democracy. With immigrants and refugees streaming to the United States from all sides, with Americans dying in the battlefields around the world "so that others might live to enjoy democracy," Americans could not but regard their country as the ideal haven for the oppressed and themselves as champions of freedom. America was viewed as a democratic success unequaled by any nation in the history of mankind. Much of this may be true; what is wrong is the conclusion drawn that Americans, and American Christians *qua Americans,* had a clear mandate from the Almighty, a "manifest destiny," to transport their specific American form of Christianity to all parts of the world. Josiah Strong's triumphalism--and triumphalism was common up to World War II--is but another type of ethnocentrism. In fact, it was a rather common belief that "pagans" had first to be "civilized," actually Westernized, before they could be Christianized.

America was looked upon not only as the "ideal" democracy but one that had proven itself beyond question through its miraculous economic and political growth. Toward the end of the last century expansion westward was almost complete. The Philippines were "liberated" for America to bring "real" Christianity to the islands. The Caribbean area was now under American control. American influence in Central America was secure. All this reflected "God's special plan" for the American churches to export *themselves,* when it was really Christ that they wished to make known.

3. *Racism.* The worst type of ethnocentrism--only too well known to all of us--is, of course, racism, and little need be said about the subject. Prejudice against the non-WASP ethnic groups, especially against the Indians, Spanish-speaking Americans, and Blacks, no doubt, constitutes one of the most unfortunate blemishes in American church history. It was not an easy matter, for instance, for the Divine Word Missionaries, as late as 1920, to open a Catholic seminary at Bay St. Louis, Mississippi, for the training of Black candidates for the priesthood, at a time when Blacks were considered fit for baptism but not for ordination or leadership (Powell, 1976). And it was only several decades ago when it was still common to label and describe simple non-Western societies as "savage."

II. INCIPIENT ADAPTATION

A. General Notion

In contrast to the ethnocentric attitude toward non-Western ways and values is the positive stance of "adaptation" or "accommodation," also referred to as "indigenization," "nativization," "inculturation" or, sometimes, "cultural relevancy" and "promissio." Adaptation admits that there are "neutral" and "naturally good" elements in non-Western cultures and "even" in non-Christian religions. In fact, it says that whatever is "naturally good" or "neutral" in a non-Christian culture is to be preserved.

B. Incipient Adaptation in Historical Perspective

One of the main factors discouraging adaptation has always been the concern for Gospel purity and the fear of error. Paul himself was constantly admonishing the apostolic churches against the dangers of syncretism (e.g., 1 Cor 10:14-22; Eph 4:22; Col 2:4-3:4; 2 Tim 2:14-26). The churches of Antioch and Athens, of Colossae, Corinth, and Crete, of Pergamos, of Rome and of Samaria, all had their struggles with syncretism (Visser't Hooft, 1963). The belief in the total depravity of fallen man (the Reformed view of distortion) has sometimes led to the conclusion that all non-Christian cultures were, to say the least, suspect, if not totally "contaminated" and "sinful," that accommodation to any aspect of a "heathen" religion was "compromise," and that contact with or toleration of anything of "pagan" origin necessarily led to Christo-paganism, a hodgepodge of Christianity and "ungodliness." (The opposing Thomistic view of deprivation, rather than distortion, was somewhat more sympathetic toward adaptation.) Similarly, fear of idolatry has made dialogue with non-Christian religions, such as Buddhism, Hinduism, and Islam, "unthinkable," as unthinkable as dialogue with the devil himself. The "Declaration on the Relationship of the Church to Non-Christian Religions *(Nostra Aetate)*" of Vatican II has unnecessarily shocked not only some Roman Catholics but also many other Christians, owing to the shocked person's ethnocentric understanding of "heathenism."

1. Roman Catholic Experience. Adaptation is, of course, as old as the Church (Elizondo, 1975:86-95). We have seen how the opposite attitude, ethnocentrism, contradicted a very basic policy of the apostolic church. Among the early Christian apologists we find the so-called "Irenics" and the "Polemics," two groups with opposing views regarding non-Christian philosophy and religion. Tertulian was able to discern in the pagan heart what he called the *testimonium animae naturaliter christianae,* "the testimony of a naturally Christian soul." Similarly, St.

Cyril of Alexandria and others looked for the *logoi spermatikoi* in paganism. As the Roman Empire crumbled as well as throughout the Middle Ages, many traditional non-Christian customs were adopted by the Church, some of which eventually became a part of our own Christian heritage. Pope Gregory the Great gave express orders to missionaries to follow a policy of accommodation toward pagan cultures. During the following centuries, the stated policy of the Congregation for the Propagation of the Faith and the official papal directives again and again condemned the missionary who saw only falsehood, immorality, darkness, depravity, blindness, and sin in non-Christian cultures. There is, therefore, a consistency in the official pronouncements of Catholic authorities throughout history down to our present day: Go, make the beautiful in the pagan heart even more beautiful; seek out what is naturally good in all cultures and as much as possible build Christian communities on such native goodness. As one of the papal encyclicals of more recent times puts it: The Church

> ...from her very beginning down to our own day has followed this wise policy. When the gospel is accepted by diverse races, it does not crush or repress anything good and honorable and beautiful which they have achieved by their native genius and natural endowments. When the Church summons and guides a race to higher refinement and a more cultured way of life, under the inspiration of Christian religion, she does not act like a woodsman who cuts, fells and dismembers a luxurious forest indiscriminately. Rather she acts like an orchardist who engrafts a cultivated shoot on a wild tree so that later on fruits of a more tasty and richer quality may issue forth and mature. (Pius XII, *Evangelii Praecones*, no. 89.)

Adaptation has, therefore, always been the official Catholic policy. What about practice? While the Jesuits, such as St. Francis Xavier in Japan, Ricci in China, Veda of Nobili in India, and the "Reductions" in South America were being accused of excessive adaptation, the accusers were espousing a very unenlightened form of ethnocentrism. The otherwise beautiful theory, generally upheld by Catholic missiologists, missionaries, and Roman authorities in practice has until recently been mostly wishful, selective, and at best incipient (Loiskandl, 1975). Accommodation only too often has remained on a rather superficial plane, affecting external forms rather than deeper meanings, functions, and basic values, with almost total disregard of the dynamics involved.

The reasons for the lack of genuine implementation of the policy of adaptation were, of course, many. The concrete and deeper implications of "adaptation" were never spelled out in

any real detail by Catholic missiologists or authorities until
Vatican II. Then, too, those who were to implement the theory
and policy were unfortunately still imbedded in or at least influenced by the colonial spirit of their times. Essentials and
non-essentials of Christianity somehow all turned out to be
"essential," the beautiful principles of accommodation notwithstanding. The distinction between "unity" and "uniformity" had
not been made clear either until Vatican II. Moreover, as an
aftermath of the Reformation and Counter-Reformation, centralization and uniformity appeared to Catholics highly desirable in
regard to many non-essentials in liturgy, training of clergy,
catechetics, Canon Law, and in many other aspects of Church life.
Pluriformity was definitely "undesirable." Finally, until the
social sciences became recognized as sciences and as applicable
to missionary problems, mission theorists, mission authorities,
and missionaries in the field did not have, nor could have had,
our present-day understanding of the nature and dynamics of culture and society. As a result, it is very difficult indeed to
find today missions anywhere in the world that could be called
genuinely indigenous, fully adapted to the ways and values of
the local people, truly incarnated. Complaints about "suppression" and cries for "liberation" in our times are largely a reaction to the inadequacy of the type and degree of adaptation actually realized. Especially in times of deep national feeling,
such inadequacy has been particularly conspicuous and painful.[3]

While recognizing this lack of depth in actual practice, it
would be unfair not to recognize some of the more advanced thinking of the last two centuries. The fact is that the first eth-
nographers of the Americas, Africa, and Oceania were mostly missionaries, often individuals who not only showed great sensitivity
to local cultures and languages but who appreciated the close relationship between local ways and values on the one hand and
missionary effectiveness on the other. In fact, the first strictly culturological work recognized as such in the history of
Anthropology was the four-volume study of Canadian Indians by
Jesuit Joseph Francois Lafitau *Moeurs des sauvages américains
comparées aux moeurs des premiers temps,* Paris 1724. (A much
earlier notable effort was that of the Franciscan missionary
Fray Bernardino de Sahagun, who had studied the customs of the
Aztecs in Mexico in the first half of the 16th century.) We
might mention also a number of examples of individuals and groups
of missionaries in the Americas with extraordinary practical
adaptive skills and an ability to communicate cross-culturally,
skills and an ability that presuppose a true sensitivity to indigenous cultures, for instance, Father Junipero Serra and his
co-workers.

A certain amount of missionary ethnocentrism lingers on in
the Catholic Church, but the days of ethnocentrism are numbered.

(1) Indigenous control of dioceses throughout the world has made rapid stride ever since Pius XII's time. The Second Vatican Council was a living picture of adaptation theory put into practice, both in regard to the composition of the assembly of bishops as well as in regard to the cross-cultural sensitivity manifest practically in all the documents that have come out of the Council. Similarly, the permanent Concilium of Bishops for guiding the 1974 Synod for the next several years is clearly representative of the present-day pluralistic spirit in the Catholic Church: Three members of the Concilium are from Europe, three from the Americas, three from Asia, three from Africa, and three are appointees of the Pope. (2) Until only a few decades ago, many, if not most, American Catholic missionaries were trained very much the way church workers were being trained for homeland activities, with the missionary taking his preconceived ideas, biases, and ethnocentrism with him to the mission field. The situation has, of course, changed dramatically, especially since World War II. Today, training in cross-cultural sensitivity has become the rule rather than the exception. Sociology and Anthropology are no longer looked upon as academic luxuries. Exposure to field experience overseas during and as part of one's theological training is now a common practice. Graduate degrees in Missiology are now available in the United States. Mission-orientation courses and continuing education seem to be innovations here to stay. (3) Research and planning centers, deeply committed to the principle of adaptation, can now be found in many parts of the so-called "mission world" itself. These are but some of the indications of the important change in the preparation of missionaries for their difficult task of working in an unfamiliar cultural milieu.

Speaking of missionary training, we might point out that the first Catholic, explicitly missionary training center in the United States was founded in 1908 at Techny, Illinois, by a young missionary society imported from Europe and known as Divine Word Missionaries. If there was anything unusual about the Divine Word Missionaries it was their commitment to indigenization, supranationalism, and the scientific study of Missiology, Ethnology, and Linguistics, not as a mere appendage to their activities but as an integral part of their traditional missionary strategy (Loiskandl , 1975a:113-114; 1975b:24-25; Luzbetak, 1976c:47-49). Three years after the Divine Word mission seminary was opened, a strictly American mission society was founded in Maryknoll, New York. The establishment of such a society was no small achievement, considering that, at the time, the U.S. Catholic Church was still itself officially listed as a "mission land."

2. *Protestant Experience*. Although American Catholics until
a few decades ago have depended largely on Roman authorities and
European missiologists for their missiological theory, American
Protestant missionary groups had a Rufus Anderson as early as
1820. Anderson was definitely ahead of his time when he stressed
that Christianity was not synonymous with Western civilization
and when he insisted that the object of mission was the creation
of self-governing, self-supporting, and self-propagating local
churches. Another important figure in this regard was Rufus
Anderson's disciple Robert E. Speer, who likewise championed the
right of local churches to organize themselves and express the
Christian faith according to their cultural and social needs.

A dramatic change, similar to that within the U.S. Catholic
Church, has taken place also, and perhaps even to a greater degree, in Protestant missionary training programs. A genuine
appreciation of native languages has been achieved several decades ago through the Wycliffe Bible Translators, the Summer
Institute of Linguistics programs, and the American Bible Society.
Training in Mission Theology and mission-oriented social sciences
have become common in divinity schools throughout the country
(Schwartz, 1973). Academic missiology, after having had a slow
start, is now showing considerable promise (Beaver, 1976).

3. *Current Ecumenical Trends*. Most importantly, for both
Catholics and Protestants, we have today (besides the Association
of Professors of Missions founded in 1950) an ecumenical American
Society of Missiology. With the admission of the Society into
the Council on the Study of Religion, missiology in America has
indeed come of age (Luzbetak, 1976a). It is sound missiology,
more than anything else, that will lead our American missionary
efforts from ethnocentrism to incipient adaptation and beyond.

III. INCARNATIONAL ADAPTATION

Today, with many sad experiences behind us, with new theological and historical insights to support us, with all the
solidly-founded culturological, sociological, and psychological
concepts, principles, theories, and methods available to us, we
can hardly be content with what we have been calling "incipient
adaptation." Today it is quite generally felt that we cannot be
satisfied with anything less than a genuine incarnational
approach to Christianizing the world.

Despite the tension, and sometimes confusion, caused by the
Second Vatican Council and by such Protestant events as the 1910
Edinburgh Conference, the Laymen's Commission, the International
Missions Council in Willingen in 1952, the Lausanne Internation-
al Congress on World Evangelization in 1974, and the internation-
al meetings of Uppsala, Bangkok, and Nairobi, such epoch-making

events have served to sharpen our missionary thinking and, to a
greater or lesser degree, to direct our attention toward genuine
adaptation, toward the incarnational concept of missionary activity, toward genuine and full selfhood of local churches.
Thanks to such historic events, we are moving beyond the only-
too-familiar problems with which we have struggled for a long
time: "Is the missionary to save souls or is his task primarily
that of planting and consolidating churches? Is he to preach
the Gospel or is he to heal the sick and feed the hungry? Is he
an evangelizer or a humanizer?" Instead, we are now spending
much more time asking ourselves such questions as: "Is the
missionary a decision-maker for the local people or is he only
an 'enabler'? Is he a partner or is he an assistant to the
local leader? Is he a father, brother, or perhaps a servant?
What does all this mean concretely? Is the Church one or many
or perhaps both? What does 'unity in diversity' mean concretely?"
It is only by struggling through such often deeply-emotional
problems that we can hope to reach a clarification of missionary
goals and priorities and arrive at the updated theory and practice which every generation of missionaries needs.

But what are the major differences between the incipient and
incarnational forms of adaptation?

A. Difference Between Incipient and Incarnational Adaptation

The difference between incipient adaptation and full incarnational adaptation is threefold: there is a difference (1) in
depth, (2) in principle agents involved, and (3) in ultimate
objective.

1. A Difference in Depth. Incipient adaptation, as we have
already emphasized, is just that—incipient and lacking depth.
As we have seen, during the greater part of the last two centuries, accommodation might have been described at best as being
superficial. On the other hand, incarnational adaptation is the
form of adaptation of the future, a direction still largely a
matter of challenge rather than actuality. The limits of indigenization, in particular, are still to be worked out. "Unity
in diversity" must be spelled out in such a way that both fidelity to God and fidelity to man's nature are both upheld, a
challenge to the missionary, mission boards and authorities as
well as to mission theologians and social scientists, but, as we
shall see, a challenge especially to the local church itself
(Visser't Hooft, 1964; Yamamori, Taber 1975).

Incarnational adaptation is, therefore, something deep, very
deep, going far beyond *external forms* of behavior and entering
into the deeper levels of culture, into the level of *meaning and
values* and into *the philosophy and mentality* of a society, the
underlying premises, attitudes, and drives (Luzbetak, 1975:17-25).

When Christ is born into a culture, Christian beliefs and practices must actually become *integrated,* i.e., become one, with
the culture whole; they must be tied in as a real part of a system. Christ must, in fact, become the very soul of the system.
Through missionary work Christ must, so to speak, be allowed to
be born again and again, not however as a Jew who lived 2000
years ago or, much less, as an American or European, but as a
true citizen of the time and place. As Cardinal Justinus Darmo-
juwono, of Indonesia, put it at the 1974 Synod of Bishops: "It
is not a question of transplanting the Church, but of planting
it in a socio-cultural context within which it ought to be at
home" (Campion, 1974:206). The first major difference between
the incipient and the incarnational types of adaptation, therefore, is depth: the Christian becomes nothing less than "another
Christ," that is, the ideal Christian is modeled after a Christ
that has been incarnated into the ways and values of the given
time and place just as Christ was born into the set of ways and
values of the Jewish people of his time. He was totally indis-
tinguishable from other Jews, having taken on the entire Jewish
culture, on all levels (form, function, and psychology) to the
extent that his divine nature and mission allowed. That is
"incarnation"--being *truly* human and *truly* divine. (Luzbetak,
1976b.)

Without entering into the subject at any length, I do wish to
offer a few words of caution regarding the type of "depth" we
are speaking about. (1) The depth we have in mind, as Mbiti
would put it, does not involve "culturizing Christianity," but
the other way around, "Christianizing culture." In his words,
"traditional cultural lordship must yield to the Lordship of
Christ" (Mbiti, 1973). "Incarnation" can never mean, as some
would have it, "experiencing Christ" and then creating a new
Gospel, basically indigenous but essentially different, at least
in some points, from that preached by the historical Christ.
(2) It should also be pointed out that cultures are dynamic and
that there is no such thing as "instant Christianization"--at
least, normally not. The depth of which we speak is achieved
through a complex process in which Grace and nature cooperate
according to their sets of "laws."

2. *A Difference in Agent.* In the incipient type of adaptation, the missionary was the "prima donna," although he usually
admitted that ultimately it was God who gave the increase. It
was the missionary who had to adapt himself and to accommodate
because those being evangelized had only secondary roles to play.
In incipient adaptation, the missionary regarded himself as the
laborer in the vineyard of the Lord and his converts as the
fruits of his labor. Although there is some biblical justification for such a self-conception, the view does not represent
the full theological truth. Nor is it good anthropology. The
two most important and immediately involved agents in mission

work are God and the people being evangelized, not the missionary. The task of the missionary is chiefly to remove obstacles in the way of the Spirit, and, like St. John the Baptist, to prepare the way for the coming of the Lord. In the incarnational approach, the missionary conceives himself merely as a catalyst, as an enabler, as a guide and consultant, as a servant. The real transformers of non-Christians into "other-Christs" are, as both good theology and good anthropology maintain, not the missionaries but the people being evangelized--the "leaven" of the Gospel, which is to permeate the whole mass, and the "innovators" of anthropology, who alone can bring about a culture change. The real heart and soul of evangelization according to the recent Bishops' Synod in Rome is to be found in the local community itself. The most suitable and in fact the only effective transformers of a non-Christian society are the local people themselves through the Holy Spirit (Campion, 1974:225, 247, 273; Carter, 1975).

Unlike incipient accommodation, therefore, the incarnational approach calls for full trust in the Spirit and full trust in the community being evangelized. The missionary recognizes that there are serious risks in this approach. He nevertheless regards such risks as worth taking, since they are the same risks that the early Church took, whether at Philippi, Ephesus, Colossae or Crete, or, for that matter, in later history throughout Europe. The evangelized should as soon as feasible be given the necessary freedom to express Gospel values in their own local cultural patterns, values, philosophy, traditions, and structures, for they alone can really know their culture and are in a position to Christianize it.

3. *A Difference in Objective.* Incipient adaptation sees the planting of self-governing, self-sustaining, and self-propagating communities of Christians as the object of mission activity, while the incarnational approach looks beyond planting of churches--at mutual enrichment as goal. Missionaries will always have to be sent *from* America to Asia, Africa, Oceania, and elsewhere, while missionaries of one sort or another will always have to be sent from Asia, Africa, Oceania, and elsewhere *to* America in order to enrich America. This is the fuller meaning I get out of St. Paul's doctrine of the Body of Christ. The older churches need the newer churches to restore their vitality and to bring new insights; the newer churches, in turn, need the older churches to be able to share in the strengths developed over the centuries and to be able to enjoy the fruits of the Spirit, Who has been active not only in apostolic times but throughout the past 2000 years. The older generation needs the younger, and vice versa, for we are all indeed *one* Body in Christ. Incarnational adaptation, therefore, does not espouse or advocate isolationism. The Church is a universal Church.

The incarnational approach views the growth of any part of the
Body of Christ as the growth of the entire Body. The part needs
the whole, and the whole needs the part. In other words, we are
speaking of *mutual* enrichment.[4] With mutual enrichment as objective, missionary activity will of necessity continue till the
end of time. Missionary action will never be a thing of the
past; it will always be relevant and necessary because *mutual
enrichment* will always be relevant and necessary. In fact, with
mutual enrichment as goal, our missionary task is really only
beginning.

B. Incarnational Adaptation in Historical Perspective

1. Catholic Experience. The position of the Catholic Church
regarding the incarnational concept of mission is quite clear.
In fact, as early as 1945, when the word "incarnation" was seldom heard in missiological circles, Pius XII spoke explicitly in
such terms:

> The Church...is placed in the center of history of the
> whole human race...As Christ was in the midst of men, so,
> too, His Church, in which He continues to live, is placed
> in the midst of the peoples. As Christ assumed a real
> human nature, so too the Church takes to herself the
> fullness of all that is genuinely human, wherever and
> however she finds it, and transforms it into a source of
> supernatural energy (*Christmas Message*, 1945).

As in Vatican II, so more recently in the 1974 Synod of Bishops,
representatives of newer churches left no doubt about the depth
and intensity of their hunger for cultural authenticity in articulating their faith. The response in both cases was positive
(Abbott, 1966; Elizondo, 1975:95-102; Paul VI, 1975:no. 20,
62-64; Carter, 1975; Connors, 1974; Campion, 1974). This outcry for an opportunity for Asians, Africans, and Latin Americans
was echoed and supported by Pope Paul VI in his Apostolic Exhortation *Evangelii Nuntiandi* (No. 20), calling for nothing less
than a deep understanding and appreciation of local cultures by
the older churches, an understanding that is achieved "not from
outside, as though it were a matter of adding an ornament or a
coat of paint" but by going to the very "core and root of life
...in the very broad and rich sense of the *Pastoral Constitution
on the Church in the World of Today* (No. 53)." American superiors of religious orders (embracing a membership of about
200,000) have recently put themselves on the line--and not only
themselves but the entire U.S. Catholic missionary movement
since most missionary activity is in the hands of religious in-
stitutes--when they unequivocally committed themselves to the
incarnational understanding of mission:

> We join in this struggle to incarnate Christianity in
> the world's cultures in such a way that one of the
> church's oldest and greatest glories, her "unity in
> diversity," will shine ever more brightly in tomorrow's
> world (cited from paper read by S. Smith, S.J., 1976
> ASM meeting.)

2. *Protestant Experience.* Among the most important Protestant missiologists at the turn of this century who moved most
toward the direction of the incarnational approach were John
Henry Barrows and Charles Cuthbert Hall. Without putting non-
Christian religions on an equal footing with the Christian faith,
Barrows was able to recognize genuine goodness and beauty in
such religions, while Hall deplored the general lack of Christian appreciation of the great Oriental religions, whose strong
contemplative bent he felt could not but enrich the Church.

The period between the two World Wars gave American Protestant
missions such thinkers as E. Stanley Jones, Daniel Johnson
Fleming, and Sherwood Eddy, three outstanding champions of missionary adaptation. We must also mention here Edmund D. Soper
who, in his *The Philosophy of the Christian World Mission* (1943),
a modern mission classic, shows great sensitivity to the need
for indigenization and pluralism in evangelism.

Among the more recent forerunners of the incarnational approach to mission work must be included such well-known mission
thinkers as Donald A. McGavran and Eugene Nida, and the mission-
ary-scholars associated with *Practical Anthropology* (e.g., W.A.
Smalley, W. D. Reyburn, J.A. Loewen). The now-defunct Kennedy
School of Missions, Wheaton College, and Jaffrey School of Mission all deserve special mention in this connection (Kraft, 1973:
111-112). Particularly active and important today in steering
American mission thinking in the direction of the incarnational
approach is the School of World Mission of the Fuller Theological Seminary (Martin, 1974).

3. *Current Ecumenical Trends.* Most encouraging are the number and quality of missiological publications of the last five
years on the incarnational approach to mission, usually ecumenical in effort. Incarnation, in fact, seems to be the basic
issue of American missiology today.

Also encouraging are the current ecumenical discussions, for
instance, on development, liberation, secularization, revolution,
modernization, humanization, peace and justice, dialogue with
non-Christian religions, signs of the times, contextualization
of theology, reverse mission, and other current missiological
emphases, all of which can be important steps toward the

deepening of our understanding of "incarnation" and "mutual enrichment," but only if we recognize that the *real* issue is incarnation and mutual enrichment.

In this connection, let me express my personal view about a
popular subject, which we cannot leave out in any discussion
of the incarnational approach--the so-called "moratorium," a
strategy of self-reliance by means of a temporary withdrawal
of all foreign funding and personnel as expressly requested by
a particular church. No matter how radical the idea may seem,
too many highly respected individuals support the idea for anyone to brush it aside.[5] Nevertheless, somehow I wish that a
moratorium would be declared on the moratorium. Somehow I wish
missiologists would grapple with the *issue* and not get bogged
down in one of the many possible strategies that might be suggested,especially one that is not generally applicable. I am
suggesting that missiologists grapple with the *real* issue. As I
see it, the real issue is not the moratorium itself but how to
achieve incarnation and mutual enrichment.

The word "moratorium" is misleading and confusing. It is
used too often merely for its shock-value. While applicable at
best only in rare cases, "moratorium" is very often spoken of
as if withdrawal of funds and personnel were a generally applicable cure-all. As such, the word provides very poor public
relations; in fact, it turns away potential mission workers and
donors. It suggests that a complete shut-down of operations is
necessary for any serious planning, reorganization, and strategy development. "Moratorium" is too negative a term, implying
far greater frustration and bitterness than is generally the
case. It implies not only dissention but an impasse between
younger and older members of the family of God, when in reality
it wishes to speak of reconciliation and of strengthening universal brotherhood--in fact, when it wishes to advocate mutual
enrichment. "Moratorium" speaks of *not* doing something when it
wishes to speak of vitality. It speaks of death when it en-
visions a "second Spring." I would suggest that we call a spade
a "spade" and be satisfied with speaking of "a temporary withdrawal of foreign funds and personnel" and only when and where
such withdrawal is in fact applicable and to the extent that it
is applicable.[6]

On the other hand, one cannot but espouse the *intentions* of
the moratorium: to enable the new churches to develop their
own strength and selfhood, to allow them the time necessary to
reflect and plan, to enable them to express the Lorship of
Christ freely and without foreign domination (*International
Review of Mission* 64:210). Selfhood, identity, and the elim-

ination of structures and policies that obstruct the Spirit and self-development are, in fact, essential aspects of the incarnational approach.

My purpose is not to stifle open discussion but to bring balance into it. I am suggesting that we fix our sights not on any particular technique, and then perhaps get lost in it, but that we constantly keep our eye on the target, the basic issue, something that is far more universally applicable and far more lasting than any moratorium, something that is meaningful everywhere and until the end of time--incarnation and mutual enrichment. We should explore *all* routes to this all-important goal, our real concern.

CONCLUSION

We have reviewed in general terms the history of American missionary ethnocentrism and adaptation over the last two hundred years. We had to speak in general terms because there has never been a single vision of mission in the U.S. during any period of its history.

My purpose was not so much to criticize the past as to challenge the American Society of Missiology to discuss and research with ever greater intensity the incarnational understanding of mission and the role of mutual enrichment as object of missionary action. Ours is an ideal forum for the various Christian traditions and missiological fields to come together to discuss, and especially to learn, together. The mission theologian must provide us with the all-important theological light, the very basis of all we do, whatever our specialty may be. Mission historians and anthropologists, as well as their colleagues in other social sciences who focus their attention on missionary concerns, must, like the mission theologian, not only keep up professionally with their general fields but, by engaging in dialogue among themselves and with the mission theologians, administrators, and missionaries, they must as meaningfully as possible apply their wealth of knowledge to mission--to the discovery of the shortest and most effective route to action leading to genuine incarnation and mutual enrichment. Only if truly professional theologians and truly professional social scientists work together, as we are trying to do in the American Society of Missiology, will we be able to develop a true science of Missiology--a genuine Ethnotheology, a genuine science that respects both natures, God's and man's.

I came not to praise. I came not to blame. I came to challenge.

NOTES

1. Gregory Baum, for instance, claims that the missionary's
    primary task is not to convert people to Christ, and thus
    change their culture, but instead to enable them "to cling
    more faithfully to the best of their religious tradition
    and live the full personal and social implications of their
    religion more authentically," or, as others would put it,
    "to make a Hindu a better Hindu." The traditional and
    generally accepted view in missiology would be termed by
    Baum as "exclusivist" and as "spiritual imperialism"
    (Baum 1974).

2. Although it is estimated that almost one-fourth of all U.S.
    Catholics are Hispano-American, only 4.3% of the college-
    level seminarians and 3.1% of the theologate-level are
    Spanish-speaking ethnics. It is also estimated that there
    are only 185 Mexican-American priests of a total Mexican-
    American population of seven million. The present-day
    openness to and positive concern for minority vocations is
    evidenced by the inclusion of a "**Part Five**: Seminary Educa-
    tion in a Multi-Cultural and Multi-Racial Society" in the
    new edition of the National Conference of Catholic Bishops
    guidelines for U.S. seminaries (NCCB 1976:no.542-550).

3. For an excellent example of the depth of feeling and pain
    resulting from Western ethnocentrism, see Mwasaru (1975).

4. This line of reasoning is very much in accord with that of
    Pope Paul's *Evangelii Nuntiandi* (No. 63): "A proper atten-
    tion to the local churches can only enrich the Church.
    Such attention is necessary and urgent, for it corresponds
    to the deep-rooted desire of peoples and human communities
    to explore ever more fully their own special character."
    See also No. 62 and 64 which emphasize the universalistic
    nature of the Church.

5. A good coverage of the "moratorium debate" can be found in
    the April 1975 issue of the *International Review of Mission*
    and in I-DOC, 1974, No. 9, 49-86.

6. A general moratorium would involve other serious practical
    and theological problems as well, for which, see, for
    instance, Tippett (1973), Anderson (1974a; 1974b), and
    Wagner (1975).

REFERENCES CITED

Abbott, S.J., Walter M. (ed)
    1966   *The Documents of Vatican II* New York: Associa-
                tion Press

Anderson, Gerald H.
    1974a   "The Significance of the Call for a Moratorium on
                Missionary Personnel and Funds" I-DOC, No. 9,
                49-51
    1974b   "A Moratorium on Missionaries" *The Christian*
                Century, January 16, 1974, 91:43-45 reprinted in
                Mission Trends 1:133-141 and I-DOC, 1974, No. 9,
                83-86

Baum, O.S.A., Gregory
    1974   "Is There a Missionary Message" *Mission Trends*
                1:81-86

Beaver, R. Pierce
    1976   "The American Protestant Theological Seminary and
                Missions: An Historical Survey" *Missiology*
                4:75-87

Campion, S.J., Donald R.
    1974   "Synod Jottings" *America* 131:186-187, 205-206,
                225, 246-247, 273

Carter, S.J., Most Rev. S.E.
    1975   "The Synod of Bishops--1974: An Assessment"
                International Review of Mission 64:295-301

Connors, S.V.D., Joseph
    1974   "Synod '74: Success or Failure?" *America*
                131:346-348

Elizondo, Vergilio P.
    1975   *Christianity and Culture* Huntington, Indiana:
                Our Sunday Visitor, Inc.

I-DOC
                "Moratorium: Retreat, Revolt or Reconciliation?"
                No. 9, 49-86

Kraft, Charles H.
    1973   "Toward a Christian Ethnotheology" in A.R. Tippett
                (ed) *God, Man and Church Growth* Grand Rapids:
                Eerdmans 109-126

Lafitau, S.J., Joseph Francois
    1724   *Moeurs des sauvage américains comparées aux moeurs
                des premiers temps* Paris

Loiskandl, S.V.D., Helmut H.
    1975a   "The Christian Tradition and Ethnocentrism"
                Verbum SVD 16:105-114

    1975b   "Scholars Among Us: Scientific Research Has Long
                Been a Hallmark of the Divine Word Missionaries"
                in John Boberg, S.V.D. (ed) *The Word in the World*
                Techny, Ill.: Divine Word Missionaries 24-25

Luzbetak, S.V.D., Louis J.
    1975   "Understanding 'Cross-Cultural Sensitivity':
                An Aid to the Identification of Objectives and
                Tasks of Missionary Training" *Verbum SVD* 16:3-25

    1976a   "Missiology Comes of Age" *Missiology* 4:11-12

    1976b   "Unity in Diversity: Ethnotheological Sensitivity
                in Cross-Cultural Evangelism" *Missiology* 4:207-216

    1976c   *The Church and Cultures: An Applied Anthropology
                for the Religious Worker* So. Pasadena: William
                Carey Library (3rd printing; originally published
                in 1963 by Divine Word Publications, Techny, Ill.)

Martin, Alvin
    1974   *The Means of World Evangelization: Missiological
                Education at the Fuller School of World Mission*
                So. Pasadena: William Carey Library

Mbiti, John
    1973   "African Indigenous Culture in Relation to Evange-
                lism and Church Development" in R. Pierce Beaver
                (ed) *The Gospel and Frontier Peoples* So. Pasadena:
                William Carey Library

Mwasaru, Dominic
    1975   "Africanization" *International Review of Mission*
                64:121-128

National Conference of Catholic Bishops
    1976   *The Program of Priestly Formation* Washington:NCCB

Paul VI
    1975   *Evangelii Nuntiandi* (Latin Text in *Osservatore
                Romano* of December 19, 1975) English translation
                "On Proclaiming the Gospel" in *The Pope Speaks:
                The Church Documents Quarterly* 21:4-51.

Powell, S.V.D., Elmer S.,
    1976   "Leading the Way: A Black Priest Pays Tribute
              to SVD Courage and Wisdom" in John Boberg, S.V.D.
              (ed) *The Word in the World* Techny, Ill.: Divine
              Word Missionaries 28-31

Schwartz, Glenn
    1973   *An American Directory of Schools and Colleges
              Offering Missionary Courses* So. Pasadena:
              William Carey Library

Soper, Edmund Davison
    1943   *The Philosophy of the Christian World Mission*
              New York: Abingdon-Cokesbury Press

Tippett, Alan R.
    1973   "The Suggested Moratorium on Missionary Funds and
              Personnel" *Missiology* 3:275-278

Visser't Hooft, W.A.
    1963   *No Other Name: The Choice Between Syncretism and
              Christian Universalism* Philadelphia: Westminster
              Press

Wagner, C. Peter
    1975   "Colour the Moratorium Grey" *International Review
              of Mission* 64:165-176

Yamamori, Tetsunao and Taber, Charles R. (eds)
    1975   *Christopaganism or Indigenous Christianity?*
              So. Pasadena: William Carey Library

13

The Role of American Protestantism in World Mission

W. Richie Hogg

In Philadelphia on July 4, 1776, the Continental Congress adopted the Declaration of Independence of the United States of America. A new nation was born. Several days earlier on June 29 and with the Golden Gate in full view, a Franciscan missionary dedicated the site for the Mission of San Francisco. The new settlement became the chief northern outpost on the Pacific Coast of a Spanish mission to the Indians. The latter had been launched two and a half centuries earlier and two thousand miles to the south from Mexico City.

Those two events in 1776 on opposite sides of a virtually empty continent seemed as unrelated to each other as both did to another that had already occurred across the Atlantic. That March in England Adam Smith had published his *Wealth of Nations* and in it advanced a striking new idea. A nation gains wealth, he argued, not by extracting it openly or covertly from another, but through the productive labor and organizational skill of its people. The ideological foundation for America's economic growth had been laid.

Two hundred years later in July, 1976, and if all goes well, a United States space probe in two stages, launched last August and having traveled 500 million miles, will place two Viking landers on Mars. They should operate for years and will relay to earth within minutes data on soil, rocks, and organisms, and also color pictures of Mars' surface and its reflection of changing seasons.

Meanwhile, during the two centuries between 1776 and 1976 on the one planet in this solar system that seems to be inhabited by human beings, the population grew from .8 billion to 4 billion persons. On every continent and from among every people, nearly one-third of them affirmed their belief in God as he is known through the Lord Jesus Christ. Of all the religions on earth such wide and diverse rootage is true only of Christianity.

Seemingly disparate, those several historical events and data are in fact related. They point again to the inextricable intertwining of events in a world history that is sustained by God and is completed in his providential purpose. One need not dwell here on that interrelationship, but the thoughtful reader will realize that it is presupposed in these pages.

I. *INTRODUCTION: PURPOSE AND CONTEXT*

This paper seeks to present a perspective on the American Protestant contribution through 1976 to a chapter of major significance in the history of the Christian world mission. It attempts this through a review of certain major developments and, given the limitations of space, inevitably must omit some that could have been included. The American Bicentennial provides the occasion for it. Specifically, this survey is prepared for the American Society of Missiology and is meant to provide grist for its discussion and analysis of much that is set forth here.

The subject must be considered within its historical context. Moreover, the mutually shaping interplay of mission and history and of theology and action/event should be probed. Yet detailed contextual examination is here impossible. Some of the relevant dynamics will be presented in related papers, and others will have to be assumed as known and evident to the reader.

Within the context of the Christian world mission, American Protestantism through 1890 fulfilled its major missionary responsibility in its homeland. Yet it also had sent a small but steady stream of missionaries overseas. They helped there to lay foundations for future work. After 1890, it responded with steadily mounting resources—personal and financial—to the overseas challenge. This produced the more visible and exciting accomplishment, but the mission at home continued to claim the larger staff and support. These two realities and time periods shape the two major sections of the paper.

The historical context for the American role in world mission
is the third and latest segment of the modern epoch. That epoch
spans the five centuries during which Western European civilization and peoples have dominated the world stage. The drama
has consisted of three acts--three clearly distinct periods but
with widely overlapping termini.

The first began with the unprecedented sixteenth century
Iberian global expansion. Underway with probing sea journeys
for nearly a century, it found its great advance from the voyages of discovery made by Columbus in 1492, Vasco da Gama in
1498, Magellan in 1519, and those who followed. The result in
McNeill's phrase was "the closing of the ecumene." Thoughtful
people began to realize that, with all its exotic diversity,
humankind is one. This first period encompassed the rise of
printing, the resulting rapid dissemination of ideas, and the
Protestant Reformation. Its long decline proceeded from the
defeat of the Spanish Armada in 1588, but it also included
the remarkable and vigorous global outreach of the Roman Catholic mission through the seventeenth century.

The second and overlapping period occupied the two centuries
between 1588 and 1789. A time of transition, it encompassed
the Enlightenment, and in it the Danes, Dutch, French, British,
and others vied with one another in worldwide exploration and
settlement. Catholic missions continued but in the later years
suffered decline, especially in Southern and Southeast Asia
where Protestant powers ousted the Iberians.

The third period was shaped by the Anglo-American dominance
of the past two hundred years, and so its beginning may be set
in 1776. In the nineteenth century England secured its global
empire, while America pushed its frontier westward and settled
its continental domain. In the twentieth century the two
powers shared pre-eminence--first England and then America.
On the North American continent, despite the earlier presence
of Spain and France, the territory between the Canadian border
and the Rio Grande came into American hands. In its religious
development, although in the twentieth century the Roman Catholic Church became the largest single church, American Protestantism was the dominant shaping force.

Meanwhile those two centuries brought an unprecedented increase in scientific knowledge that produced a radical change
in the human understanding of history, the universe, the planet,
and man. Technology and communications transformed living
patterns and shrank the earth. Theories and practice of
government changed. In short, the age was one of revolution,
and its impact was global.

Those twenty decades between 1776 and 1976 embraced "The Great
Century" of Christian mission in which Anglo-Americans took the
overwhelming lead. Yet, at the same time, much of the Western
base from which that outreach had sprung was being eroded by a
secularism that fostered an alien view. It held that human life
without need for God can find fulfillment on earth.

The great breach came between Christian faith and the secular
faith which rejected it. Often nominal Christian profession
masked secular values. Latourette designated that duality "The
Great Century: Growing Repudiation Paralleled By Abounding
Vitality and Unprecedented Expansion."[1] Martin Marty calls it
"The Modern Schism."[2]

Finally, one notes that as the period of Western hegemony
over the world was ending, a new historical epoch was dawning.
On a planet made physically one, all the world's peoples had
been thrust together in interdependence. Made one by science and
technology, they were divided by religion and ideology. That
produced their often unwilling but growing pluralism. The rising
prominence on the world stage of the peoples of Asia, Oceania,
Africa, and Latin America marked the dynamic accents of the new
age. One of its most prominent features for Christian faith was
the rise of a self-conscious world Christian community spread
among the two-thirds of the world's people who gave their alle-
giance to different lords.

All the above and more relate to the part played by American
Protestantism in the Christian world mission in the past two
centuries. We turn now to view that role briefly from two
perspectives: first, the mission to America and, second, the
mission from America.

II. *The Mission To America*

Most Protestants, when thinking of mission, regard America
only as sending missionaries abroad. Yet during the past two
centuries, the greatest missionary effort in history among a
single people was concentrated within the United States. In
what is now the world's fourth most populous nation, that mission
has produced the largest national group of those who call themselves Christian. That reality deserves further probing.

A. *The Colonial Period.* In this country's history the Pil-
grims and Puritans rightly hold a position of honor. So too do
Quakers, Baptists, Reformed, and others. The legacy of their
spirit has given this nation much that is unique in its character. Moreover, from that earliest and often strongly Calvinistic
heritage came the first missions to the Indians. Although long

ignored, their theological and methodological importance for the
Protestant world mission has been advanced recently, among others,
by Pierce Beaver[3] and Charles Chaney.[4]

Yet one hard fact stands. The majority who arrived here came
not for religion but for new opportunity, life free of binding
restrictions, land, achievement, and gain. Like other British
colonists elsewhere many had little interest in Christianity or
the church.

Despite concerned Anglican efforts from England to meet this
need through the Society for the Promotion of Christian Knowledge
(1699) and the Society for the Propagation of the Gospel (1701),
the weakness of the transplanted church life for American Christians by the third generation and for new arrivals was everywhere
evident. The majority of the colonists had no connection with
the churches, and in the congregations spiritual life had sunk to
a low ebb. Contrary to current popular myth, in many areas the
colonial church was weak, mocked and ridiculed, and ignored as
irrelevant.

Considerably changing that situation in the half-century before 1776, the Great Awakening made itself felt throughout the
colonies and shaped the evolving national conscience. Richard
Niebuhr interpreted what happened as a profound theological
shift from an earlier emphasis upon the primacy of God's sovereignty to the primacy of his grace as manifested in the kingdom
of Christ.[5] That dynamic helped to shape American life. No
isolated event, the Great Awakening was closely interrelated
with German Pietism and the Evangelical Revival in England.

A major force in American history, the Great Awakening produced many results, two of which require noting here. First, it
emphasized the need for individual, personal transformation under God and thus introduced to America a new perspective on evangelism. Second, it unleashed enormous power channeled through
voluntary associations for Christian action in society and for
outreach in mission. In this, in its impact on the Indians, and
in the revivals which followed after it, it gave shape to the
American mission at home and overseas.

B. *The New Nation's Free Churches and Their Mission.* The
birth of the nation really required two decades—from the Boston
Tea Party in 1773 to the Paris Treaty of Independence in 1783
and then to the Second Inaugural of Washington and Adams in 1793.
Through those years the nation's long travail proved painful for
the churches. Involved in and often divided on the issues of the
day, they were so absorbed in the nation's needs and disruptions
that their recent vigor sharply declined. The Anglicans, among

whom had been many Loyalists, were in disarray. The populace was overwhelmingly British (92%), and those of English background comprised 83.5%. The churches reflected this.

During this period two events occurred which shaped the church and mission in America. The first in 1776 involved human dignity and equality. For 150 years the colonies had been importing Africans for slavery, but used blacks in the Revolutionary War to fight for American independence. Yet in 1776, with South Carolina holding the key vote and to achieve union, the Continental Congress forced deletion of Jefferson's proposed abolition of slavery from the Declaration of Independence.

The Declaration affirmed the "self-evident" truth that "all men are created equal" and are "endowed by their Creator with certain unalienable rights," among them "Life, Liberty and the Pursuit of Happiness." Yet its application became and remains a debated and disruptive force in America's religious and political life. In accord with biblical teaching, the nation's foundation document affirms human dignity for all. Every attempt by the majority to bend or deny that affirmation has inflicted or exacerbated powerful wounds. Americans extended the continental United States to the Pacific, but treatment of the ethnic minorities within their midst--Indians, Hispanics, Asians, blacks, and others--has remained a test of white American Christian profession in its national and world mission.

The second seminal event during these two decades, occurring in 1789, created religious freedom within the nation in quite new form. In that year the Congress appended to the newly ratified Constitution the Bill of Rights. In it the First Amendment declares: "Congress shall make no law respecting an establishment of religion, or prohibiting the free exercise thereof." That determination reversed nearly fifteen centuries of civil and church history from the time of Constantine. It also differed greatly in intent and form from what is often said to be the "similar" French action that year.

Separation of church and state in America freed the churches from state intervention and support. The long road to the Constitution's provision for complete religious freedom stretched back to the Peace of Augsburg in 1555 and to England's Toleration Act of 1689, but the Christian Enlightenment[6] joined the Rational Enlightenment to complete it. The ancient axiom that political and social solidarity in a nation require religious uniformity had been broken. Although a few states required some years to align their state constitutions, the foundation for genuine, but often painful, pluralism was laid. With no government support, the churches, as they had been in the first three centuries, became self-supporting voluntary bodies.

Two effects quickly became apparent.

First, the denominational system resulted. Complete freedom
in America made denominations of the transplanted state churches
from Europe, including the Roman Catholic. Others arose spontaneously. Moreover, successive waves of immigration from Europe
created new denominations, as the German and Scandinavian Lutherans notably demonstrated. The European pattern of the great
state church and the small non-conforming bodies or sects did not
appear.

Instead, a whole group of churches flourished on a basis of
equality. Most regarded themselves as denominations or branches
of the church, but not as "the church." Each made its own way in
society. Each could evangelize freely and pursue any endeavors
made possible by the voluntary support of its members. This encouraged "American activism."

Second, a remarkable but little noted development of profound
consequence had begun to appear by 1789. The American churches
recognized that they lived amid a mission field for which they
held major responsibility. This in turn rested upon a voluntary
support base. The situation was not unlike that to which the
European churches awakened in 1945. The latter suddenly realized
after World War II that despite a baptismal enrollment nearly
matching the population, the living church was a tiny minority of
5% to 10%. Europe was declared a mission field. The American
proportion and position were similar in 1789.

Some perspective may help. In 1745 Wesley in England, de-
fending his preaching in the streets and outside the factories,
argued the futility of speaking to empty pews. England's Industrial Revolution was transforming rural multitudes into urban
masses as the working proletariat. Few among them ever came to
church. Their conversion required the Evangelical Revival. Two
centuries later in 1945, the Church of England's *Towards the
Conversion of England* noted that only 10% to 15% of the populace
was linked to the churches and, paraphrasing Wesley, declared,
"You cannot convert people who are not there."[7]

In 1943 Abbé Henri Godin published his bombshell (English
Trans., *France, Pagan?*) and declared France to be "a mission
land" within which 8% of the people were practicing Christians.
With startling rapidity a similar story emerged from Germany,
Scandinavia, Italy, Spain, and elsewhere in Europe. The outward
remnants of Christendom's shell in Europe had long masked the
truth.

In a new American nation 165 years earlier, the churches had
faced a similar reality. They saw themselves realistically--a

small minority of perhaps 7-10% amid a rapidly growing population outside the church and with minimal interest in the gospel. Free churches in a free land, and quickened by the Second Great Awakening (1800-1835), they launched a mission that continues today. Parenthetically, one notes that the frequently cited comments on religion in America made by the perceptive De Tocqueville came during his visit from France in 1831-1832, with the full effects of the Second Great Awakening abundantly obvious.[8]

C. *American Mission and the Growth of the Church*. For many, Latourette's "Great Century" evokes images of churches in Asia and Africa. Yet few have noted that the century's most noteworthy exhibit of missionary results was the United States itself. Mission reaches to those outside the faith and in need of evangelization--precisely the reality the American churches in the 1790's perceived and pursued.

Quality of Christian life and achievement constitute important measures for judging mission. There are others, including growth. Behind two centuries of steady numerical growth in church membership in America's wholly voluntary setting lies one tangible norm with considerable meaning. It is used here not as a total but rather a simple and vivid measure.

Church statistics are notoriously difficult to gather and to collate with equivalency. The designation of communicants, members, and constituency or community may be used in varied fashion. Catholics count all those baptized as members. Most Protestants count only those formally received into membership, not baptized children. Allowing for these and other difficulties, and with an admonition to prudent caution in their use and interpretation, the following widely-used figures are set forth.[9] AT the least, they indicate a decisive trend in one measure for the effectiveness of the mission to America.

TABLE I

CHURCH MEMBERS AS
A PERCENTAGE OF POPULATION IN THE USA[10]

Year	Percentage
1776	05-06%
1800	07-10%
1850	16-20%
1900	36%
1920	40%
1940	46%
1960	59.5%
1970	60%
1976	59.2%

The above figures at best are approximations and also incorporate a factor difficult to balance. Certain churches represented in the earliest figures had a disciplined membership.
In some cases those attending services were often greater in number than the members. Later figures more nearly represent a
constituency.[11]

The important element remains the obvious basic trend. That
membership doubled after the Second Great Awakening (1800-1835)
is understandable. The considerable increase between 1850 and
1960 is noteworthy. That period, with its massive population
growth, included the settling of the West, migrations from
Europe, urbanization and industrialization, conflicts from the
Civil War through two World Wars to the Korean War, and uphea-
vals and depressions. Catholics grew most rapidly through
immigration following 1860. The steady growth here charted suggests a massive and intensive mission effort shared in by Protestants and Catholics alike.

Two other surveys provide useful supplements. In 1957, the
Census Bureau asked the question only of those fourteen years of
age and older, "What is your religion?" It reported that 96% of
the American people indicated a denominational or religious
"preference" which did not necessarily imply membership. Among
an adult population of 119 million, some 30 million regarded
themselves as Roman Catholics and 70 million as Protestants.
Some related to Eastern Orthodox and other Christian bodies and
some to other faiths.[12] No matter how one assesses the religious status of this majority, it represents a significant rate
of identity with the Christian faith.

More recently the annual Gallup Poll on Church-Going indicated that for the 1971-1975 period, 40% of American adults
attended a church or synagogue during a typical week. During
1970-1975 young adults, eighteen to twenty-nine years of age,
were attending at a rate of 30%. Even more striking, participation in prayer groups, Bible study, and the like, in addition to
church attendance, involved 20% of the adults and 18% of the
young adults.[13]

Everyone is clear that the "secular schism" exists. Crime is
up. Public morality sags. Yet statistical evidence also points
to a notable penetration of Christian faith. It discloses a
significant minority actively practicing the Christian faith as
measured by church attendance and participation in Christian
groups. This is by no means the full story. Yet is similar
evidence available from any other industrial country? The mission to America is still operative and seems still to show mea-
surable results.

Nevertheless, as noted above, statistics on church membership and participation constitute only one norm in judging the penetration and depth of Christian faith in the nation's life. A considerable proportion of those who claim church membership are nominally Christian and by the admission of their own denominations need to be re-evangelized.

Peter Berger's 1961 study, *The Noise of Solemn Assemblies: Christian Commitment and the Religious Establishment in America* (Cf. Amos 5:21-24), provides an example of the probing and evaluation that sociologists of religion offer for one seeking to understand those statistics. The role of America's "Civil Religion" and the degree to which it is identifiable with or is divergent from Christianity provides another difficult to apply but important tool for that continuing effort.[14]

D. *The Mission to the Frontier.* The nineteenth century American home mission centered on the westward-moving frontier.[15] The story is as vast as the land it covered and as diverse as those who settled it. In the process missionaries encountered Indians, and there was always outreach to them; but the chief drive was to evangelize the pioneers, virtually all of whom were white and beyond the reach of settled congregations.

Fundamental to this unparalleled effort was the belief in almost all denominations that the church itself constituted a missionary movement in its homeland. Underlying that was the further conviction that this land and people had been especially favored by God and that America would play a special role as a Christian nation.

From the outset the effort steadily gained, and as mission churches became settled congregations, those most committed to the missional ecclesiology saw that the church must have well organized missionary societies and agencies to pursue the task always beyond the reach of the local congregation. These societies appeared. Thus in varying proportion on the frontier the mission involved mingled efforts by local churches and national societies.

Several cooperative agencies arose, including the American Home Missionary Society in 1826. Until the Civil War, it was the largest mission, but by 1861 all its founding members except one had withdrawn, and it became a Congregational society. The field was seemingly without limit. Denominational interest was high, denominational societies flourished, and the denominational network moved westward. There was room for everyone.

Baptists and Methodists seemed most suited to the frontier, and those two bodies grew more rapidly than the others. Their

effective evangelism, spontaneous and popular services, and major use of lay leadership and lay preachers held great appeal.
Methodist circuit riders remained unmarried, traveled cease-
lessly, and lived summer and winter in the saddle. Such were
the rigors of their work that into the 1830's their average age
at death was 29.

The churches concentrated their mission in this country and
along the frontier. In 1874, for example, the Missionary Society
of the Methodist Episcopal Church (Northern) supported in whole
or in part more than 3,000 missionaries in the United States.
In the same year, and including those in its Women's Society,
that church had 145 missionaries overseas--75 men and 70 women.
Yet at home it had 257 in special "language work" among Germans,
Scandinavians, Chinese, and Indians.[16] In short, home missions
claimed major attention from the American churches.

Only one specific feature of this entire enterprise can be
singled out for mention, namely, schools. At every level they
constituted a notable part of this outreach. Indeed, one of the
great achievements of the mission-founded churches was their
establishment of colleges and universities. From coast to coast
these were built for the training of clergy and for the preparation of an educated laity. Their contribution is incalculable.[17]

E. *The "Other Mission" and the Twentieth Century.* Not all
the nineteenth century mission focused on the frontier. Much of
it related to those who were neither Anglo-Saxon nor white and
in some cases to those whose heritage involved another religion.
Millions of immigrants of Roman Catholic background from Southern
and Central Europe poured into the U.S.A. after the Civil War.
Protestant missions among them were limited and may have assisted
some in the transition to a new land; but no large group of them
became Protestant. Work among Scandinavians and Germans by non-
Lutherans led many to join other than Lutheran churches. In
some cases this in turn led to the planting of American Protestant churches in Scandinavia and Germany as converts--sailors,
farmers, and tradesmen--returned to their homelands and spontaneously spread their new-found faith.

Among Asian immigrants, who often suffered grievously from
the stigma of the "Yellow Peril" label, missions were moderately
successful. Some Asian converts went to Hawaii to spread the
faith and began churches there. Asian-Americans have continued
this work in recent decades within the continental United States
and in Hawaii.

Protestants began their outreach to Hispanic Americans with
the colonization and annexation of Texas. At least in part, they
also saw the mission to the Mexican-Americans as an avenue to

the area south of the Rio Grande. Increased by continued migration chiefly from Mexico, Puerto Rico, and Cuba, an indigenous
Hispanic Protestant community today is experiencing healthy ferment.

Much of the American encounter with the Indians constitutes a
seldom mentioned stain on this nation's history. Through the
missions to Indians much good has been achieved. Yet far too
many of these efforts have been naively well-intentioned but
poorly understood and with commensurable results. The detailed
story of the Indian missions has been treated in another paper.

Meanwhile, as the nineteenth century advanced, needs for mission were changing as were the patterns of response. Indeed,
the process had been underway since 1870. By 1890 frontier
settlement had been completed, and that mission of geographic
extension ended. The new frontier was in the city among the
millions of new immigrants from Europe and in pockets of poverty.
The new pattern became intensive mission to human need.

On the eve of the twentieth century, the Spanish-American War
in 1898 brought Puerto Rico, Cuba, and the Caribbean into the
zone of national concern. At the same time, the Philippines
became a special responsibility of American missions in Asia.
The United States annexed Hawaii in 1898, and in 1959 it gained
statehood. Meanwhile, Alaska's importance loomed steadily
larger, and in 1959 it, too, gained statehood. To meet these new
and steadily changing needs the churches sought to adjust their
response in mission.

F. *The Mission Among the Blacks*. The long encounter between
blacks and whites in America is unique. Deep within the national
psyche it has produced an active, volcanic moral issue. Equally
unique in its own way is the mission among the American blacks.

Also treated in another paper, the significant growth and contribution of black Christianity in America recently has begun to
emerge in its true light. Concerned missionary efforts from
white Christians form an indispensable part of the picture. Yet
more importantly, black Christians appropriated the gospel, represented it, and largely advanced it among themselves. Although
some black churches conduct missions in Africa, most of their
effort has been concentrated here.

One of Latourette's most arresting observations relates to
the unprecedented growth, when viewed in world context, of the
self-propagated black church in America. By 1916, the 4.6 million black Protestants in America, 90% of them Baptists and
Methodists, equaled the number of *all* Protestants in the churches
of Asia and Africa established there between 1815 and 1914 by

the combined Protestant missions of the Continent, Britain, and
the U.S.A. "Among no other body of peoples of non-European
stock did nineteenth century Christianity make such large numerical gains."[18] The proportion of Christians in the black
population has continued closely to match the proportion of
Christians in the national population.

One qualitative measure of that numerical picture appeared
recently. In its Bicentennial Issue, *Ebony* named "The Ten Most
Important Blacks In American History," those "upon whose shoul-
ders all blacks today are able to stand." Seven were closely
identified with the Christian faith, including Harriet Tubman,
Frederick Douglass, and Associate Justice of the Supreme Court
Thurgood Marshall, an Episcopalian who helped to produce the
legal foundations for civil rights legislation. Mary McLeod
Bethune and Booker T. Washington founded colleges, and Bishop
Richard Allen founded the African Methodist Episcopal Church.
Within the past two decades Baptist clergyman Martin Luther
King made an unparalleled impact on the nation.[19]

G. *Some Concluding Notations*. Here several matters may be
referred to briefly.

First, in personnel and finance the mission to America has
been larger than that from America. Contrary to the belief of
many, the American churches have not favored overseas work to
the neglect of mission in the homeland. For the past 175 years,
the available evidence suggests, the major denominations have
maintained a larger national mission than that overseas.

In 1932, for example, denominations in the Home Missions
Council had 22,000 home missionaries and had a budget of
$27.5 million. In contrast, member bodies of the Foreign Mis-
sions Conference were supporting about 11,000 missionaries on
a smaller budget of $22.5 million.[20] Again, in 1939 when three
members of the Methodist family formed the Methodist Church,
the united body had nearly 5,600 home missionaries and less than
1,500 overseas.[21]

More detailed research in this area is needed than was
feasible for this paper. Access to adequate data for the past
twenty-five years has not been possible, and in that time there
may have been a shift. Yet the general evidence seems to confirm the judgment through 1950.

Second, the national mission effort has made its own contribution to the larger cooperative endeavor of the American
churches. It has occurred not only at the city and state level,
but also at the national level. With leadership from Charles L.
Thompson, Executive Secretary of the Presbyterian (U.S.A.,

Northern) Board of Home Missions, it created in 1908 the Home
Missions Council. In the same year the Council of Women for
Home Missions also emerged.

In 1911 those two bodies began to function together in
partnership, in 1940 united, and since 1950 have been part of
the National Council of Churches. Their purpose was to facilitate cooperation among the agencies for national mission through
common counsel and unified planning. Some of the notable
achievements of the churches in the resulting common endeavor
have involved work with Indians, migrants and sharecroppers,
Asian-Americans, and blacks. Professor Robert Handy's *We Witness Together* presents this story as it unfolded in the first
half of the century.[22]

Third, a dynamic conviction--some would say "mystique"--
informed much of the theology and drive of the mission to
America, and from America. Put briefly, it was the belief that
America is an elect nation, divinely chosen for a unique role in
the world. The new people being formed in the wilderness were
convinced that they had a God-given destiny, and they interpreted that within their own biblical perspective.

Americans came to understand this as their calling under God
to embody the purity and power of Protestantism--basically
Anglo-American Protestantism--for the world. The anti-Roman
Catholic temper therein derived in no small part from the long-
standing English antipathy toward Rome and included the more
recent suspicion and fear directed toward the French and Spanish
Catholic presence in North America. Some of it came from the
stance of the papacy regarding the modern world, including "The
Syllabus of Errors" of Pius IX, and "The Christian Constitution
of States" of Leo XIII as some were interpreting its application to the United States.

That belief in the American destiny as standard bearer of
civil liberty and pure faith for the world grew for more than a
century after 1776. It helped to form the American mind. It
also enabled the events and acquired territories of 1898 to be
interpreted as providentially bestowed. Yet the American
reality, given form by massive immigration from Europe, was
increasingly pluralistic. Belief in "the mission of America"--
intertwined with but distinguishable from that of its churches--
still expresses itself with power. But it has had to accommodate
to an altered vision.

Manifest Destiny emerged in the 1840's and related to the
American drive from Missouri to the Pacific. Yet the phrase was
soon invested with the dimensions of the larger dream and is
often used now to designate the latter. This is no new

phenomenon, for similar expressions have been voiced among
others by the Chinese, Egyptians, Greeks, Romans, Iberians,
English, Germans, and Russians. Yet the "destined mission" of
the nation reached the peak of its American Protestant expression late in the nineteenth century. With the American frontier
won, the national mission refocused on the cities, and the new
frontier emerged in the world mission. That conjunction deserves noting and reflection.[23]

Fourth and finally, as the above suggests, American Christians, i.e. the majority of the populace holding voluntary church
membership, received the Christian faith through diverse denominational missions with a common concern: to bring the gospel
and its fruits to all the peoples of the nation. Contributions
freely given by people of modest means through denominations to
support that enterprise have amounted to hundreds of millions of
dollars. Greater amounts have been given directly for specific
work.

How effective has it been? One relies again, in part, upon
the statistics of the tangible, not for themselves but for the
spirit and devotion that produced what they represent. Early
in this century Congregationalists, Methodists, and Baptists
judged that from 80% to 90% of their "Western" churches arose
from home missions. Three decades earlier in 1873 Presbyterians
estimated that west of Pennsylvania they owed 90% of their
churches to home missions.[24]

The results of that mission are legion. For now only one
need be mentioned. From the base here built, and even from a
minority within it, has come the greatest voluntary outpouring
of life and treasure ever seen to spread the gospel to all the
peoples of the world. The human agents of that mission have compounded fault and sin, error and superiority in their efforts at
obedience. Yet through such faith, conveyed in earthen vessels, God has fashioned a world Christian community, and the
mission is being repeated in Korea, Chile, Africa, the Pacific,
and elsewhere. In the long sweep of history, even as it was
for certain other lands, perhaps that is among the greatest
results of the mission to America.

III. *The Mission From America*

To present within a few pages the salient features of
American Protestantism's role in world mission from the founding
of the American Board in 1810 to the present poses a formidable
challenge. So, too, does the effort to delineate the strictly
American in the closely related and interwoven British and
American work. For convenience in these pages the term "North
American" refers only to Canada and the U.S.A. What follows

then is a brief listing of certain major distinguishing elements
in the Protestant mission from America.

A. *The Predominance of American Personnel and Giving.* Since
the early 1920's North Americans have comprised the largest segment of the Protestant overseas mission. During the past twenty
years they have represented about 64-67% of the total. Equally
noteworthy, for probably the past century North American and
British missionaries, including those few from Australia and New
Zealand, have steadily represented from 73% to 88% of the entire
Protestant force and since 1900 have not been below 81%. Major
stages in this development are partially indicated in Table II
below.

TABLE II

NORTH AMERICAN, BRITISH, AUSTRALIAN, AND
NEW ZEALAND MISSIONARIES AS A PERCENTAGE OF
TOTAL PROTESTANT MISSIONARIES OVERSEAS[25]

Year	North American Personnel		N. Am. + British, Australian & N.Z. as Percentage of Total	Total Protestant Missionaries Overseas
	Number	Percentage of Total		
1900	4,891	27%	81%	18,164
1910	7,219	34%	E. 84%	21,307
1925	13,608	49%	E. 86%	28,011
1938	12,146	48%	85%	25,343
1952	18,576	52%	---	35,522
1956	23,432	67%	88%	34,792
1960	29,380	66%	85%	44,411
1973	35,070	64%	84%	E. 54,500

E. (Estimate)

Those so inclined may draw from these figures their own comparisons and contrasts. Indeed they are included, in part, as a
stimulus to reflection.

For more than fifty years, North Americans have constituted
approximately 50% or more of the world force. Moreover, between
1900 and 1972 they have sharply reversed percentage roles with
the British. Significant internal changes in the doubling of
North American missionaries between 1952 and 1972 will be noted
later.

Equally impressive is the growth in voluntary giving by North
Americans to sustain this enterprise. In 1900 it amounted to
$6.6 million. In 1910, when the world total reached $30 million,

it was $13 million, or 43%, and the combined American and Brit-
ish amount was 81% of the total. By 1914 it was $19 million,
or 49% of the nearly $39 million world figure, and within sev-
eral years became the major portion of all Protestant missionary
funding. By 1925 it had reached $48.6 million or 70% of the
world total and thenceforth represented the great portion of
Protestant missionary funding.

The Depression dropped this giving in 1932 to $22.5 million
but it recovered, and in 1952 had reached $83.7 million. By
1960 it had advanced to $170 million, and in 1972 it had spurted
to $392 million. In 1976 it may be well over $400 million.*
Even allowing for the impact of inflation on them, those figures
represent a sizeable enterprise.[26] From 1910 onward North
American and British combined giving ranged from 81% to 89% of
the total Protestant giving for world mission.

In short, the heavy flow of Protestant world mission came
through the stream of the Anglo-American peoples and churches.
Through World War II Britain had a worldwide empire and in its
churches, in addition to theological motivations for mission,
resided a deep sense of responsibility for those in the empire.
The Americans had no empire as such. Yet the conquest of the
frontier, the creation of their own dynamic nation, the deep
sense of national purpose, and the enormous global power and
influence of their nation after World War II fostered the conviction that America could change the world for the better.

Recent events had subdued that mood by 1976. Yet one must
ask to what extent the powerful surging forces in the nation's
life had shaped the size and drive of the American Protestant
mission? That question admits no easy answer, but it must be
confronted openly. Meanwhile, for well over a century the
emphases, ethos, and patterns of the Anglo-American churches
have had a substantial impact among those churches growing in
Asia, Africa, and Latin America.

B. *The Mission Integral to the Church.* Protestant missions
in Europe and Britain developed through voluntary societies outside the official structure of the church. To be sure, they
represented a church or denominational constituency, and their
founders had been nurtured by the church, but their members

----

* If compared in size to a corporation's sales or revenues,
a $400+ million income and expenditure figure would place the
American Protestant overseas missionary enterprise about 410th
in the "Fortune 500" list of America's largest industrial
corporations. On this basis, it would rank approximately with
The New York Times (*Fortune,* May, 1976, p. 334).

represented a concerned minority. The general pattern among German-speaking Protestants was a regional or territorial society, e.g., The Berlin Mission, The Basel Mission, and The North German Missionary Society. The pattern in Britain was largely that of the independent denominational society. Thoroughly Anglican in their constituencies, the high church Society for the Propagation of the Gospel, the evangelical Church Missionary Society, and other societies reflecting special concerns have operated with the full cooperation of the Church of England, but as autonomous agencies.

The American pattern has been different. With no established church and with a populace not deemed to be Christian by birth and therefore needing the gospel, Christians in the young nation saw themselves quite literally as missionary communities. This was so for Baptists, Methodists, and others. Old School Presbyterians declared the church to be a missionary agency with responsibility for its own outreach. In 1835 the Episcopal Church affirmed the same, incorporated its formerly autonomous and voluntary missionary society, and decreed that all Episcopalians were thereby members in it.[27]

The American churches made their mission societies or boards integral to the church. With this, missionary promotion became internal, official, and church-wide. Inevitably, that shaped the American Protestant theological understanding of mission: the church itself is responsible for mission. This was a factor in the American inability to grasp the issues being debated in Europe on the integration of the International Missionary Council into the World Council of Churches in 1961.

Yet it has also raised problems. Whether women's boards have been integrated or not, the church normally is regarded as having a common mission agency, focus, and policy. Those in the constituency who reflect different theological orientations or missionary concerns may desire another option. This has led to splits and new denominations. In part it also accounts for the appeal of the newer independent missions to many within denominational constituencies. In contrast, Roman Catholic societies reflect considerable diversity.

C. *Voluntary Lay Support for Missions.* In the older Roman Catholic pattern, the king was financially responsible for missions in his territories. Yet as Protestant missions arose—the Danish-Halle mission in India was one exception—they received no state support. British, Dutch, and German colonial administrators subsidized mission schools, but did so primarily through a sense of responsibility for the welfare of their subjects, to encourage their appreciation of opportunities offered by colonial rule, and to provide a needed educated class, not

primarily to spread the Christian faith. American mission
schools overseas--and in some cases in the U.S.A. among the
Indians--willingly received such subsidies.

Yet in contrast to the sums spent by the Spaniards and Por-
tuguese for missions and in the absence of government help, Protestant missions depended totally upon voluntary support.
Catholic societies enlisting lay giving also appeared in Europe
and in America in the nineteenth century. In the American
churches this meant energetic fund raising through education
and drives. If one distinguishes between general church funds
allocated to missions and those raised directly within the church
for mission, a minority of members, estimated to be from 10% to
33%, giving modestly but steadily, has provided the great bulk
of missionary funds.

Women have maintained the chief interest in overseas outreach
and have encouraged family contributions to the missions of the
church. Simultaneously they also have supported through women's
societies their own special concerns to aid children, young
girls, and women overseas. As their work flourished, the more
the regular mission benefitted in interest and income. Directly
and indirectly, it appears, women have been responsible for the
bulk of missionary support. To enlist equivalent interest and
giving among men, the Laymen's Missionary Movement was founded
in 1907, and other bodies with similar intent have emerged.

The surge in giving in recent years undoubtedly relates to
the American economy, inflation, and centralized church budgets
with apportioned allocations. Yet the great increase has come
from outside the central cooperating denominations and often
from non-denominational agencies drawing upon a constituency
within those denominations.[28]

D. *The Impact of World Mission of the U.S.A.* Since the sixteenth century the Christian world mission has influenced the
West. One recalls the published defense in the 1690's by the
Protestant Leibniz of the Jesuit mission in China. Protestant
missions since 1800 have greatly stimulated popular and scholarly
Western interest in other lands, peoples, and religions. Especially among their supporters, missions have developed world-
mindedness and a sense of world community. This in turn has
shaped the thinking of others.

Missions have also been a factor in foreign relations.
Again, as recently as World War II, probably half of the American scholars and experts in the languages and cultures of the
Near East and Far East had a missionary background. Some
government ministers and statesmen have been shaped at least
in part in their work by direct of indirect missionary

influence. This important area is difficult to measure precisely, and requires investigation.[29]

Yet contemporary cultural and political historians have ignored almost completely the missionary role and impact on international relations and in the American scene. Within his concern for China studies and pointedly noting this oversight and lack of interest, Professor John K. Fairbank of Harvard in his 1968 presidential address to the American Historical Association urged that this omission be corrected. He designated the missionary "the invisible man in American history."[30] Practicing what he preached, he has encouraged doctoral students to investigate this field. Some of those dissertations make a notable contribution and have already been published.

At another level and across the decades the Missionary Education Movement, Friendship Press, and other agencies have produced mission study books. Often they have provided the best available brief, popular accounts of other countries and have been used annually by several hundred thousand persons. This education of a constituency to think globally and of needs other peoples face represents part of the impact. The recent resettlement of Vietnamese refugees in this country was greatly facilitated by just such missionary influence.

Nonetheless, a widespread negative image of mission and missionaries exists and is especially noticeable among university and seminary students. Errors and faults are many. Valid anthropological critiques are important and can only be helpful. The mission is open to much proper criticism, and it must be faced responsibly, but mission as the mocked and unjustified whipping boy is quite another and a serious matter. James Michener's *Hawaii*, as book and film, similar works, and the studies of too many anthropologists whose "objectivity" includes an uninformed animus have created a view of the missionary as a cultural villain. This requires response. In analyzing *Hawaii*, Alan Tippett has shown one way in which that response can be made.[31]

E. *Varied Relations With Governments.* Church and state—that also reads "mission and governments"—always have interacted. Nationally and internationally the American Protestant experience fits that pattern. The subject raised here is so vast that any brief statement, without amplification and qualification, is fraught with danger. Recent scholarly probing confirms the complexity. Yet several observations—and they are only that—can be made.

First, as the American missionary movement grew and had to deal with Washington, the boards discovered their need to speak unitedly. Government agencies would shun a chorus of individual voices, but would hear a representative spokesman. That fact spurred the cooperation represented by the Foreign Missions Conference of North America. It was in regular contact with the State Department and other bureaus on missionary concerns relating to the Spanish-American War, Boxer Indemnities, the Russo-Japanese War, the World Wars, and much else in between. It also had access through Washington to ambassadors from other nations.

Second, on the other side of that coin, government also has sought help from missions. Across the years missionaries in various parts of the world have aided government agencies with translations and with knowledge about a given area. During World War II some missionaries from Japan and some who had been reared there in missionary homes served in intelligence and language work. The recent recognition that the C.I.A. has gained intelligence from certain missionaries may be argued by some to fit within this picture; but its vigorous repudiation by the church and by some government officials is the best measure of how it is viewed.

Third, the pattern in host countries has varied widely. The majority of missionaries have been concerned for the human rights of the people among whom they worked and have sometimes opposed or sought to change related government policies. In colonial lands most American missionaries probably sided with and encouraged the aspirations of nationals for independence. Indeed, some were deported for their activities, and the pledge is well remembered that had to be signed by missionaries in British India promising no involvement in Indian political matters.

Practically speaking, except for the years 1898-1946 in the Philippines, American missionaries have served in countries where their governement has had only diplomatic or consular presence. They have sought diplomatic protection, but on occasion have rejected the counsel of their own government. This often has led to tension. On the whole they have cooperated with the governing power and those of its directives that maintained order and showed concern for justice.

Fourth, the charge of missionary involvement in imperialism requires response. In a nutshell, in the intertwining of history such was inevitable. Yet as the above paragraphs suggest, the involvement for American Protestants--and others--has been considerably different from that to be seen in earlier centuries. One partial but important example must suffice. As Asia was "opened" to the West, most Protestant missionaries viewed the victories of Western arms or diplomatic power as providential.

Such in 1898 was the case with the Philippines. They also
viewed China, as Xavier had three centuries earlier, as the key
to evangelizing East Asia.

The handful of missionaries clustered at Canton and held off
by a nation that steadfastly rejected all Westerners--diplomats,
businessmen and missionaries--condemned the opium trade, but welcomed the opening made by the Opium War of 1839-1842. The
treaties of 1842-1844, at the urging of at least two American
missionaries, granted all missionaries a place in the five
treaty ports along China's east coast. A few urged further
Western intervention. After the War of 1856, most welcomed the
"Unequal Treaties" of 1858 and 1860 which, through a clause in-
serted by a French missionary translator in the Chinese copy,
gave Christians access to and property rights in all China.
There had been since the sixteenth century a continuing presence
of Roman Catholics, but the Chinese today remember the forced
entry between 1839 and 1860 of Christianity.

Yet the total picture is vastly larger. It incorporates remarkable human devotion and concern for the Chinese, and after
the Boxer Uprising the refusal of the China Inland Mission, the
largest body and the one which had suffered most, to receive any
indemnities. It also includes the return, apparently from
missionary suggestion, by the United States of the first Boxer
Indemnity installment for the education of Chinese in their
homeland. There is also the seldom remembered return by America
to China of the balance of the Indemnity. In considerable measure that was due to the untiring efforts of Mary Woods of the
Episcopal Mission with members of Congress.[32]

Today the situation has changed vastly. Despite what is
termed "economic neo-colonialism," the old familiar Western
imperialism is dead, and the colonial holdings in the Third
World no longer exist. Western missionaries now must maintain
relations with independent governments, an increasing number of
which oppose their presence.

Christianity and its missionary outreach were on occasion
deliberately and often inescapably involved in the five centuries of Western colonialism which died rapidly after World
War II. Yet with its passing, the churches in the former colonial areas are stronger than ever. Despite allegations to the
contrary, the faith in the Third World obviously is not dependent upon whatever links it had with Western empire. History
may well disclose that just as the gospel moved forward among
new peoples during the period of Anglo-American ascendancy, it
continued to do so even as that period receded into the past.

F. *Areas of Concentration.* The shifting concentration of
North American missionaries in different areas deserves noting—
and an appraisal not possible here. Table III below does not
attempt completeness, but seeks to indicate basic distribution
by concentrating on certain major areas.

TABLE III

OVERSEAS CONCENTRATION OF
NORTH AMERICAN MISSIONARY PERSONNEL[33]

	1890	1915	1938	1956	1973
China	198	2,862	3,090	-----	-----
Japan	146	858	686	1,567	1,931
Korea	6	386	400	346	474
	350	4,106	4,176	1,913	2,405
Pakistan	---	-----	-----	298	306
India	262	2,105	2,036	2,127	1,247
Philippines	---	204	290	760	1,187
Near East	111	685	836	832	*
Africa	103	620	1,637	5,618	7,671
L. Am. & Caribbean	108	1,352	1,863	5,121	9,592
Pacific			498		860
Europe				253	1,871

---

* Absorbed in Asia and Africa Figures

The first column of Table III reminds one of the relatively
small American overseas mission in 1890. Then one notes the
stunning increase in missionaries in the twenty-five years between 1890 and 1915. The number in East Asia increased 9 times
and those in India by 8 times. Both Africa and the Near East
showed better than six-fold increases, and those in Latin America
increased nearly 12 times. All that reflects the powerful impact of the Student Volunteer Movement on the North American
missionary enterprise.

Second, Table III suggests that by 1915 approximately 80% of
the North Americans were concentrated among people of high culture and ancient religions in the Near East, India, China, and
Japan. China especially had magnetic attraction. Yet Christianity has never made notable gains among such people. Indeed,
other religions when operating in a purely voluntary way and
without the force of arms have experienced the same phenomenon.

Third, after World War II the shifting concentration of missionary personnel to Africa and Latin America gained momentum. This is evident in the 1956 and 1973 columns. Today, 34% of the North American Protestant missionaries are concentrated among 9% of the world's people in Latin America, and another 27% are concentrated among 10% of the world's population in Africa. Some 51% then are concentrated among 19% of the world's people. In Asia, with well over 60% of the world's population, the proportion has slipped to 30%. Yet notable increases have occurred in the Philippines, Korea, and Japan. The bulk of this massive post-World War II shift has occurred through the bodies which are not part of the Division of Overseas Ministries of the National Council of Churches, USA (DOM).

Finally, one notes a change in striking contrast with what obtained early in this century. In 1914 North American missionaries were heavily concentrated, with 71% in Asia and with 67% in China, Japan, Korea, and India alone. If one makes allowance for the Philippines, the situation today is sharply reversed. Forty-four percent (44%) of the North American missionary force is concentrated in Latin America and the Philippines, both long regarded as overwhelmingly Catholic, and in Europe, usually regarded as the heartland of Christendom. If one adds Africa, the concentration in those three areas, plus the Philippines, totals 71%--a complete reversal. The factors producing that change also bear pondering.

Table IV below is reproduced from the *Mission Handbook, 1973* for convenience and indicates the comparative distribution of missionaries today by major areas.

TABLE IV

COMPARATIVE DISTRIBUTION
OF MISSIONARY PERSONNEL, 1972[34]

	Population, 1972 (millions)	N. American Protestant Missionaries	U.S. Roman Catholic Missionaries
Africa	364 (10%)	7,671 (27%)	1,107 (15%)
Asia	2,154 (61%)	8,700 (30%)	2,014 (27%)
Europe (& USSR)	717 (20%)	1,871 (06%)	39 (01%)
Latin America	300 (8.5%)	9,592 (34%)	3,429 (46%)
Oceania	20 (.5%)	860 (03%)	826 (11%)
	3,555 (100%)	29,290 (100%)*	7,415 (100%)

* Total for whom areas of service were reported.

G. *The Bible in World Mission.* One special area of contribution relates to the Bible. Its centrality for Protestants is axiomatic, and its use and distribution have occupied a large place in the mission. Indeed the translating and publishing of the Scriptures in the world's languages has coincided with the rise of Protestant missions. They have held that every believer should have the Scriptures in his or her own tongue, and that they should be available as an instrument of evangelism in every possible language.

That perhaps 97% of the world's people have some portion of the Scriptures in their mother tongue is too readily taken for granted. It is a miracle! Fulfilling that intention often has meant learning an unwritten language, reducing it to writing, producing diglot grammars and dictionaries, and spending a lifetime gaining shades of meanings and finding equivalents for concepts and words that do not translate. Then follow translation, publication, and distribution. The almost inevitable concommitant is an educational program to make literacy possible.

Since its birth with the British and Foreign Bible Society in 1804, the Bible Society movement has played a unique role in mission. When the American Bible Society began in 1816, the movement spread. Formed in 1946, the United Bible Societies now link fifty-six national bodies and maintain four regional centers.

A table will portray most readily the remarkable story of Bible translation for mission.

TABLE V

LANGUAGES IN WHICH SINCE 1450
THE SCRIPTURES HAVE BEEN PUBLISHED[35]

Year	Languages	Portions, Gospels	The New Testament	The Bible
1450	33	15	4	14
1800	71	16	15	40
1830	157	65	40	52
1900	406	204	91	111
1937	1,008	617	212	179
1951	1,250	716	297	237
1974	1,549	924	368	257
1975	1,577	930	386	261

Between 1800 and 1830 the Scriptures were translated into 86 new languages. The production of those three decades exceeded the total of the previous eighteen centuries! That period also marked the concerted beginnings of Protestant missions, the Bible Societies, and the prodigious translation labors of Carey, Marshman, and Ward, the Serampore Trio.

The great increase between 1800 and 1900 speaks for itself. Among the 335 new languages into which the Scriptures were translated in that century, 219 were reduced to writing specifically for that purpose.[36]

The enormous growth of this endeavor in the twentieth century is apparent. The reduction of languages to writing as a vehicle for evangelization has greatly accelerated. Indeed, the remarkable Wycliffe Bible Translators, founded in 1934 and with their current force of 3,500 growing by 160 yearly, concentrate on providing the gospel through this means to the small and remote tribes.

Today some portion of Scripture is available in more than 1,577 languages, which represent the tongues of about 97% of the world's people. Yet 90% of those people use the 50 major languages of the world. The Bible Societies, which aid national agencies and through which nearly 219 million Scriptures were distributed in 1972, are concentrating on this segment of the work. Worldwide they seek to provide better and more easily understood translations (e.g., *Good News for Modern Man*).

No one really knows how many languages or dialects in the world remain to be reduced to writing and into which the Scriptures can be translated. Indeed when one probes dialects and sub-dialects, defining what constitutes a language becomes a problem. Wycliffe is concentrating on those tongues, perhaps 2,000 or more, among the small fraction of tribal peoples largely overlooked by the world. For the past six years Wycliffe has been placing once every twelve days a new team among another pre-literate people to advance the process. Wycliffe and the Bible Societies are concentrating their work in two quite different areas and thus avoid duplication of effort.

The above suggests at least two corollaries. First, because of the Christian mission, more languages have been reduced to writing in the past 175 years than in all the prior history of humankind. In the accompanying development of literacy and literature, hundreds of ethnic groups have learned to read the Bible and have been able and encouraged to record their oral traditions to provide an initial indigenous literature. Those anthropologists who score the Christian mission as a destroyer of cultures seem entirely to have overlooked the meaning of this fact. Moreover, many of the languages reduced to writing

have been given form through Romanized script. Within the world
community and for those who must learn other languages, this is
a unifying and facilitating factor.

Second, most of this work has been done by Anglo-Americans.
Thus, among many recently pre-literate or illiterate peoples,
those learning a second or third language are likely to learn
English. This also has enabled them to participate more
readily in international exchanges and gatherings in which
English is often the basic or common language. One notes also
that before 1900 the British spent more effort on translation of
the Scriptures, and the Americans in their vast new land concentrated more heavily on distribution. That pattern has
changed in the twentieth century.

H. *The Important Role of Women.* For centuries Roman Catholic monks had provided the church with its corps of missionaries,
but the rise of Protestant missionary societies created a new
missionary structure. Within it when men went overseas, their
wives went with them. The mission gained a new dimension. In
Near Eastern and Asian cultures, especially in India, foreign
men seldom could approach women directly, and that extended to
medical care. Women's wants were best met by other women, and
the missionary wives fulfilled this role.

As needs mounted, opportunities grew for single women to
serve. After 1865 they entered the work increasingly. The
Student Volunteer Movement enrolled them in still larger numbers.
With help for their housework and children, wives have functioned in their own right as missionaries. [That pattern has
been shifting in recent years as more wives have chosen to
exemplify the role of full-time Christian homemaker and mother
while engaging in substantial spare-time service.] Yet single
women had greater mobility and could give undivided attention to
their work. Each group has made a noteworthy and unique contribution.

The following figures reflect the approximate numerical
strength of women in the overseas mission. Their proportion in
1830 was 49% and by 1880 had reached 57%. By 1923 they represented 61%, in 1929 about 67%, and in 1956 some 60%.[37] From
1920 through 1956 their proportionate strength ranged between
60% and 67%. Of the missionaries overseas in 1956, for example,
the nearly 6,300 married women were 36% and the 4,055 unmarried women were 24%. Yet for the past twenty years the proportion of single women has been declining.[38]

In their homeland women had helped to conquer the frontier
and in the process worked as hard as men, but they gained the
right to vote only in 1920. Overseas and amid the same cultural

mindset, the missionary women held a lesser status than the men.
This was compounded by the additional distinction in the church
accorded to ordained men. Yet the women coped without complaint
and worked just as diligently.

Free of family obligations, the single women undertook almost
every job the mission was doing, fulfilled a unique role with
women and children, and proved their full missionary capability.
The women's boards in the U.S.A. supported them and their work,
as well as that of the married women. The resulting strong,
personal links also included those women among whom the work
progressed and produced a sense of mutual Christian involvement
on opposite sides of the world.

In lands where the education of girls and women was widely
judged to be needless or even harmful, determined effort produced elementary schools, and from them came girls' high schools.
These led soon to outstanding women's colleges--Ginling in China,
Isabella Thoburn in India, Ewha in Korea, and others. From them
came the well trained women who in turn multiplied the outreach.
Women in America thrilled to these achievements and sensed
deeply that they were engaged in the advancement of women
throughout the world.

The same pattern appeared in medicine. In India and in other
areas only women could treat women medically. Dr. Clara Swain
and Dr. Ida Scudder developed hospitals and medical training
schools in India. From these and other hospitals the nursing
corps was trained. It is no accident that until World War II,
virtually all nurses in India were young Christian women, and
that in some Asian lands up to 50% of the physicians are women.
By 1910 of the more than 1,000 missionary physicians overseas,
one-third were women. To this day a ratio like that does not
exist in the U.S.A.

The Christian mission brought Western higher education and
medicine to Asia and then to Africa. This is one of its great
and best known accomplishments. In Asia women missionaries
made both available to women and then trained their Asian sisters to carry on the work. Accepting certain inequalities in
church and society with grace, but operating determinedly as if
these did not exist, Christian women--Eastern and Western--in-
vested the mission with solid achievement and brilliant highlights.

The large role of women in the mission undoubtedly has
shaped it. They brought heightened emphasis upon education of
all kinds, orphanages, special care for the handicapped, and
medicine at all levels. This in turn has made a substantial impact upon the surrounding society. Whatever value one may

assign to the latter, one thing is clear. The strengths now
demonstrated by the church in the Third World are owed in considerable measure to these women. They walked the road to human
dignity with their sisters in the Third World and enabled them
to provide the church with its sustaining human rootage.

I. *The Spread of Denominationalism and the Growth of Cooperation.* As the bulk of Protestant mission increasingly flowed
through Anglo-Americans, their denominations were transplanted
overseas. As Latourette early noted, by the twentieth century
the mission was moving with growing resources chiefly through
Congregationalists, Baptists, Presbyterians, Methodists, Disciples, and similar bodies rather than through the great national
churches of the European Reformation. The Anglicans always had
loomed large, and in time Reformed and Lutheran Churches were
also spreading from an American base, but the new trend was
unmistakable, has continued in its present manifestations, and
has accelerated through bodies not associated with these denomi-
natons.

In short, a larger variety of Christian churches was
spreading around the world than ever before. As they took root,
they did not reproduce the church/sect alignment typical in
Europe and for which Troeltsch gave classic expression. Instead they reproduced themselves in the predominantly American
pattern of denominations with no state support,[39] but in a
pluralistic setting that involved other major religions.

That denominational diversity, so natural to American Christians, posed problems overseas. In Germany, for example, in an
area where 95% are Lutheran and 2.5% are Reformed, a council of
churches makes little sense. Yet in India where Christians
represent less than 3% of the population, and in an area where
from ten to twenty Protestant bodies may be at work, a council
of churches has a much more obvious role to fulfill. Indeed,
it appears to have ecclesiological significance. The American
pattern of church councils was reproduced widely.

In Asia the problems of denominationalism loomed large. Over-
lapping, competition, differences incomprehensible to those outside, and financial problems in developing needed Christian
institutions quickly became issues. The theological conviction
arose that proclamation of God's reconciling power in Jesus
Christ was being denied by the churches themselves before
those to whom they witnessed. That belief and urgent practical
considerations led to comity,[40] to union enterprises in education, medicine, and publishing, to regional and national
agencies of cooperation some of which became councils of
churches, and to church union itself.[41]

Missionaries found need for consultation and cooperative
planning in missionary conferences,[42] and they and nationals
together referred frequently to need for a united church of
Christ in the nation. One outcome of this has been the growth
of church unions in Asia, the most notable of which are the
Church of South India (1947) and the Church of North India
(1970). From William Carey's first challenge for all to pray
for the mission, to his call for a world missionary conference
in 1810, to the growth of cooperation and unity in mission, the
ground was being prepared for the emergence of the Ecumenical
Movement. It roots in and is nourished by the world mission.[43]

J. *The Student Movement and John R. Mott.* From the founding
of The Brethern at Williams in 1808 to the rise of the Student
Volunteer Movement for Foreign Missions (SVM), Student Christian
Movements (SCM), and the World's Student Christian Federation
(WSCF) late in the nineteenth century, to the current crop of
student conferences, students and student movements have played
a prominent role in stimulating missionary spirit in North
America—and indeed throughout the world.

Undergirded by the Intercollegiate YMCA, the American SCM held
its first conference at Dwight L. Moody's Mount Hermon School at
Northfield, Massachusetts, for a month in the summer of 1886.
Missionary spirit was high, and there the SVM was born with its
first hundred volunteers, among them John R. Mott. From that
moment, the SVM grew steadily. Its members signed a pledge,
"It is my purpose, if God permit, to become a foreign missionary." Only a minority of those who signed went overseas,
but the others became a formidable missionary force in their
home churches.

In 1888 Mott, already at 23 the national intercollegiate
secretary of the YMCA, became chairman of the SVM and Robert E.
Speer became its traveling secretary. The SVM and the SCM
spread to Britain, Europe, Australia, and to India, China, and
Japan. As Christian student enthusiasm and concern mounted in
universities around the world, the need to focus its constructive power became apparent. In 1895 the WSCF, largely through
Mott's initiative, became the international coordinating link
for the national SCM's.

Meanwhile, the SVM watchword, "The evangelization of the
world in this generation," became the dynamic center for the
whole inter-related student movement. Widely misquoted and
misunderstood, then and now, it was not a prophecy of fact. Nor
did it envision the *conversion* of the world. It was rather a
call to recognize the responsibility that each generation of
Christians has to make the gospel available to all in that
generation. No others can fulfill that task. For the first

time the physical means were available to facilitate that aim. Its intent was not to flood the world with Western missionaries, but to triple the force, to recruit and train national pastors, and to speed the development of indigenous churches which alone could fulfill the evangelistic task among their own people.[44]

Mott, a Methodist layman, missionary statesman, extraordinary administrator, and evangelist, guided the SVM as its chairman until his resignation in 1920. Although it had passed its peak by 1925, it sent more than 25,000 university graduates--the great majority of them North Americans--overseas through their denominational boards. In addition, perhaps five to ten times that number who had been members remained at home but as supporters. Moreover, other thousands who never joined the SVM felt its influence and entered missionary service. Table III above (columns for 1890 and 1915) provides evidence of the SVM's contribution in its early years to the number of North American missionaries. The strength of the SCM in the Asian universities and the appeal of the Asian potential also help to explain the high concentration of missionaries in the Far East.

K. *The Rise of International Missionary Cooperation.* Missionary conferences dealing with problems and strategy in Asia, conferences of missionary administrators in Europe, and growing need for consultation on common concerns led in 1893 to the formation of the Foreign Missions Conference of North America (FMC). Mott and Speer were active in its development, and it agreed upon the understanding of authority operative in the German *Ausschuss,* namely, that any decisions reached represented counsel. Their acceptance by the boards (churches) would be wholly voluntary. That, in turn, became the understanding of authority operative in all ecumenical structures. Including Canadian and American boards, the Episcopal Church and the Southern Baptist Convention, the Assemblies of God, Seventh Day Adventists, and the Church of the Nazarene, as well as the China Inland Mission and the Sudan United Mission, the FMC was the largest and most representative agency of its kind. Its membership varied over the years, but when it became a division within the newly-formed National Council of Churches, U.S.A., in 1950, the Canadian boards and certain others dropped their membership. In its early years, the FMC contributed to Edinburgh, 1910, and to the national and international structures of missionary cooperation.

Meanwhile, Mott had become the organizing genius for the World Missionary Conference, Edinburgh, 1910. He credited the SVM's watchword and the entire missionary-oriented SCM as being the key factors leading to that unique event. It became the source of the organized Protestant and Orthodox manifestations of the Ecumenical Movement in the twentieth century.

Edinburgh, 1910, is often referred to as "a home base conference." Yet in 1912-1923 Mott, convening twenty-one conferences from Colombo to Tokyo, in effect, reproduced Edinburgh,
1910, throughout Asia. In size the meetings averaged less than
one hundred carefully chosen and delegated members, of whom 14%
were women and 35% were Asians. From these sessions the ground-
work was laid for the National Christian Councils in Asia.
Through his carefully organized world tours, Mott encouraged the
development of an extended network of National Christian Councils
(NCC's).

In 1921, although it had in fact been functioning since 1910,
the International Missionary Council was founded, with the NCC's
and missionary conferences as its members. This world council
of national councils sought to encourage the most effective
strategic development of the Protestant world mission. As the
IMC's Chairman, Mott functioned as its chief executive officer.
From Edinburgh, 1910, came the Faith and Order Movement. The
Universal Council on Life and Work begun in 1925 in its development depended heavily upon the IMC. Although many others were
involved, and notably the Archbishop of Canterbury, William
Temple, the cooperative missionary enterprise contributed
uniquely to the emergence of the World Council of Churches in
1948. Undergirding that and even more important was its development of a strong consciousness of world Christian community
among the churches on all continents. Its leadership was widely
international, but its key figure had been the American layman
John R. Mott whose vision was "the evangelization of the world
in this generation."[45]

L. *The New Evangelical Student Movement.* The theme of
world evangelization re-emerged after World War II through a new
student movement which has had considerable missionary impact.
It arose through the Student Foreign Missions Fellowship (SFMF),
which was born in 1936, and the Intervarsity Christian Fellowship (IVCF), begun in 1939 under the leadership of C. Stacey
Woods. In 1945 the two merged, and the SFMF became the IVCF's
missionary arm.

Similar developments in Europe and elsewhere led in 1947 to
an international student conference convened at Harvard where
the International Fellowship of Evangelical Students (IFES) was
born. C. Stacey Woods became its general secretary, a post he
was to hold for more than two decades.

Although its roots reach beyond the 1930's into the late
nineteenth century, this post-World War II Evangelical Student
Movement has reproduced the pattern of its prototype. As a
national movement the IVCF parallels the old SCM. The SFMF is
comparable to the former SVM. With its evangelistic concern,

The IFES stands as the counterpart to the earlier WSCF. Significantly, this Evangelical Student Movement claims as its heritage the work and witness of Dwight L. Moody, John R. Mott,
Robert Wilder, and Robert E. Speer. It also has made its own
the Watchword of the SVM, "The evangelization of the world in
this generation."

   In North America the IVCF/SFMF also has convened its own noteworthy series of student missionary conferences. The first of
these met at Toronto in 1946. Since 1948 they have met tri-
ennially at Urbana, on the campus of the University of Illinois.
They grew steadily in size, and in the years since 1961 have
enrolled between 5,000 and 10,000 students. One researcher
provides the program of an early SVM conference for comparison
and contrast and suggests that in scholarship and breadth, in
probing spiritual and social problems, the SVM Quadrennials
were unique.[46]

   These IVCF/SFMF conferences have aided the overseas mission
drive of the evangelical agencies, the remarkable growth of
which is noted in the next section. Yet it is too early for a
probing assessment of their full impact. Based upon questionnaires, one detailed study of the 1967 conference pointed to
some diverse and "unorthodox" theological views among those
attending. For example, 63% did not believe that one who had
not heard the gospel was "eternally lost."[47] Observers and
students have noted the lack of a student role in the planning
and leadership of these conferences. The latter have drawn
students from the North—from Canada and from Maine to California—but few from the South and fewer from among blacks. Their
influence appears to have been considerable.

   M. *New Missions and the Evangelical Spirit.* The three decades since the close of World War II have brought a massive
change in the configuration of American missionaries sent overseas. Since 1952 the number of those sent by members of the
Division of Overseas Ministries of the National Council of
Churches (DOM), regarded as representing the large central core
of cooperating American church bodies, has fallen. Except for
the Associated Missions of the International Council of Christian Churches which have declined precipitously, all other
sources of missionaries show a remarkable increase. Table VI
below presents the picture.

TABLE VI

NORTH AMERICAN PROTESTANT MISSIONARY PERSONNEL:
DIVISION OF OVERSEAS MINISTRIES,
NATIONAL COUNCIL OF CHURCHES, USA,
AS RELATED TO ALL OTHER PERSONNEL[48]

Year	FMC/DOM*	DOM Affiliates	All Other	Total
1925	11,020**	------	2,588**	13,608
1952	7,405	2,439	8,160	18,576
	572			
1960	7,709	2,111	19,056	29,380
	504			
1970	5,676	3,258***	25,003	34,460
	523			
1973	3,569	2,908	28,149	35,070
	444			
1976	2,776	2,234	30,119	35,458
	329			

*With the formation of the NCC, USA in 1950, the FMC was offi-
cially dissolved, and those bodies in it which wished to be part
of the NCC structure remained. The FMC's Canadian Boards had to
relate themselves nationally and now constitute the Commission
on World Concern of the Canadian Council of Churches. Their
missionaries in the years from 1952 to 1976 are shown in a
separate figure under that for the DOM, reflecting the North
American pattern of the former FMC.

**These figures are approximations. No attempt has been made
to determine the number for the Affiliates, but among those
groups at the time supporting the FMC financially, although not
constitutional members, were the Africa Inland Mission, the
China Inland Mission, the Sudan Interior Mission, and the Women's
Union Missionary Society. Their missionaries are included in
the "All Other" category. *The Foreign Missions Conference of
North America, 1928, Report* (New York: FMC, 1928), pp. 190-191.

***In 1970 the three DOM Affiliated Boards sending the largest
number of missionaries were the Seventh Day Adventist (1,426),
the Lutheran Church--Missouri Synod (639), and the American
Lutheran Church (573).

Comments on Table VI must be kept to a minimum. It clearly discloses that American Christians have been sending missionaries overseas in steadily increasing numbers. The increase has come from boards and agencies not related to the DOM, but, as is well known, many in the DOM/NCC churches also support these missions. It is too early to assess the total figures which are flat for the 1970's, but in the past similar periods of longer duration have appeared.

Yet the long-term trend in the internal shifting ratic of those being sent overseas is evident. The decline continues in overseas missionaries from the DOM constituents and related bodies. The number of missionaries from boards and agencies not related to the DOM steadily increases.

The contrast is striking. In 1925 the cooperating bodies of American Protestantism provided 81% and all other agencies supplied 19% of the North American missionaries overseas. A half-century later the DOM group contributed 14.5% of the missionaries and all others accounted for 85.5%. Interestingly, in 1973 the DOM bodies provided 33.5% of the North American expenditures, a figure which reflects in part their relatively heavier commitment to educational, medical, and other institutions and to churches.[49]

To probe the reasons behind this phenomenon and its meaning is tempting, but would unduly extend this presentation. Indeed, its purpose is to stimulate such reflection. Yet two observations can be made. First, the bulk of American Protestant funds (66.5%) and personnel (85%) for mission overseas is going through conservative evangelical channels. This shapes the representation and image of Protestant missions in the Third World. But at present this proportion does not have a corresponding relationship to church size there, for many of these missionaries are concentrated among relatively small groups of Christians, while the older and larger churches there may have few Western missionaries among them.

Second, one observes that the DOM bodies generally have been making a theological transition with notable operational consequences. The shift marks a move away from a Western Christian evangelistic crusade to the world and toward an engagement with the world in what is regarded as a total evangelistic response to the world's needs and the religious beliefs of its people. It presupposes a profound change in today's world and in the relationship of its peoples to one another. It views the North American role in world mission not in terms of large numbers of professional missionaries, but rather through fewer skilled specialists and particularly through the work and witness of the worldwide lay Christian diaspora in secular posts.[50]

In addition to the DOM, two other large cooperative agencies
serve the needs of many boards and societies. The Interdenominational Foreign Mission Association (IFMA) began in 1917 and
brings together many of the faith missions. That movement began
when Hudson Taylor founded the China Inland Mission in 1865.
Yet IFMA missionaries have had their most rapid growth since
1945. The Evangelical Foreign Missions Association (EFMA) was
formed in 1945 and represents conservative evangelical bodies.
The number of missionaries represented by the EFMA has also
grown rapidly. Since the Wheaton Conference in 1966, the IFMA
and EFMA have cooperated closely.

The most amazing growth in the sending of missionaries has
come among unaffiliated agencies. Between 1952 and 1970 they
had increased 3.8 times to 11,000. The Southern Baptist Convention with some 2670 missionaries in 80 countries and the
Wycliffe Bible Translators with 3500, some of whom are from outside the U.S.A., are the two largest bodies in this group.

Part of this increase relates to the founding in recent years
of many new mission agencies. By the time of Edinburgh, 1910,
in North America 102 societies were operating. From then until
the outbreak of World War II, 126 more had been formed. Since
then an additional 279 have emerged. Most of the latter are
very small, but for now seem to be flourishing.[51] From another
perspective, the ten largest missions, six of which are denominational, account for 38% of the North American overseas personnel, and the top 26 account for approximately 56%. The remaining 317 agencies share responsibility for 44% of the personnel.[52]

Most of these newer bodies are meeting a need among a generous and concerned constituency. Many people want to contribute
directly to and be closely related with missions in which they
deeply believe. How effectively many of these and the missionaries they send out strengthen the mission in today's world
may not be known for some time. Yet the question deserves
serious reflection.

One reports frankly and with sadness that some among these
are parasitic. Some are contentiously divisive, and their appeals for support reflect an "anti-this" or "anti-that" spirit.
Some would be embarrassed to have any responsible board of
review examine and make public their financial records. They
pose a problem.

One new element requires noting. Non-denominational
agencies, which have long appealed to individuals within the
denominational constituencies, increasingly are seeking recognition from denominations, synods, or churches as approved

channels for part of a congregation's missionary giving. This
development poses certain basic questions for the American denominational boards which have regarded their status within the
denomination as inviolate. Is more diversity, such as that
seen in the Anglican societies and in the Roman Catholic Church,
needed? If so, the churches face some practical and ecclesiological issues in dealing with autonomous non-denominational
agencies.[53]

Underlying all this is a tide of fundamental importance--
the growing spirit designated "evangelical." The line runs
directly from the World Congress on Evangelism, Berlin, 1966,
through the regional conferences which followed, to the International Congress on World Evangelization, Lausanne, 1974.
Moreover, the Catholic bishops dealt with world evangelization
in their recent Synod, and the impact of both was clearly felt
on the Fifth Assembly of the World Council of Churches at
Nairobi in 1975.

Significantly, the watchword of the SVM, "the evangelization
of the world in this generation," has been widely perceived to
have vital meaning for the contemporary church. Its first
major restatement in recent years appears to be in *Lumen
Gentium*, the foundational document for Vatican II.[54] For
Pentecostals it is a matter of belief. It emerged at Berlin and
at Lausanne. It was stated at Bangkok[55] and was clearly reflected at Nairobi. Contributing to this on the Protestant side
have been the Evangelism-in-Depth Program, with its genesis in
Central America, and the Church Growth Movement with its center
in the Fuller School of World Mission. Here is a focused
spiritual stirring of major import.

N. *The Worldwide Spread of Pentecostalism*. Within the world
Christian community the most explosive movement may be Pentecostalism. It already has reached significant proportions, has
spread to every continent, and is growing most rapidly in Latin
America and Africa. In addition to "traditional" Pentecostalism,
Charismatic Renewal within the Roman Catholic Church and among
Anglicans, Lutherans, and other Protestants brings new awareness of the power of the Holy Spirit into churches that once dis-
dained Pentecostalism.

One dare not pin a national label on the Pentecostal Movement,
but it is widely regarded as having had its origins in the
American Holiness Movement--with *its* roots in Wesleyan Chris-
tianity--and as having begun in the Azusa Street Mission in Los
Angeles in 1906. Although there may now be two hundred Pentecostal bodies in America, the Assemblies of God, the largest,
and the Church of God (Cleveland, Tennessee) are two major
representative groups.

One striking feature was its almost instantaneous spread around the world. T. B. Barratt, a Norwegian Methodist minister, influenced by the Azusa revival, returned to Norway with the Pentecostal fire and saw it spread from there into other Scandinavian countries. Almost immediately it moved into Britain and Europe. Meanwhile, W. C. Hoover, a Methodist missionary in Chile, began the growing movement in that land.

Two Swedish workers from Chicago felt called to Brazil in 1910 and there began the Brazilian Assemblies of God. In that same year an Italian-American immigrant also went from Chicago to Brazil and there launched the Christian Congregation of Brazil. Throughout Latin America and the Caribbean the movement has spread rapidly and today probably embraces at least 15 million persons. Some estimate its Latin American constituency to be 25 million.

Discovering an already prepared base, missionaries brought the Pentecostal Movement to South Africa in 1908. Through African leadership it spread quickly and today is found throughout Sub-Saharan Africa. Indeed, many of the rapidly growing independent African churches are Pentecostal in nature whether or not they have any direct tie with the international movement through its regular world conferences. This writer judges that the African Pentecostal community is probably as large as that in Latin America and may outgain it.[56]

Pentecostals send missionaries overseas, but the movement's great strength has been through compelling individual and corporate witness. Its congregations emphasize individual evangelistic responsibility, spontaneous worship, and supportive community. Its language is not translated but is idiomatic and living. Its forms are indigenous and its people display an impressive vibrancy. Its problems are readily noted, but the power of its inner life expressed daily often contrasts sharply with that found in "respectable" churches.

Pentecostalism raises ecclesiological and theological issues. The traditional genius of the Roman Catholic Church for holding together within its unity diverse movements and expressions of Christian faith has shown itself again in the Catholic Charismatic Renewal. That church has viewed this burst of new life as a recovery of intense fellowship and caring *koinonia* within and for the church, not as a divisive force. It has explored the theology of the Holy Spirit and of Charismatic Renewal *within* the church. The resulting strength has been that of nuclear fusion rather than fission. Indeed, Roman Catholic theologians have provided the most effective and knowledgeable theologizing on Pentecostalism to be found.[57]

More than twenty years ago the perceptive Lesslie Newbigin
suggested that Catholicism had laid primary stress upon apostolic
structure and Protestantism upon apostolic message. In so doing
both were seeking to safeguard the uniqueness and finality of
God's salvific action in Jesus Christ. Yet the evident action
of the Holy Spirit in the church requires an enlargement of that
bi-polar encounter to include a third element: the presence of
the living God in the church through the power of the Spirit.[58]
The life of the church is no less important than its form or
message.

The church must now explore anew the doctrine of the Holy
Spirit. It has been virtually untouched since the days of
Nicea and Constantinople. The signs of the times require it.

The Chalcedonian Christological formulation of 451 became
normative for the church. Yet it emerged because three distinctive emphases--not one of which would have sufficed alone--in
creative engagement made it possible. Is it too much to suggest
that a somewhat similar encounter now may be necessary to affirm
the wholeness of the church for its mission in the world? Perhaps such would incorporate the essential Pentecostal gift--a
heart and community transformed in the Spirit--as basic to the
life of the church.

IV. *Conclusion: The Church in the Third World*

The above pages provide little indication of theological and
other motivating forces, for these have been dealt with by other
participants. The writer has made no effort to explore negative
factors. Instead, he had attempted to present certain major
features evident in the American Protestant world mission. In
whatever worth these possess for the oikoumene, they reflect
gifts and opportunities God has granted to American Protestants
in this period of their history. The contributions have been
achieved in concert and mutual involvement with Christians from
other lands.

The greatest contribution of all is that made to the growth
of the church in Asia, Oceania, Africa, and Latin America. It
is part of a five-century effort in which Catholics and Protestants especially, but also Orthodox have shared.

From Russia through Europe to the U.S.A. and across to
Australia and New Zealand, Christians number 650 million. Yet
unrecognized by many, Christians have been growing in number in
the Third World steadily and now rapidly. There today they
total more than 600 million. For the first time in history,
these Christians almost equal those in the West. Within a

decade they should equal and by the end of this century should
noticeably exceed the number of Western Christians. Their majority should continue to grow.

Christianity already is universal. No longer can it be
called "the white man's faith." In his providence God has used
a large number of white people as instruments to achieve that
end.

In short, we live amid the most massive shifting of its center of gravity that the Christian faith has ever seen--from the
old Christendom to the Third World. This also represents a
fundamental transition in world history and in the dynamics
that shape global history. The impact, scarcely evident yet,
will be profound.

What does it involve? Here the briefest hints must suffice.

First, far more important than numbers is the vitality--the
surging vigor--of much Christian life in the Third World. The
Western church offers centers of renewal, creativity, scholarship, and superb resources for the entire church. Yet it is
widely viewed as declining, irrelevant, and with little power
in society. Although its churches display all the usual human
faults, and some are very weak, quite the opposite is the case
in much of the Third World. The axis of dynamic Christian life
now is moving from the West to the Third World. That is a
notable shift.

Second, certain demographic and logistical realities suggest
some new challenges to the faith. Their implications provide a
study in itself, but need not be pursued here.

Third, the shift involves a new and enlarged encounter between Christian faith and Marxist ideology and also between the
gospel and the traditional faiths of mankind. Constantine's
arrival seemed to dispose of the issue symbolized by Tertullian
("What has Jerusalem to do with Athens?") and Clement of Alexandria. The meaning of the seminal Word (*spermatikos Logos*) runs
directly from Justin Martyr through Clement of Alexandria and
Aquinas to Vatican II.[59] The relation of the Christian gospel
to other faith systems remains divisive for Christians, will be
an issue of mounting importance, and requires the concerted
theological concern of the entire church.

Fourth, the church faces anew its understanding of the work
and presence of the Holy Spirit. This relates not only to the
issue of encounter but also to the meaning of the evidences of
the Spirit's working. What is the meaning of the Holy Spirit

for the church's life-witness, structure, mission, and encounter
with the world?

Fifth, Christians in the Third World are increasingly appro-
priating the gospel in their own way—even as Greeks, Romans,
Germans, and Americans have done. What Third World Christians
view as central and most urgent theologically is at many points
very different from that seen in Western perspective. The
varied theologies of the Third World are fresh and vibrant. To
the service of the gospel they bring the diversities and richness with which God has endowed all humankind. The gospel is
neither black, brown, red, yellow, nor white. It is God's Word
to all and needs to be heard from all for its symphonic wholeness. Indeed, is this not one element in God's purpose for
humankind to which the evangelization of the world points?

Finally, what used to be called Christendom no longer exists.
The world of the past two centuries has changed and is no more.
God's mission abides. The mission is thus in a transition so
vast that the uncertainties constitute a crisis. The transient
patterns of the past 175 years do not constitute the norm for
the future of mission.

God is unchanging, and man in his nature and need for God is
unchanged. The alignments of history have shifted as have the
theological issues thus brought to the fore. The mission is
larger and more complex than ever before, and its norm—even
as it was for Abraham—is that faithful obedience which can
follow God's leading into a new land.

Let those who have ears hear what the Spirit is saying to the
churches.

NOTES

[1]K. S. Latourette, *A History of Christianity* (New York: Harper, 1953).

[2]M. E. Marty, *The Modern Schism* (New York: Harper, 1969).

[3]R. P. Beaver, *Church, State, and The American Indians: Two and A Half Centuries of Partnership in Missions Between Protestant Churches and Government* (St. Louis: Concordia, 1966).
----- ed., *Pioneers in Mission . . .: A Sourcebook on the Rise of American Missions to the Heathen* (Grand Rapids: Eerdmans, 1966).

[4]C. L. Chaney, *The Birth of Missions in America* (South Pasadena, Calif.: William Carey Library, 1976).

[5]H. R. Niebuhr, *The Kingdom of God in America* (Chicago: Willett, Clark & Co., 1937), pp. 45-126. See especially pp. 118, 125. Chaney, *op. cit.*, p. 49, also notes Niebuhr's interpretation.

[6]Cf. Niebuhr's phrase, *Kingdom of God in America,* p. 124.

[7]*Towards the Conversion of England* (London: Press and Publications Board of the Church Assembly, 1945), p. 3.

[8]Alexis De Tocqueville, *Democracy in America* (New York: Knopf, 1945), I:314-319.

[9]They have been used among others by these representative writers: K. S. Latourette, *A History of the Expansion of Christianity* (New York: Harper, 1937-1945, 7 vols.) IV:385; F. H. Littell, *From State Church to Pluralism* (New York: Doubleday, 1962), p. 32; S. E. Ahlstrom, *A Religious History of the American People* (New Haven, Conn: Yale University Press, 1972), p. 952; E. S. Gaustad, *Historical Atlas of Religion in America* (New York: Harper, 1962), pp. 52-53, 158.

[10]Table I is reconstructed from the following: Latourette cited *(Expansion,* IV:385 and elsewhere) the percentage of Christians in the population from 1800 to 1910, using the figures given in H. C. Weber, ed., *Yearbook of American Churches, 1933 Edition* (New York: Federal Council of Churches, 1933), p. 299. Weber's figures from 1800 through 1890 in chart form, which may have been compiled by G. L. Kieffer, follow closely those of Daniel Dorchester, *Christianity in the United States* (New York: Phillips & Hunt, 1888. Rev. eds., 1890, 1895). Littell, *State Church to Pluralism,* p. 32, also uses the figures in Weber for the period 1776-1900. Ahlstrom, *A Religious History,* p. 952,

lists the percentage figures from 1910 to 1970 directly and indirectly from editions of the *Yearbook of American Churches.*

Gaustad, in his carefully detailed *Historical Atlas,* provides early figures three to four percentage points higher than those in Weber, but from 1900 ff. his figures align closely with those in Weber and in continuing editions of the *Yearbook of American Churches.*

Because percentage figures for church membership in the *Yearbook of American Churches* include Jewish, Buddhist, and other affiliations, the figures given in the table reconstructed here have been revised downward accordingly. Figures for 1960 and 1970 are taken from the 1961 and 1971 *Yearbooks* which, in turn, reflect church statistics for 1959 and 1969. The 1976 figure is from the 1976 *Yearbook.*

[11]Winthrop S. Hudson, *Religion in America* (New York: Charles Scribner's Sons, 1965), pp. 129–130.

[12]Gaustad, *Atlas,* pp. 164–165.

[13]Kenneth A. Briggs, "Young Adult Church Attendance," *New York Times,* January 4, 1976.

[14]Robert N. Bellah, "Civil Religion in America" in Donald R. Cutler, ed., *The Religions Situation: 1968* (Boston: Beacon Press, 1968), pp. 331–356. "Commentaries" *ibid.,* pp. 356–393. See also Peter L. Berger, *Religion in a Revolutionary Society* (Washington: American Enterprise Institute for Public Policy Research, 1974).

[15]C. B. Goodykoontz, *Home Missions on the American Frontier* (Caldwell, Idaho: Caxton Printers, 1939). Latourette, *Expansion,* IV:172–223. The many histories of the church in America also deal with this major development.

[16]*Annual Report, Missionary Society of the Methodist Episcopal Church, 1874* (New York: The Missionary Society, 1875), pp. 142, 183. Cf. W. R. Hogg, "The Missions of American Methodism" in E. S. Bucke, ed., *The History of American Methodism* (Nashville: Abingdon Press, 1964), III:114.

[17]Latourette, *Expansion,* IV:418–419 and D. G. Tewksbury, *The Founding of American Colleges and Universities Before the Civil War* (New York: Columbia University, 1932).

[18]Latourette, *Expansion,* IV:327–356.

[19]Among the others, Elijah Muhammed founded the Nation of Islam. Marcus Garvey led the Back To Africa Movement. William du Bois, scholar, founder of the N.A.A.P.C., and national

spokesman for blacks, was the son of a Presbyterian minister. *Ebony*, XXX:10 (August, 1975), pp. 130-134.

[20]Hermann N. Morse, *Home Missions Today and Tomorrow* (New York: 1934), pp. 12-15.

[21]Hogg, *loc. cit.*, p. 114.

[22]R. T. Handy, *We Witness Together: A History of Cooperative Home Missions* (New York: Friendship Press, 1956).

[23]The following are useful interpretations and point to the best primary sources: Gerald H. Anderson "Providence and Politics Behind Protestant Missionary Beginnings in the Philippines" in G. H. Anderson, ed., *Studies in Philippine Church History* (Ithica, New York: Cornell University Press, 1969); E. M. Burns, *The American Idea of Mission: Concepts of National Purpose and Destiny* (New Brunswick: Rutgers, 1957); Conrad Cherry, ed., *God's New Israel: Religious Interpretations of American Destiny* (Englewood Cliffs, N.J.: Prentice-Hall, 1971); W. A. Clebsch, *From Sacred to Profane America: The Role of Religion In American History* (New York: Harper, 1968); W. S. Hudson, *Nationalism and Religion in America: Concepts of American Identity in Mission* (New York: Harper, 1970); M. E. Marty, *Righteous Empire: The Protestant Experience in America* (New York: Dial Press, 1970); Frederick Merk, *Manifest Destiny and Mission in American History: A Reinterpretation* (New York: Knopf, 1963); and A. K. Weinberg, *Manifest Destiny: A Study of Nationalist Expansionism in American History* (Chicago: Quadrangle Books, 1935. Paperback ed., 1963).

[24]Goodykoontz, *Home Missions on the American Frontier*, p. 407.

[25]Table II is reconstructed from the following sources:
1900 J. S. Dennis, *Centennial Survey of Foreign Missions* (New York: Revell, 1902).
1910 J. S. Dennis, H. P. Beach, C. H. Fahs, *World Atlas of Christian Missions* (New York: SVM, 1911).
1925 H. P. Beach and C. H. Fahs, eds., *World Missionary Atlas* (New York: Institute of Social and Religious Research, 1925).
1938 J. I. Parker, ed., *Interpretive Statistical Survey of the World Mission of The Christian Church* (New York: International Missionary Council, 1938).
1952 R. P. Beaver, "The Protestant Foreign Missionary Enterprise of the United States," Missionary Research Library, [Henceforth, MRL], *Occasional Bulletin*, IV:7 (May 8, 1953) and as amended by Price and Moyer in 1956. Professor Beaver conceived and launched this important series.

1956 F. W. Price and Kenyon Moyer, "A Study of American Protestant Foreign Missions in 1956," MRL, *Occasional Bulletin*, VII:9 (November 16, 1956).

1960 F. W. Price and Clara E. Orr, "North American Protestant Foreign Missions in 1960," MRL *Occasional Bulletin*, XI:9 (November 23, 1960). The figure given was 27,219 and was adjusted upward in *North American Protestant Ministries Overseas, 1970, 9th Edition* (Monrovia, Calif.: For the Missionary Research Library by Mission Advanced Research and Communication Center [MARC], 1970), p. 2.

1973 E. R. Dayton, ed., *Mission Handbook: North American Protestant Ministries Overseas, 1973, 10th Edition* (Monrovia, Calif.: Prepared and edited for the Missionary Research Library by MARC, 1973). In this compilation Canadian missionaries numbered 1,013 and those from Australia 3,200—for the latter, the highest ever. The estimate of the total given by the writer in the above reconstruction assumes 3,400 missionaries from the Third World, or 6% of the total (pp. 71, 95), and 4,600 from Europe (cf., p. 95).

[26]R. P. Beaver, "Missionary Motivation Through Three Centuries," in J. C. Brauer, ed., *Reinterpretation in American Church History* (Chicago: University of Chicago Press, 1968), pp. 115-116, provides a helpful compilation from several sources. See also Dennis, Beach, Fahs, *World Atlas*, 1911, p. 78; H. P. Beach and B. St. John, eds., *World Statistics of Christian Missions* (New York: Foreign Missions Conference of North America, 1916), p. 54; Beach and Fahs, *World Missionary Atlas*, 1925, p. 69; and Dayton, ed., *Mission Handbook: North American Protestant Ministries Overseas, 1973, 10th Edition*, p. 74.

[27]Cf. Goodykoontz, *Home Missions*, p. 238-261.

[28]R. P. Beaver, *All Loves Excelling: American Protestant Women in World Mission* (Grand Rapids: Eerdmans, 1968), *passim*. Cf. Valentin H. Rabe, "Evangelical Logistics: Mission Support and Resources to 1920," in J. K. Fairbank, ed., *The Missionary Enterprise in China and America* (Cambridge: Harvard University Press, 1974).

[29]James A. Field, Jr., "Near East Notes and Far East Queries," in Fairbank, *Missionary Enterprise in China and America*, pp. 43-55. This perceptive article is one example of what can be done. Also see K. S. Latourette, *Missions and the American Mind* (Indianapolis: National Foundation Press, 1949), pp. 28-40.

[30]J. K. Fairbank, "Assignment For the Seventies," *American Historical Review*, Vol. LXXIV, No. 3 (Feb., 1969), pp. 876-878.

[31]Alan R. Tippett, *Aspects of Pacific Ethnohistory* (South Pasadena, Calif.: William Carey Library, 1973), pp. 169-177, 184-185.

[32]K. S. Latourette, *History of Christian Missions in China* (New York: Macmillan, 1929), pp. 521-525, 818. Latourette, *Expansion*, IV:257-369. See also S. C. Miller, "Ends and Means: Missionary Justification of Force in Nineteenth Century China," in Fairbank, *The Missionary Enterprise in China and America.*

[33]Table III is reconstructed from the following sources:
1890 E. M. Bliss, ed., *Encyclopedia of Missions* (New York: Funk and Wagnalls, 1891), II:479, 631-632, as repro- duced in Field, "Near East Notes. . .," Fairbank, ed., *The Missionary Enterprise in China and America*, p. 36.
1915 Beach and St. John, eds., *World Statistics of Christian Mission*, pp. 62-77.
1938 M. S. Bates, *Data on the Distribution of the Missionary Enterprise* (New York: International Missionary Council, 1943), p. 6. Based upon Parker's *Interpre- tive Statistical Survey*, 1938.
1956 Price and Moyer, MRL, *Occasional Bulletin*, VII:9 (November 16, 1956), pp. 18-19.
1973 Dayton, ed., *Mission Handbook: North American Protestant Ministries Overseas, 1973, 10th Edition*, pp. 84, 85, 97-99.

[34]Reproduced from Dayton, ed., *Mission Handbook: North Ameri- can Protestant Ministries Overseas, 1973, 10th Edition*, p. 84.

[35]Table V is constructed from the following sources: E. M. North, *The Book of A Thousand Tongues* (New York: Harper, 1938), pp. 1, 2, 23, 38. [A reprint edition appeared recently with a preface by E. A. Nida (Detroit: Tower Books, 1971).] *Ecumeni- cal Missionary Conference, New York, 1900*, II:22, 23, 32. E. A. Nida, *God's Word in Man's Language* (New York: Harper, 1952), pp. 2, 94, 95. *Here's What the American Bible Society Is All About* (New York: American Bible Society, 1975), p. 7 in a sixteen-page booklet. *Scriptures of the World...A Compilation of 1,549 Languages...1974* (Stuttgart: United Bible Societies, 1975), p. 5. *American Bible Society Record*, May, 1976, pp. 10-11.

[36]*Ecumenical Missionary Conference, New York, 1900*, II:23. The general concerns treated in this section of the paper are developed usefully and in another fashion by F. W. Price, "The Bible In the Christian World Mission," MRL, *Occasional Bulletin*, VIII:9 (October 18, 1957).

[37]The figures for 1830, 1880, and 1929 derive from a survey
of six denominations and appear in W. G. Lennox, *The Health and
Turnover of Missionaries* (New York: Foreign Missions Conf. of
N.A., 1933), p. 28, as cited, with that for 1923, in Beaver,
All Loves Excelling, p. 109. These percentages approximate those
arrived at in earlier research by the writer. The 1956 figure
derives from Price and Moyer, MRL, *Occasional Bulletin,* VII:9
(November 15, 1956), p. 26. Beaver's work in this area is noteworthy.

[38]Cf. Beaver, *All Loves Excelling,* p. 199. See also Marian
Derby, "Where Have All the Women Gone?", MRL, *Occasional Bulletin,* XXII:3, (March, 1971).

[39]See Sidney Mead's classic essay,"Denominationalism: The
Shape of Protestantism in America," in his *The Lively Experiment:
The Shaping of Christianity in America* (New York: Harper & Row,
1963).

[40]R. P. Beaver, *Ecumenical Beginnings in Protestant World
Mission: A History of Comity* (New York: Thomas Nelson, 1962).

[41]H. R. Weber, *Asia and the Ecumenical Movement, 1895-1961*
(London: SCM Press, 1966).

[42]W. R. Hogg, *Ecumenical Foundations* (New York: Harper,
1952), pp. 16-35.

[43]H. P. Van Dusen, *One Great Ground of Hope: Christian
Missions and Christian Unity* (Philadelphia: Westminster, 1961).
Cf. Hogg, *Ecumenical Foundations.*

[44]J. R. Mott, *The Evangelization of the World in This Generation* (New York: SVM, 1900); Robert P. Wilder, *The Great Commission: The Missionary Response of the SVM's in North America and
Europe* (London: Oliphants, 1936).

[45]Hogg, *Ecumenical Foundations.*

[46]Denton Lotz, *The Evangelization of the World in This Generation: The Resurgence of a Missionary Idea Among the Conservative Evangelicals* (Hamburg: The University of Hamburg, 1970).
This doctoral dissertation by an American Baptist is photo-
printed and traces the story of the Evangelical Student Movement and the Urbana Conferences, pp. 358-408. See p. 407 and
Appendix XIX for the 1904 SVM program.

[47]P. F. Barkman, E. R. Dayton, and E. L. Gruman, *Christian
Collegians and Foreign Missions* (Monrovia, Calif.: MARC, 1969).
Based upon questionnaires distributed three months after Urbana,

1967, of which 5000 were returned. It provides considerable insight into the student participants, their attitudes, and their theological views. The two largest groups attending were Baptists (16%) and Presbyterians (13%). The "Summary", pp. 84-86, provides a good orientation and entry into this book's 424 pp.

[48]Table VI is reconstructed from the following: W. R. Hogg, *One World, One Mission* (New York: Friendship Press, 1960), pp. 75-76; Beaver, "The Protestant Foreign Missionary Enterprise of the United States," MRL, *Occasional Bulletin*, IV:7 (May 8, 1953), pp. 1, 5-6, 16; Price and Orr, "North American Protestant Foreign Missions in 1960," MRL, *Occasional Bulletin*, XI:9 (November 23, 1960), pp. 10-11; *North American Protestant Ministries Overseas, 1970, 9th Edition*, p. 4; Dayton, ed., *Mission Handbook: North American Protestant Ministries Overseas, 1973, 10th Ediction*, pp. 80, 421-427. Data for 1976 from *Mission Handbook, 1976, 11th Edition* supplied by Burt N. Singleton, Jr., in a letter, January 14, 1977.

[49]DOM and Canadian and related bodies in 1973 made expenditures of $104+ million overseas. The total of all North American Protestant expenditures was $311 million. Dayton, ed., *Mission Handbook: North American Protestant Ministries Overseas, 1973, 10th Edition*, pp. 421-422, reconstructed.

[50]See David M. Stowe, "Changing Patterns of Missionary Service in Today's World," MRL, *Occasional Bulletin*, XX:1 (January, 1969). Stowe here reflects upon the shifting balance in missionary sending as shown in *North American Protestant Ministries Overseas, 1968, 8th Edition*. See also the Staff of the DOM, "An Analysis of the Context of World Mission Today," MRL, *Occasional Bulletin*, XVII:9 (September, 1966) and Eugene L. Stockwell, "Reflections on the Contemporary World Mission," MRL, *Occasional Bulletin*, XXVI:4 (May/June, 1976). Stowe was and Stockwell is chief executive officer of the DOM. These three articles provide insight into DOM perspectives.

[51]Dayton, ed., *Mission Handbook: North American Protestant Ministries Overseas, 1973, 10th Edition*, pp. 88-90.

[52]*Ibid.*

[53]Cf. Ralph D. Winter, "The New Missions and The Mission of the Church," *International Review of Mission*, LX:237 (January, 1971), pp. 88-100.

[54]*The Dogmatic Constitution on the Church*, 1964, pars. 1, 17, and 33-35 (Section on The Laity).

[55]Report of Section III, "Churches Renewed in Mission,"
(Report of Section III: II:C:1), *International Review of Mission*, LXII:246 (April, 1973), p. 219.

[56]The best comprehensive survey of this movement is W. J.
Hollenweger, *The Pentecostals: The Charismatic Movement in the Churches* (Minneapolis: Augsburg Publishing House, 1972. Original edition in German, 1969); Christian LaLive d'Epinay, *Haven of the Masses* (London: Lutterworth, 1969) provides a unique sociological study with theological insight into Chilean Pentecostalism.

[57]Among many excellent Catholic publications in this area of benefit to the entire church are Donald Gelpi, S.J., *Pentecostalism: A Theological Viewpoint* (New York: Paulist Press, 1971); [Kilian McDonnell, ed.] *Theological and Pastoral Orientations on the Catholic Charismatic Renewal, Malines, 1974* (Notre Dame: Word of Life, 1974); Leon J. Card. Suenens, *A New Pentecost?* (New York: Seabury, 1974).

[58]Lesslie Newbigin, *The Household of God* (London: SCM Press, 1953), pp. 87-110.

[59]Justin Martyr, *First Apology*, XLVI, and *Second Apology*, XIII. Cf. Vatican II, *Declaration on the Relationship of the Church to Non-Christian Religions*, par. 2. See also Clement of Alexandria, *Stromateis*, I:5:28; cf. Origen, *De Principiis*, III:6. See also William Temple, *Readings in St. John's Gospel* (London: Macmillan, 1945), p. 10, comments on John 1:9-13.

14

The American Role in World-Wide Mission: The Roman Catholic Church

Simon E. Smith, S.J.

Given the broad range of topic and perspective represented at this ASM meeting it seems to me that both the historical and contemporary have been adequately honored. For this reason and also because I feel strongly that it is less than responsible for any of us to rest content with the historical and the contemporary at the expense of the future, I shall focus my remarks toward the future.

Perhaps that was the intention of those who constructed the program--I don't really know--but I wish to read the title of my half of this last session "The American Role in Worldwide Mission: Roman Catholic Church" in such a way that it looks forward. My prognostications, or at least my hopes, are not at all devoid of a sense of history, but they try to be hope-filled, concrete, grounded in experience and forward-looking.

I base my remarks almost exclusively on a formal presentation made by the Global Ministry Committee of the Leadership Conference of Women Religious (LCWR) and the Mission Committee of the Con-ference of Major Superiors of Men (CMSM) for last month's Annual Assembly of the U.S. Catholic Mission Council in this same city. Since I had a certain role in the composition of that paper, en-titled "Our Hopes and Concerns for Mission," I feel that I am speaking not solely in my own name and not solely in the names of those two groups which represent in themselves most of the Catho-lic religious of this country and therefore most of the Catholic missionaries of this country: a rather formidable group if one considers that together these religious orders have upwards of 6600 men and women religious in foreign missions.

How, then, do we see the future of our American role in world-
wide mission? There are many points of departure for such an
exercise. We could build our theories around Scripture texts.
I personally feel that that could be a most valuable exercise
for this group which constitutes the ASM, particularly because
we could thereby uncover some radical differences of opinion, of
approach, of method.

For example, as a sometime New Testament exegete I find a
great personal difficulty in the way we of ASM often treat Scripture. To be very frank, I am often amused, sometimes even ap-
palled at what I consider to be a rather simplistic approach to
such key texts as the "Great Commission" (Mt 28:18-20 and parallels). I do not know of any competent exegetes in the Roman
Catholic Church who today consider that basic text to be a dom-
inical saying.[1] Part of the reason for our position lies in the
"official" vindication of historico-critical method, particularly of form- and redaction-criticism, evident in the publication
of an Instruction of the Pontifical Biblical Commission "On the
Historical Truth of the Gospels," dated May, 1964.[2] That highly
nuanced approach to Scripture, particularly to the *ipsissima
verba Jesu*, was carefully and consciously enshrined in Vatican
II's teaching on revelation.[3] But that is only one example and
possibly a digression.

As Catholics we could also take as our point of departure
various official Roman documents on mission.[4] The most recent
one, by Paul VI, is only a few months old: *Evangelii Nuntiandi*
(December, 1975)[5] and it marks some significant advances in official missiological teaching. It is partly a result of the
1974 Synod of Bishops on the topic of evangelization and thereby
reflects some of the thinking of representative Catholic bishops,
many of them from "mission" countries.

But neither of these classical approaches was chosen by the
LCWR and CMSM when we set about delineating our hopes and concerns for mission. Rather, we looked to our own experiences,
shared them with each other, remarked at how they converged at
so many points and from that sharing of experiences spelled out
our hopes for the future.

That our hopes are more than just vague dreams is assured by
two factors: (1) they are grounded in our extremely varied experiences as missionaries and (2) we ourselves as religious
superiors or decision-makers are the ones who will forge policies
for the future. Thus our hopes become an agenda. And we share
them with you as a blueprint for a future American Catholic role
in worldwide mission.

From this point on I quote freely and verbatim from the LCWR/CMSM document, aware that it may yet be published, yet convinced that it needs to be shared with ASM without waiting for formal publication.

CENTRAL HOPE

Within the overriding hope and striving of every Christian to proclaim the Good News of salvation in Jesus, to share the experience of his redeeming love, to know the power of the Spirit in our world—all of which I presume to be germane to the full membership of the ASM as well as of the Roman Church—the U.S. missionary religious hope that we as a missioned church will respond creatively and enthusiastically to the growing awareness of other cultures, of the needs of other peoples and of how much we have to receive from them.

a. Faith Incarnate in Culture

So many of us have in the past gone forth with great zeal to bring Christ to others whom we presumed knew him not. How often have we done so in the naive assumption that we had but to proclaim that Christ (whom we so confidently "possessed") to a world in darkness and that world would respond with enthusiastic faith and commitment and thus be saved! The history of missionary activity[6] is eloquent testimony that we do not exaggerate this point, however simplistic it may sound right now.

But our goal here is in no way to denigrate the past. It is rather to point out that the *present* is structured differently and the present faces us with new challenges to inter-cultural sensitivity, to our own humility and ultimately to a renewal in our self-understanding as a church in mission.

The 1974 Synod of Bishops was, in many ways, an extraordinary experience for the participants. New, vigorous voices were heard from the African and Asian episcopacies represented there. What they said in many forceful ways was a *cri de coeur* for cultural authenticity in articulating their faith.[7]

Paul VI's December, 1975, Apostolic Exhortation, *Evangelii Nuntiandi*,[8] is eloquent in response to the Synodal Bishops when it affirms a radical and profound understanding of culture.[9]

We of LCWR and CMSM share the Pope's sensitivity to both the complexity and the profundity of cultural factors encountered in the evangelization process. From our own personal experiences on mission, from the experiences of our peers in our respective congregations,[10] from the experiences of many lay missionaries of our acquaintance, we have become much more aware than ever

before of the need for greater sensitivity to the values expressed by and structured into cultures other than our own. We
assert the need of a positive approach to such cultural values.
We cannot insist too much on the need to understand such factors
from inside the given culture before we undertake to reject or
even condemn them.[11]

We are not speaking here of what is commonly known as adaptation or acculturation. Our insight goes much deeper and is not
content with surface adaptations, any more than is Paul VI, who
speaks as follows:

> ". . . what matters is to evangelize man's culture and
> cultures (not in a purely decorative way as it were by
> applying a thin veneer, but in a vital way, in depth and
> right to their very roots), in the wide and rich sense
> which these terms have in *Gaudium et Spes* (#53), always
> taking the person as one's starting-point and always coming
> back to the relationships of people among themselves and
> with God."[12]

We realize how deep such cultural factors go when we reflect
on the history of the earliest expansion of the church,[13] on the
famous "Chinese Rites" controversy, or on the contemporary
struggles of some African churches.[14] We join in this struggle
to incarnate Christianity in the world's cultures in such a way
that one of the church's oldest and greatest glories, her "unity
in diversity," will shine ever more brightly in tomorrow's world.

b. Needs of Other Peoples: Development and Justice

As missionaries, many of us have gone forth to work in foreign
lands responding to a genuinely felt "call" to expend our tal-
ents, energies and even our lives for the sake of others. That
true heroism has been demanded and forthcoming in such ministries is now a commonplace of missionary history.

Yet, as is clear from what is written in the previous section,
our contemporary experience and reflection have led us to new
perceptions of what it means to "work for the sake of others."
At the risk of oversimplifying by using a worn cliché, we would
describe the shift in our perception as one that has moved from
a notion of working *for* others to a notion of working *with* them.
The distinction is not as simplistic as it sounds. Put briefly,
if bluntly, we have become aware that our efforts to work for
others have often been experienced by those others as patron-
izing.

Where this has been most apparent is in areas where poverty and underdevelopment are extreme. Our humane response to the awesome degradation of poverty, be it in Rio or Calcutta or Manila or Lagos, is often a desire to "do something" about it right away.[15] The record of accomplishment of U.S. missionaries in both small and large development efforts in third-world countries is one we can justly be proud of. Sanitation, irrigation, marketing, literacy, low-cost housing, natal care, education, health and social services, etc.--all types of development projects have been undertaken by missionaries for their third-world communities.

And there lies the rub: we have done such projects *for* these people and the people remain recipients, not instigators, beneficiaries, and not creators. We do not for a moment suggest that it is wrong to work for others. But we do suggest, again from our experience, three considerations.

First, our efforts to work for others have often led us unconsciously to impose on them a solution for their problems that is either foreign to their own ways or at least not of their own making. And this has often had the unwanted side effect of reaffirming a sense of dependence, if not inferiority, which we now feel is contrary to the spirit of the very Gospel we are trying to communicate.

Second, we feel that today's missionaries should be characterized as co-workers *with* people. This implies the need to identify with the people as strongly as possible in order to overcome the we/they dichotomy in our thought-patterns which is ultimately destructive of the unity and harmony characteristic of the Body of Christ whose building-up we serve.

Third, we are convinced that the people with whom missionaries work must be allowed, helped, stimulated, encouraged to develop along the lines and according to models which they select, even if this procedure is less efficient or more expensive.

Beyond such considerations of our attitudinal stance, though, there is a far greater and more urgent area upon which we must comment. The experiences we have had in missionary work, almost all of it in third-world countries, has led us to reflect with the bishops and the Holy Father, as well as with our peers and the very people in those countries with whom we have worked, on the causes of the extreme poverty and injustice we have encountered and in some cases even experienced ourselves. Beyond the immediate alleviation of human need, be it physical, moral, spiritual or whatever, lies the necessity to change the very structures of society which perpetuate such evils.

It is not our intention here to embark on any lengthy social
analysis, much less explore the economic and political dimensions
of poverty and underdevelopment. Not only is that beyond our
competence, but it has been ably done by many others.[16]

Rather, we join with the Bishops of the 1971 Synod in recognizing the sinfulness of the structures of society in today's
world.[17] We accept and affirm from our experience the accuracy
of the Latin American Bishops' characterization of many situations of structured injustice as "institutionalized violence."[18]
Moreover, we join with the Catholic Bishops of the Antilles in
a frank and humble confession of guilt for whatever part we may
have had, by commission, omission or unaware complicity, in the
perpetuation of such sinful structures.[19]

We are quite well aware of the fierce complexity of such
issues as the maldistribution of wealth and power in today's
world, the massive (sometimes negative) impact of U.S. technology, militarism and consumerism in most developing countries,
the ever sharpening debate on the relative merits of capitalism
and socialism,[20] the present search, via the U.N. and other organisms, for the construction of a new international economic
order,[21] etc. But there comes a moment, and it is long past,
when one can recognize in all humility and simplicity, that,
whatever the complexity of the issues, "any society in which a
few control most of the wealth and the masses are left in their
want is a sinful society."[22] It is this simple but profound
realization that has radically altered our perspective on our
missionary work.

We have been sent to evangelize and in today's world where
the maldistribution of wealth and power have reached such intolerable proportions, we cannot preach Jesus Christ apart from
this reality of injustice. Though each of us should know it now
by heart, we need to repeat the affirmation of the 1971 Synod of
Bishops that

> action on behalf of justice and participation in the trans-
> formation of the world fully appear to us as a constitutive
> dimension of the preaching of the Gospel, that is, of the
> mission of the Church for the redemption of the human race
> and its liberation from every oppressive situation. [23]

Or as the Asian Bishops put it:

> Engaged in tasks for justice in accordance with the spirit
> and demands of the Gospel, we will realize that the search
> for holiness and the search for justice, evangelization and
> the promotion of true human development and liberation, are
> not only not opposed, but make up today the integral preach-
> ing of the Gospel. [24]

Or as the Jesuits state it in their recent General Congregation:

> We can no longer pretend that the inequalities and the in-
> justices of our world must be borne as part of the inevitable
> order of things. It is now quite apparent that they are the
> result of what man himself, man in his selfishness, has done.
> Hence, there can be no promotion of justice in the full and
> Christian sense unless we also preach Jesus Christ and the
> mystery of reconciliation he brings. For us, it is Christ
> who, in the last analysis, opens the way to the complete and
> definitive liberation of man. From now on, therefore, it
> will not be possible to bring Christ to men or to proclaim
> his Gospel effectively unless a firm decision is taken to
> devote ourselves to the promotion of justice. [25]

Or, finally, as Paul VI reiterates in his apostolic exhortation
on evangelization:

> Between evangelization and human advancement--development
> and liberation--there are in fact profound links. These
> include links of an anthropological order, because the man
> who is to be evangelized is not an abstract being but is
> subject to social and economic questions. They also include
> links in the theological order, since one cannot dissociate
> the plan of creation from the plan of Redemption. The latter
> plan touches the very concrete situations of injustice to be
> combatted and of justice to be restored. They include links
> of the eminently evangelical order, which is that of charity;
> how in fact can one proclaim the new commandment without
> promoting in justice and in peace the true, authentic ad-
> vancement of man? [26]

Similar citations can be added these days almost *ad infinitum*.
We of LCWR and CMSM feel, however, that our own international
experience as missionaries has given us a peculiar ability to
resonate with these statements. They are fleshed out for us in
the sufferings of the people we have served as missionaries.
Such eloquent statements of the Pope, the Bishops and others
have a clear and concrete meaning for us that springs from our
sharing in the lives of the very poor and oppressed, the victims
of global structures of injustice. We recognize that the debates of the last decade on evangelization *versus* development
have been superseded by the profound realization that in many
ways today evangelization *is* integral human development,[27] that
engagement in the struggle for justice *is* itself a form of the
preaching of the Gospel.[28]

So our hope is for ever more creative and enthusiastic responses to the needs of other peoples, responses which will recognize the indivisibility of the process of evangelization and

engagement in the struggle for more just and humanizing structures in our world.[29]

c. Receiving

A third major facet of our central hope is based on our experience of the richness of the cultures we have encountered in
our missionary works. We have found ourselves experiencing
some new horizons of humility as we learn to listen with new
ears and to realize how much we have to *receive* from those to
whom we went to give.

Yet, as North Americans, we find that the charism of receptiveness, a willingness to receive, does not come easily or last
long. The marvelous national confidence we share with other
U.S. citizens as a characteristic of our own culture often gets
in the way of our ability to listen, to learn from others, or
simply to be passive for a while.

This is further complicated by a confidence born of our Catholic faith, historically so sure of itself, which equips us with
a message and a zeal to share it as missionaries. All too often
we have proclaimed Christ and his church so loudly and confidently that we have failed to perceive that the receptor culture
perhaps has its own experience of the same God we preach.

The recognition by some leading bishops at the 1974 Synod
that God speaks where he will, not always where we expect,[30]
is a profound insight. It is not a new insight. Indeed, it is
as old as the Old Testament. But in our zeal as missionaries
we often fail to let it sink in. We are not speaking here of
some of the more deplorable forms of cultural imposition which
have been known in the history of missions, but of a deeper
level of sensitivity to the Spirit breathing already in cultures
to which Christ is yet to be proclaimed.

For example, it took centuries for Christians to recognize
that Yahweh and Allah and God are all one. Granted the theological distinctions to be made, it is astonishing, on later reflection, how insensitive we may have been in failing to appreciate the underlying recognition of the one God of us all which
characterizes these three "religions of the book."

Similarly, we are learning these days to listen more carefully to the voices of Buddhism, Hinduism, Taoism, etc., and to
discern in them a voice whose timbre resonates with the voice
we know as the one God's.[31] We are not succumbing to syncretism. We are listening. We are aware that we are on the threshold of a new breakthrough in missionary consciousness, one that
treats other religions with the utmost respect and reverence,

one that hesitates to label "pagan" or "heathen" what is or
may be a genuine channel of God's communication to men.

Our sensitivity to these facets of cultural-religious experience of others leads us to new postures as missionaries. We
now know how long it takes anyone of us to assimilate in depth
the beauty and uniqueness of another culture and thereby to
penetrate to an awareness of how that culture experiences God.
Just as we have become more attentive to our own personal experience, we are learning to enter and share the experiences of
others, most especially their experience of God. This shared
experience, valued for what it is, becomes the point of departure for a new kind of missionary activity. We are ready to
give only when we have learned to receive.

The same attitude of receptiveness has other, perhaps less
profound dimensions, those related to cultural values of other
peoples. We are religious who, by our experience in other cultures, have come to a radical re-assessment of our own values
as North Americans. No longer do we feel that profit, productivity, achievement, efficiency, speed, accomplishment and the
many other values of our society less worthy of mention, are
our primary values.

We do not regret our U.S. citizenship! But, as North Americans overseas, we have experienced both the criticism and the
appreciation of other peoples and it is this experience that
has led us to sort out some of our personal values by reflecting
on those facets of our corporate personality as Americans which
other peoples appreciate and laud by imitation and also on those
facets which justly give offense to others and for which they
cannot praise us.

As North Americans, on the other hand, we are proud of our
high ideals of "liberty and justice for all," of "life, liberty
and the pursuit of happiness." Our overseas experiences have
taught us to be less cavalier about assuming that those ideals
have become realities, even in our own country. Because of our
international experiences we discover ourselves better able to
read and understand the U.S. Bishops' Bicentennial publication,
Liberty and Justice for All,[32] without being threatened or
reacting in anger. Unfortunately, we have, as U.S. citizens, a
long way yet to go for the full achievement of those ideals.
It is our hope that what we have learned from other cultures
will help us to contribute to and to modulate the articulation
and better structuring of those ideals in our society.

Another most important gift we feel we have received, particularly from the cultures of the East, is a renewed sense of
contemplation, an ability to strike new chords in our relation-

ship with God even while remaining involved with the people we
try to serve. We feel this particular gift is of primary importance for people of our own culture. It is more than just
making a retreat or communing with nature. It is a facility
for deep, comtemplative union with God, even in the midst of the
hectic pace of life in this country.

Certainly contemplation has always been part of our Catholic
heritage, at least since Antony and Pachomius in the third and
fourth centuries (and surely in Jesus' own life; cf. Mt 4, 17
and parallels). But our North American way of dichotomizing
contemplation and action has led us, it seems, to slice up our
lives and to categorize or atomize the flow of our lives. From
the East we are learning ways to integrate contemplation and
action for the enrichment of both. For Christians this is a
most precious gift and we value it highly.

The lessons we have learned from the poor with whom we have
worked are, in many ways, more humbling and poignant. The
truly incredible human beauty shining through the misery of the
poor, of the destitute who have no visible reason for hope, of
those who are victims of forces they cannot control.....that
beauty has left us often speechless with awe. We who have been
taught by our own culture that happiness is having, or that possessions bring peace, or that success is measured by salary and
social status, have received from the world's poor a most
salutary jolt to our self-confidence. We have been led by them
(more than we ever could be in our comfortable, affluent social
matrix at home) to free ourselves from the devils of greed, ac-
cumulation, avarice, desire for material goods, etc. We are
learning how relative our "needs" are; we are learning to re-
sist the "created needs" forced on us by consumerism; we are
learning to be freer with less and thereby to grow closer to
him who had "nowhere to lay his head" (Mt 8:22). The poor, who
have nought to give, have gifted us with a new freedom: freedom
to be, to be able to be without lots of things, to be able to
be in simplicity of life, to be able to share, not the things
we possess but the beings we are. This gift is a gift of life.
A gift worthy of Jesus who tried to teach us the same thing,
but we couldn't quite hear him. We met him in the poor and
are richer for it. But this beauty has not and cannot diminish
our indignation at the powers that keep people poor nor our responsibility to work with them to change their lot.

We hope that these things we have experienced, these gifts
we have received from others can be somehow shared with the
North American church at large. We hope that our North American
church can learn, as we are trying to, to receive. We hope, in
other words, that our church can appreciate that mission is not
all giving, not all a one-way street. Perhaps the greatest

thing a U.S. missionary can do is not to give but to learn to receive.

This, then, is our central hope: to respond creatively and enthusiastically to the growing awareness of other cultures, of the needs of other peoples and of how much we have to receive from them. What we say in the thoughts that follow is based on this central hope. What we say in succeeding pages has this central hope as a basic filter, as the primary modulator of our hopes and concerns.

RELATED HOPES

In view of the previous exposition of where our experiences and reflections have brought us, and conscious that our central threefold hope informs all our other hopes, we wish to articulate and share some of those other hopes. They are interrelated and, in varying degrees, dependent on our central hope. Some of them reflect current trends in the church, others speak of long-range desiderata.

a. Formation and Re-Formation[33]

We are unanimous in our conviction that "formation" is not a once-for-all phenomenon but an on-going, never-ending process. In a certain sense, none of us is ever fully "formed" until we have entered the fulfillment of our life's journey and orientation in the beatific vision. In another sense, we are each a cell in the Body of Christ, in the *ecclesia semper reformanda*, and therefore continually in need of change, up-dating, new horizons and challenges, in a word: continual renewal.

In our view, and from **our experi**ences with formation programs, chapters, continuing education programs, etc., there are three separate areas of formation which we wish to address.

First, the re-formation of each one of us. By this we mean the deep, radical, personal conversion which adherence to the Gospel demands of any Christian. The call of Vatican II[34] for a return to our respective sources and charisms as members of religious orders or congregations has been heard and implemented in various ways. The process of renewal continues. We hope it never ends.

Yet each one of us, whether religious, lay, bishop or pope, has a responsibility before God and the church for undertaking that continual conversion demanded by the very fact of our baptism into Christ. The new awareness, which theologians have shared with us, that conversion is a *process*, necessitates a sense of humility and a willingness to continue growing in our conversion.

Second, the more difficult area of how we "form" our own young religious. We hope for a greater integration into the formation programs of our respective congregations, of several dimensions which we mention here only briefly.

A sense of the global is today essential in any formation program. We feel it is inadequate to form religious without some sense of the universal mission of the church. We feel, further, that a global awareness is particularly necessary for those religious who will *not* be going on missionary duty. In other words, we feel that for a religious whose ministry will be exercised here in the U.S., a real awareness of the global dimensions of the church's activity in many cultures, of the global dimensions of injustice today and of the universality of the human family is absolutely essential for competent ministry.

How this awareness is to be achieved is up to each congregation. Our experience as missionaries and our high valuation of cross-cultural experiences, though, leads us to prefer that formation programs include some extended period of ministry in another culture than one's own. We are aware of the criticism that such programs (e.g., Sisters of Nazareth, Jesuits) have encountered, but we judge them by their fruits and have found them to be a valuable investment in preparing adequate ministers for work abroad *or* at home.

We hope, in other words, that those who are engaged in structuring or restructuring formation programs will take seriously the need for all congregations, whether mission-oriented or not, to form their members with a realistic, experience-based awareness of the global dimensions and responsibilities of ministry today.

Third, we rejoice at the efforts many congregations are making at corporate re-formation. We rejoice, further, that the leadership of the Pope and the Bishops is having its effect as congregational goals and structures are articulated in response to the signs of our times. Not only are congregations recapturing their primitive charisms, but they are re-interpreting those charisms in the face of today's needs, of the challenges presented by the encyclicals, the Synods and by many pastoral letters of Bishops' Conferences.

Our hope, then, is that this process will continue and be recognized as necessarily on-going. Renewal is a never-ending process. If our efforts at corporate renewal are done in a context of global awareness and of creative response to the needs of our suffering fellow-humans, we are confident that the healing presence of Jesus will radiate anew through religious congregations.

Yet we feel that there is need to insist that congregations, whether mission-sending or not, realize that mission is not something to be left to the missionaries. Every Christian is in a radical sense "missioned." It has been our sad experience that religious congregations have tended to leave mission to the missionaries. But every Pope in memory and the New Testament itself impress on us the responsibility of *all* Christians for mission. ". . . the whole Church is missionary, and the work of evangelization is a basic duty of the People of God."[35]

Whether they pursue a strictly mission goal or not, communities dedicated to the active life should sincerely ask themselves in the presence of God, whether they cannot broaden their activity in favor of extending God's kingdom among the nations. . .[36]

We hope, in other words, that the efforts of our various religious congregations to renew themselves will take seriously the responsibility for mission incumbent on each of them. And we are ready to assist these renewals in any way we can.

b. Mutuality of Mission

While some talk of a moratorium on missions,[37] others see a bright future for mutual missioning. We of LCWR and CMSM recognize that there are valid reasons leading to the call for a moratorium: prolonged dependence of new churches on personnel and funds from abroad, certain extreme attitudes of paternalism, lack of trust, cultural impositions, etc. We do not wish here to enter that debate. What we have said in the opening pages of this exposition gives adequate indication of our feelings about sensitivity to other cultures, to justice in inter-community relations and to a sense of receptiveness for there to be little doubt that we deplore whatever excesses of missionary zeal have provoked a call for moratorium.

But we do not support that call. From a strictly ecclesiological point of view we feel that everybody ends up a loser if a moratorium is called. From within the Roman Catholic Church in any case moratorium is unlikely.

What is likely, and what we support with enthusiasm, is the growing practice of mutuality of mission, whereby priests, religious and lay members of one-time mission churches respond to a call to serve other churches in the very countries which once sent missionaries to them. Indian or African or Asian voices in U.S. Catholic pulpits are still a rarity except on special occasions. But we strongly desire to hear more such voices for we need the realization of universality which such an experience engenders, we need to be enriched by learning how

other cultures experience God and Christ, we need the healthy
criticism that comes from cross-cultural exchange among equals,
we need the salutary awareness of how culture-bound our own
understanding of Christianity has become. We thus see a purify-
ing and enriching outcome for all parties if such mutual missioning is encouraged and we hope both to initiate it and encourage
it in our own congregations and to see it supported by bishops
and pastors at all levels.

Our hope in this regard is grounded in our experience of
mutual exchanges of personnel within our own religious communities. The advantages of such mutuality far outweigh any initial
awkwardnesses, expenses, logistical problems, etc. Once we
have moved beyond token exchanges of personnel into a general
pattern of common ministry of one *ecclesiola* to the other, we
are much closer to the experience urged on us by Paul in his
letters to the early Christian communities he nurtured.[38]
Moreover, we can reach a new experience of solidarity across
diocesan or national boundaries and come to a fresh appreciation
of why Paul was so concerned about the "collection"[39] as more a
concrete expression of mutual solidarity than merely a charitable donation from a well-off community to a less well situated
one.

Finally, we hope that such mutual exchanges of personnel and
funds can lead to a more realistic and shared apportioning of
both, in terms of the greatest human needs of the total People
of God and not in terms of local priorities (sometimes at the
expense of greater needs elsewhere which simply are not known
locally).

c. Creative Collaboration in Mission

Directly related to the previous hope for mutuality of
mission is a facet of such movements which we wish to isolate
for specific attention. Over the last few years a collaborative
effort among several foreign-mission societies is creating a
new form of mutuality. The Mexican Foreign Mission Society
(Misioneros de Guadalupe), the Yarumal Society of Colombia, the
Quebec and Scarboro Foreign Missionary Societies of Canada, and
Maryknoll have been engaged in extensive contacts over the last
few years. At Medellín in 1975 they were joined by a new
Brazilian missionary institute ("Missionary Star of Brazil") and
at that meeting the five others offered personnel and financial
assistance to the Brazilians to help them get underway.

In January 1976 Maryknoll carried this collaboration a step
further by sending two of its best men to work on the training
and development efforts of the Brazilian group, and the other
societies will add their own forms of assistance. In August of

this year a further meeting will be held in Montreal and will
include some European-headquartered mission societies. The Montreal meeting is to lead to further integration of training programs and other forms of collaboration. This movement, far from
a dream or a vague hope, is a concrete series of hard commitments which is tending toward something new in the Roman church:
a joint Brazilian-Mexican-Colombian-Canadian-U.S. outreach. The
image it projects is one of the universality proper to the
church.

This new concrete thrust of creative collaboration grounds
our hope for other similar initiatives from within our own congregations and the U.S. church at large.

d. Local Lay Leadership

The issue of the place of lay leadership in the structure
and function of the church is complex and confused. Nor is it
our goal here to discuss it at length. We frankly articulate
it, though, as a question of lay leadership, not just "the place
of the laity."

We have watched with interest and eagerness the growth of
certain indigenous movements in third-world churches whereby
natural community-endorsed lay leaders have emerged as ministers
to their own communities. The example of the Aymara churches
in the Bolivian and Peruvian altiplano is well known and rightly
lauded. Similar movements are growing in the Caribbean, among
U.S. Indian populations, in certain African sees, etc.

It is all too easy to consider such movements as emergency
measures in the face of an extreme shortage of ordained priests.
We feel that such a reaction fails to appreciate the ecclesiological significance of what is actually happening. Shortage or
superfluity of ordained priests is ultimately a secondary consideration to the reconsideration of roles that is underway.
The proper assumption of responsibility and the consequent exercise of a variety of ministerial roles by natural lay leaders of
local churches is but a faithful, creative and responsible echo
of the initial experience of the primitive Christian communities.[40] That it is being encouraged and fostered by both local
bishops and missionary congregations is a sign of healthy flexibility and growth, a clear response of initiative and creativity
from within local communities and a possible antidote to paternalistic precedents (however unwitting), which gives the Spirit
greater rein for more effective action in the community. We
hope to see even greater efforts in this direction encouraged
by responsible church authorities so that an even greater
variety of ministries, exercised by an increasingly representative body of lay leaders will let the full panoply of charisms
be seen in all its glorious heterogeneity.

On the domestic scene there are analogous hopes grounded on
analogous movements. We situate such efforts of our local U.S.
churches not so much in any attempt to de-hierarchize our church
as in a genuine response by lay leaders to the impulse of the
Spirit received at baptism which impels each Christian to proclaim the Gospel in word and deed to others. This sense of mission, exercised in a variety of lay ministries, is true to the
New Testament and the magisterium.[41] No baptized Christian is
exempt from the universal call to preach the Gospel, to comfort,
to heal, to minister in an immense variety of ways. That certain dioceses of our country are providing exemplary leadership
in fostering full lay participation in ministerial, administrative and even decision-making roles is a sign of great encouragement to us.

We hope, therefore, that such efforts will continue and
spread. We hope, in addition, that the experiences of such
efforts to foster lay leadership in third-world or mission
countries will benefit our local U.S. dioceses in many ways.
We have much to learn from each other.

e. Diversity of Ministries

As a corollary to the previous topic, we wish to isolate a
factor for further consideration. It is our conviction that
mission is to be achieved through *community* where diverse
ministries are encouraged and where individual members will
minister to the community and to others beyond it. This is
already the experience of Christian communities for centuries.
But we feel it needs great emphasis today and even greater
encouragement from church authorities. Within the given diocese there are a variety of ministries: contemplative ministry,
the witness of poverty, the call to prophecy, the role of advocacy for the poor and oppressed, etc. None of these or analogous ministries is by nature restricted to any specific group
within the community. We feel that there are more or less
common (erroneous) assumptions that the contemplative life is
the prerogative of contemplative religious, that advocacy in
the public forum is more properly the role of the laity, that
celibacy is for clerics and nuns. Such assumptions are not
only contrary to fact, but can severely restrict the prerogative
of the Spirit to breathe where he will.

So we hope for even greater recognition that *all* Christians
are called to minister and that *no* Christian is exempt from
being sent. As we discern together the signs of the Spirit's
activities in the Christian community, we hope we can be progressively more free in response to whatever calls he gives.
Our hope in this regard is not utopian. We see some of our
religious congregations entering into new forms of affiliation

with lay individuals and groups, we see religious undertaking ministries once considered the preserve of the laity and vice versa, we see dioceses like Los Angeles and Boston and Kansas City continuing and expanding their already exemplary missionary activity, we see U.S. youth creating new and exciting roles of service, we see lay volunteers clamoring for overseas ministries, and on and on. Our hope, then, is for greater encouragement of such efforts to diversify the one ministry which is that of Jesus Christ.[42]

f. Life-Style

That we of CMSM and LCWR have had our struggles with the life-styles of religious communities over the last decade is fairly common knowledge. But those struggles, including both our successes and our failures, have been uncommonly productive. We are still in process. We can, however, isolate two areas which bear directly on our mission concerns and we present them as grounds for our hopes for the future.

First, our abrupt rupture of the isolating structures of religious institutions (convents, seminaries, monasteries, etc.) has led us, not without pain and loss, to a new experiential awareness of the need for flexibility, variety and creativity in our life-styles. We realize now, after a decade of experimentation, that there can be no return to the isolation of our former ways of life for the simple reason that it would be ultimately irresponsible. It served a good purpose at one time, but that time is no more.

Our bold step into the world as religious has demanded new and more responsive probing of our identities as Christian witnesses and ministers. Our lives have been deeply affected in many positive ways. Our ability to function in various ministries has profited immeasurably from our rediscovered identification with the problems, sufferings, joys and hopes of those we serve. Our insertion into various Christian communities as fellow-pilgrims and no longer as a breed apart treated with gingerly respect and distance, has meant a significant increase in renewed zeal, more flexible responses to real needs, freer engagement with the structures of families and the *polis*, as well as some vibrant rediscoveries and redefinitions of our various primitive charisms as religious congregations. Because this relatively abrupt desertion of the restrictive structured isolation of the past has been so salutary, we intend it to continue. Most of our congregations have taken seriously the need to restructure ourselves for greater service by fostering opportunities for deeper insertion into the ordinary life-styles of the Christian communities where we find ourselves.

Our hope is that this shift in our style of life will continue to help us forge with the local communities a common witness to the world of the vibrancy of Christian service in a world sorely in need of such support and challenge. The opposite of isolation is involvement. We hope our new levels of involvement in the world can provoke other Christians, lay and religious, to take seriously the role of Christ's Body as a leaven in the world community of today struggling for a greater measure of justice and peace tomorrow.

Second, our exodus from the protections of an institutional life-style and our involvement in the world of ordinary people both here and abroad have brought home to us the tremendous need we have to simplify our life-styles in prophetic witness against the destructive folly of consumerism. In our missionary experience, as noted earlier, we are learning how to live content with less material goods, how to free ourselves from the opium of material consumption, how to free ourselves from the "need" to accumulate possessions and protections. Hopefully, this will grow by our increasing identity of life and lot with the poor. It has been furthered by our reflections about starvation in today's world and the related issues of how wealth, resources, goods, etc., are so poorly shared among God's people.

We hope to continue our efforts at evolving simple life-styles. We hope also that the witness of our actions will provoke imitation and further solidarity with the poor.

g. Advocacy

As in the past, so today in many local churches there has been no dearth of devoted Christians, priests and laymen, missionaries and natives, men and women, who have fought for the rights of the poor and of minority groups. Today in many countries the church is involved in the fight against every type of discrimination or oppression, claiming for all men fair and equal access to economic, cultural, social and spiritual benefits. [43]

Many Catholics still shy away from the thought of a priest or a nun in a picket line or a protest rally. Many others feel very strongly that it is not only inappropriate but positively wrong for religious to engage in anything but their "proper" duties, i.e. sanctuary, school, convent or whatever. Our remarks on justice in the first part of this paper and the two statements just preceding, on our hopes for diversity of ministries and changes in life-style, should leave no room for surprise that we espouse a strong, public role for religious in the promotion and defense of human rights of individuals and groups.

The forms such advocacy will take are a question of community discernment in each individual case. Further, not all advocacy is done in picket lines or protest rallies: indeed many of them are counter-productive. But the solidarity with the poor and oppressed which we hope characterizes our respective congregations leaves no room for backing out of the responsibility to struggle with the same poor and oppressed in their efforts to redress whatever wrongs they suffer. The guidelines for such advocacy suggested in the document on "The Church and Human Rights" are sound and responsible. The leadership already provided the North American church by the many valuable position papers and public statements on social justice issues which have been published by the National Conference of Catholic Bishops and the United States Catholic Conference[44] deserve creative imitation and implementation.

Our hope here is that such leadership will, on the one hand, extend itself to a broader range of issues on the global scene and, on the other hand, lead to greater involvement by religious and laity in the struggle for justice and peace. The time is over when we can rest content with things as they are. The ever-increasing suffering of millions of people demands a response by those who claim to follow Christ, who died for the allegedly subversive activity of bringing the good news to the poor, proclaiming liberty to captives and new sight to the blind, and setting the downtrodden free.[45]

From the dignity of the human person who has been created in the image and likeness of God, the Father of all men, and who has further been redeemed by the blood of Christ, must arise the spontaneous witness of all Christians to their faith. They should, as followers of Christ, demonstrate their awareness of their responsibility to defend the rights of their neighbors, male and female, individuals and groups, regardless of race, sex, class, religions, or political opinion. [46]

"The defense of human rights to which the church is committed implies protest against any violation of these rights, past or present, temporary or permanent. This is all the more necessary when the victims of such injustice cannot defend themselves."[47]

We of LCWR and CMSM express our hope that the other members of the Catholic Mission Council and those they represent will join us in our advocacy of the rights of the voiceless victims of injustices at home and overseas, especially those with whom we work in our various missions.

I omit one last hope we expressed for greater collaboration between the religious orders of men and women and the U.S. bishops because it is rather parochial and fits more the immediate context of the Annual Assembly of the U.S. Catholic Mission Council for which the preceding statement was prepared.

But allow me to conclude with the last section of our statement, since it is of paramount relevance to the ASM. In it we try to express our one fear, our single "concern," as we called it.

We have but one concern. It relates to every hope we have expressed. It can be stated briefly and forthrightly. Indeed, we prefer to state it with the utmost brevity to assure its impact.

We of LCWR and CMSM are dreadfully concerned that one single factor, one basic attitude could crush all our hopes. Even more, that one factor we fear, if it grows or spreads, can undo the church herself.

The one thing we fear is myopia.

Shortsightedness, narrow vision, limited horizons, introversion, isolation, retreat from challenge, parochialism, insecurity, fear..... all these facets of myopia (which can be reductively considered forms of egocentrism, the very essence of sin) are the direct antitheses of what we hope for from the church in mission.

Why spell it out with lots of words and risk clouding its reality? For every hope we have expressed above, the perfect antidote is to retreat from the reality of today's world, to turn in on ourselves and our narrow, local concerns. We see already in the Catholic church certain signs of such myopia which ground our concern. We see windows being gently closed, initiatives silently snuffed, creativity bridled, fear masquerading as prudence and caution, isolationism coated in patriotic rhetoric, insecurity parading as concern for orthodoxy, pluralism damned as syncretism, introversion lauded as high spirituality, etc.

We forbear lengthening the litany. Let a few cases suffice to illustrate the disease. The white, middle-class sector of the U.S. Catholic church is turning in on itself. In the face of hardship and lack of resources, when hard decisions do have to be made, the white church seems unable to shatter its insularity, to break out of its self-interest, to respond freely to the greatest human needs. We see decisions being made to close schools in the black ghettos.[48] We read of six million Catholic children in this country (mostly minority youngsters)

getting little or no formal religious education.[49] We see
local or national priorities in church budgets eating up so
much money that expenditures for international service are reduced to mere tokens. We see a National Catechetical Directory
being planned with little or no awareness of any meaningful
reality, let alone responsibility, beyond the boundaries of the
U.S. We even hear of plans for a massive effort at evangelization of the "unchurched" within the U.S., an effort we can
support only if it does not consume our energies and focus our
vision on our own local concerns.

Myopia is a disease.

Myopia is evil.

Myopia is unChristian.

We dread myopia.

I need add nothing more. The same myopia can curse us of
ASM. In sharing with you the hopes and concerns of U.S.
Catholic religious in this way, I personally hope I have
communicated what we see the future of U.S. Catholic mission to
be. More than that, I hope that such sharing and others like
the now annual programs of the Overseas Ministries Studies
Center in Ventnor on the future of U.S. missionary activity[50]
will themselves be instruments of growth for the church.

NOTES

1. See, e.g., G.W. MacRae, S.J., "The Mandate to Evangelize:
    The Mandate in the Roman Catholic Tradition," *Midstream* 8
    (4, '70), pp. 92-104, especially his remark on p. 102:
    ". . . contemporary Catholic authors do not hesitate to
    subject the whole passage [Mt 28:18-20] to the same search-
    ing criticism that it receives in other hands, and to con-
    clude that it owes its form, if not much of its content also,
    to the Matthean church itself." MacRae refers here to two
    other respected Catholic exegetes: W. Trilling, *Das wahre
    Israel* (Leipzig: 1959) and A. Vögtle, "Ekklesiologische
    Auftragsworte des Auferstandenen," *Sacra Pagina* (Paris:
    1959), II, pp. 280-294 and the same Vögtle's "Das christo-
    logische und ekklesiologische Anliegen von Matthaus 28:
    18-20," *Studia Evangelica*, II (Berlin: 1964), pp. 266-294.
    A more recent treatment of the pericope (by one of the "other
    hands" to which MacRae refers) is J.D. Kingsbury, "The Com-
    position and Christology of Matt 28:16-20," *Journal of
    Biblical Literature* 93 ('74), pp. 573-584, whose thesis is
    "that the evangelist Matthew has himself composed vss. 16-
    20 and that he has done so in large part with a view of his
    Son-of-God christology."

2. "Instructio de historica Evangeliorum veritate," *Osservatore
    Romano*, May 14, 1964, p. 3. The full Latin text and an
    English version can be found in *Catholic Biblical Quarterly*
    26 ('64), pp. 299-312. See also the superb commentary on
    the document by J.A. Fitzmyer, S.J., "The Biblical Commis-
    sion's Instruction on the Historical Truth of the Gospels,"
    Theological studies 25 ('64), pp. 386-408. See especially
    p. 401 of the latter: "The most significant thing in the
    whole document, when all is said and done, is that the Bibli-
    cal Commission calmly and frankly admits that what is con-
    tained in the Gospels as we have them today is not the words
    and deeds of Jesus in the first stage of tradition, nor even
    the form in which they were preached in the second stage,
    but only in the form compiled and edited by the Evangel-
    ists . . . . It is good to recall that this redacted form
    of the sayings and deeds of Jesus which the Evangelists give
    us is the inspired form."

3. "Dogmatic Constitution on Divine Revelation" [*Dei Verbum*] in
    The Documents of Vatican II, ed. W.M. Abbott, S.J. (New
    York: America Press; London: G. Chapman, 1966), pp. 111-
    132. See especially # 19.

4. For example, the encyclicals *Rerum Ecclesiae* (1926) of Pius
    XI and *Evangelii Praecones* (1951) of Pius XII.

5. It is available in English as *On Evangelization in the Modern World* (Washington, D.C.: United States Catholic Conference, 1976).

6. Cf., for example, K.S. Latourette's seven-volume *History of the Expansion of Christianity* (N.Y.: Harper & Row, 1937 ff.).

7. Cf. "The 1974 Synod of Bishops," *Omnis Terra*, No. 64 (Dec. '74), pp. 51-62, for some characteristic interventions of bishops from third-world sees.

8. See n. 5 above.

9. *Ibid.*, # 20.

10. Cf., for example, the brief document entitled "The Work of Inculturation of the Faith and Promotion of Christian Life," in *Documents of the Thirty-Second General Congregation of the Society of Jesus* (Washington, D.C.: Jesuit Conference, 1975), pp. 44-45.

11. Instructive here is a recent work by a well-known missiologist, E. Hillman, C.S.Sp., *Polygamy Reconsidered* (Maryknoll, N.Y.: Orbis, 1975). Without necessarily agreeing with his position totally, one can appreciate the book as an example of sensitive, sound methodology in dealing with a cultural phenomenon of the gravest importance. See also Virgilio Elizondo, *Christianity and Culture: An Introduction to Pastoral Theology and Ministry for the Bicultural Community* (Huntington, Ind.: Our Sunday Visitor, 1975).

12. Paul VI, *Ibid.*, # 20.

13. Cf. Acts, especially chapter 15.

14. Cf. Bp. Peter K. Sarpong, "Christianity should be africanized, not Africa christianized," *African Ecclesiastical Review* 17 (6, '75), pp. 322-328.

15. See here Peter Berger, *Pyramids of Sacrifice. Political Ethics and Social Change* (N.Y.: Basic Books, 1974) for a statement of the dilemmas one encounters in trying to "do something" to alleviate such poverty.

16. One could do worse than start with G. Dunne, *The Right to Development* (N.Y.: Paulist, 1974). See also and especially *The Church in the Present-Day Transformation of Latin America in the Light of the Council*, 2 vols. (Bogotá: General Secretariate of CELAM, 1970), available in U.S.A. from USCC, Division for Latin America, Washington, D.C.

17. *Justice in the World* (Washington, D.C.: USCC, 1972). See also the commentary and guidelines for practical implementation outlined in W.R. Callahan, S.J., *The Quest for Justice* (Washington, D.C.: Center of Concern, 1972).

18. *The Church in the Present-Day Transformation of Latin America in the Light of the Council*, Vol. 2, p. 78.

19. *Justice and Peace in a New Caribbean. A Joint Pastoral Letter from the Bishops of the Antilles Episcopal Conference*, given at Trinité, Martinique, November 21, 1975 (Kingston, Jamaica: Antilles Episcopal Conference, 1975), # 13.

20. Cf. "A Statement of Conscience by Christians and Jews," in *Global Justice and Development. Report of the Aspen Interreligious Consultation, Aspen, Colorado, June 1974* (Washington, D.C.: Overseas Development Council, 1975). See also *Justice . . . . Caribbean*, ## 29-43 on "Socialism and a New Society," and Bp. Benedict Singh's (Guyana) "Pastoral Letter on Socialism," reprinted in *Scarboro Missions* 56 (11, '75), pp. 12-15.

21. See, for example, the brief introduction and evaluation of this issue by R. Heckel, S.J., "Towards a New International Economic Order," *Justitia et Pax* [Bulletin of Pontifical Commission Justice and Peace] No. 20 (Dec. '75), pp. 3-6, or the recent lucid exposition by M. Schultheis, S.J., "The United States and the Changing International Economic Order," prepared for the Interreligious Task Force on U.S. Food Policy, *Impact/Hunger* No. 4 ('76) [110 Maryland Ave., DC].

22. *Justice . . . . Caribbean*, # 34.

23. *Justice in the World*, introduction.

24. *Evangelization in Modern Day Asia. The First Plenary Assembly of the Federation of Asian Bishops' Conferences* (FABC) Taipei, Taiwan, Republic of China, 22-27 April, 1974 (Hong Kong and Manila: FABC, 1974), # 23.

25. *Documents . . . . Society of Jesus*, "Our Mission Today: The Service of Faith and the Promotion of Justice," # 27. See also the very detailed treatment of P. Land, S.J., "Justice, Development, Liberation and the Exercises," *Recherches Ignatiennes/Communications*, 2 (6, '75) [published in Rome by Centrum Ignatianum Spiritualitatis]. The "Exercises" of the title refers to the "Spiritual Exercises of St. Ignatius of Loyola," a classic text (by the founder of the Jesuits) for what is commonly known as a "retreat."

26. *On Evangelization in the Modern World*, #31. See also the remarks of R. McCormick, S.J., " . . . the connecting link between evangelization and liberation in all forms would be, I believe, man's dignity as we know it from the Christ-event and the Church's concern in evangelization is man and if man is being countereducated by economic, social and political structures (counter=told of his real lack of worth and dignity), then she must speak and act. In this sense liberation is absolutely essential to evangelization," "Notes on Moral Theology," *Theological Studies* 37 (1, '76), pp. 117-118.

27. See the article by S. Rayan, S.J., on this topic in *Mission Trends No. 2: Evangelization*, ed. G.H. Anderson and T.F. Stransky, C.S.P. (N.Y.: Paulist and Grand Rapids: Eerdmans, 1975), along with 21 other articles on the topic of evangelization. *Mission Trends No. 1*, published in 1974, has 23 equally thought-provoking articles on mission topics. The two volumes together constitute an excellent primer of current thinking on missiology and related matters by leading churchmen the world over.

28. " . . . since there can be no love without justice, action for justice is the acid test of our preaching of the Gospel," "Our Mission Today," # 28.

29. The excellent positions on humanizing and dehumanizing structures in our world which we of LCWR and CMSM elaborated with the major religious superiors of the Canadian Religious Conference and the Latin American Confederation of Religious in Bogota in the fall of 1974 provide amplification on why we use here the term "humanizing." See *Witnessing to the Kingdom in a Dehumanizing World*, "Donum Dei," No. 22 (Ottawa: Canadian Religious Conference, 1975), especially pp. 179-182 and 187-190. And see the excellent position taken by M.A. Fahey, S.J., in "The Mission of the Church: To Divinize or to Humanize?" which he delivered in Washington at the Catholic Theological Society of America convention and which will be published in the 1976 *Proceedings* of that Society.

30. See n. 7 above for some good examples.

31. See the remarkable statement of the Asian Bishops about these religions: "How can we not acknowledge that God has drawn our peoples to Himself through them?" *Evangelization in Modern Day Asia*, # 15. See also the valuable collection of articles by G.H. Anderson, *Asian Voices in Christian Theology* (Maryknoll, N.Y.: Orbis, 1976).

32. *Liberty and Justice for All. A Discussion Guide* (Washington, D.C.: National Conference of Catholic Bishops, 1974).

33. Roman Catholic religious orders use the term "formation" to refer to those processes and structured programs of initiation or incorporation into religious orders whereby the aspirants or candidates for incorporation spend from two to a dozen years imbibing the spirit of a given order: its charism, priorities, attitudes, peculiarities, sense of identity, etc. Such a process is often (less felicitously) referred to as "indoctrination," though doctrine as such plays a fairly minor role in the process.

34. "Decree on the Appropriate Renewal of the Religious Life" [*Perfectae Caritatis*], *The Documents of Vatican II*, especially # 2. And see the distinction between adaptation and renewal which Archbp. McEleney highlights in his "Introduction" to the decree, pp. 464-465.

35. "Decree on the Missionary Activity of the Church" [*Ad Gentes*], *Ibid.*, # 35.

36. *Ibid.*, # 40. See also Paul VI, *On Evangelization in the Modern World,* # 69.

37. The literature on this one topic of moratorium is already vast and promises to grow. See especially "Moratorium: Retreat, Revolt or Reconciliation?" in *IDOC/ The Future of the Missionary Enterprise,* No. 9 ('74), pp. 49-86 as well as *International Review of Mission* 64 (254, '75) which is completely devoted to this theme.

38. Ephesians 4; Philippians 2:19 ff.; Colossians 1:21 ff.; 3:5-6.

39. 2 Corinthians 8-9.

40. Cf. Acts 1:8; Romans 12:6-8; 1 Corinthians 12:4-11, 28-30; Ephesians 4:11.

41. See n. 40 above for the NT and note 35 for the position of Vatican II in *Ad Gentes*, which is further elaborated in # 2 of the same decree and echoed in the "Decree on the Apostolate of the Laity" [*Apostolicam Actuositatem*], *The Documents of Vatican II*, # 1: "Our own times require of the laity no less zeal [than in the NT]. In fact, modern conditions demand that their apostolate be thoroughly broadened and intensified."

42. See M. Brennan, "Women's Liberation/Men's Liberation," *Origins* 5 (7, '75) 97–105, a paper given at the 1975 CMSM Annual Assembly which speaks competently and creatively about the shattering of categories and precedents which was a characteristic of Jesus' ministry. The same paper has been reprinted in *New Visions New Roles: Women in the Church* (Washington, D.C.: LCWR, 1975), pp. 21–34.

43. "The Church and Human Rights," Working Paper No. 1 (Vatican City: Pontifical Commission "Justitia et Pax," 1975), # 77. This document was reprinted in part in *Origins* 5 (11, '75), pp. 161–170.

44. Some of those issued last year, for example, treated "Food Policy and the Church: Specific Proposals" (Sept. 11), "Handgun Violence: A Threat to Life" (Sept. 11), "Statement on the United Nations and the Republic of South Africa" (Oct. 9), "Resolution on Farm Labor" (Nov. 20), "The Economy: Human Dimensions" (Nov. 20), "The Right to a Decent Home" (Nov. 20).

45. Cf. Luke 4:18.

46. "The Church and Human Rights," # 102.

47. *Ibid.*, # 78.

48. See the powerful statement of the National Office of Black Catholics on "The Collapse of Catholic Schools in the Black Community," in *Origins* 5 (33, '76), pp. 528–532, which asserts that the dismantling of Catholic schools in the Black community can "give unmistakably clear notice to *all* black people—Catholic and non-Catholic—where its [the church's] priorities are: the white suburban population," p. 530.

49. Cf. *NCCB/USCC Report*, 2 (4, '76), pp. 1–2.

50. For example, last month's special consultation on "Emerging Models of Christian Mission."

BIBLIOGRAPHY

Anon., "Moratorium: Retreat, Revolt or Reconciliation?, *IDOC/ The Future of the Missionary Enterprise*, No. 9 ('74).

Anon., "The 1974 Synod of Bishops," *Omnis Terra*, No. 64 (Dec., '74), pp. 51-62.

Asian Voices in Christian Theology, ed. G.H. Anderson (Maryknoll, N.Y.: Orbis, 1976).

Berger, P., *Pyramids of Sacrifice. Political Ethics and Social Change* (N.Y.: Basic Books, 1974).

Brennan, M. "Women's Liberation/Men's Liberation," *Origins* 5 (7, '75), pp. 97-105.

Callahan, W.R., S.J., *The Quest for Justice* (Washington, D.C.: Center of Concern, 1972).

"The Church and Human Rights," Working Paper No. 1 (Vatican City: Pontifical Commission "Justitia et Pax," 1975).

The Church in the Present-Day Transformation of Latin America in the Light of the Council (Bogotá: General Secretariate of CELAM; Washington, D.C.: United States Catholic Conference, Division for Latin America, 1970).

Documents of the Thirty-Second General Congregation of the Society of Jesus (Washington, D.C.: Jesuit Conference, 1975).

The Documents of Vatican II, ed. W.M. Abbott, S.J. (N.Y.: America Press; London: G. Chapman, 1966).

Dunne, G., *The Right to Development* (N.Y.: Paulist, 1974).

Elizondo, V., *Christianity and Culture: An Introduction to Pastoral Theology and Ministry for the Bicultural Community* (Huntington, Ind.: Our Sunday Visitor, 1975).

Evangelization in Modern Day Asia. The First Plenary Assembly of the Federation of Asian Bishops' Conferences (Hong Kong and Manila: Federation of Asian Bishops' Conferences, 1974).

Fahey, M., S.J., "The Mission of the Church: To Divinize or to Humanize?" *Catholic Theological Society of America. Proceedings*, Vol. 31 (In publication).

Fitzmyer, J.A., S.J., "The Biblical Commission's Instruction on the Historical Truth of the Gospels," *Theological Studies* 25 ('64), pp. 386-408.

Heckel, R., S.J., "Towards a New International Economic Order," *Justitia et Pax*, No. 20 (Dec., '75), pp. 3-6.

Hillman, E., C.S.Sp., *Polygamy Reconsidered* (Maryknoll, N.Y.: Orbis, 1975).

Justice and Peace in a New Caribbean. A Joint Pastoral Letter from the Bishops of the Antilles Episcopal Conference (Kingston, Jamaica: Antilles Episcopal Conference, 1975).

Kingsbury, J.D., "The Composition and Christology of Matt 28: 16-20," *Journal of Biblical Literature* 93 ('74), pp. 573-584.

Land, P., S.J., "Justice, Development, Liberation and the Exercises," *Recherches Ignatiennes/Communications* 2 (6, '75).

Latourette, K.S., *History of the Expansion of Christianity* (N.Y.: Harper & Row, 1937 ff.).

Liberty and Justice for All. A Discussion Guide (Washington, D.C.: National Conference of Catholic Bishops, 1974).

MacRae, G.W., S.J., "The Mandate to Evangelize: The Mandate in the Roman Catholic Tradition," *Midstream* 8 (4, '70), pp. 92-104.

McCormick, R., S.J., "Notes on Moral Theology," *Theological Studies* 37 (1, '76), 70-119.

National Office of Black Catholics, "The Collapse of Catholic Schools in the Black Community," *Origins* 5 (33, '76), pp. 528-532.

New Visions New Roles: Women in the Church (Washington, D.C.: Leadership Conference of Women Religious, 1975).

Paul VI, *On Evangelization in the Modern World* (Washington, D.C.: United States Catholic Conference, 1976).

Pontifical Biblical Commission, "Instructio de historica Evangeliorum veritate," *Osservatore Romano*, May 14, 1964, p. 3; *Catholic Biblical Quarterly* 26 ('64), pp. 299-312.

Rayan, S., S.J., "Evangelization and Development," *Mission Trends No. 2: Evangelization*, ed. G.H. Anderson and T.F. Stransky, C.S.P. (N.Y.: Paulist and Grand Rapids: Eerdmans, 1975), pp. 87-105.

Sarpong, P.K., "Christianity should be africanized, not Africa christianized," *African Ecclesiastical Review* 17 (6, '75), pp. 322-328.

Schultheis, M., S.J., "The United States and the Changing
International Economic Order," *Impact/Hunger*, No. 4 ('76).

Singh, B., "Pastoral Letter on Socialism," *Scarboro Missions* 56
(11, '75), pp. 12-15.

"A Statement of Conscience by Christians and Jews," *Global
Justice and Development. Report of the Aspen Interreligious
Consultation, Aspen, Colorado, June 1974* (Washington, D.C.:
Overseas Development Council, 1975).

Synod of Bishops, *Justice in the World* (Washington, D.C.: United
States Catholic Conference, 1972).

Witnessing to the Kingdom in a Dehumanizing World, "Donum
Dei," No. 22 (Ottawa: Canadian Religious Conference, 1975).

15

Response to Father Smith

Charles H. Germany

Will you let me have a personal word at the outset. My presence
today as a commentator is on invitation from Dr. R. Pierce Beaver.
We honor him in this meeting of the American Society of Missiologists as he retires from his responsibilities at the Overseas
Ministries Study Center in Ventnor. I want personally to take
this occasion to express appreciation to Pierce for his life and
his work as good friend, supportive colleague, leader and guide.

My comments on the two papers presented will be made in two
phases. First, I want to say something about the two papers in
relationship to each other. Then, second, I want to say something about each of the papers individually.

First of all regarding the two papers in their relationship
to each other. It is remarkable the extent to which the two
papers complement each other. Richey Hogg's paper is basically
historical in its sweep. Simon Smith's paper looks primarily
toward the future task of mission. It is helpful that the two
papers are in this way different, and complementary. Each has its
distinctive turf.

In the very fact of the differences of the papers, however, exists a problem for us. The two papers co-exist. They do not talk to each other. Simon Smith's paper is preoccupied with the future; Richey Hogg's paper essentially deals with the past. Readers are left with the task of forcing the papers to say hello and start talking to each other. Does Richey Hogg's reading of history lay the ground work for Simon Smith's future? Does Simon Smith's future have the freedom and discipline it needs in terms of a responsible grounding in the past?

Years ago Professor John McKay wrote a remarkable small philosophy of history entitled <u>Heritage and Destiny</u>. In the book he developed his "Boatman's philosophy." John McKay spoke of his vacations spent in a seaside setting. Each day it was necessary for him to row across the sound to buy supplies at the general store. Sitting in the rowboat, one faces backward. He learned that by lining up two points in the range of mountains behind him he was able to row directly across the sound to his intended destination. A responsible reading of the past, he concludes, is inescapable in setting the course of the future. We hope in the discussion which follows we may be successful in getting Richey and Simon into dialogue so that the past as so remarkably developed and described by Richey may question the challenging future outlined by Simon and vice versa.

Now, first, to turn to Richey Hogg's paper. It is easy to be appreciative of Richey and difficult to be critical. A long-standing personal friendship with Richey dates back to the early 1940s when we were seminary students of the same generation. We worked together in the Inter-Seminary Movement. We became candidates for missionary service under the Methodist Church at the same time. We paced the corridors while the candidate review committee made their decision regarding the future of both of us. Through the years later it has been good to visit Perkins School of Theology from time to time and to know the quality of relationship between Richey and the students of the Seminary, touched with love, respect and gentle humor.

Let me say some of the aspects of Richey's paper most appreciated. The paper is a remarkable resource document. It is simply filled with data and with charts that will be helpful for us all.

The section on <u>Perspective on Mission to America</u> - Home Missions was helpful. Certainly people in my own church, the United Methodist Church, need the balancing insights summarized on pages 8 and 9 of the paper. I believe that members of my church do not fully know the extent to which the concerns and energies of Christian mission have been directed to the challenges

of mission within our own nation. This perspective is needed
for balance.

Again, the section on <u>Perspective on Mission from America</u> -
World Mission, was exceedingly helpful. The section puts in
detailed context the place of U.S. personnel in mission. It
helpfully focuses on the place of mission in the church in the
United States as being integral to the very life of the church
itself. It describes helpfully the influence of world mission
on the United States of America.

The section on <u>Relationships with Governments</u> provides a
helpful background for contemporary concern with the C.I.A. issue
and mission involvement and Senator Mark Hatfield's tragic
abandonment of his legislative cause.

The section on The <u>Bible in World Mission</u>, the role of women,
the role of denominationalism, the student movement, the international missionary cooperation as expressed in the emergence of
the international missionary council -- all are informative
sections, rich in historical detail. The final section on <u>New</u>
<u>Mission</u>, with concern for the evangelical spirit and Pentecostal-
ism rounds out a remarkable presentation of mission and America's
role to the present time. One is exceedingly appreciative of
this background.

What I missed and what I personally hoped for from Richey is
that he will find the time to carry further what he has already
done. Richey made a choice. It was as if he were making a trip
to India with limited time. He was forced to travel by air,
stopping down briefly here and there. But, he had a long
itinerary and thus was not able to spend very much time anywhere.

First of all, I missed the analytical and evaluative within
the rich historical detail provided by the paper. Take, for
example, the issue of America's manifest destiny and the imperial
mystique which undergirded much of the great missionary outreach
from the United States. Richey concludes on page 16 that "Today
the situation has changed vastly. Despite what is termed
'economic neo-colonialism,' Western imperialism is dead...."
Well, can we say with such certainty that Western imperialism is
indeed dead? The further task necessary is to wrestle with the
issue of continuing American power and the implications of
subtle and at times not so subtle cultural imperialism, with the
attendant influence of America in value domination in our world.

The concern expressed is seen in the resource of statistics
in the paper. One desires more of the analytic and the evaluative. The paper treats data on numbers of missionaries. One

would be interested in the relationship of missionary numbers to
styles and goals of mission, for example in relation to goals of
self-determination on the part of Asian, African and Latin
American churches. It would be helpful for the paper to probe
the significance of North American-U.S. influence in the internationalization of mission in relation to the problems of ethnocentrism. The paper has statistics on women missionaries. It
points out that from 1920 to 1960, sixty to sixty-seven percent
of missionaries were women. What has happened? What has been
lost from mission by the lessening of the presence of single
women missionaries? Has a factor of creative tension been lost?
In this very society of American missiologists, where are the
women? Why are they not here?

The paper deals with the role of the student Christian movement and missionary strength. We need to hear from Richey, from
his background, the meaning and the significance of the demise
of the university Christian movement in conciliar churches.

There are new issues in mission to America that call for
analytical and evaluative treatment from Richey. Early America
accepted the melting-pot theory. The scene since has shifted,
as the paper indicates, but, what are the forms of unity within
American society which can and must exist within an affirmation
of ethnic diversity?

Finally, I missed in Richey's paper a coherent perspective of
mission for the future. What is the task? What are the goals?
The patterns of relationships, the critical mission stance for
the next decade?

This hope, then, Richey, that you find the time to do a third
section building on mission to and mission from America. This
section would be the U.S. church and society in international
inter-action -- an effort to design a world view in mission that
holds the two together.

I turn now to comment on the paper of Simon Smith. First and
foremost, appreciation is in order. The paper is coherent and
sensitive. The architechtonics are excellent. It is exceedingly
well constructed.

First, some sweeping comments: The perspectives of the paper
are exciting -- faith incarnate in culture, the needs of others
in the theme of development with justice, the importance of
receiving, the basic reality of hope in mission. I found the
paper helpfully in line with the growing emphasis today of
analyzing experience as an essential approach to mission concerns,
rather than study of documents, or study of biblical texts which

begin and end there, or even the detailed history of mission.

The paper is clear about sinful structures of society which impact mission. The section on <u>Formation and Reformation</u> is informative. Voices of other religions, seen as gifts of the Spirit for us provides a provocative thought. I found the lessons from the poor simply beautiful. The comments on life-styles were helpful, the necessity that the missionary orders move out from the institutions into the life of humanity marks an affirmative direction. The emphasis upon the advocacy task in mission was helpful. The danger of myopia in mission directed even to the very Society meeting here was a worthwhile reminder. It is easy for the institutional church and for specialists in mission to become myopic.

Though they are not central, problems for me were present here and there. I did not see clearly the distinction made between mutuality and collaboration. Further elaboration of this point would be helpful. The emphasis upon local lay leadership was good, still as a religious it is unclear as to the full implication. How can clergy relate to the laity without over-shadowing? The most important statement I want to try to make about Simon Smith's paper concerns the task of missiology for tomorrow. It is precisely at this point that, in my judgment, the fundamental question for us all resides. Specifically, how can the Christian church in mission come to understand and to articulate in word and life the wholeness of the Gospel in mission?

I took the liberty of sharing Simon's paper with a new and exceedingly able colleague just coming to the staff of the World Division of the Board of Global Ministries in our church. He will come to give expression to a new portfolio on Church Development and Renewal. He will be concerned primarily with the evangelization task of the Christian faith. I want to take the liberty of sharing the comments of this staff colleague because I think they will be helpful to Simon Smith and to our discussion. My colleague writes, "Simon Smith talks of 'engagement in the struggle for justice' as 'itself a form of the preaching of the Gospel.' (page 6) He is concerned that Catholic missionaries 'may proclaim Christ and His Church so loudly and confidently' that they may fail to perceive that the receptor culture perhaps has its own experience of the same God we preach.' (page 7) He considers it a 'new breakthrough in missionary consciousness' to treat 'other religions with the utmost respect and reverence.' (page 7) He wants the church to understand that 'mission is not all giving' and that 'the greatest thing a U.S. missionary can do is not to give but to learn to receive.' (page 9) These are merely examples of which many more could be given. All of these

are good, and I really have no basic quarrel with them. But the
problem is that many of these phrases and ideas are getting to
be a bit old hat now. They constitute the new orthodoxy. Our
Protestant problem is that we have been saying these things for
so long now that we have lost in many cases the sense that we
really do have something important to offer to the world, namely
the Gospel of Jesus Christ, and that the building up of the
church in the Christian community has something to commend it."

My colleague continues, "We are now struggling with the
question as to how this concern for political, social and
economic issues (or to put it in other terms: justice and
liberation) relates to the uniqueness of the message of God's
coming among us in Jesus Christ."

Because we struggle so to relate the personal and the social,
conversion and social justice, we simply have got to learn to
say better and do more to demonstrate that the Gospel in mission
is one reality in Jesus Christ, in the words He spoke and the
word He was and is, in the life He lived.

The American Society of Missiology

The American Society of Missiology was founded in 1973 after two
years of preparatory meetings and twenty years of talk about the
need of such a society. Today it has over 500 members.

The purposes of the Society as stated in the Constitution are:

- to promote the scholarly study of theological, historical,
  social, and practical questions relating to the missionary dimension of the Christian church;

- to relate studies in missiology to the other scholarly
  disciplines;

- to promote fellowship and cooperation among individuals
  and institutions engaged in activities and studies related to missiology;

- to facilitate mutual assistance and exchange of information among those thus engaged;

- to encourage research and publication in the study of
  Christian missions.

The Society is a member of the Council on the Study of Religion,
and publishes a scholarly quarterly journal, *Missiology: An
International Review*, which has a worldwide circulation of approximately 3,000 subscribers, including 800 libraries. The editor
is Dean Arthur F. Glasser, 135 N. Oakland Avenue, Pasadena, California 91101. Subscription to the journal is included in the
Society's annual dues of $14.50. Subscription to *Missiology* only

is $10.00 per year. This journal is indexed in Christian Periodicals Index, Index to Religious Periodical Literature, Religious and Theological Abstracts, and Bibliografa Missionaria.

Address inquiries about membership and subscriptions to Missiology, 1605 E. Elizabeth Street, Pasadena, California 91104.